WASHITA
LOVE
CHILD

ALSO BY DOUGLAS K. MILLER

Indians on the Move:
Native American Mobility and Urbanization
in the Twentieth Century

WASHITA LOVE CHILD

THE RISE OF
INDIGENOUS ROCK STAR
Jesse Ed Davis

Douglas K. Miller

Liveright Publishing Corporation

A Division of W. W. Norton & Company
Independent Publishers Since 1923

Frontispiece: Jesse Ed Davis performing at the Santa Monica
City College Amphitheatre, 1973. Photo by Howard Tsukamoto.
(Courtesy of Bob Tsukamoto)

For information about permission to reproduce selections from this book,
write to Permissions, Liveright Publishing Corporation, a division of
W. W. Norton & Company, Inc., 500 Fifth Avenue, New York, NY 10110

For information about special discounts for bulk purchases, please contact
W. W. Norton Special Sales at specialsales@wwnorton.com or 800-233-4830

Manufacturing by Lakeside Book Company
Book design by Brooke Koven
Production manager: Julia Druskin

ISBN 978-1-324-09209-4

Liveright Publishing Corporation, 500 Fifth Avenue, New York, N.Y. 10110
www.wwnorton.com

W. W. Norton & Company Ltd., 15 Carlisle Street, London W1D 3BS

10 9 8 7 6 5 4 3 2 1

For Exa and Kit,
with whom every night is Saturday night

Must have been a sweet dream
brought you here

—JOHN LENNON, "Mucho Mungo (Mucho Jesse)"

TRACKS

FOREWORD

I FIRST MET Jesse Ed Davis in the late '80s. I was in Los Angeles briefly for a solo performance. John Trudell asked if I'd record some tracks for him while I was in town. That's when I found myself in a garage studio in Culver City recording voice tracks for possible use in one of Trudell's albums with Davis. I had just released a cassette tape from Watershed Foundation of my poetry, *Furious Light*, with jazz players I had met during the time I lived in Denver. Soon I'd be learning saxophone and fronting my own poetry and music band, Joy Harjo and Poetic Justice. I was initially inspired by the iconic poet Jayne Cortez and her band the Firespitters, whose drummer, Denardo, was her son by Ornette Coleman. Her confrontational political outspokenness and the jazzy Afro punchiness of the band matched the rocking and rolling Native blues pairing of John Trudell and Jesse Ed Davis. Jesse and I had an easy connection because we were both Indians from Oklahoma. We had common history. He was laid-back, and warmly friendly. His role that day was as recording engineer and producer. A few years later I'd open a newspaper while having brunch in San Francisco with a friend, and see a nearly hidden news item announcing Jesse's overdose in a laundromat in Venice, California. It was and still is difficult to reconcile that kind of death with the gentle yet intensely present giant who was a legend of an artist. Since then, I like to imagine him with guitar in hand on his family land by the Washita River.

In *Washita Love Child*, Jesse Ed Davis is resurrected in story. We come to know him as a man who loved his people, formed from a powerful mix of tribal histories and family that included the Kiowa, Comanche, Cheyenne, Seminole, and Mvskoke peoples, and how he became one of the most sought-after guitarists in the world of rock and roll, jazz, and blues music. Holding any kind of power is dangerous even as it is dazzling. It is responsibility. Jesse was tremendously creative, yet with creativity comes destruction because we live in a world of duality. There is no light without dark, or dark without light. Silence defines rhythm. That line in between is the trickster's realm. Navigation is tricky because the gift is potent and demanding. It needs to be fed; it needs to be shared. And what of the human who, with a guitar, grows wings, whose guitar is his weapon, even as it is the singing of his ancestors, and the vehicle that will take him to creative heights that most never attain, all over the world, to perform with other giants in the industry? Touch down, and the vision appears lost. To stay in those heights is impossible because, in the end, we are human. That is the story you will find here, the unwinding of a tale of incredible accomplishment married with self-destruction, yet the hero persists into history, perhaps even cheating death. That is the nature of legends. They continue through time.

Any biography of any Native subject in this country is entwined with its historical becoming. To be Native means that in any telling, you walk through the traps of stereotypes, through the slough of racism, or you disappear into the mists of romanticism. There appears no way around it. Our tribal stories are so individual and complex, yet when we are out in collective American society, we are compacted into flat characters, if we are even seen at all. Jesse Ed Davis's ancestry contains the story of America, just as the guitar he mastered is a major storytelling instrument of this country, whether it is via rock, blues, country, or jazz. The roots of these genres owe much to the Mvskoke peoples who made up most of the population of the Southeast before removal. That shuffle swing leads you right back to Jesse's Mvskoke and Seminole ancestors.

Because of the everyday experience of being American Indian in

America, Jesse went the route of becoming a musician who just happened to be American Indian rather than touting his Indianness and building his music around identity. He didn't market himself as Indian. Yet, his love of music was passed down through his parents and grandparents, and he was very familiar with various Native musical forms as well as popular music on the radio as he was growing up. What really shines in Douglas Kent Miller's storytelling is his rendering of how a musician emerges from generations of family and musical traditions. We come to understand how land, history, and complicated and accomplished family history gave birth to the brilliant Davis. We can hear all of this in Jesse's guitar, how he was born postwar into a Native family that was immersed in their tribal cultural expressions and knowledge systems yet embraced the all-American middle-class postwar ideal. The systems often do not mesh and those spaces can give birth to new music. Oklahoma was made up of many cultural currents from the South, West, Southwest, Midwest, and Great Plains. Jesse's music gave him a way to maneuver with the fuel from this cultural trajectory, first playing with local bands, then jamming with Taj Mahal, then on to releasing his own music, to performing with the royalty of rock and roll, then finally coming home to the Grafitti Band and John Trudell.

Jesse was given a foundation in music with his mother's piano lessons and his father's occupation with Dixieland music. He competed on the Oklahoma powwow circuit, including dances in Colony, Oklahoma, where his Cheyenne ancestors lived. He once mentioned to Taj Mahal, who gave him his first big-gun opportunity, that many of his guitar fills and song arrangements were born from the grooves he borrowed from his dancing days. Oklahoma was central to his story. Jesse once said about his home state: "It's still the Wild West out there. It's really provincial." His musical prowess would take Jesse far away from Oklahoma and the Washita River into the circles of the best players in the world, to collaborations and friendships, including those with John Lennon, Bob Dylan, and Jackson Browne. Doorways opened to his genius. His discography includes several Taj Mahal albums, the New Breed, Junior Markham & The Tulsa Review, Delaney & Bonnie, Bob Dylan, Charles Lloyd, Leon Russell, John Lee Hooker, Albert King,

Gene Clark, George Harrison, Joe Cocker, B.B. King, three albums with John Trudell, and many, many others. He produced three solo albums: *¡Jesse Davis!*, *Ululu*, and *Keep Me Comin'*. Yet, at the heart of it, he would always be that Indian kid from Oklahoma, navigating history, racism, and short-minded snipes about anything or anyone Native. That journey has proven to be too much for far too many.

In the end, we all return home, whether it is literally or metaphorically. Perhaps *Washita Love Child* helps return Jesse Ed Davis home to his place in the larger story of American music, of Native music, of the soul of music and how it wants to live, no matter the personal and communal challenges. Jesse's story has many branches, some realized and some still waiting to flower. Going home means finding landing despite the contradictions, despite what falters, despite the twists and turns of failure and accomplishment.

Jesse sang that he was born in a tipi along the Washita River. That was his heart song. He was a love child, born of a generation, of a people, carrying a gift to share that was larger than his life. In 1986 he bragged to his friends he was going home, back to family lands by the Washita River. It was always there in his music, in his giant spirit, bearing a guitar in his hands.

—Joy Harjo, MVSKOKE NATION
MARCH 23, 2024

PREFACE

THERE'S AN OLD ADAGE in the music business that suggests a musician has their entire life to write their first album, and six months to write their second. I experienced the opposite. I wrote my first book, *Indians on the Move*, about Native American people like Jesse Ed Davis who relocated to major cities in the twentieth century, in finite time under great pressure. But the book now in your hands, I've been writing my entire life.

Music forms the center of my earliest, blurriest impressions in life. When I was a little kid living in Germany where my dad was stationed in the army, he often brought records home from the post exchange. He wasn't a music fanatic like me. But he, like my mom, had been a teenager in the 1970s, and they knew their way around the FM dial. In our small apartment, my dad would place big headphones over my little ears and hook me into his Pioneer turntable. I came to life, smiling, laughing, and dancing while my dad napped on the couch in his green army fatigues. I think this is why I still love the TV show *M*A*S*H*. If my dad was sleeping, at least he was home. Standing there, soaking in the sounds of what we now call classic rock the way other kids read board books or built with blocks—these were my happiest times with my father, though I can't quite call them memories.

A few years later, in a time more like a memory, we left Tacoma,

Washington, and drove back home to Moline, Illinois, where I was born. I clearly recall the road trip soundtrack: Bob Seger, Queen, and Jackson Browne. The latter cassette included a song called "Doctor My Eyes." Even at that age, I studied liner notes on the tape case. As I grew, I learned to read liner notes like road maps. I became obsessed with music, almost pathologically so. For years, I dreamed of a life in music, sitting behind a drum kit comprised of Lincoln Logs boxes, or strumming a plastic KISS guitar, using my dad's belt as a strap and a nickel for a pick, running back and forth to the TV screen to imitate the musicians I saw on MTV. Music filled my life with joy even during its darkest chapters. Music guarded my thoughts and emotions from trauma in my home. It was an alternative world I could enter through an ever-growing case of cassettes in my bedroom when I wanted to escape, but couldn't. As a teenager, I began drumming in bands with friends. Later, I picked up a guitar and wrote songs, achieving a rewarding, if modest, career as a musician that somehow turned into me becoming a history professor. It's a long story.

I can't help but think my entire career, as both a musician and a scholar of Native American history, was supposed to lead me to this project. One night, while listening to Gene Clark's *White Light* (1971), which features Jesse as both producer and player, I began thinking about Jesse as a subject in both music history and Indigenous history. Indeed, there are so few books about Native people in the late twentieth century, and even fewer that consider prominent cultural figures. Jesse's story is fundamentally one about a Native kid from Oklahoma who set out to become an authentic bluesman, and all the triumphs and travails that entailed. In so many ways he doesn't fit the profile of a typical Native American history subject. His story instead reminds us that it's worth expanding our view of Native people, while inviting new subjects into the fold. As valuable and popular as they are, this is not another story about Native American resisters in the nineteenth century who rallied around great chiefs, or Native American objects and victims of settler state power and policies in the twentieth century. My conviction is that there are other important stories to tell, and doing so can be refreshing.

Jesse is equally intriguing as a music subject. He reminds us that we should also further consider the production of popular music that both shaped and soundtracked transformational times in American culture and society. Jesse represents an emerging appreciation for the players who backed the stars and conducted a lot of the daily labor required to make popular records. Sometimes he was at the front of the stage or on the front of the album covers, but his work behind the scenes is just as significant. For these reasons and more, Jesse is deserving of a book. I was delighted to meet and embrace the support of so many others who agree.

In terms of actually putting this book together, I began doing so during a global pandemic. What a strange thing to do then, to explore and rehabilitate someone else's life—someone I never met. Now I'm sitting in Medicine Park, Oklahoma, finishing it. I'm very close to Rainy Mountain, sacred in Jesse Ed Davis's ancestral Kiowa histories, and Rainy Mountain Kiowa Indian Baptist Church and Cemetery, where Jesse's ancestors are buried. Also nearby, Fort Sill's morning artillery exercise is shaking my little cottage down by Medicine Creek. Some of Jesse's Comanche, Cheyenne, and Kiowa ancestors were prisoners of war at Fort Sill, where their children were forced into a boarding school that, for many, was also kind of like a prison.

While making this book, I counted a lot of dreams in which Jesse visited me. Numerous others experienced the same. A remarkable number of people had dreams about Jesse the night before I first contacted them and invited them to contribute. On every occasion, Jesse's visits were pleasant, excepting one nightmare, wherein the two of us were broken down on the side of Interstate 35 in a touring van, unable to get the engine started, fearing we were going to miss our gig. I endured that misfortune a few times in my own career as a touring musician, but here it was obviously a sign that I worried about completing this book and properly recounting and honoring Jesse's story and legacy.

Indeed, discovering Jesse proved difficult. His relative obscurity in contemporary music media seemed at odds with the stature he once exhibited. When I began, I doubted the potential for a book. But my developing sense was that he was important beyond a handful of available articles about him, many of which contain several basic factual errors. Given that he didn't leave much of a paper trail, I wondered if

Jesse was simply too unknowable. Finding him, I realized, would begin with the vast collection of music he made and the stories and insights carried by people who knew him. I would have to create an archive virtually from scratch. Gathering hundreds of albums, photos, letters, videos, radio programs, newspapers, magazines, interviews, and more, I was driven by the fundamental sense that, if I wanted to read a book about Jesse Ed Davis, then I would have to write one.

If the heart of this book is in the stories it tells, then the soul is in the music. In music criticism, there's another old adage, possibly apocryphal in its varying attributions to Frank Zappa and John Lennon, which suggests that writing about music is like dancing about architecture. The process might tell us something, but music and writing are different languages. I did not and cannot write about every Jesse Ed Davis album, song, and session. This would spoil the experience for you; it would rob you of your own discoveries. Instead, with the authority of someone who daily, across five years, swam in the ocean of music Jesse made, I prefer pointing you in the right direction while highlighting some touchstones. Occasionally, I prevail on songs that are underappreciated or overshadowed by some of his more famous achievements. If this book results in just one outcome, I hope it will be more people listening to more of his music.

Finally, this book is a note to my loved ones. If music has functioned as a photo album in my life, then I hope this book is a picture of me. My son can always find me here. At age five, he already practices an assortment of instruments, writes songs, performs live in our living room, manages his music playlists, and builds his own record collection. Where music speaks the language of my heart, I now more than ever witness its greater power in harmony.

—Douglas K. Miller

JANUARY 2024

PRELUDE

Farther on Down the Road

THE MADISON SQUARE GARDEN house lights are dimmed for soundcheck. While exhaling his own puff, platinum blond Leon Russell, the rollicking musician from Oklahoma, leans in to light the former Beatle George Harrison's smoke with a fading match. Fire catches. Then George, strapped into a cherry red Les Paul, turns to his left, releases his own toke, and sparks Jesse Ed Davis's Winston with the lighter he had been holding the entire time. Practically a comedy routine, it's more an expression of the camaraderie these musicians enjoyed when playing together. They were all quick with an assist.

Davis, a Native American guitarist from Norman, Oklahoma, sports a white t-shirt overlaid with a sleeveless denim cowboy shirt draped under his long black hair. One of the most sought-after sidemen of the decade, Davis had initially been invited to fill the big shoes of an ailing Eric Clapton, who, with a little help from his friends, made the gig in the nick of time. With showtime rapidly approaching, Jesse had just emerged from a hotel room where he had received a crash course in the setlist from bass guitarist Klaus Voormann. "C to F, this goes here, that goes there . . ." Voormann recalls. "He was easygoing. Fantastic."[1]

Extending a flame to Jesse was now the least George could do. This wasn't just any gig. Beer and Coke cans crowned an assortment of keyboards, pianos, and amplifier stacks arranged haphazardly across the stage, waiting to blast the sounds of the greatest concert of the decade, George Harrison's 1971 Concert for Bangladesh.

That night, Leon, George, Jesse, Klaus, Clapton, Ringo Starr, and other esteemed musicians performed some of the most beloved music of the era. Producer Phil Spector recorded from a mobile truck parked outside, capturing his signature "Wall of Sound," using forty-four microphones onstage, an elaborate feat for live concerts at that time. The venerable drummer Jim Keltner remembers how Jesse created the center of their big sound: "It was the Jesse Ed groove."[2]

George took the stage and launched straight into "Wah-Wah," an exasperated tune about his relentlessly overshadowing former group. In a regal white suit, holding a weary white Stratocaster guitar, this was George's first live appearance since the Beatles quit the road in 1966. Jesse marveled at the opportunity to appear onstage with George and Ringo. "That's gotta be one of the great sideshow musical tragedies, for my money anyway," Jesse said, referring to the Fab Four's breakup. "I loved the Beatles. They meant a lot to me."[3]

Basking in George's rare presence, many in the crowd also wondered if the rumors were true that Bob Dylan would make a surprise appearance. As George experienced with Clapton, Dylan's dithering made George dreadfully nervous right up to showtime. John Lennon had already bowed out with just one week's notice and Clapton barely made the show on time.[4]

Fresh from cutting "Watching the River Flow" and "When I Paint My Masterpiece" with Leon Russell and Jesse Ed Davis, Dylan too had rarely appeared live since 1966, the year of his electric tour with the Band, when so-called fans called him "Judas" for betraying his folk music roots. This was a big band in a big moment on a big stage. The first big concert event for a humanitarian cause, it prefigured Farm Aid, Live Aid, Live 8, USA for Africa's "We Are the World," and other massive music benefit endeavors across subsequent decades. "I thought it was going to be a catastrophe," Jesse recalled.[5]

Everyone exhaled when Dylan finally strode onstage with an acoustic guitar and harmonica. The concert was not a catastrophe. The large ensemble of musicians from around the world prevailed. "It was one high-level experience from beginning to end," Ringo proclaimed. Jesse, now donning a blazer and flares, eyes closed, grooving with his signature Telecaster guitar, fit right in, radiating confidence and exhilaration, forming their rhythmic core. At the after-party, Phil Spector performed impromptu piano jams accompanied by gonzo Who drummer Keith Moon. Jesse marveled at it all.[6]

In his description of the event, he was almost "someone else that night," floating above the stage in an out-of-body experience, "like a dream." "Just the opportunity to play with these people was enough," he suggested, "but to play together for the purpose that we were doing, I thought was probably one of the highest points of my career—musical, emotional, spiritual, you name it. It was just a wonderful day."[7]

It had only been five years since 1966, when Davis first sprinted from his Oklahoma birthplace down Route 66, hoping to break into the Hollywood music business. The Bangladesh concert now marked his arrival. His adoring California girl Patti Daley watched her "Kiowa Chief" from the front row at Madison Square Garden. Whether witnessing Jesse live at the concert or noticing him through the popular corresponding live album and film, more people began asking, "Who was that Indian guy?"

Fast forward to 1987. Jesse Ed Davis is now giving George Harrison an assist—not with a cigarette, but a loaner guitar at a second legendary concert. It's a much smaller gig, not in New York City but on the opposite coast at North Hollywood's Palomino Club, an old Western swing saloon where Merle Haggard used to down beers. Bob Dylan again hesitates to join the band. Finally climbing onstage, he tells Jesse he can't do his own songs because he's too drunk to remember the words. He isn't kidding. His ad hoc bandmates discreetly turn his amp down during songs. Dylan makes George sing "Watching the River Flow," before prodding John Fogerty, who appears from the crowd, to play his Creedence Clearwater Revival standard "Proud Mary" for the first time in fifteen years. "If you don't sing it, people are going to think it's a Tina

Turner song!" Dylan exhorts. A flustered Fogerty finally abides. "You know, that didn't feel too bad," he confesses afterward.[8]

On this occasion, it was George and Dylan who were guests on Jesse's stage. The Grafitti Band* Jesse led with Dakota poet and activist John Trudell was backing Jesse's old music partner, his "Captain," the exalted blues musician Taj Mahal. But if this was another star-studded concert event, it was noticeably different. Jesse was now walking with a cane, and he spent most of the set sitting down. Still, standing or sitting, he unleashed several riffs, licks, and solos from his and Taj Mahal's old repertoire and even sang lead on their aching cowrite "Farther on Down the Road." If the music didn't match the Bangladesh concert, then in the more relaxed atmosphere, absent such grand expectations, it sure seems like it was more fun. Watching the grainy VHS recording of Taj, Bob, George, and Jesse onstage together at this second fabled gig, it first occurs to me that, by 1987, these veteran rock and rollers were all grown up. But then I realize they were still so young.

One night, hanging together in the studio shortly after the Palomino gig, Dylan told Jesse he wanted to see the gig tape. Grafitti Band bassist Bob Tsukamoto had a copy. Jesse hopped on the back of Dylan's Harley and Tsukamoto followed them to Jesse's apartment in Mar Vista. With the video player located in the austere apartment's bedroom, all three climbed onto Jesse's bed and began watching. On the nightstand rested a copy of *Rolling Stone* magazine with Dylan on the cover. It was the July 17, 1986, issue in which he called Jesse and John Trudell's *aka Grafitti Man* the best album of the year.

A decade removed from his initial career crest as one of the most coveted guitarists in popular music, Jesse had rolled out to sea on a drowning wave of drug dependence. Now he was coming back to shore. "I'm Jesse Ed Davis and I'm real proud to be an Indian, and this is something I hope that doesn't go by you," he declared that night at the Palomino with his old friends gathered in support.[9]

That Jesse needed to affirm his Indigenous pride was not merely a

---

* The group misspelled their name. This will be explained later.

reflection of how far he had drifted. Rather, it indicated his determination to make his experience and identity as an Indigenous person, his Indigeneity, a fundamental aspect of his reintroduction to music audiences. Only a few months later, his extraordinary life and career ended in tragedy, with a heroin injection in a Los Angeles laundry room. That fact has made it difficult to prevent his death from becoming the story of his life. But while his death was indeed a tragedy, his life surely was not.

WASHITA
LOVE
CHILD

OVERTURE

My Ship Has Come In

No one played like Jesse Ed Davis. As frontman, sideman, guitarist, pianist, producer, bandleader, and more, the multi-talented musician recorded or appeared with more than one hundred major artists, including Bob Dylan, John Lennon, George Harrison, Ringo Starr, Taj Mahal, the Rolling Stones, the Allman Brothers, Jackson Browne, Eric Clapton, B.B. King, Emmylou Harris, Leon Russell, Harry Nilsson, Leonard Cohen, Rod Stewart, Joe Cocker, Cher, Gene Clark, Arlo Guthrie, and too many others to list here. In addition to making three solo albums during the early 1970s, he became one of the most sought-after guitarists in Hollywood, contributing to over one hundred major releases, including eight top-ten albums, seven top-ten singles, and dozens more top-twenty and top-forty records. "My discography would be as long as my arm, probably," he said. That was an understatement.[1]

By age twenty-five, Jesse was already beloved among guitar players by virtue of his work with Taj Mahal. Covering guitar, piano, organ, horn arrangements, and even handwritten album notes, Jesse was such an instrumental force that Taj sometimes called their group the Davis Band. It was specifically Jesse's scorching slide guitar on Taj Mahal's version of "Statesboro Blues" that inspired Duane Allman to adopt the technique, long before the latter became widely regarded as the greatest bottleneck slide player in the world with the Allman Brothers Band.

That's Jesse's spirited electric guitar solo on Jackson Browne's first top-ten hit "Doctor My Eyes." Those are Jesse's seductive acoustic guitar licks on Rod Stewart's sultry number-one hit "Tonight's the Night." In 1973, Mick Jagger had Jesse waiting in Los Angeles with his bags packed, ready to fill Keith Richards's spot on a Rolling Stones tour, before Keith escaped a twenty-five-count drug bust in the nick of time. "Jesse's music? Those are my roots," testifies guitarist Elliot Easton, whose group the Cars topped the music charts for a decade. In a rare interview, Fleetwood Mac founder Peter Green adds, "I tell you who I like a lot and that's Jesse Ed Davis." "Indian Ed'll lay more guitar on you than any of them blues guitar people you can name," taunted cosmic cowboy Gram Parsons. "Indian Ed is the cream of the crop; he's better than Clapton and Hendrix put together."[2]

Such accolades and endorsements alone merit serious attention, but then his story merits a book. Jesse Edwin Davis III was born in Oklahoma in 1944 to a family that was practically nobility in its community. Like a million other kids from his generation, he dreamed of becoming a rock and roll star after seeing Elvis Presley. When attempts at college and military service failed, he split for California and soon found himself playing with the biggest rock stars in the world. Before long, however, Jesse was swept into a rising tide of debilitating drug addiction. Ten years later, he began orchestrating a comeback after joining forces with a powerful poet he sang about long before they ever met, only for their formidable partnership to end prematurely. Everything moved too fast, with a strange collage of characters and subjects—including Johnny Cash, the Beatles, Little Richard, Andy Warhol, Bob Hope, Gary Busey, the FBI, the Los Angeles Police Department, the Kiowa Six, the Stanford Seven, John Lennon's assassin, and an Aquarian cult—marking his days and nights. And if this inspires skepticism, these are only the greatest hits.

To be fair, Jesse sometimes undermined his own credibility. He was prone to self-mythologizing. Did he really play on the Monkees' hit "Last Train to Clarksville"? "Oh no," laughs the Monkees' Mike Nesmith. "I've heard it was everyone from Jesse Ed to Charles Manson." Jesse didn't need to embellish his résumé. The reality was far more impressive. But then, Jesse didn't move to California for the fact; he went there for the fiction.[3]

Jesse Ed Davis wasn't your average rock star. Though he performed poorly as an English major at university, he loved reading. He displayed an impressive vocabulary and impeccable penmanship. His knowledge was intimidating. "Have a good day and learn things," he recited daily. To date, he's the only musician I've heard refer to the *Rubaiyat of Omar Khayyam* from the stage. Other favorites included his Kiowa cousin N. Scott Momaday's *House Made of Dawn* and *The Way to Rainy Mountain*, Dashiell Hammett detective novels, roguish Hollywood star Errol Flynn's autobiography, and Ross Russell's magisterial biography of Charlie Parker. Jesse was especially intrigued by Parker's redheaded Jewish trumpeter Red Rodney, who, in terms of his ethnicity, seemed dissonant in a music world where he was known as "Albino Red." He became hooked on heroin, not unlike Jesse himself.[4]

To Jesse, the meaning of life was simple: eat good food, play good music, and have fun. His song "Every Night Is Saturday Night" wasn't just a party tune; it was a serious personal philosophy, though it sometimes became reckless. "I made too much money too soon, and too young," he once observed. Jesse was a quintessential Virgo: hardworking, but equally hard on those around him. He subjected himself and others to abrupt pivots between wanting to feel as intensely as possible and not wanting to feel at all. "There's just a darkness in me," he confessed to friends when they tried to help. "Being an artist," he said, "you have to feel deeply. You have to feel more deeply than your average person. You have to feel more deeply to even *want* to be an artist."[5]

Jesse was indeed an artist, but he was also a man of many contradictions. He knew his talent, but he was insecure. He was an innovator who championed tradition; he loved Christmas and simple pleasures like beaches and amusement parks. He could talk on the phone for hours, but then disappear for days. He went out of his way to help friends, but he also hustled them. He produced a large network of musicians, but he compartmentalized his life. He was proud of who he was, but his omnipresent mirrored sunglasses made it seem like he wanted to hide or disguise himself. He was physically imposing, but his humor was disarming—his smile was a song unto itself.[6]

Jesse Ed Davis was also Native American. Though Jesse himself insisted on being understood first as a musician, then as a Native American musician, the fact of his Indigeneity makes his life and legacy all the more compelling and important, especially given how few Indigenous artists have reached his level of influence, recognition, and success. In a century often portrayed as a period of ongoing distress and decline for Native people, Jesse and his Kiowa, Comanche, Cheyenne, Mvskoke, and Seminole ancestors from Oklahoma exemplified new possibilities for Native Americans. They prevailed through creativity and persistence. While speaking the language of sovereignty and self-determination, Jesse and his kin exercised power and shaped their worlds through renewed modes of cultural production and collaboration, as well as renewed labor and professional opportunities, including sports, religion, science, art, education, politics, medicine, acting, and finally, music.

From his first major gig supporting chart-topping rockabilly and country artist Conway Twitty, through European tours with Taj Mahal, George Harrison's 1971 all-star Concert for Bangladesh, and an arena tour with Rod Stewart and the Faces, Jesse appeared on some of the biggest stages in the world, from Los Angeles, Chicago, and New York to England, Germany, and France. At a time when few other Native American musicians appeared on concert stages, radio waves, and record store walls, Jesse achieved monumental visibility and audibility. In both Hollywood studios and the courts of British rock royalty, Jesse Indigenized the transatlantic crosscurrents of popular music in the late twentieth century, and even cocreated an altogether new style of Indigenous music. If not exactly a diplomat, Jesse was no mascot or sojourner. He was a producer, insider, and key collaborator.

Whereas twentieth-century Native American history is often presented as a policy narrative emphasizing American Indians as colonized people subject to federal assimilation campaigns, I instead position Jesse's story as a cultural narrative—one that portrays him more as an Indigenous person than an Indigenous object. In the 1960s and '70s, Native people typically only appeared in national media through the lens of Red Power activism. The significance of groups such as the American Indian Movement (AIM), which flourished during Jesse's commercial peak, cannot and should not be understated in the collective fight for self-determination in education, health care, child welfare, environmental protection, and more. But Jesse's music was more of an ally than an adversary or alternative to those causes. His music projected an equally important expression of Indigenous humanity through artistry.

If Jesse sang less about American Indian people than many contemporary white artists, it was because he didn't need to. Jesse's mere existence was subversive, both offstage—in an industry where Native workers and artists were once foundational—and onstage, where a generation of young music fans could see Native people were still here, precisely when the bestselling *Bury My Heart at Wounded Knee* (1970) implicitly suggested otherwise. Though his fame never surpassed that of Native musicians such as Jimi Hendrix or Robbie Robertson, who achieved greater commercial success, Jesse's total range, the sheer volume and diversity of his work, extended much further.

Though lacking a large cohort in popular music, Jesse belonged to a generation of Native leaders and luminaries in different areas who challenged conventional wisdom about how and where Native people could fit in postwar America. These included political activists and leaders such as Wilma Mankiller, Dennis Banks, LaDonna Harris, and Winona LaDuke; writers such as Joy Harjo, Vine Deloria Jr., and N. Scott Momaday; and artists and entertainers such as T. C. Cannon, Charlie Hill, and Wes Studi, many of whom Jesse knew personally.

Even so, given his remarkable success as an Indigenous rock star, it's tempting to conclude that Jesse is exceptional as a historical subject.

In fact, he is representative in ways previous histories have intentionally or unwittingly foreclosed. Perhaps one reason Jesse isn't better remembered is that the general public has been conditioned to think of Native Americans in the late twentieth century in injurious stereotypes. Jesse's experience in Los Angeles as a self-described "urban Indian" did not inevitably become a story of skid row and dislocation. Instead, his experience speaks to a larger theme of Indigenous mobility and ingenuity. Similarly, his music calls for integration and cultural exchange rather than separation and protest. Jesse was more of an interlocutor than a Red Power activist.

Jesse nevertheless rose to fame in the context of the Red Power era. In 1969, when John Trudell and Indians of All Tribes claimed Alcatraz Island, Jesse was an emergent guitarist backing Taj Mahal. When the occupation ended in 1971, Jesse's first solo album hit shelves. His second solo album corresponded with the Bureau of Indian Affairs takeover in Washington, DC, in 1972. In 1973, his jubilant third solo album appeared while Native people were dodging bullets at Wounded Knee. With friends in high places and major album and production deals, Jesse could have provided the soundtrack to Red Power. We might wonder why he didn't. In the end, we might consider whether anyone really could.

The music Jesse made wasn't so much a national anthem as an expression of Indigenous sovereignty but a "Natural Anthem," the title of an instrumental tune from his third solo album, as an expression of Indigenous culture. "Jesse spoke through his guitar and his demeanor," suggests Little Feat keyboardist Bill Payne. In doing so, Jesse created a soundtrack for a different kind of Indigenous takeover that emerged out of twenty years of urban relocation, the racialization of Native people as a minority group within Lyndon B. Johnson's Great Society, a federal shift to a tribal self-determination policy, and an expanding generation of young Indigenous people who attended college and broke into the American middle class and mainstream media consciousness. Jesse's lyrics and music illuminated a still largely unfamiliar set of Indigenous experiences, ones that were a little more Saturday night in the city than Monday morning on the rez and filled with a little more joy than pain.[7]

For Jesse, the world of music promised a retreat from the world of Oklahoma, where being Indian shaped almost everything about his life. At the same time, the music industry in the 1960s and '70s was a place where being Indian could come into relief in unpredictable, sometimes undesirable, ways. It presented a danger in that it could become an inescapable persona or caricature, to say nothing of possible discrimination and violence. Jesse's studio collaborator Van Dyke Parks held that the fact of his Indigeneity was more foundational than final. Jesse's power both emerged from and transcended his background. "Jesse Ed had all of that, the mystery of empire and the progress of [a] prophet," Parks recalls. "Yes, he wanted to survive, he needed a meal, but he was beyond that. He was greater than his opportunity. . . . I knew immediately when I met Jesse Ed [that] he was a charismatic man, that is, you felt you were in touch with someone who knew God."[8]

Many former bandmates remember Jesse as the first Native person they ever met. Some of the very same people who insist that Jesse's Indigeneity was immaterial among socially enlightened artists would sometimes seamlessly pivot to mention of Jesse's Native features—a "fierce" expression, like his Comanche ancestors, or his beautiful black hair. New acquaintances called him "Indian Ed" or "Chief Davis." The nicknames were conceived in affection, but Jesse desperately "wanted to be a part of this other world where that shit doesn't matter," stresses his Mohawk friend and early guitar influence Robbie Robertson. "The biggest obstacle that Jesse had to deal with was being an Indian," adds Jesse's Dakota music partner John Trudell.[9]

That is to say, Jesse had to protect himself. His pride in being Indigenous was never in doubt. He knew about his peoples' pasts and how he fit within their ongoing stories. He didn't have to discover or rediscover himself: Jesse was born Indian, on the banks of the Washita River, in a Kiowa-Comanche tipi, as he told it. It's more than a narrative device when I demonstrate his numerous name changes across the following pages. Indeed, many Native cultures practice name changes that signify new stages of experience and maturity. "Snookie" became Eddie, who became Ed, before he finally settled on his birth name, his father's name. Jesse went to California to become Jesse, who was first and foremost an authentic bluesman and rock and roller. That's how he wanted to be remembered.

What made Jesse an exceptional talent, in so many words, was an extension of the person playing the guitar. His sound reflected his spirit: playful, slightly dangerous, and always full of life. He played with a soft touch in his picking hand. His right-hand rhythm was especially fluid as he balanced his subtle attack with a cranked amplifier that made his guitar extra responsive. Playing his volume and tone knobs like instruments unto themselves, he searched for the best possible placement of each note within a song's chordal spectrum. His slide guitar technique only expanded his tonal palette, affording him a broad dynamic in terms of volume, color, and sound. Now contrast his left hand, which played strongly on the neck and fretboard. In these respects—forceful left hand, sympathetic right hand—Jesse approached the guitar more like a piano, his first instrument.

In fact, Jesse derived significant influence from musicians who didn't play guitar, citing blues pianist Otis Spann as his overall greatest influence. (Conversely, Jesse once suggested his favorite guitar player was saxophonist Junior Walker.) Jesse embraced a diversity in his playing that reflected the multitude of settings he experienced, particularly in the geographical and cultural crossroads of Oklahoma. Indeed, his string bends were so muscular that they occasionally slipped into a shade of bluesy dissonance with a forceful imprecision that allowed his funky character to come through. With an idiosyncratic command of his guitar, Jesse liked to work quickly and encouraged producers to keep his and his bandmates' mistakes when their mistakes demonstrated soul. For Jesse, soul was more important than perfection.[10]

As a hybrid rhythm and lead player, Jesse prioritized enhancing a song's effect without confusing or overwhelming its essence. He was a minimalist who focused on melody, an approach borrowed from the early rock and roll 45s he listened to in Oklahoma, in which the guitar was still a rhythm instrument that set the spine of a song. This characteristic talent made him especially attractive to British musicians who grew up listening to those same 45s, often left behind by American soldiers before they returned home after World War II. As kids, many famous British musicians dreamed about America, and what's more American than a Native American?

Jesse stood out among guitarists in his selectiveness with notes. He wasn't afraid to hang back if he didn't think he could improve what was already happening inside a song. "When he played and I played drums behind him it just sounded like the real shit," says Jim Keltner, who played more sessions with Jesse than any other musician. Keltner considers Jesse one of two true geniuses he worked with, the other being jazz legend Albert Stinson, who also died from heroin addiction. Guitarists Bonnie Raitt and Bob Britt both describe Jesse in just one word: badass.[11]

ANSWERING THE PHONE in his Los Angeles apartment in 1986, decades after leaving home in Oklahoma City, Jesse Ed Davis was anxious to share some news with the caller. "My ship has come in," he beamed. "I got sixty acres that's come down from the Kiowa," his mother's tribe. "As luck would have it, I don't know if you know any legends of the old General George Armstrong Custer, but there was an old thing that went down called the Washita Massacre," he explained. Jesse's sixty acres included a ridge in the flood plain overlooking the site of the massacre. "I didn't know that until a few days ago," he added.[12]

But Jesse had always known stories about what happened to his Kiowa, Comanche, and Cheyenne people in the Washita country, including the murder of many women and children in 1868. He also knew about his Seminole and Mvskoke ancestors who fought to defend their homelands in the southeastern United States before being marched at gunpoint to Indian Territory during the 1830s.

"I'm fixing to move back to Oklahoma," Jesse announced to the caller. He was on a comeback trail, after all, making new music with Native artists, attending powwows, thinking about dancing again, and planning to enter the sweat lodge. At night, he dreamed about a life playing guitar in a little café on an Indian reservation, or moving into an old mansion on a hill back in Oklahoma. Alas, as his friend Bob Dylan once sang, "You can always come back, but you can't come back all the way." Although, maybe that isn't exactly true. Perhaps Jesse had his own thoughts on the matter. "Keep me coming, back again," he sang.

One

NATURAL ANTHEM

This was all Indian land. The Comanche and Kiowa were here before there was an Oklahoma City.
—RICHENDA DAVIS BATES

J ESSE ED DAVIS'S PEOPLE came along many paths from many places. They did extraordinary things, lived dynamic lives, and shaped history. Many of them could sustain books of their own. Jesse's Kiowa, Comanche, Seminole, Mvskoke, and Cheyenne families include an exceptional number of notable chiefs, medicine people, knowledge keepers, artists, writers, musicians, athletes, war veterans, business leaders, and more. They hunted, farmed, worshipped, sang, danced, and drummed. They governed and made treaties. They fought to defend their lands. They were visible and audible in every direction. Some rest in the Wichita Mountains, some in the Rainy Mountain Kiowa Indian Baptist Cemetery, some in Fort Sill, some on a hilltop near the old Arbeka Trading Post, and some, including Jesse and his parents, rest in Oklahoma City. Their histories are as complex as they are compelling.

In the nineteenth century, the families Jesse was born to survived violent colonization of the American West. In the twentieth century, through profound sacrifice and bold ingenuity, they rebuilt their families, homes, communities, and nations, and remade themselves as People. Taken together, they demonstrate the range of possibilities for Jesse's life and allow us to consider how Jesse might have thought about his position relative to his Indigenous ancestors and his place in the world—where he could go, who he could become.[1]

Jesse's family stories intersected at one place, one word, Washita, which became shorthand for his own sense of who he was and where he came from. Washita country is Kiowa, Comanche, and Cheyenne country in western Oklahoma. The Washita River meanders through it. To the south, the Wichita Mountains appear almost like sleeping bison on the horizon when they first come into view, and bison herds still roam there today. But Washita is more than a winding river. It also invokes survivors who experienced trauma that transcended generations, trauma that was quite literally in Jesse's blood.

"We're going to go way down home now," Jesse told an audience in Rochester, New York, in 1973, before launching into his autobiographical number "Washita Love Child." "I guess everybody's hip to Wounded Knee by now." Certainly they were. Reports from the frontlines of an armed conflict, still underway, between US Marshals and FBI agents backed by armored personnel carriers against a hundred or so Native Americans, including many Vietnam veterans, in the Wounded Knee hamlet on the Pine Ridge Reservation, had appeared on the nightly news for almost two months straight. Jesse continued, "A long time ago there was another massacre on the Washita River back in Oklahoma, God's country."[2]

Before dawn on November 27, 1868, Civil War veteran Colonel George Armstrong Custer charged four columns of roughly seven hundred cavalrymen into the sleeping Washita River village to the soundtrack of "Garryowen," an old Irish drinking song from Limerick. "We'll break windows, we'll break doors / the watch knock down by threes and fours / then let the doctors work their cures / and tinker up our bruises," so the song went. Cheyenne women and children hid in the riverbed while Cheyenne soldiers fought back. They were overmatched. Custer prevailed, continuing to hunt down fleeing Cheyenne and allied Native people throughout the next day. Custer's victory at the so-called Battle of the Washita resulted in twice as many Native women and children killed as male defenders.

After Civil War general William Tecumseh Sherman learned of

the US military assault on the Washita camp, he congratulated area commander General Philip Sheridan and suggested that he would have "all these Indians begging for their lives" by Christmas. Sheridan and Sherman blamed the massacre on Cheyenne Chief Black Kettle, a peace chief who survived the 1864 Sand Creek Massacre in Colorado but failed to escape the Washita Massacre when he and his wife were shot in the back attempting to ride away. The US military officials delighted in their belief that they had defeated Native people responsible for recent hostilities in the region. But it was projection. It had in fact been the US military that murdered women and children on that winter morning when Cheyenne, Comanche, and Kiowa people ran for their lives. Still, only a few years later, the US military had the gall to describe the Kiowa and Comanche as defiant people who resisted reservation confinement, while federal agents used food rations, guaranteed by treaties and land cessions, to extort more concessions.[3]

Jesse's ancestors who survived the Washita Massacre never forgot what they experienced there. They couldn't. Jesse never forgot either. When he formed his own music production company as part of his first solo album contract in 1970, he christened it "Washita Productions," as though his art and imprimatur were a tribute to, and made possible by, his Cheyenne, Kiowa, and Comanche people's survival just over one hundred years prior. Jesse used his Washita Productions label and letterhead until the day he died.

JESSE'S COMANCHE ANCESTORS, who still call themselves "Lords of the Plains," once dominated portions of the southwest in an expansive geographic area the Spanish called Comanchería. The Comanche governed the region through economic and military prowess. European horses and weapons, mostly coming from Spanish and French traders, led to a profound transformation on the Southern Plains west of the Mississippi during the eighteenth and nineteenth centuries. Horses fostered greater mobility and efficiency for tribes that became even more dependent on the buffalo, both for their own immediate survival and for the expanding market in hides. Moreover, new weapons helped Plains and Southwestern tribes such as the Comanche, Apache, Navajo, Ute, and Kiowa defend their prized hunting grounds.

At the beginning of the eighteenth century, the Comanche were a small tribe of hunters living in northern New Mexico. They had only recently arrived, after fleeing tribal warfare and political disputes on the central Great Plains. Soon, however, mostly as a result of their massive herds of horses and skills as mounted warriors, they began dominating a massive trade network. Through their own complex political system, they operated a major trade center in the Upper Arkansas River Valley that served as a redistribution point for trade goods circulating from the Rio Grande all the way to the Mississippi.

Many Indigenous tribes engaged in the practice of adopting captives seized during battle. This stemmed from a need for marriage partners outside the tribal genetic profile and a desire for replenishing populations after disease struck. By the late eighteenth century, however, tribes such as the Comanche, Navajo, Apache, and Osage began conducting raids for the purpose of taking captives, not to adopt into their respective tribes but to sell to other parties, typically the Spanish or French, who in turn sold them into slavery. In some cases, the French sold Southwestern Indian captives to the British, who might subject the captives to slavery as far away as South Carolina, where they then might even be sold to the West Indies. The practice reflected the maelstrom of colonial markets and general malevolence inherent to colonization.

In time this market dominance resulted in Comanche people incorporating neighboring tribes, including their old Kiowa enemies, into their political and economic systems. The Comanche became a territorial power, in effect staging a colonial role reversal in which the Comanche people expanded and dictated the terms of trade and violence while Europeans resorted to resistance and retreat. The Comanche proved so powerful that they significantly explain why the Spanish and then Mexican governments failed to ever establish real authority in the greater New Spain and New Mexico territory.

By the 1860s, resulting from warfare with Cheyenne and Arapaho people to the north and diminishing trade prospects with unstable Mexico to the south, Comanche people had lost their geopolitical primacy and made treaties with the United States for permanent homelands in Indian Territory. Many Comanche bands concentrated north of the Red River, abundant with cattle grazing lands. The famous and controversial Comanche Chief Quanah could be found here after leading his people through the Red River War in 1874. Jesse Edwin Davis II, Jesse's father, counted Quanah as an ancestor. Quanah later became a successful cattle entrepreneur and railroad investor. At his impressive Star House, originally erected near Fort Sill, Quanah hosted his friend Teddy Roosevelt. From one angle, Quanah willed his people through almost impossible ordeals, through battlefield leadership and then economic entrepreneurship. But from a different angle, he enriched himself at his people's expense. If the reality is somewhere in the middle, then it might be that capitalism comes with costs. Or, from a more practical and less academic perspective, as one of Quanah's great-great-granddaughters stressed to me, "They were going to kill us all."[4]

Quanah's daughter Laura moved the Star House to Cache and sold it to a non-Comanche family in 1958. It still stands today, although in severe disrepair from floods, time, and neglect exacerbated by an ongoing dispute over rightful ownership. Through a gate, behind an old trading post, past the twisted, rusty remains of the abandoned Eagle Park amusement center's Little Dipper rollercoaster, sits the dilapidated home—an emblem of one chapter of Comanche people's history, like the 1867 Medicine Lodge Treaty or Jesse Ed Davis's Telecaster guitar.

On his father's side, Jesse's great-great-great-great grandfather, a Comanche *paraibo* (leader) named Parrawasamen (Ten Bears) led his people in both treatymaking and military defense of ancestral lands, once even leading a counterattack against the US in retaliation for the invading nation's assault on a band of Kiowas, Jesse's mother's people. Mvskoke actor Will Sampson portrayed Parrawasamen in Clint Eastwood's *The Outlaw Josey Wales*. So did Dakota actor Floyd Westerman in *Dances with Wolves*, though Kevin Costner refashioned him as a Lakota leader. During the 1980s, in his concurrent music career, Westerman shared live bills with Jesse's Grafitti Band.[5]

Parrawasamen was a reluctant signatory at the 1867 Medicine Lodge Treaty meeting in Kansas. Alongside Kiowa and Apache leaders, he and his Comanche delegation secured United States peace and protection from illegally encroaching settlers in exchange for moving to a reservation in Indian Territory and a cessation of raids and captive-taking. At the meeting, General Sherman warned the Native representatives that they "can no more stop this than you can stop the sun or the moon. You must submit, and do the best you can." In his most famous speech, Parrawasamen considered the meaning of "best you can":

> My people have never first drawn a bow or fired a gun against the whites. There has been trouble between us. My young men have danced the war dance. But it was not begun by us. It was you who sent the first soldier. . . . The Comanches are not weak and blind, like the pups of a dog when seven days old. They are strong and far-sighted, like grown horses. . . . You have said that you want to put us on a reservation, to build us houses and to make us medicine lodges. I do not want them. I was born under the prairie, where the wind blew free and there was nothing to break the light of the sun. I was born where there were no walls and everything drew free breath. I want to die there, not within walls. I know every stream and every wood between the Rio Grande and the Arkansas River. I have hunted and lived all over that country. I live like my fathers before me and like them I live happily.

Parrawasamen's protest proved prescient. Going forward, the United States failed to honor its treaty agreements. Faced with starvation and sickness when annuity goods and food rations didn't arrive, Comanche people had no choice but to feed themselves through a new series of raids. So catastrophic was the outcome in Indian Territory and the resultant arguments back in Washington that Congress altogether forswore further treatymaking with Indigenous nations in 1871. Instead, Congress began treating Native people as internal subjects, though not citizens—and then proceeded to complain about its "Indian problem."[6]

Parrawasamen's grandsons Permansu and Tah-pui bring us closer to Jesse Ed Davis. Permansu, also known as Comanche Jack, became a cattle rancher and business partner with Quanah. After the 1874 Red

River War, Permansu served as a tribal policeman while providing leadership in the Comanche peyote faith. He was especially responsible for integrating Jesus into the ceremonies and teachings. Permansu's trips to Washington with Quanah to negotiate leasing agreements with Texan cattle ranchers made him as controversial among Comanche people as Quanah. Both became rich from their endeavors and found themselves at odds with some Comanche people and most of the Kiowa people to the north regarding the question of leasing their lands to Texas cattle ranchers.[7]

Jesse Ed Davis's paternal great-great-grandfather and Permansu's older brother Tah-pui (meaning "To Scout on Foot"—settlers mispronounced it as "Tah-pony") was subchief of the Yappaituka band of Comanche people. He missed the twentieth century by one year, dying from a smallpox epidemic in 1899 that took many members of his family. Permansu buried Tah-pui on top of a hill in what became the Mountain View Addition within Lawton, not to be confused with the town of Mountain View to the north. In 1903, as Lawton grew around the burial site, local business leaders demanded that Tah-pui and his nine relatives' remains, along with the bones of an unidentified Kiowa person, be moved to a cemetery. Permansu paid a local Christian missionary $100 for help. Today Tah-pui and his relations rest somewhere in the Deyo Cemetery, west of Lawton, in the shadows of the Wichitas, though the exact location of their shared grave is known only to Comanche elders.[8]

Tah-pui was survived by his son Esa-wyoh-yah, translated as Running Wolf, who was forced to assume the name Eustace Merrick while attending the infamous Carlisle Indian Industrial School in faraway Pennsylvania during the early twentieth century. Eustace (or Eustis) Merrick would later become grandfather to a Comanche boy named Jesse Edwin Davis II. When the latter became a popular fine artist, he reclaimed his grandfather's name, using the spelling "Asawoya" when he signed his prize-winning paintings.[9]

ALICE BROWN DAVIS, Jesse's Seminole great-great grandmother from the Tiger Clan (prominent for producing leaders), was no less remarkable

than his Comanche ancestors. Davis served as the first female chief of the
Seminole Nation and led her people through the disastrous allotment
policy and the Great Depression. Born within the Cherokee Nation in
Indian Territory in 1852, Davis was the daughter of a Seminole woman,
Lucy Gray-Beard, and a Scottish doctor named John Brown, who was
born in Edinburgh and educated at the University of South Carolina
after immigrating to the US. The federal government appointed Brown
as a physician to the Seminole people during their forced removal from
Florida to Indian Territory during the 1830s.

Alice's brother John Frippo Brown was an ordained minister. He
had been a Confederate officer during the Civil War and later served
as principal chief of the Seminole Nation in Indian Territory with support from his friend Teddy Roosevelt. In 1905, Alice joined other Seminole people in a diplomatic visit to Mexico City to discuss land grants
Mexico made for Seminole people who helped defend Mexico against
attacks from other Native nations. She also visited Palm Beach, Florida,
to serve as a language interpreter in a high-profile murder case concerning her relative De Soto Tiger. In 1922, President Harding appointed her
chief of the Seminole Tribe of Oklahoma, making her the first female
chief of any Indian nation in Oklahoma, and possibly the first in North
American history.

Alice Brown married George Rollin Davis, whose ancestors were
Irish. "There was a Mick in the woodpile," Jesse jested. "That's how I got
the name Davis."[10] Known to his family as "Roll" and Native people as
"Big-Davis," George stood six feet tall, waving beautiful surgeon's hands,
gazing through laughing blue eyes. In 1895, Alice and Roll split when
he got another woman pregnant. One night he slipped away, leaving
Alice to tell people he died in a fight over cards on a gambling train.[11]

For many years prior, George and Alice Davis ran the Arbeka Trading Post, near Henryetta, in Okmulgee County. The trading post sold
pots and pans, soap, candy, crackers, coffee, pecans, flour, meat, and
specialized in felt hats. Children enjoyed making treats there by sand-
wiching a gingersnap between two crackers. Skunk and possum hides
hung from the ceiling and emitted a foul odor. Cowboys passing through
could occupy a cot on the front porch, singing songs into the night, and

wrestling in the morning. The mail came through the trading post. So did Al Jennings, future silent film star and leader of the dissident Jennings Gang that robbed trains, banks, and trading posts throughout Indian Territory. The gang once stayed overnight at the Arbeka Trading Post. It's unclear whether they exacted any payment from the proprietor who was gracious enough to allow the outlaws to rest their horses and catch some shuteye.[12]

As a hub of commerce and information, the post granted the Davises a certain degree of influence in their community and in the Oklahoma Seminole Nation.[13] Despite its central importance, however, the trading post lay in a remote location. One relative remembered it as a rough life and landscape: "We made roads, forded streams by just driving into them. . . . I had a feeling of being lost in the woods, but strangely thrilling instead of being in any way alarming. The country in a thirty or so-mile radius of Arbeka was quite broken and sharply so. . . . We drove over and around everything."[14]

Alice and George Davis also owned the nearby Bar X Bar Ranch, which held seven thousand cattle. When he became old enough, their son, the first Jesse Edwin Davis, became the ranch foreman, earned prestige as a champion rodeo rider and roper, married a Mvskoke neighbor girl named Ella Knight, and would later be great-grandfather to Jesse Edwin Davis III, though they would never meet. Jesse Edwin Davis had a reputation as a dangerous young man who supposedly had notches on his pistol, though there is no evidence that he ever committed a crime of that nature. He probably stuck to gambling and drinking, which wasn't uncharacteristic of young men in his time and place.[15]

Jesse had a brother named Jack, who achieved a modest career in music playing cornet on the traveling tent-show circuit, working from Texas to Montana in the Worthen and Allen shows. The leading female star, Ione McBride, fell in love with Jack, married him, and convinced him to try acting. Up in Roundup, Montana, Jack joined a film studio, making $30 per week playing not an Indian but a cowboy, and also wrote a couple of screenplays. Jack dreamed of becoming a star and ensuring that his mother would never have to work again. It didn't happen. His screenplays were not contracted, the acting work dried up, and he was soon back on the music circuit. Not long after, Jack disappeared, abandoning his wife and baby, who had been on the road with him. He only resurfaced when he wrote home to ask for a little cash, as he often did. He was ashamed of his inability to support his family: "Something always happens to keep me in debt and absolutely powerless to help them. My thoughts almost drive me insane. What would you advise me to do, Mama?" Alice sent him money to pay his musician union dues. After years performing through-out the West, Jack finally settled in California, working as an actor.[16]

Meanwhile, Jack's brother Jesse Edwin Davis remained a rancher throughout his life, rarely straying far from Arbeka, with the exception of service in the original 1st Separate Troop A Cavalry out of Okemah and service in World War I. He became very sick in 1921. Some records indicate influenza; others suggest some sort of respiratory disease, possi-bly tuberculosis. "He will cough at intervals all night," his mother Alice wrote from his bedside. Alice tried sending him to a government hospi-tal out west, hoping a drier climate might help. Jesse's sisters prescribed everything from milk, honey, and calamus root to cod liver oil and raw eggs. Alice stayed by his side until April 21, 1921, when the first Jesse Edwin Davis died in the Arbeka ranch house. Alice held his hand until his heart stopped. "His chief aim in life was to give pleasure to others," his obituary stated—not unlike his great-grandson Jesse Edwin Davis III. "Good-bye till morning comes again / The shades of death brings thought of pain / But could we know how short the night / That fall and hides thee from our sight / Our hearts would sing the glad refrain / Goodbye till morning comes again," his family sang at his funeral.[17]

JESSE'S CHEYENNE ANCESTORS are more obscure, both in his lineage and available sources, but it is apparent that they were also prominent and remarkable people, including an impressive line of powerful women from a Cheyenne community in Colony, Oklahoma. Jesse's great-grandmother was Martha Little Bear, also called Sage Woman. Her daughter with Eustace Merrick, son of the Comanche subchief Tah-pui, married Jesse's Seminole-Mvskoke grandfather William "Willie" Graham Davis. Mar-tha's sister, Mary Inkanish, became a master beadworker who taught people the technique in the hope of preserving it. Jesse Edwin Davis II's artworld friend, anthropologist Alice Marriott, spent significant time with Mary and coauthored a book about her life and times. Like her great-grandnephew Jesse Edwin Davis III, Mary Inkanish grew closer to her Native culture and roots toward the end of her life.

Martha and Mary's generation blended modern homes with tipis in early-twentieth-century Colony. Mary was one of the first Cheyenne people to live in a house and drive a car. Though Jesse Edwin Davis II sometimes felt he didn't know enough about his Indigenous culture, he did know about his great-aunt Mary Inkanish and emphasized her when discussing his background. Jesse, his wife Vivian, and their young son— then still "Eddie"—would emulate her when they moved to Oklahoma City and appeared to neighbors in their Park Estates neighborhood to be the most progressive people on the block, with the newest appliances, fanciest cars, and trendiest clothes.

Martha and Mary's mother Little Bear/Yellow Woman Stone was a holy woman, or Mah-hee-yuna, who served the Sun Dance. She had Mary and Martha with a man named Block, who had opened a trading post in Colony. Block was a mysterious man, possibly French-Canadian, who stayed with Little Bear just long enough to have the two girls and then disappeared. Little Bear never discussed her marriage to a Frenchman from Canada and her daughters knew nothing about him, not even his complete name, beyond some vague bits of information from people around town. We don't know why Yellow Woman Stone married him, but she seemed to regret it.

Martha and Mary had a second maternal figure, possibly an aunt, in Shell Woman, who had fought at the grisly 1864 Sand Creek Massacre in Colorado and killed four US soldiers. These were tough women; Cheyenne girls like Mary and Martha learned not to cry at a very young age. At the Sand Creek and Washita Massacres that Jesse Ed Davis's Cheyenne ancestors survived, crying could be a matter of life or death.[18]

JESSE'S KIOWA ANCESTORS worshipped the Sun. He enjoyed explaining this to Jehovah's Witnesses when they visited his home in Marina del Rey during the early 1970s. If he was toying with them, he was also consistent with his people's beliefs. The Sun *is* the most powerful force, or *dw'dw'*, in Kiowa culture. Sun Father gave birth to Son of the Sun, which divided into the Split Boys, one of whom became the Ten Medicines, maintained by ten Kiowa medicine keepers, who counted some of Jesse's ancestors among them.[19] Kiowa people also acknowledge the Big Dipper constellation, known to them as Kiowa kinspeople in the night sky: the Seven Sisters who escaped the wilderness. Jesse's opening instrumental jam, "Big Dipper," on his third solo album *Keep Me Comin'* may refer to them. Or maybe the song title is merely a gesture to the speedy Big Dipper rollercoaster that was a feature attraction at the Springlake Amusement Park near Jesse's home in Oklahoma City.[20]

Kiowa people emerged from the headwaters of the Yellowstone River in present-day Montana. Jesse told certain trustworthy friends the Kiowa origin story, wherein the trickster Saynday turned the Kiowa people into ants so they could pass from the underground world into our present world through a hollow cottonwood log. One large, pregnant ant became stuck, and many Kiowa ant people became trapped in the passage and perished. This explains why there have always been a relatively small number of Kiowa people in this world. Those who survived passed from darkness into light and learned to hunt buffalo. By the late eighteenth century, alongside Apache allies, they occupied the sacred Black Hills of present-day South Dakota, before rival Lakota and Cheyenne forced them from the Black Hills to the Southern Plains, where they first fought against the more powerful Comanche people before making an alliance.[21]

In 1867, under the threat of annihilation, Jesse's Kiowa ancestors signed the Medicine Lodge Treaty, doing their best to preserve as much land and power as possible while agreeing to a defined reservation within Indian Territory. Like their Comanche counterparts in the negotiations, they met the challenges the treaty both reflected and perpetuated. In his enduringly powerful work *The Way to Rainy Mountain*, Pulitzer Prize–winning Kiowa author N. Scott Momaday, a relation of Jesse's through their great-grandmother Kau-Au-Ointy, an Indigenous Mexican captive, described the people, place, and time as a "landscape that is incomparable, a time that is gone forever, and a human spirit, which endures." Jesse would have known this passage. At the end of his life, after he had traded away so many earthly possessions, he still held on to his signed copies of Momaday's books.[22]

Churches among the Kiowa became important places for remembering personal histories and nurturing the enduring human spirit. More than places of Christian worship, churches were central social institutions in a community comprised of people praying for deliverance from pain and hunger. If a passionate embrace of the Christian faith seems counterintuitive, even traitorous, in hindsight, it made sense then, and persistence has created a logic unto itself. "They came at a time when the Kiowas were searching, they were lost," said Delores Toyebo Harragarra, a modern member of the Kiowa nation. "This came along and they embraced it and they never left it." It was fortunate, Harragarra reflected, that the first missionaries arriving from Chicago in the 1890s recognized that the Kiowa were a musical people and encouraged them to make songs in the Kiowa language.[23]

Jesse's maternal great-grandfather Gui-Pola (Mature Wolf), popularly known as Kiowa George Poolaw, was an arrow maker, sweat lodge doctor, and keeper of the Kiowa calendar, which documented past events through pictographs. In this respect, Kiowa George was a historian. He was one of the Kiowa tribe's last official medicine men and a member of the Buffalo Medicine Cult. These Kiowa men practiced healing inside medicine tipis, where they invited the power of a guardian spirit. They danced to a drum beat they made with their medicine bundles and sang medicine songs, bringing music to the sick. Jesse Ed Davis might be said to have done the same, bringing people into a communal space, making rhythm, singing songs that celebrated life and the healing needed to sustain it. In his own way, Jesse offered people good medicine music.[24]

Kiowa George also served as a scout with the all-Indian 7th Cavalry at Fort Sill and fought in the Spanish-American War. The full range of military service and accolades among Jesse's relations on both his mother's and father's sides cannot be captured here. Suffice to say that Kiowa George's grandson and Jesse's uncle, Pascal Cleatus Poolaw, remains the most decorated Native American veteran in the history of the United

States armed forces. Serving in World War II, Korea, and Vietnam, Pascal earned four Silver Stars, five Bronze Stars, three Purple Hearts, and a total of forty-two medals and citations.[25]

Kiowa George later acted in the 1916 film *Old Texas*, produced by Texas cattle rancher George Goodnight, who wanted to depict and preserve his triumphant effort at saving a small herd of bison in the Texas panhandle, after long contributing to the slaughter of roughly fifteen thousand of them. In the film Kiowa George performs a buffalo hunt and makes the kill shot. As many as eleven thousand local spectators showed up to watch the Kiowa perform their hunt on Goodnight's ranch.[26]

Kiowa George's son Horace, a famed Kiowa photographer, and others among the Poolaws, Jesse's mother Vivian Saunkeah's maternal family, represented a new generation of Native people who embraced technological innovation and popular media in order to achieve representation in a dramatically changing world. As much as any Native family, the Poolaws demonstrated Indigenous peoples' capacity for engaging modernity on their own terms. "I do not want to be remembered for my pictures, but through my pictures I want my people to remember themselves," Horace Poolaw's daughter Linda recalls her father saying. "Granpa" Horace Poolaw, remembers his grandson Thomas, was a "man who wore many hats."[27]

That characterization is true for many members of Jesse's Kiowa family, especially Jesse himself, who was much more than an Indian guitarist. Jesse demonstrated diverse skills as he helped his people remember something about themselves, something more about a vibrant spirit than trauma. Jesse's Kiowa ancestors were cosmopolitan people who lived and traveled from Montana to Mexico, engaging with many different peoples, societies, cultures, and economies across centuries. What distinguished Jesse's Kiowa family wasn't their approach—they were more representative than exceptional in that respect. It was instead their talent.[28]

We can hear these histories in Jesse Ed Davis's guitar. His ancestors knew something about the blues, evident in some of the great Native guitar players then and now, including Alex Palmer, Gene Tsoodle,

Chebon Tiger, Dusty Miller, Ace Moreland, the numerous players featured in the film *Rumble*, and more. As Jesse's cousin N. Scott Momaday wrote, these generations of Kiowa people experienced a "crucial time of change when the Plains culture was brought down and the Kiowa, along with other tribes, had to enter upon another, harder plane of existence. It was a brutal transition, an accommodation most difficult, final, and unforgiving."[29]

CHIEF AMONG JESSE'S inspiring ancestral forebears were two especially remarkable grandfathers who motivated him to challenge all boundaries and attempt greatness. Jesse's paternal grandfather, William Graham Davis, was born in 1900 near Okemah in Okfuskee County. "Open range, there was no fences in those days," he later reminisced. He grew up on the ranch his father Jesse Edwin Davis managed and began herding cattle atop bareback horses at age five. Farm work can lend itself well to football. At the Haskell Indian Institute in Lawrence, Kansas, one of the most prominent off-reservation Indian boarding schools in the country, William Graham Davis, known as "Willie" to his peers, earned valor on the gridiron as a 210-pound bomb-catching receiver for the Haskell Braves, even achieving honorable mention in "Father of American Football" Walter Camp's All-American team selections that year. He also played center on the Haskell basketball team. His athletic accolades helped offset some of his classmates' and teammates' resentment toward him as a representative of the so-called civilized tribes— Seminole and Mvskoke Creek. His athletic ability no doubt benefited him when he served in the 114th Field Artillery 30th Division Battery E in World War I.[30]

Before finishing at Haskell in 1920, William Graham married a Comanche-Cheyenne girl named Richenda (pronounced Be-chan-da) Emma Merrick. Though not uncommon among Native women, the otherwise unique name came from Carlisle Indian School supervisor and federal boarding school architect Richard Henry Pratt, who demanded that Richenda's father Eustace name his daughter after his own girl named Richenda, possibly a feminized derivative of his own name. This is the same Richard Henry Pratt notorious in Native American history for suggesting that "Friends of the Indian" like him needed to "kill the Indian and save the man" with the federal policies they devised for Native people. This hideous notion was actually a novel concept at a time when many Americans didn't believe there was a valuable human inside American Indian people at all.[31]

In the 1920s, after a brief run as a professional basketball player with the Kansas City Athletic Club, where Harry Truman was a member, William Graham Davis returned to football, playing for the Hominy Indians of Oklahoma professional team, making between $100 and $150 per game. Barnstorming around the country, the team featured players from fifteen different tribes, including one Alaskan Native. Funded by Osage oil money, they played their home games in a pasture on a grid cordoned by a metal cable. Fans drove their cars right up to the edge and sat on their hoods. Those who struck it rich from the oil boom donned fur coats. The Hominy Indians' greatest moment came in 1927 when they played the reigning NFL champion New York Giants in Pawhuska in front of a crowd of two thousand. The Indians were no easy opponent. Known as the "Terrors of the Midwest," they were on a twenty-eight-game winning streak. Willie Davis caught the first touchdown pass, which helped ensure a 13–6 victory that sent the crowd rushing onto the field.[32]

When World War II arrived, William Graham Davis again enlisted for service, this time in the Navy alongside his two sons Jesse (or Jess) Edwin Davis II and Madison Berkley Davis, known respectively as "Bus" (short for "Buster") and "Dutch" in their mutual football circles. William Graham served as coxswain, third class petty officer. During the war, unlike his sons who shipped out, he worked in the Norman Navy Air Station's buildings and grounds department and coached his son Jess in football on the side. Beginning in 1943, William Graham began shuttling to Hollywood, where he landed work as a set builder for Paramount, MGM, and Warner Brothers. Then in 1945 he moved to Los Angeles and stayed for twenty-nine years, for a time enjoying the company of a houseguest in the form of his grandson Jesse Ed Davis, who possibly learned leatherworking from his grandfather during his stay while hoping to break into the music business.[33]

William Graham mentioned working on *Gone with the Wind* (1939), which seems impossible given the timeline—possibly a blurry memory or an embellishment of a truth that was already impressive enough. His memory of working on *And Now Tomorrow* (1944) is more convincing, given his vivid account of meeting the film's stars Alan Ladd and Loretta Young and building one of the film's central sets—the winding staircase Loretta Young's character descends. The film's screenplay was written by Raymond Chandler, who became a favorite author of William Graham's grandson Jesse Ed Davis, perhaps even stemming from this episode. William Graham shook the hands of many stars, including Young, Ladd, Bing Crosby, and Dean Martin, surprised to find them "just as common as an old shoe" and "not stuck up at all." In Los Angeles, he also fashioned a friendship with legendary Sac and Fox athlete Jim Thorpe, whom he casually knew from Indian Country. They would sit and talk about old times, especially their sports careers. William Graham retired from the motion picture industry in 1973 and returned to Wewoka, where he helped build the Seminole Nation Museum and continued speaking both the Mvskoke and English languages. He died in Oklahoma City in 1992.[34]

JESSE'S MATERNAL GRANDFATHER Jasper Saunkeah was one of the most prominent leaders of the Kiowa Nation in the twentieth century, guiding his people as tribal chairman during the Great Depression and Indian New Deal, while also serving as a US Marshal. He did this from Oklahoma City, where he and his family relocated in 1932, precisely two decades prior to the federal urban relocation program that moved Native people to cities for work, social, and education opportunities.

Kiowa people had generally demonstrated remarkable adaptability and resilience. At the turn of the twentieth century, "Folks who had literally been nomadic hunters were hiring lawyers and fighting court cases," Kiowa scholar Kent Sanmann stresses. "I doubt most lawyers of that time would have been able to do the reverse and switch to bison hunting." Jasper's grandfather survived on bison. That alone demonstrates the remarkable and profoundly rapid transformation Kiowa people experienced in the immediate decades prior to Jesse Ed Davis's birth.[35]

Jasper Saunkeah (meaning small man or boiled man) was born in Carnegie, Oklahoma, but, as he explained, there wasn't exactly a visible town there at the time. When he retired after twenty years as a US Marshal, one newspaper suggested, he was practically an Oklahoma landmark. He too wore many hats, as a cofounder of the American Indian Exposition (initially the Southwestern Indian Fair), district game ranger, Riverside Indian School official, church leader, farmer, and US Marshal, in total serving the Kiowa tribal government, Oklahoma state government, and US federal government for thirty-eight years. Most significantly, from 1939 until his retirement in 1953, he served as "chief of the Kiowas," though, reflecting his determination to be taken seriously as a contemporary person, he insisted that people refer to him as "chairman of the council."[36]

Saunkeah's public service began when he became chief of police for the Kiowa agency in 1915, quickly becoming known as the person other Kiowa people could call to help when they got in any trouble with state law enforcement. In the 1920s, he had a reputation as one of the most progressive farmers in Kiowa County. He was prominent in the church, too, traveling around the country with his wife Anna Poolaw for national Baptist conventions and Shriner conventions, the latter indicating his relative position among the urban elite. As superintendent of the Riverside Indian School, he represented Native people at the Anadarko Thanksgiving pageant and helped direct a stage performance that told a story of Natives, newcomers, and peace.[37]

As Jasper Saunkeah gained power through new modes of authority and influence, he didn't deny his people. He protected them and their lifeways. As a game ranger from a chapter of the Oklahoma Game Protective Association he personally organized, Saunkeah carried a sawed-off shotgun and on at least one occasion had to appeal to it when ejecting criminally trespassing hunters from a quail refuge he supervised southeast from Anadarko. In 1947, he flexed muscle as deputy US Marshal when he threatened illegal alcohol traffickers who went to Anadarko to sell to Native people. It was the "first and last warning," he declared. After Jasper swept through, the police chief reported, beer sales dropped almost one hundred percent.[38]

His leadership among Kiowa people also granted him real influence in the state Democratic Party, within which he chaired the Kiowa Democratic Club. In 1928, he organized a powwow event for Democratic US senator Elmer Thomas. In return, Jasper used this political connection to score campaign promises from the senator, including money specifically for the Riverside Indian School, where Jasper was an administrator, and a bill to provide monies for Indian students to attend public schools throughout the state. His reputation among Kiowa people was further bolstered when he led his nation in a victorious $1.5 million lawsuit against regional oil companies.[39]

Jasper's experience in various positions of leadership proved valuable and pivotal during the introduction of the federal Indian Reorganization Act (IRA), which brought him to Washington to speak on the Senate floor. The IRA was one of the most consequential federal policy initiatives of the twentieth century. In exchange for organizing governments that reflected the one in Washington and ratifying a constitution to reflect the United States Constitution, Indian nations would receive access to a revolving credit fund, money for education and other areas of development, and a reorganization of the tribal land base to protect it from allotment.[40]

Saunkeah initially voted to reject the IRA in 1934, but his vote didn't reflect his own position on the question. He felt he had no choice as tribal chairman but to back the overwhelming number of Kiowa people who at first resisted it. He decried the general lack of New Deal support for Kiowa and other Native people, and he saw some solutions in the IRA. He continued trying to sway his people in an essay he wrote for *Harlow's Weekly*, wherein he worried about the land base held in trust and how the otherwise imminent end of governmental supervision, problematic as it was, would only result in more land being swindled away by unscrupulous white folks, as it had been in the past. "We have seen our brothers and sisters . . . fleeced by the ever-greedy land-grafters who swarm the country of the Indians," he said. "Business education is the only salvation for the Kiowa Indians," he projected. (Notably, his daughter Vivian earned a degree in business administration.)[41]

In 1935, having convinced his people that the federal policy initiative would be worth their investment and compromise, Jasper supported the new Oklahoma Indian Welfare Act—a separate version of the reorganization act that specifically applied to Oklahoma. Speaking again before the Senate Subcommittee on Indian Affairs in Washington, Jasper emphasized the measure in the bill that promised to not only preserve the land trust agreement and return some Indian land but also actually altogether stop the allotment process that had divested Native American people of ninety million acres of tribal land since the passing of the General Allotment Act in 1887. He believed something needed to be done to improve life for the more than half of people in his Kiowa jurisdiction who were landless. The average per capita income for Native people in Oklahoma at the time was $47.[42]

Jasper also led Kiowa Nation claims against the United States through the Indian Claims Commission, established in 1946 as a means for Indigenous nations to bring legal suit against the settler nation over broken treaty agreements and other matters. While the US refused to return land in the many cases it lost, it did provide substantial cash settlements, which soon often became part of extortion efforts to compel tribal nations to dissolve their tribal governments and essentially stop functioning as semi-sovereign nations. This became known as the termination policy, which Nixon formally overturned in 1970, but whose potential reawakening still lurks in relations between the US and Native nations. Upon retiring, after a long multifaceted career, Jasper and his wife Anna Poolaw elected to remain in Oklahoma City, where their children had grown up.[43]

Beyond these historic achievements, Jasper somehow made time for social and cultural events too. His grandson Jesse Ed Davis wouldn't be the first member of his family to go perform music in Los Angeles. Jasper himself went there in a chartered bus in 1938 to appear at the National American Legion convention. Jasper and his fellow Kiowa performers took to the stage in buckskin at the Hollywood Bowl and

visited movie studio lots, where his future grandson's paternal grandfather currently worked. At a second scheduled event, Jasper formally
adopted Bing Crosby into the Kiowa tribe live over a radio broadcast.[44]

Meanwhile, Jasper became a founder and president of the American
Indian Exposition, a major social event that grew out of the defunct
Caddo County Fair and became an all-Indian fair. His daughter Vivian
was Exposition princess in 1942. Vivian also accompanied her father to
Kansas in 1947 at a Medicine Lodge Treaty ceremony.[45]

Jesse sometimes told people his grandfather Jasper brought down the
brutal serial murder tandem Charlie Starkweather and Caril Fugate,
the couple depicted in Bruce Springsteen's song "Nebraska" and Ter-
rence Malick's film *Badlands* (1973). In 1958, Starkweather and Fugate
killed eleven people before law enforcement captured them in Lincoln,
Nebraska. Jasper couldn't take credit for it, however, as he retired from
the US Marshal service in 1953. It is instead likely that Jesse confused
or embellished the fact of Jasper's role in bringing down "Butcher Billy"
Cook, who, in 1950, abducted and later killed five people in Oklahoma after they picked him up as a hitchhiker. The story is depicted
in Ida Lupino's *The Hitch-Hiker* (1953), the first noir film directed by
a woman.[46]

In 1952, Jasper spoke up about the refusal among Oklahoma City's
white citizens to rent property to American Indians for powwows. Media
coverage mocked Jasper's effort, using bigoted language to depict Native
people searching for a place where they can "pound their tom-toms
without objections from the palefaces." As Jasper matter-of-factly put it,
"Once or twice a month we would like to hold an Indian program." The
paper translated that as "Indians Demand Right to Beat Tom-Toms."
This was a subtle but important reminder of the world Jesse and his
family confronted. The local population accepted and even highlighted
Indian people when they performed assimilation or portrayed characters
from the past. Though Native people may have lived on their own terms
in Oklahoma City, the media and political narrative was determined on
non-Indian terms. It was okay to slip into buckskin for a public event,
but for the white community, who dictated the terms of acceptable social
events, an Indian powwow was too much. So Jasper protested, likely

anticipating the media would caricature his plea, while realizing that maneuvering within that sphere was imperfect but worth it.[47]

Jesse's families could make it look easy. These were prominent people not just within their Native communities but within Oklahoma City and beyond. But the distinguished and dignified outward appearances and series of achievements, including Jesse's own, could mask formidable challenges Jesse and his families experienced. Jesse was often quiet about his people's pasts. But that didn't mean he didn't know and feel them. The same may have been true of his ancestors.

When Jasper Saunkeah passed away in September 1959, Jesse Edwin Davis became serious about guitar. In traditional Kiowa practices, the deceased are buried in the ground, from which life emerges. Then they go on their journey while women wail in grief as cedar and smoke comfort those who remain behind. The family observes a traditional year of mourning, which includes a cessation of social activities. "Eddie" turned to rock music to comfort him and carry him through the year while his family kept a low profile. He and his parents were devastated. But while Eddie mourned his grandfather's death, Elvis Presley was alive. It was then that Eddie put down his violin and picked up a guitar. He couldn't resist. As he recalled, he had been "caught by the rock n roll bug."[48]

Two

A KIOWA-COMANCHE TIPI

JESSE ED DAVIS'S PARENTS and others like them formed a bridge between an older generation that still recalled violent conflict and a future generation of Native people who would again profess outward pride in being Indian after years of programs designed to make them stop being Indian. This wasn't easy. Whether or not Jesse's parents imagined their only son would become a music star, their own immense talents and extraordinary stories suggested that their son would be capable of great things. Indeed, Jesse's parents would make it difficult for Jesse to aspire to anything less. He worried about disappointing them.

Like their son after them, Jesse's parents had numerous nicknames. Usage depended on who was in the conversation and when, but in almost every case, they were terms of affection. Jesse's parents carried all of the ambition, talent, tenacity, foresight, and sense of purpose as their elders. They were college educated and knowledgeable about tribal culture. They were career professionals and powwow dancers. They advanced Indigenous culture in both public displays and private settings. They loved playing and collecting music, liked a good time, and sought to elevate people around them. If Jesse was intimidated by them, he was also deeply proud of them.[1]

Jesse Edwin Davis II, also known as Papa D, Papadee, Jess, Big

Jess, and his football nom de guerre Bus, was a tough and serious man, physically imposing, well over six feet tall, 240 pounds, and strict about manners and etiquette. He was also a man of many talents, including painting, music, and photography. He expressed himself through various artistic media, but hid himself when he was creating it. He grew up on farms and held 160 acres of land in Comanche County, south from Fort Sill and just north of West Cache Creek, but he was just as comfortable in the city. In any setting, he led by example, teaching his son Eddie independence, an appreciation for the arts, and the value of disarming humor.[2]

Eddie Davis loved his father and reflected his many talents. Like his father, Eddie cultivated knowledge in many areas, adored Dixieland jazz, practiced numerous musical instruments, enlisted in the armed services, played the tackle position in football, and even exhibited an impressive hand at art, specializing in drawing, lettering, sketching, and later leatherworking. As a boy, Eddie quite literally followed his father's footsteps when he performed at powwows as a straight dancer—a Southern Plains–style that grew out of traditional war dances. Jesse Edwin Davis III so resembled a miniature Jesse Edwin Davis II that the two actually won an annual father-son lookalike contest in 1948.[3]

Born in Anadarko in 1921 and baptized at the Anadarko Presbyterian Church, Bus moved semi-frequently while growing up, spending time in Okemah, Wewoka, Tonkawa, and briefly Oklahoma City during the early 1930s when his father William Graham worked as a pipe fitter for an oil company. When settled, he spent most of his time on the family farm in Seminole County, much like his Davis elders.[4]

Like his father, the toughness Bus developed through farming made him formidable on the gridiron. In 1937, as a 212-pound sophomore, he caught the eye of state football scouts who ranked him a top prospect at tackle, the best some had seen in a decade. Rather than a college football program, however, Bus got swept up in the war. After high school, he entered training as a radio ham with the New Deal National Youth Administration (NYA) Radio School as part of a work-study program in Tonkawa. The NYA school funneled graduates to the war effort where they served as radio operators and technicians. The roughly two hundred student workers learned basic technical experience in radio construction and communications, transmitting and receiving coded messages, handling a soldering iron, and repairing and rebuilding receivers, while earning somewhere between $10 to $25 per month. The NYA camp also provided social opportunities through sports, dancing, and music. It isn't surprising that radio and music became central features of the future Davis home.[5]

In 1942, together with his father William Graham, a World War I veteran, and his brother Madison, Bus enlisted for service with the United States Navy. He was first stationed in San Francisco before fighting in Guam. Home from the war in October 1943, he finished his term at the Norman Naval Air Station, where he began taking courses in fine art at the University of Oklahoma (OU). "Tough as nails," he also returned to football, playing tackle for the Norman Navy Zoomers regional semiprofessional football team. Bus's father attended every practice and sometimes helped with coaching, occasionally taking to the field during practice as a limber and inexhaustible forty-four-year-old former star. When not fighting on the gridiron, Bus somehow found time to fight fires while serving the Norman Navy Air Station Fire Department.[6]

At OU, Bus stood out. The only student in his yearbook not wearing a suit, to say nothing of being one of few recognizably Native students, he found community in both his art program and the university's Sequoyah Club, founded in 1914 as a social outlet for Native American students who sought to preserve Indian culture and advocate for their advancement in education. Bus's brother Madison served as president and led pipe ceremonies during halftime at OU football games. Bus served as "Medicine Man" (Vice President) of the Sequoyah Club's umbrella unit, the Ittanaha Organization—a consortium of ten Indian Clubs from various Oklahoma colleges. He remained loyal to the Sequoyah Club long after graduation, sometimes dancing and making live paintings at their community events.[7]

While studying fine art, playing football, leading a student organization, and putting out fires, Bus also put his radio operator skills to use as a guest host for the *Indians for Indians* radio show based in Nor-

man. In 1941, Sac and Fox chief Don Whistler created the show by and
for Indigenous people to report news, announce events, and play music
from Indian Country. It transmitted to over fifty thousand American
Indian listeners on Tuesday afternoons from WNAD at the University
of Oklahoma. At the time, it was the only program in the United States
that broadcast using Indigenous languages.[8]

We hear Bus speak with an archetypal Oklahoma accent, though
that might only mean something to other Okies. Given its geographic
location and Indigenous populations, accents in Oklahoma can be as
diverse as the state's music. Bus's cadence was taut with sentences curl-
ing upward. Not as syrupy as a stereotypical Southern drawl, it was a
little friendlier than a Texan accent, similar to how Oklahoma blues
was a little friendlier than the meaner-sounding Texan version.[9] When
guest hosting, Bus introduced singers who appeared on the program—
"Thank you, Charlie, that was very good singing. . . . If you could sing
a couple more songs, that would be okey doke"—and delivered news
about upcoming dances, powwows, Fourth of July celebrations, war veteran gatherings, church associations, all-Indian baseball games, Indian
princess pageants, parades, dedications to Native people in the armed
services, and the annual American Indian Exposition. The latter was
"really a big thing. Everybody should see it once before going to the
happy hunting ground." Signing off, Bus said, "Until then, this is Jesse
Davis saying so long and tune in next week."[10]

Bus's brother Madison also served as a guest host. Their role in the
radio program reflected their place and time as Native people. They
were connected to traditional ways, yet as Native Americans who sought
attention as a surviving people in a changing world, they embraced tools
and technologies that broadcast their continued existence. It's another
example of how Eddie's families' recent pasts provided models for using
art to express cultural persistence. Within his immediate Davis family,
he could turn to a grandfather who worked in Hollywood and a father
and uncle who hosted radio programs, to say nothing of the musical
talent Eddie's parents shared.

If there was any space left on Bus's palette, then he reserved it for a
Kiowa girl who brightened his world. Vivian Saunkeah was practically

Indian royalty, a former leader of the same university Sequoyah Club, and currently managing the administrative assistant desk in OU's Zoology Department. They attended powwows together, told each other stories about their tribal culture, and mutually stressed proper manners. Most important, they loved blues music. "Daddy had a hard time / Mama made his eyes shine," their future son would sing about them.

Jess and Vivian married on February 2, 1944, at the bride's home in Oklahoma City. Vivian wore a blue wool dress with a pink corsage and Bus wore his seaman first class Navy uniform before an altar featuring palms and snapdragons. Vivian's father Jasper and her friend Mary Ruth Toyebo served as witnesses. Toyebo would go on to marry Fred Tsoodle in 1946, and Tsoodle would go on to work at Tinker Air Force Base, like Bus. These were energetic young Native couples, confident in their places in the world. "We can be good Americans, making a decent living and still keep our Indian culture," as Fred Tsoodle said, characterizing their cohort. He placed responsibility for success or failure directly in Indians' hands: "They'll have to do it themselves. They have to adjust . . . buckle down. It's within ourselves." Over twenty years later, the Tsoodles and Davises featured in an Oklahoma City news story—not the first time for either couple—about Kiowa Indians who had allegedly "assimilated into 'the mainstream of society.' "[11]

The largest paper in Oklahoma portrayed such "urban Indians" like most other news media in the 1960s. The *Daily Oklahoman* emphasized Indian people's misperceived inability to adjust to modernity, exemplified by city life, as a symptom of some sort of pathological failing. It created a caricature of the fallen Indian in the city, caught between two worlds, struggling to negotiate technological developments, cowering at car horns. "His problems usually follow him to the city," the paper warned, "and although there are many exceptions, the Indian's problems often multiply." Native Americans live in a "twilight zone" between modernity and an "ancient culture," the story continued, proceeding to describe Jesse's people as bitter, hateful, miserable, distrustful, resentful, impoverished, ignorant, dislocated, and withdrawn, before, contradictorily, complaining that generalizations about Indians can "give the wrong picture."[12]

Some of these tropes impacted Jesse's thinking about his parents. He sometimes suggested they were among the first generation of Indian people to assimilate into white society. On the subject of assimilation, he didn't express any disappointment or regret. Referring to the catastrophic land allotment policy, he only mentioned how his family "ended up with some nice bits of property. . . . My parents were assimilated and college educated, and I have a wonderful education." Jesse was in general proud of his family's achievements and dynamic lives:

> My grandparents were actually born in tipis on the Washita River. They went through all Custer's Washita Massacre and all that horseshit. . . . When my parents grew up they went to Indian school at Riverside Indian School in Anadarko. They grew up speaking their Native language. When they went to the Indian school they were whipped and spanked if they spoke their Native language. Now they grew up telling me to speak English and they didn't teach me my Native language.

Even so, Jesse didn't often volunteer personal reflections on his experience as an Indigenous person. When he insisted on being understood as a musician who is American Indian, as opposed to an *American Indian musician*, he assumed his place in a family that survived the nineteenth century and thrived in the twentieth. But he also recognized the futility in trying to act or appear Indigenous on anyone else's terms, especially when the terms were so capricious. "Now at the Riverside Indian School, since their culture is slipping away, they're teaching all the Indian kids to speak their Native language," Jesse explained. "So, it just goes to show you that Uncle Sam doesn't know what he wants." It might be more accurate, or at least more empowering, to quote Bus Davis's Choctaw painter peer and fellow World War II veteran Chief Terry Saul, who observed Indian culture at midcentury not in a state of assimilation but rather a state of revolution.[13]

In 1951, while still residing in Dwelling Number 402 at the Norman Naval Air Base, Bus landed a middle-class job at Tinker Air Force Base where he could put his painting and drawing skills to use in the graphic arts department, sometimes seeing his illustrations grace weapons of war. In 1956, he made the "600,000 in 60" slogan that accompanied hundreds of thousands of pieces of media. The phrase referred to Oklahoma City's collective cheerleading for a population of six hundred thousand by the year 1960. Locals were proud of their exceptionally fast-growing city, contrasting it with the Steinbeckian "Okie" motif that had become short-hand for condescending and disparaging attitudes toward people from the state. World War II changed Oklahomans' image of themselves, especially given their hand in winning the war. The 45th Infantry had achieved great battlefield valor and Tinker Air Force Base now stood as the largest air base in the nation. Rapid socioeconomic transformations also inspired movements for civil rights as Oklahoma City history teacher Clara Luper and NAACP Youth Council members led the very first lunch counter sit-ins, at the Katz Drug Store. This nonviolent strategy toward desegregation inspired future sit-ins, including those in Greens-boro, North Carolina, in 1960.

As they cultivated a place in American postwar modernity, these New Okies reclaimed that epithet with a new sense of pride. An "Okie" would no longer mean Tom Joad, the downtrodden Dust Bowl refugee in Steinbeck's *Grapes of Wrath*. According to *Daily Oklahoman* editor E. K. Gaylord, "O stands for opportunity and optimism, K is for king-pin of the southwest, I for industry and intelligence, E for enterprise and eagerness." It's not insignificant that a Native American person repre-senting several Indigenous nations from Oklahoma contributed art to a movement urging a new Oklahoma, just as it was not insignificant that his son, also representing several Indigenous nations, became central to the creation and popularity of the Tulsa sound.[14]

If the fastest way to get to know Jesse Ed Davis was through his music, then perhaps the same was true for his father when it came to art. Bus painted with oil and watercolor and trained with Oscar Jacob-son, the influential OU fine art professor who sponsored the famous Kiowa Six, whose work showed throughout the United States and Europe. One of Jacobson's last students, Bus practiced the Kiowa Six's "true Indian" flat-painting style. He began showing his work in 1949, while finishing his degree, and went on to win awards in Oklahoma and Wyoming. His work also showed individually in Montana, New Mexico, and North Dakota, and toured galleries around the country as part of a larger collection. He signed his paintings "Asawoya," meaning Running Wolf, resurrecting the name a boarding school took from his Comanche grandfather.

Though Bus benefited from Jacobson's mentorship, the distinguished professor exaggerated his student's place on a cultural evolution plane—a somewhat passé notion for a humanities scholar at that time. Jacobson erroneously suggested that Bus was raised by white folks. Jacobson also confused acculturation with assimilation before equating assimilation with whiteness. Wrongly suggesting that Bus only revealed his Indian heritage through his art, Jacobson predicted that his student "will doubt-less find his future career in the White man's world and become com-pletely absorbed in it."[15]

It is true that Bus sought to explore Indigenous culture more deeply after frequently moving with his family as a kid, attending public schools, training in a New Deal project, serving in World War II, and going to a major university. But none of those experiences were truly antithetical to being Indigenous. Mobility, varied education pedagogies and epistemologies, technological development, and armed defense of a nation were all fundamental parts of Indigenous peoples' lives well before European colonists ever arrived in North America pretending to have invented those practices.

In 1949, Bus loaded the family car and took Vivian and their son Eddie on a summer-long road trip throughout the US West to visit var-ious reservation communities and learn more about Native American people, culture, and history. "I have seen a lot of Indians," he claimed upon returning. "I believe that I am now more one of them."[16]

Bus's paintings typically depicted powwow dancers, Comanche horsemen, and Cheyenne dog soldiers. In 1957, his casein painting "Aftermath" won the grand prize at the twelfth annual contemporary American Indian painting exhibition at Tulsa's Philbrook Museum. This distinction automatically scheduled him for an individual showcase, as well as a spot on the jury for the following year's competition alongside anthropologist Alice Marriott. In 1959, Bus's painting "The Sentinel," depicting a Cheyenne soldier, took first place in one category and the silver cup in another at the Sheridan, Wyoming, Indian Days Arts and Crafts Exposition. It also earned him first honorable mention that year at the Philbrook. Critics noted a particular degree of delicacy and elegance in his work.[17]

For the spring 1962 issue of *Oklahoma Today* magazine, Bus illustrated popular Native American history writer Stan Hoig's story about the sacred Cheyenne Medicine Arrows that dated back to Cheyenne people's life in the Black Hills at the turn of the nineteenth century. The four arrows, which Cheyenne soldiers carried into battle, offered power over either animals or humans. The winter 1962 issue of *Oklahoma Today* featured more of Bus's work, in this case "The Long Snow," depicting hungry Native hunters on horseback in cold winter bringing home a bounty of rabbits. He "seems almost to paint from subconscious memory," an accompanying statement suggested. By the early 1960s, Bus's painting career was tapering off as he began pursuing new interests in photography and music. His next major painting assignment wouldn't come until 1970, when his son asked him to produce the cover art for his debut LP.[18]

EVERYONE LOVED Jesse Ed Davis's mother. Jesse downright adored her. While he emulated his father's sense of humor, he absorbed his mother's sweetness. Vivian Saunkeah Davis enjoyed her own nicknames: Aunt Bea to family, Mamacita to friends. "She wouldn't have it any other way," Taj Mahal bassist Gary Gilmore insists. "One of the warmest human beings on the planet," Taj Mahal recalls. "I mean, seriously, an amazing person."[19]

Vivian radiated kindness. As both a prominent person among Kiowa people and a visible leader within the Oklahoma City Indigenous community, she was an accomplished student, musician, and dancer. A kind of first-call session player in her own right, news media and Oklahoma City business and government leaders often recruited Vivian to represent the state's large Indian population at public events and ceremonies. Once, in support of a war bond drive, she conducted both a formal ceremony and comedy routine with Bob Hope in which she adopted him into the Kiowa Nation with a war bonnet and the name "Chief Eagle Beak." She described how every feather in a Kiowa war bonnet represented courage and honorable action that produced peace—a lot of responsibility for a slapstick comedian.[20]

To non-Native people, Vivian represented the archetypal Indian princess. Her father was "chief" of the Kiowa Nation, her family achieved great social stature in Indian Country and beyond, and her father adored her. Such hallmarks of the trope date back at least to Pocahontas. But Vivian experienced those qualities more as reality than myth.

Vivian's parents and extended kin were prominent in virtually every Kiowa social pillar, including the church, the business community, education, and politics. She could easily shuffle from a seat at a diplomatic table to a piano bench. She was the first Kiowa woman to earn a bachelor's degree at the University of Oklahoma, and she long remained an important figure in the OU Alumni Association. She gained a wide frame of reference for understanding Kiowa people's place in the world and she earned it growing up in a rapidly transformational time in their lives. Her son Jesse would benefit from his mother's experience and perspective. She was the kind of mother who could imagine and support her son making a career in music.

Vivian Saunkeah was born in 1921 near Anadarko, Oklahoma, in Kiowa Country, where she inherited land along Rainy Mountain Creek. She grew up in the Riverside Indian School, where her father Jasper was an administrator, attended the Rainy Mountain Baptist Church, where many of her ancestors are buried, and the Popejoy School of Music in Anadarko, where she trained with the area's most venerated piano teacher, Dora Streight Popejoy, head of the Oklahoma Federation of Music Clubs.[21]

Ms. Popejoy hosted annual piano recitals featuring the best young talent in the state. At a concert in 1932, Vivian performed "Joyful Peasant (Jolly Peasant Returning from Work)," a playful number by the troubled German composer Robert Schumann. Vivian's rendition broadcast live on Oklahoma City's WKY, which would later sponsor one of her son's first-ever live music performances. Among Ms. Popejoy's other impressive piano students was a young boy named Russell Bridges, who arrived at the school at age four in 1946. He later became one of Jesse Ed Davis's greatest collaborators, the "Master of Space and Time," Leon Russell. Perhaps when we talk about the Tulsa sound that Leon and his band of Okies, including Jesse, fashioned in the late 1960s, we might do well to remember Dora Popejoy.[22]

In 1932, Vivian's family moved to Oklahoma City, where her father began serving as a US Marshal and could exercise greater political influence for the Kiowa Nation. Vivian switched from Anadarko Junior High to Harding Junior High, but she didn't seem to miss a beat, and her family stayed connected to Kiowa culture and community. If anything, Oklahoma City (OKC) gave her family a greater platform for sharing and advancing Kiowa culture, even if it sometimes had to be delivered in character to gain attention.

Vivian traveled far and wide with her father to attend major social, political, and cultural events. That same year they took up residence in OKC, Jasper and Vivian drove out to Kansas with Vivian's grandfather Kiowa George, now an elder tribal historian, for a ceremony to honor the 1867 Medicine Lodge Treaty. In 1934, Jasper and Vivian ventured to St. Louis to dedicate the Municipal Auditorium as part of the National Folk Festival. The same Oscar Jacobson who would later become Bus's fine art professor introduced Jasper and Vivian at the festival. The father-daughter tandem made their own costumes for the event. The large audience gasped at the vibrant display when Jasper and Vivian appeared alongside Kiowa gourd dancers and culture keepers who conducted a ceremony to honor the Kiowa Chief Satanta's leadership in the nineteenth century. Appearing in two sets, Vivian performed at a major folk festival. Thirty-four years later in Newport, Rhode Island, her son would do the same with Taj Mahal and the Great Plains Boogie Band.[23]

Vivian also traveled with her mother and father to Dallas. They represented the Cedar Creek Methodist Church in Carnegie, a sort of second church for the Saunkeahs, who were members at Oklahoma City's stately Trinity Baptist Church, where Vivian was baptized at age seventeen in 1938. Vivian and her parents participated in a program about American Indian people at the northern Texas city's Trinity Methodist Church.[24]

Vivian did not always travel with her father, however. On one occasion, she trekked to Mexico with her best friend, and in 1939 she appeared at the New York City World's Fair, representing the American Indian Exposition her father cofounded. A New York reporter described her as one of "three pretty Indian maidens in native buckskin dress." At the fair, the Guard of Honor—consisting of twenty-six mounted horsemen representing nineteen tribal nations recruited from three Indian boarding schools—escorted Vivian and her two Native companions. Earlier that summer, the Guard of Honor had escorted England's Queen Elizabeth and King George at the fair. Now they ushered Vivian and her troupe from the main entrance to Perylon Hall. Under the theme "Dawn of a New Day," it was the first world's fair to focus on the future, as opposed to the past. Because Native American people are almost always portrayed as a relic of the past in popular media and culture, especially at that time, it is significant that here in New York City, which today boasts the largest Native population anywhere in North America, a troupe of young Native people from Oklahoma was part of a spectacle about the future. With Vivian, they couldn't have chosen a better representative.[25]

In 1938, Vivian graduated from Classen High School, where she had been vice president of a Pan-American Club that promoted interest in Latin America, a place that would become deeply familiar to Vivian's Saunkeah cousins when they became missionaries there for many years. She briefly enrolled in the Oklahoma College for Women before transferring to OU in 1940. There Vivian was "Princess" of the Sequoyah Club, making her a regular feature of parades and pep rallies, where she appeared in tribal dress and ran Indian ceremonies for the public. Before football games she regularly led the "all-night beating of drums" and "making of medicine." In 1941, she was elected to the position of "Sachem" in the statewide Ittanaha Indian Clubs Association, in which her future husband would also serve.[26]

Still Vivian made time for extracurricular activities, bouncing back and forth from Norman to Oklahoma City to continue appearing with her father and supporting tribal initiatives. In 1942, she worked with the Missionaries Linguistics Institute to teach exchange students the Kiowa language. In 1943, she became honorary colonel of a preflight basic training program in OKC. She also kept up with her public tribal adoption ceremonies, including the famous ventriloquist Edgar Bergen and his dummy Charlie McCarthy.[27]

Upon graduating from OU in 1942, Vivian stayed connected to the university making $125 per month as an administrative assistant in the Zoology Department before taking a job with the IRS, then Tinker Air Force Base, and finally Hughes Tool Company, where she served as executive secretary until she retired. She also remained a longtime luminary in the OU Alumni Association.[28]

By age thirty-three, Vivian had experienced what must have felt like a lifetime of dramatic, sometimes sudden, changes. She likewise saw her Kiowa people rise to meet transformational challenges in a compressed period of time. But beyond her marriage to Bus in early 1944, nothing impacted her life more than the birth of her only child, her "Washita Love Child," Jesse Edwin Davis III, later that year on September 21 in the Norman Naval Air Base hospital. "I was a war baby," Jesse said.[29] When he grew up and became a rock star, he only slightly mythologized the story of his birth, like this:

> *I was born on the banks of the Washita River*
> *In a Kiowa-Comanche tipi*

"That is kind of an easy song to write, an autobiographical tune," Jesse once suggested. English scholar Steve Ellerhoff notes how this centerpiece song, recorded in 1970 for Jesse's first solo album, shares lyrical themes and patterns with Sam Cooke's towering civil rights anthem, "A Change Is Gonna Come." "Washita Love Child" became Jesse's personal anthem, about how he could overcome injustice and make his mark on the world as an Indigenous person. It also carries further possible meanings. Jesse's proclamation, "Lord it was just us three," can also refer to the three-member family he had then only recently formed with Patti Daley and her son Billy, whom Jesse parented and loved as his own.[30]

Jesse wasn't literally born on the banks of the Washita River, but the river is a metaphor for his ancestors' lives. He was born, as a spirit unbound by time, at the Washita River Massacre, where his ancestors hid from gunfire in the river banks. "I was born in the Washita River country," Jesse stated, "and this song really says it all I guess." His identity as a Kiowa person ran from his ancestors' escape along the Washita through his fingertips when he played guitar. "The Indian in his DNA had something to do with the blues he played—no one played so melodic," Jesse's Taj Mahal bandmate drummer Chuck Blackwell reasoned. "I can imagine what the experience would have been for Jesse, his brilliance," the Dakota poet John Trudell reflected. "It was magic what he could do with a guitar. I mean it was something that was in his DNA."[31]

In March 1949, while Bus finished his art degree at OU, with Vivian still working for the Zoology Department, the *Daily Oklahoman* newspaper ran a story on the Davis family and their bright prospects. Their son was in the picture, literally, and the reporter wondered what his future might be, born to these exceptional parents: "Eddie, four years old, hasn't started to school yet, but he is sure to take his college work at OU. Just what will be his profession hasn't been decided yet."[32]

Three

SIX-GUN CITY, OR, YOU CAN TAKE THE BOY OUT OF OKLAHOMA . . .

JESSE ED DAVIS could sense prejudice from a mile away. Within Oklahoma, he endured racism directed at Native American people. Beyond Oklahoma, he withstood stereotypes and condescension directed at Okies. He learned to protect himself long before he entered the music business. When he arrived, he didn't tolerate humor at his expense. "I grew up in Oklahoma City," he once informed an interviewer. "I see, so you're no country boy, right?" the interviewer taunted. "Well, I got a college degree; what does that matter?" Jesse countered. He raised his slightly incomplete college degree as a shield, just as his grandfather did when highlighting his two sons' degrees as central achievements. "You were raised in the city?" the interviewer asked again, seemingly struggling with the possibility. "Yeah," Jesse answered, "urban Indian."[1]

Jesse had mixed experiences growing up in Oklahoma City, and behind his shield, he seemed to have mixed feelings about it. Being Native shaped his life in ways that would inform his art and his place in other worlds outside Oklahoma. As far as most friends from Oklahoma were concerned, Jesse lived a sort of all-American middle-class postwar ideal. But his life was more complicated than that. Jesse and his family often had to conceal their pain. In the end, that would hurt Jesse. Friends tried to understand, but mostly they only had cryptic asides to work from. Or perhaps Jesse wasn't so much elusive as he was unsure as anyone else about the particular headwaters of the hurt that coursed within him. He could only tell friends there was a "darkness" somewhere inside him. This could sometimes be difficult for friends and family to reconcile. Growing up in Oklahoma, Eddie's life was contrasted with so much light.

JESSE'S FAMILY MOVED to the city according to their own ambitions and networks. They employed the "moccasin telegraph" that Native people cultivated in the early twentieth century to help each other achieve social, education, and work opportunities. Throughout Indigenous peoples' histories in North America there have always been examples of urbanity, sometimes to degrees that rivaled or surpassed other versions around the world. But Eddie's families were among the first to experience Oklahoma City as a metropolis where most inhabitants assumed they were a world away from Indian people living on "reservations"— though that land had been carved up for decades by the federal allotment policy, which had sent Native people onto new paths toward survival. There were not many Native American people living in Oklahoma City, or at least there weren't supposed to be, according to settler logic. These are only some of the fundamental realities and assumptions Eddie, and then Jesse, would navigate as a so-called urban Indian.

In a somewhat confounding statement, possibly a witticism, made at the peak of his music career, Jesse told a radio DJ he was "always a little weird, anyway, being an Indian in Oklahoma." On one hand, Oklahoma is Indian Territory. You're reminded in every direction you look. Yet even in Indian Territory, city folk still saw Indians as aberrations. Perhaps Jesse's reflection speaks less to his people's legitimate historical and ancestral claims to belonging in Oklahoma City and more to the surrounding society's determination to portray urban Native American people in a state of temporal and geographic dislocation. After all, Native American people were not supposed to be capable of modernity, and nothing represented modernity quite like cities.[2]

As an adult, however, Jesse didn't see Oklahoma City as a paragon of modernity. He thought it was stuck in the past—the same accusation settler folks made about Indigenous people. "Oklahoma's kind of like six-gun city, you know?" Jesse characterized it. "It's still the Wild West back there. It's really provincial." And it was, or at least some people there wanted it to be. Some still do. It's reflected in the culture and politics. Oklahoma self-mythologizes its history of Cowboys versus Indians to the point of pageantry. But then, every state has some exaggerated story about fighting Indians. To some degree, Jesse self-mythologized his experiences too, or at least exaggerated them. He didn't exactly grow up in a tipi.[3]

Oklahoma has always been much more diverse than its place in popular culture and politics has led people to believe. As in any state, there's a certain amount of historical amnesia here, driven by both outsiders' assumptions and insiders' always complicated, often calculated, occasionally shameful motives for crafting fiction. When Jesse referred to a "six-gun city," he didn't mean an outlaw poker game or shootout in some film his grandfather worked on. He meant the prejudice and pain Indian people experienced at the hands of those cowboys. "Since I've grown up, ya know, I really look back and see a lot of the racial things I went through that were really heavy, formative trips in my life," Jesse said. Referring to his parents' hard work and determination to defy colonization on every level, Jesse acknowledged the cost: "Their lifestyle enabled us to live in the better part of town. As a consequence, I was most of the time the only Indian guy in school and I got a lot of pain and bitterness and resentment about that."[4]

THE INDIAN TERRITORY Land Runs introduced a wide cast of characters, often from hardscrabble backgrounds, to a place that is now home to thirty-nine Indigenous nations. Oklahoma was also home to an important and poignant legacy of Black Towns settled by freedpeople that are less visible today. From the end of slavery in 1865 until the Tulsa Race Massacre in 1921, Oklahoma included more Black-founded, -occupied, and -governed towns than anywhere else in North America. As refugees from slavery and the Jim Crow South paradoxically functioned as settlers in their own way, they thought of Oklahoma as a "promised land," and actively recruited more Black migrants to populate their burgeoning communities with churches and schools at their centers. After statehood in 1907, the social and legal flexibility and racial fluidity guaranteed by Oklahoma's territorial status diminished, and many Black citizens experienced disfranchisement not just within the triangulated race, class, and gender power matrix but within a square that also included land ownership, or lack thereof, as a barrier against Black uplift. With some citizens moving on to Canada, Mexico, and even Africa, the tax bases contracted, railroad access declined, and many Black Towns virtually disappeared.[5]

Life in Oklahoma was characterized by competing sovereignties, communities, and families, comprised of people trying to avoid subjection to the lowest rung on the socioeconomic ladder. The volatile weather provided no comfort. Locals like to suggest that, if you don't like the weather here, then just wait five minutes. It's quietly one of the most environmentally and ecologically diverse places in the nation, but in a way that can be harsh, made infamous by the series of dust bowls in the 1920s that sent Okies searching for survival elsewhere. The 115-degree heat, suffocating humidity, and extreme winds are punishing enough, and then there are the tornadoes, whose whirling forces of misfortune practically define the state to outsiders. The environment here cynically breeds character while it fiendishly attempts to kill its own people. Couple this with a certain element of boredom and you have a place where almost everybody played a little something musically, not merely for fun but for sanity and posterity. This lends Okie music a spirit of joie de vivre. Especially true in Oklahoma, music is celebratory and cathartic.

Jesse's opportunities to experience live music were abundant growing up in Oklahoma City. He enjoyed support and exposure at home from two parents who collected records, played numerous instruments, and encouraged their son's enthusiasm for it. Moreover, Oklahoma City provided an active music scene at the center of the state's rich cultural landscape. Many esteemed musicians emerged from Oklahoma City, Tulsa, and the rest of the state alongside Jesse. They flourished in every genre, including rock, pop, jazz, country, folk, blues, and gospel. Something extraordinary continues to happen here in terms of nurturing music and musicians. From Chet Baker to Charlie Christian, Oklahoma's remarkable musical diversity is a reflection of the profound historical diversity embedded in the red clay. In Jesse's time, a vibrant community of Oklahoma musicians challenged each other. They didn't just learn music; they also "stole everything [they] could," Jesse's early bandmate John Selk recalls. But that's less a confession of a crime than a reflection of Oklahoma itself, a place that absorbed and transformed cultural currents from the South, West, Southwest, Midwest, and Great Plains. Oklahoma isn't exactly any of those places. It's a crossroads, with a big cross at its center.[6]

JESSE'S BOYHOOD BEGAN in the college town of Norman, where people refer to the football stadium as "the church." While Bus completed his fine art degree and Vivian worked as an administrative assistant, the Davis family lived in Norman Naval Air Station barracks #805. Across an asphalt parade ground lived Jesse's boyhood Choctaw friend Bill Saul. They had much in common. Their fathers were World War II veterans and promising fine arts students enrolled at the University of Oklahoma on the GI Bill. People referred to both future award-winning painters as "Chief," though only Terry Saul fully embraced the term, using it as his professional name. Young Eddie Davis had a nickname then, too, the first in his own series of changing monikers, not unlike his parents. In Norman, he was affectionately known as "Snookie."

During the blistering hot summer, Bill Saul and Snookie would head outside early in the morning for playtime, sharing toys and kindergarten conversation in the shade of a military reviewing stand before the oppressive heat sent them back inside. On a Saturday in April 1949, the two boys experienced their first cataclysmic event, and the lingering fear that accompanied it. A series of tornadoes ripped through Oklahoma and northern Texas, killing three people and injuring sixty-seven others. In Norman, among the cities hit hardest, a tornado razed several of the barracks where the Sauls and Davises lived and destroyed fifteen fighter planes in the Naval Air Station's 185th Squadron hangar, causing over a million dollars in damage. Buildings broke "like match sticks" while automobiles flew more than a thousand yards through ravaging winds surpassing two hundred miles per hour. The twister developed so quickly that a man practicing on the pistol range was picked up and carried away.[7]

In 1950, after Bus completed his degree, he and Vivian landed middle-class jobs at Tinker Air Force Base. This led the family up the road to Oklahoma City, where they first stayed with Vivian's parents, Jasper and Anna, before getting a place in Uptown. Moving in these new urban circles, the Davises made efforts to preserve their connections to Indian Country. The family vacationed in Jemez Springs, New Mexico, where some of Vivian's Kiowa relations from Oklahoma lived. Located north of Albuquerque and west of Santa Fe, the spectacular springs belong to Jemez Pueblo people, who share some cultural ancestry with Kiowa people through the Kiowa–Tanoan language family and long histories of Kiowa trade throughout the region. Growing up, Eddie also competed on the Oklahoma powwow circuit, including dances in Colony, Oklahoma, where his Cheyenne ancestors lived, and where he once took second place in a fancy dance championship against his Kiowa relative and future fellow musician Thomas Mauchahty-Ware. During his first career peak with Taj Mahal, Jesse mentioned to his intrigued bandmates that many of his guitar fills and song arrangements were born from the grooves he remembered from those dancing days.[8]

Like his mother before him, Eddie Davis began joining his grandfather Jasper in public ceremonies and media appearances. In 1953, when Eddie was nine, he assisted Jasper with the induction of University of Oklahoma All-American football star Billy Vessels into the Kiowa tribe. Eddie wore his old-style fancy dance regalia, including a porcupine and deer hair roach with an immature golden eagle feather, beaded headband, choker, armbands, cuffs, belt, moccasins, a breechcloth, a feather bustle, and Angora goat leggings.[9]

In the context of his music career, Jesse would be reluctant to dress up as Indian, at least not to market himself. "You know, music is one thing and a powwow is another," Jesse's second wife Kelly would stress. "A lot of people [say], you know, 'He was a great guitarist for an Indian.' No, no. He was a great guitarist who happened to be an Indian. He didn't equate one thing with the other." Jesse's sense of Indigenous self was personal and important to him. His relative comfort with sharing or practicing it depended on his ability to control it. This would be tested growing up in Oklahoma City.[10]

IN 1955, the Davis family purchased a brand-new home on Casper Drive in northeast Oklahoma City's Park Estates custom-build addition. Their diverse network of neighbors included an air force officer, an oil company employee, a civil service commissioner, a veterans' affairs supervisor, an advertising agent, a television station assistant, a railroad service representative, a shoe salesman, insurance agents, and other Tinker Air Force Base employees. Even in a climate of Cold War conformity, the Davises didn't stand out as the only Native family on the block. "There were Seventh Day Adventists just next door too," remembers Eddie Davis's close friend Caroline (Carol) Furr, who lived across the street, "and no one thought that was odd."[11]

Indeed, the Davises were the most stylish and modern family on the block. Neighbor friends recognized Bus's talent as a professional artist. One of his paintings hung above the fireplace in the Furrs' living room. The hip Native American family also had the newest appliances and a driveway rotation of impressive cars, including a Corvair Monza Spyder convertible with turbo-charged rear engines. "That was a radical car back then," Eddie's bandmate and friend Mike Boyle stresses. "They seemed like more modern people than we did," Carol Furr recalls. "When you went to the Davises' house, it was more . . . it wasn't the Jetsons, but it was distinctly something I didn't have." The Davises' three-bedroom ranch home in the center of the development still stands today.[12]

Within their home, the Davises were family oriented and disciplined in their routine and business. Neighbors noticed that Vivian and Bus were important people in their Indigenous communities. Many extended family members and prominent people from Indian Country regularly visited the Davis home on Casper. To outside observers, however, the Davises were quiet about their achievements and prominence.[13]

Other important features of the Davises' life surrounded their neighborhood. Eddie attended the brand-new, state-of-the-art Longfellow Elementary School that had been constructed in the northwest corner of Park Estates the same year as the Davis home. He was the only Native student enrolled—possibly the only non-white student. On weekends, Bus played live music late into the night at a club a few blocks from the Davis home. Southeast across a large field stood the grand Springlake Amusement Park. Blending with the sounds of jazz and blues records his parents spun, Jesse could hear the strains of live music from the Springlake stage, the harmonious whir of the rollercoaster, the sound of excited voices on hot summer nights.

Visiting the Davis home was like walking into a music club and record store rolled into one. A drum set stood in the corner of the family room, and typically a guitar or two were lying about. Against the wall, Vivian's piano was the centerpiece. She taught lessons for fun and extra cash. Eddie was one of her students. She still had the piano Eddie learned on thirty years later, in 1988, when she showed it to her son's friends Taj Mahal and the guys from the Grafitti Band.[14]

In his studio behind the house, Bus occupied his drafting table and worked on art projects, often into the night. The studio was almost never locked, but it was clear to visitors that they were not invited. Eddie was intrigued by his father's work, but he was also intimidated by it. As an adult, Jesse sometimes revealed his own talent for painting and drawing, but he rarely practiced it, perhaps feeling intimidated by his father's superior skill. "I think that's why he played guitars so much," reflects singer Bonnie Bramlett. That tension is precisely captured in Jesse's kindergarten workbooks. He loved coloring cats, dogs, chickens, and other standard kindergarten fare. But on every page, he added his own drawings of guitars.[15]

On weekends Bus moonlighted as a musician. He learned numerous instruments, and enjoyed challenging himself. He briefly played trombone and trumpet, but primarily occupied a trap set—a small drum and percussion kit popular in early big-band jazz. In addition to Friday night living room jams Vivian and Bus organized at the Davis home, Bus had a main spot, the House That Jack Built, in walking distance up the road. The neighborhood lounge was one of the first venues to gain a class C liquor license in 1959, when state laws slightly relaxed. At the private club, members took turns both performing and dancing to Dixieland jazz music. In 1961, Spanky McFarland, of children's shows *Our Gang* and *Little Rascals* fame, bought the club and changed the name. It didn't last. As a child star, Spanky had popularized the folksy phrase "Okey dokey." As an adult, he earned a reputation for robbery, gambling, and check forgery. The club shut down after Spanky got busted for illegal kickbacks to wine vendors in California.[16]

Within their home, Bus and Vivian amassed a formidable collection of 78 and 45 rpm records—Ted Lewis, Bix Beiderbecke, Trummy Young, Earl "Fatha" Hines, the New Orleans raconteur trumpeter Bunk Johnson, and more. "My dad's a Dixieland fanatic, and he's got a ten-foot stack of 78s of everybody from that era," Jesse told an interviewer in 1970. "I think we've got more money tied up in records than anything else." The "Dixieland music," or traditional New Orleans jazz, that Eddie Davis heard his father play evidently left an impression. Jesse recruited New Orleans music legend Dr. John to perform on his second album, and his third solo album, *Keep Me Comin'*, is soaked in southern horns that he arranged himself. Jesse's foundation in Dixieland music "hints at why [Jesse] got around what he did on the guitar," reasons his collaborator Jackson Browne.[17]

Eddie Davis fell in love with all the music around him. His parents nurtured his music interests within their home. Oklahoma City offered a vibrant environment for young kids picking up instruments during the explosion of rock and roll and an expansive Oklahoma market whose diverse influences and sounds reflected its unique geographic position and history. With radio stations, record stores, instrument shops, a recording studio, and an elaborate circuit of venues that supported a wide range of music, Oklahoma City provided every necessary ingredient. Of course, it all depended on a generation of young kids who would buy into it, as both consumers and performers.

BEFORE THERE WERE radio, records, and electric guitars, Jenkins Music catered to Oklahomans who played music with their families and friends from right within their homes. During the nineteenth-century Indian Territory days, it was expected among adults to possess some musical talent for entertaining each other on weekends. Jenkins overlanders traveled from Kansas City south to the Indian Territory prairie, delivering instruments by covered wagon to remote communities and homes. After rail lines connected Kansas City to Oklahoma City, the music goods traveled by train, and eventually a total of four Jenkins stores opened in Oklahoma City, including the flagship store downtown on Main Street. During World War II, when instrument production yielded to military resources, Jenkins made tombstones for fallen soldiers. Eddie Davis frequented Jenkins Music, where he eyed instruments and listened to vinyl on record players the store set on the sidewalk out front to lure patrons. The guitars, banjos, pianos, mandolins, violins, and flutes Jenkins sold became as important to Oklahoma as the tools that tilled the red earth.[18]

The buckle of the Bible Belt, Oklahoma City naturally had an angle in the Christian music recording industry. Partnering with Nashville, Oklahoma became both a destination and hub. If finished gospel music records eventually trucked out of Nashville, they initially began in Oklahoma, where an extensive call list of musicians worked seven days a week reading flashbacks and crafting high-quality orchestrated tracks. On a weekly basis, music label personnel flew back and forth between Nashville and Oklahoma City, carrying analog reels of songs recorded in Oklahoma's capital and prepared for release in Nashville. Oklahoma was also a wellspring of popular gospel songs, such as Albert Brumley's classic "I'll Fly Away," which he wrote while working a cotton patch in Rock Island, Oklahoma. "These melodies will come to you if you make a habit of trying to create them, just like writing letters," Brumley recalled about the gospel and folk music standard. "Writing songs was a lot easier than that cotton patch."[19]

Along with instrument retailers and a class of professional musicians, there were plenty of outlets for purchasing, hearing, and seeing music in Oklahoma City. The more traditional WKY hosted an abundance of live music, including Vivian Saunkeah's piano recital back in the 1930s and what would soon be young Eddie Davis's first public music performance with a professional band. Boasting a more diverse playlist, the more progressive KOCY, branding itself a "dragon-slayer" of prejudice, was "unafraid to explore that undiscovered area between rock-and-roll and jazz." Before them, central in breaking the color barrier, KBYE played Black rhythm and blues music and broadcast local Black community news through the Abram and Willa Ross show it acquired in 1955. The Rosses were more than music DJs and news anchors. They were anchors within the Black community, people one could go to for medical attention or inside tips on safe places for Black folks to dine when passing through. The Rosses were even the first number someone would call if their house were on fire. "We never pull punches on anybody," they promised. At a public ceremony in 1966, William T. Big Snake, chief of the Ponca nation and a Congressional Gold Medal recipient for his work as a code talker in both world wars, honored Abram Ross. They had worked together in the NAACP, co-leading a Black-Indigenous Oklahoma civil rights alliance. Big Snake wanted to ensure that Black Oklahomans knew they were not alone in experiencing discrimination at home and that they had allies in the Indigenous community.[20]

The radio station that most captured Eddie's imagination didn't broadcast from Oklahoma City, however. On their way home late one night from a family road trip to Memphis, Eddie gazed out the backseat window into darkness when Bus tuned in WLAC. They caught John R.'s show, featuring Black rhythm and blues music. Part DJ, part promoter, part manager, John Richbourg, better known as John R., became an important influence on the era's more famous DJs Wolfman Jack and Alan Freed. He was so skilled at parroting Black hep-cat talk, a practice Eddie Davis would soon adopt, many listeners assumed John R. was Black. (He wasn't.) It made no difference to Eddie. He never forgot that moment, hearing the music he needed to play.[21]

In addition to a lively radio lineup, the most exciting music groups of the day came through Oklahoma City. At the Springlake Amusement Park near Eddie's home, one could see Johnny Cash, Jerry Lee Lewis, or Conway Twitty for just 50¢. "We lived there," Eddie's high school friend Mike Smith characterized their obsession with the park. Bob Wills and His Texas Playboys, too, blew through on their way back and forth to Tulsa, where they played popular big-band Western swing at Cain's Ballroom. At the more upscale venues, big-band jazz music thrived. Most popular was Benny Goodman with his masterful and foundational jazz guitarist Charlie Christian. Raised in Oklahoma City, Christian first worked clubs in the Deep Deuce district, where he became one of Jesse Ed Davis's earliest music heroes.[22]

Eddie loved seeing live music with his father. Together they caught shows from low-key BBQ joints on up the food chain. The first of the two most important concerts Bus took Eddie to see was the Count Basie Orchestra in 1955 at the Municipal Auditorium downtown. When Eddie began picking up guitar seriously a few years later, he emulated what he witnessed at the Count Basie show. Musician Scott Colby, whose *Slide of Hand* (1987) album claims the distinction of featuring Jesse's last-ever studio session spot, recalls Jesse telling him that he learned to play guitar by copying the melody lines from Count Basie's horn section. He would spin Basie records over and over, starting and stopping, picking up leads by ear.[23]

Jesse's grounding in big-band jazz and adoration for the style, sound, and presentation are key to understanding his musical artistry and, to some degree, his success. He grew up on those records, and his earliest public gig was with a big band. The rock and roll bands he led in high school and college operated according to a core group supported by a large rotating cast of substitute musicians. His groups often played live in big-band arrangements with guitars, keyboards, drums, and horns, backing a revolving lineup of singers. Jesse preserved these trends in his solo career, which consistently featured a wide roster of musicians on each album, creating a big jubilant sound and spirit. His live appearances could feature as many as ten musicians onstage, sometimes including two drummers, an uncommon configuration in the Los Angeles music clubs he worked. Years later, when Jesse first began working with Leon Russell, he asked the Hollywood studio veteran to teach him to write horn charts, knowing a punctuating trio of horn players would be central to his sound. Beyond his solo career, Jesse thrived in large ensemble settings and albums with large connected spheres of musicians at their core, such as the Concert for Bangladesh and his work with John Lennon. Jesse's experiences as a working musician, from his teenage years until his death, demonstrated his preference for collaborative and communal projects.

A second concert at the Municipal Auditorium made an even bigger impression. In April 1956, Bus took eleven-year-old Eddie to see Elvis Presley perform a sold-out concert for 6,500 screaming fans at the cost of $1 per ticket. Wearing a yellow-trimmed sport coat with black velvet lapels he bought earlier that day in Tulsa, the "King of Cats" romped through "Long Tall Sally" and "Blue Suede Shoes," working the stage in "animal fashion," while kids danced, trembled, and screamed, Eddie among them. At one point, Elvis threatened to stop the show due to the audience's inability to stay in their seats. "I give them what they want," he told a local reporter. "I just let myself go and they like it and I love them for it." Young Eddie Davis was completely enthralled. "Elvis Presley happened," he described that pivotal moment in his life. "I wanted to be Elvis Presley so bad."[24]

There were local music heroes, too, for Eddie to watch up close and solicit their professional advice between sets. Wes Reynolds, who had earlier attended the same high school as Eddie, was a wild man who fronted a group called the House Rockers. Watching Reynolds perform, Eddie noticed his Telecaster and the sounds he wrangled from it. "[He] was a real hillbilly," drummer John Ware recalls. "He was the personification of what became rockabilly. He had a couple of loud amps and a Stratocaster and he was skinny." Bus also introduced Eddie to some of the older jazz musicians from the circuit he worked. Most important was the Black pianist Wallace Thompson, who played the Club Capri and took time to teach Eddie some blues and boogie licks on the piano. "Uncle Wallace" also turned Eddie on to the legendary Chicago blues pianist Otis Spann, who became "a really heavy influence in my life," Davis later acknowledged.[25]

There was no shortage of clubs in OKC. Patrons might frequent the classy Onyx Club, where first Ronnie and the Hawks, and then Levon and the Hawks liked to play when they came to town; or K. Denton's Esquire Club, which featured Sunday jams, where Lou Rawls or Richard "Groove" Holmes might guest; or the Embers across the street. On the east side, one could catch Grant Green or Kenny Burrell at Treva's.

Jess took Eddie around to all the clubs, and Eddie would later play all of them.[26]

WITH TWO MUSICIAN PARENTS, in a home brimming with records, and a vibrant musical community around him, Jesse Ed Davis had every incentive to pick up a guitar when rock and roll got hold of him. But after graduating from the plastic toy instruments that littered the house, he would first need to put down his violin. Though Bus and Vivian loved blues music, they wanted Eddie to play piano and violin, like Vivian did when she was a girl. Bus also hoped that learning music would keep his son out of trouble and away from alcohol as he grew older. Shortly after the Davises moved from Norman to Oklahoma City, Eddie inherited an old violin that had been languishing in his late aunt Minnie Poolaw's attic. His mother signed him up for violin lessons, which he mostly tolerated until eighth grade, when he brought home a note to Vivian from his violin instructor: "I'm sorry. I don't think this is going to work out." The violin finally "went out the window," as Jesse put it. By then his enthusiasm for it had entirely waned, and not just because of new commitments to playing football and competing in track and field like his father and grandfather before him.[27]

Around the time Eddie was in sixth grade, his father began taking guitar lessons, just another in a rotating assortment of instruments he taught himself to play. Eddie watched his father's fingers pick his Martin acoustic guitar, possibly the same 000-28 model Jesse played during his studio career in Los Angeles years later. Soon Eddie began sneaking the guitar from the closet before his father returned home from work. "For some reason I didn't want him to know I was playing," he later remembered. "He wanted me to be a piano player." He did in fact begin taking piano lessons around that time, but he "couldn't take the teacher, she was from the battle ax school." With piano, he was better off learning from Uncle Wallace and his mother.[28]

Meanwhile, Eddie could not contain his fascination with the guitar. His parents finally answered his prayer and put one in his hands. The details of this story changed each time the adult Jesse Ed Davis shared it. It is true, as he once told a live audience in New York, that he began in front of a mirror not with a guitar but a ukulele, strung around his neck with a rope, pretending to be Elvis Presley, Jimmy Reed, and Chuck Berry—the latter's "Roll Over Beethoven" among the first songs he learned to play. In another version it was an electric Silvertone from the Sears catalog in seventh grade. In yet another iteration, it was a $10.95 Stella guitar. The exact instrument notwithstanding, the story always involved a mirror. Eddie studied his reflection while absorbing the sounds coming over the radio waves.[29]

The story about his first guitar was perhaps intentionally similar to that of another one of his heroes. Muddy Waters sometimes told a story about buying a cheap Stella guitar from the Sears catalog. Although Jesse was Kiowa-Comanche from Oklahoma City, he was no different from the countless musicians of myriad backgrounds who decided that, if they want to be a great blues musician, like the legends of previous decades who commanded Jesse's turntable, then they'd have to invent or reinvent themselves and become one. Self-mythology is fundamental to the project. Tall tales are a tradition in the blues. And some of the best tall tales involve a guitar.

Eddie began venturing to Jenkins Music to take a few lessons with a veteran Oklahoma City jazz and country picker named Julian Adkins, who went by "Jess." Like Eddie's father, this other Jess was a World War II veteran. Home from the war, he landed a gig as "Cowboy Jess" on local radio and television shows, including *The Chuck Wagon Gang*, and occasionally backed singing cowboy stars such as Gene Autry and Jimmy Wakely. When Eddie began training with him, Jess's main gig was session guitarist for WKY-TV and radio. As a combination solo artist, session guitarist, and sideman to the stars, Jess Adkins must have taught Jesse Davis just as much about how to make a living as a musician as he did about playing guitar. Alongside Uncle Wallace's blues piano riffs, Jess Adkins's lessons in country and jazz licks became a well from which Jesse would draw for the rest of his life.[30]

Eddie picked up chords, scales, and techniques from his teacher, but his particular style and sound emerged from the countless hours he committed to playing guitar. When his grandfather Jasper died in 1959,

Eddie embraced guitar as a means to pass the time as his family ceased social activities for one year in the spirit of mourning. Guitar "struck a hidden chord deep within my soul," Jesse recalled, describing his conversion upon his grandfather's passing. By age seventeen, guitar was "all I lived for."[31]

Eddie's school and neighborhood friends roamed around outside and could go together to the amusement park nearby, but Eddie mostly wanted to play guitar and spin records. He soon made friends with other like-minded young musicians through Jenkins Music and its local competitor Larsen Music. He also befriended other kids at school who shared his devotion to guitar in particular, and music generally. Meanwhile, he retained his father's musical partnership at home. Bus and Eddie played together, and both were quick studies on guitar. When Bus asked Eddie's friend Jim Layton to teach him the same "Johnny B. Goode" lick he showed Eddie, Bus retreated to his art studio and then reemerged twenty minutes later playing it perfectly.[32]

In seventh-grade classmate Mike Brewer, Jesse found his first regular music partner. Brewer would go on to make hits such as "One Toke over the Line" as one half of the folk-rock duo Brewer & Shipley. For now, he and Eddie Davis passed hours after school working on Kingston Trio covers. Brewer also admired Eddie's coveted copies of Chuck Berry records, which they wore out every day after school before hitting the record stores to buy more. Together, they also joined weekend sleepover jams with other young guitarists, playing bluegrass, Western swing, rock, pop, folk, and more. The marathon sessions began as soon as school let out on Friday. It wasn't just that anyone who fell asleep would be subjected to standard teenage pranks; it was that no one could put down their guitar. They didn't watch TV. They occasionally went fishing. Their lives almost entirely revolved around guitars.[33]

IT'S DIFFICULT TO piece together Jesse Ed Davis's first live music performance. This is partly attributable to time. If he were here today, he might not be much help. "My memory is really foggy from the third grade to the tenth grade," he confessed in 1972. And as with most musicians, there can be competing definitions of what qualifies as a first real gig. Jesse recalled an early public performance with a guitar occurring at a sixth-grade school assembly to celebrate grammar school graduation. He played with a couple of friends, including Mike Brewer, in a covers group that emulated popular folk revivalists. Jesse remembered playing his father's Martin acoustic guitar: "That's my earliest recollection of really playing." Still, he admitted, "I really don't remember when I first started."[34]

Two years prior, in 1970, Jesse told the same story about a school assembly, but said it happened during seventh grade. "That was my real debut on stage," he said. "They thought I was a ham." Eddie, Mike Brewer, and their friend James Burke formed a high school group called Them, modeled on the Kingston Trio, and not to be confused with Van Morrison's early Belfast group. The trio all sang and played guitar, with Jesse on the Martin. They played school functions, a senior retirement home, and a music store parking lot. Brewer and Burke both recall playing the Northeast Viking Variety show, though Burke remembers it being senior year of high school. Memories are possibly complicated by the fact that grades seven through twelve were all housed within one school.[35]

At the variety show, the trio performed a cover of the Five Satins' "In the Still of the Night," with Brewer crooning vocals that made girls in the audience cry. They paired it with a bawdy rendition of the perennial sea chanty "What Do You Do with a Drunken Sailor," which, coupled with Eddie's demand that they play this gig under the name "Sipes 3," made the trio worry they would receive a visit from the principal after the show. Sipes was the name of the most notorious brothel in town. It's an early example of Eddie's affinity for the dirty blues, characterized by ribald humor and innuendo, that would later feature in some of his work as a professional artist.[36]

There's another early show that Jesse either forgot or didn't count. Singer Diana Allen remembers young Eddie and Mike Brewer backing her when she fronted L. Woody's Band on August 1, 1959, at the popular Twilight Beach swimming pool and recreation area frequented by teenagers from throughout the Oklahoma City metro area. Allen had just gone solo after years leading the first OKC girl pop vocal group, the Polyannas, which had cut a semisuccessful single and worked the Chatterbox and Shangri La clubs. With DJ Bill Jones and the WKY Radio Swim and Dance Party series sponsoring the show, roughly five hundred people turned out to win free records for swimming, dancing, and diving competitions around the largest pool in the region, featuring imported sand to form a mock beach, a twenty-foot slide, and chemically treated water. Allen sang "Broken-Hearted Melody" by one of Eddie Davis's favorite artists, the great Sarah Vaughan. They had rehearsed at Eddie's house, playing the record repeatedly to learn their parts. Despite being so young, Eddie was confident as a guitar player. "He was remarkable," Allen remembers him. "It was impressive to be at his house and see his father's paintings, and of course he was American Indian, though he had a crew cut at the time. I only remember him as a talented, friendly young man." At the gig, Eddie and Mike dressed in Bermuda shorts and short-sleeve sport shirts with guitars strapped around their necks. This was still a couple of years before the California beach-rock scene exploded with the Trashmen's "Surfin' Bird" and the Beach Boys' "Surfin' Safari." Eddie Davis probably couldn't have guessed that he would one day reside in the Beach Boys' California and collaborate with Brian Wilson.[37]

AT NORTHEAST HIGH SCHOOL, it wasn't like in the movies, where jocks bully the weird kids into music and art. Eddie Davis excelled in both worlds. Eddie was something of a paradox, with a letter jacket, and flat-top haircut, and guitar. As possibly the only Native kid in an almost all-white public school, Eddie could appeal to his musical talents for social value, but he had more than music in his arsenal. Like his mother and father, he succeeded in numerous areas and transcended social and cultural expectations to become one of the most visible and popular kids in school.

Eddie was a bright kid who knew how to navigate different social settings. His parents understood the challenges their son might face as a Native American student attending public schools, where he might be one of only two or three Indigenous students in an otherwise predominantly white middle-class setting. And when not leading by example, Bus would influence Eddie through hard discipline. Bus was friendly and jovial—until Eddie got into trouble. One night during senior year, Eddie and some friends broke into an ice machine at the Dog N Suds drive-in restaurant, their version of Arnold's from *Happy Days*. They figured out how to pull down one bag at a time. By the third or fourth bag, all of a sudden, police lights illuminated the scene. All the boys were arrested and taken to the station. Bus showed up, and he wasn't pleased, to say the least. "It took a while for him to settle down," remembers Eddie's friend Mike Smith.[38]

It helped that Eddie wielded a cunning sense of humor. But then, his taste for comedy could be contrasted with a controlled disposition. Friends thought of him as a "man of few words." Eddie's mercurial modes reflected a life in which he had to quickly navigate shifting social settings. He occasionally took friends to Kiowa powwows during summer, though, like most teen boys at the time, he was more interested in hot rods and girls than ancestral cultural traditions. And then the guitar kept calling from the closet. Eddie could never wait for dinner to end so he could pick it up again.[39]

Simultaneously cultivating talent in other areas, the 5'10" 174-pound Eddie Davis ran distance for the high school track and field team and played tackle, the same position his father played, on the football team. Eddie also joined the Literature Club, Great Books course, Speech Club, Future Engineers Club, the Hi-Y Christian Club to promote Christian character, Thespians, for which he appeared in *You Can't Take It with You*, *Harmonious Voices*, and other productions as an actor, all while co-leading a folk music trio.

Eddie was an all-American overachiever, a popular kid in a school with classes too small to form cliques. More significantly, he was quickly earning respect from other musicians at school and around town. As rock and roll swept through Oklahoma City, Eddie achieved a reputation as a guitar player to see and hear. "In the early days, Eddie was a guitar player and a real wiseass. He was better known for the former than the latter, but only by a little," his eventual college bandmate Chris Frederickson recalls.[40]

Eddie engendered goodwill within his school, where his Indigeneity might have been a liability if not for his talent, charisma, and the fact that a handful of Black students occupied the bottom rung of the social ladder. "Had anyone made an issue of Eddie being Native it would not have gone well," bandmate Mike Boyle recalls. Within his school, Eddie was proud of being Native, and even signed his friends' yearbooks as "CHIEF," the same nickname friends used to refer to his father. No one resented Eddie for benefiting from a tribal scholarship. No one resented him at all. To his neighbor friend Caroline Furr, he was just the boy next door. But impressions alone cannot tell a story.[41]

Outside of school, Eddie was vulnerable to racism and prejudice. This was always apparent when he was cruising the strip, that great postwar American teenager pastime that persisted into the late twentieth century. Eddie's first set of wheels was a two-door white '55 Chevy hot rod, column coupe, center post, with pinstripes and flipper hubcaps. The car's rumbling exhaust attracted a police officer in exclusive Nichols Hills one afternoon when Eddie was out cruising with his pal and bandmate Chris Frederickson. After some back and forth, the cop who pulled them over said, "You trying to get in trouble, son?" Eddie snapped back, "You trying to write a book, cop?" The officer pointed to his handcuffs. That was Eddie, says Frederickson. "He had a sharp tongue and a chip on his shoulder."[42]

Eddie's acerbic wit couldn't rescue him from every situation. After a group of kids at the movie theater bullied him for being Indian, he began bringing his older Kiowa cousin Ray Doyah with him for protection. On other occasions, Jesse appealed not to humor or a bigger cousin but to a machete. He used it to scare away teens from rival high schools who were looking for a fight on the Classen Boulevard hot-rod circuit. Eddie would give them an intimidating stare, and slowly draw his machete from under his driver's seat where he kept it hidden. When menacing gangs took off in a flash, Eddie wouldn't say a word; he'd just slide the machete back under his seat. The threats were real for young

Eddie Davis. Sometimes in a state of inconsolable panic, afraid of racist bullies stalking him, he refused to leave his house.[43]

Jesse Ed Davis later recounted the bullying he endured and the courage it took to overpower it. On his third solo album, 1973's *Keep Me Comin'*, Jesse included a song called "Ching, Ching, China Boy" that he wrote about two bullies from Northwest Classen High School named Bobo Nance and Little Dan who had been "punchin' 'em down all day long." The two tyrants used to taunt Eddie with racist slurs in which they confused Eddie with being Asian. "I'm not yellow . . . I'm red," Eddie pled. Paying no mind, they told Eddie if he didn't start swinging, then "you'd better duck." He didn't. Instead, he landed a roundhouse, "just my style," on Little Dan. Eddie then turned to Bobo Nance, who began crying while begging to "bury the hatchet." It wouldn't be the last time Jesse Ed Davis had to physically defend himself. In the meantime, maybe Bobo Nance learned his lesson. Jesse would see and hear him again. Bobo became "Bo" Nance, a popular news director and sports anchor for WKY radio and television.[44]

FOR EDDIE'S FIRST serious girlfriend—and eventually fiancée—it didn't matter that Eddie was Native. Mary Carol Kaspereit, who called him Jesse, was interested in his cultural background, but it wasn't a critical factor in their relationship. They dated in high school, became engaged in college and, like his future partners, stayed in touch and remained friends for life. They fell in love within a social milieu that still prioritized formality and carefully observed if not chaperoned relationships between teen boys and girls. In fact, familial concern about Eddie's background as an American Indian would ultimately damage their relationship.[45]

The couple first met at the Springlake swimming pool during junior high, when Northeast included grades seven through twelve under one roof. They became boyfriend and girlfriend in eleventh grade when Jesse invited Mary Carol to prom. They broke up and got back together, and then broke up and got back together. "You know how it is," she chuckles. "There was always some drama." Their relationship was bur-

dened by distance, as she first went to college in Missouri, while Eddie
was enrolled at the University of Oklahoma and increasingly devoting
his time to music. When she transferred home to attend the University
of Central Oklahoma, Eddie proposed marriage. "That just seemed
to be what you did," she recalls. "You went to college and then you
got married."

Eddie was handsome, but Mary Carol also admired his passion. They
bonded over their mutual status as only children and did things all
young couples did at the time. They cruised around, went swimming,
frequented the amusement parks, and regularly met Vivian at lunchtime for sandwiches. And of course they went to hear live music. At the
Show of Stars concert events at the Municipal Auditorium, they watched
from the balcony as Del Shannon sang "Runaway," Eddie leaning in,
analyzing every note. The radio was never off. "No, listen to *this*!" he
repeated all day. In a gust of postwar teenage romance, Mary Carol
didn't anticipate Eddie's Native background becoming a problem. "I
didn't think anything of it, but I realized later that people did," she
regrets. People around her thought it strange to date an Indian guy.
This didn't occur to her, partly because her parents had many Black
colleagues and friends through various civic organizations. Moreover,
the clerk for the Oklahoma Supreme Court and his family, who lived
next door to the Kaspereits, were Native American. Her parents were
somewhat progressive on race. If anything, Mary Carol wondered if *she*
could belong with *Jesse*.

Mary Carol experienced an early lesson in difference. Like countless
other kids growing up in the shadow of Hollywood tropes and romantic
stories of American Indian people, she played "Indian" outside one day
when the Native American neighbor girl asked her what she was doing.
Mary Carol explained that she was doing an Indian dance. The Native
girl replied, "Who's ever heard of a redheaded Indian?" When Mary
Carol and Eddie became a couple, lessons in difference became more
personal and painful. Away at college in Missouri, she kept a picture of
Eddie on her dorm desk. "Oh, who's that?" her friend from Iowa gestured. "That's my boyfriend. He goes to OU." "Oh, I didn't know you
dated Indians in Oklahoma."

When Mary Carol and Eddie became engaged, her parents didn't object. But they were concerned with Eddie's temper, and they wondered what kind of life their daughter might have with him if he became a full-time musician. They worried Mary Carol wouldn't finish college, not unlike many new women college students who got married during early 1960s culture shifts. More pressing, Mary Carol's mother informed her that some family members were whispering about her engagement with Jesse. It began affecting Mary Carol's family relationships. While they were out for a drive, with Eddie's engagement ring on Mary Carol's finger, her mother turned to her: "I don't know what all your relatives on the East Coast are going to think about this." It's such a common cinematic trope in stories about star-crossed lovers, one might forget this happens in real life. "What?" she countered. What would her relatives in New York and Philadelphia think? "Well, it's not always customary for . . . " her mother tried. Mary Carol was crushed.

Though she remembers her own, Mary Carol can't speak for Jesse's experiences in these settings. Interracial couples certainly aren't obligated to sit around and talk about the color line during every date. But there were clues that Jesse experienced his own hurtful encounters with people who had strong feelings about who and where he was supposed to be. When the embattled couple got into arguments, Jesse often repeated a heartbreaking refrain: "It's the Indian in me you don't like." It wounded their love, even if it wasn't true. He would say this again with future partners.

When Eddie and Mary Carol thrived, it was in spite of their blind spots and weaknesses. When others in their circle of friends called Eddie "Chief," it seemed harmless, and Eddie sometimes encouraged it, partly because his dad experienced the same. But Native families like the Davises navigated a social atmosphere of deep patronization and condescension, at a minimum. Eddie could be forgiven for thinking whatever was wrong with him was due to his being Indian. He followed generations of Native people who were told they needed to be fixed by some government program, social theory, religion, or other alleged cure.

The family out east and the girl from Iowa didn't know any Indian people. They only knew certain portrayals of American Indian people, all of them impoverished in some way. The racist "Lo, the Poor Indian" caricature, drunken and destitute, persisted well into the early 1960s when Mary Carol and Jesse were together. Meanwhile, thousands of Native Americans moving to major cities during this era encountered people, from new neighbors to social scientists, who fetishized their relative success at "adjusting" to urban life and modern appliances. Jesse would have to protect himself when heading deeper into those worlds.

Racial tensions came into further relief in 1961, when Mary Carol and Jesse's Northeast high school became Oklahoma City's principal site of conflict over school integration. An optometrist named Alphonso Dowell sued the school board over Northeast's refusal to admit his son, Robert, unless Robert took a supplementary course not required of other transfer admits. Dowell lived in a dependent school district that did not include any high schools at all. When it came time to begin high school, OKC Public Schools sent him to the Black school Douglass High, but Alphonso Dowell wanted his son at Northeast, a better school in terms of distance and academic achievement. After all, white students from Dowell's neighborhood attended Northeast. After a couple of years, Dowell won the case, decided in a federal court, but by that point Robert had already finished high school elsewhere.[46]

A step toward open enrollment resulted not in desegregation but an almost complete recirculation. There were maybe four Black students at Northeast when Jesse graduated in 1962. By the end of the 1960s, there were maybe four white kids. In 1972, the Supreme Court compelled Oklahoma City to institute a busing program. Until then, those who resisted integration referred to the schools with newly high Black populations as "Dowell schools" and blamed their failings on the Black community.[47]

Of course, Jesse wasn't Black, but he also wasn't white. His experiences with race and racism would facilitate deeper bonds with musicians of color in his future groups, including Taj Mahal, Bill Rich, Bobby Torres, and Carl "Rogel" Summers. Long before he worked with those musicians, teenage Eddie Davis befriended one of the first Black students to attend Northeast, a saxophone player named Ira Hall, who got

Eddie deeper into blues music in tenth grade. Hall went on to become one of the first Black students at Stanford—the Stanford Seven—and the first Black executive at IBM. When Hall was finishing at Northeast, he asked the dean of students to write letters of recommendation for his applications to Stanford, Harvard, and MIT. The dean refused, urging Hall to go Oklahoma State like everyone else. After gaining admission to all three of his dream schools, Hall chose Stanford, but he didn't find a great welcome there either. Eventually he won people over, soon becoming class president. It had been a long road from an experience in Oklahoma in 1947 when he was three years old and his family was woken in the middle of the night at gunpoint. When Jesse referred to the "heavy, formative trips" he experienced on the receiving end of racism growing up in Oklahoma City, he wasn't only referring to himself.[48]

PRECISELY WHEN YOUNG Eddie Davis was posing with his grand-father to induct celebrities into the Kiowa nation, tens of thousands of Native people were in the process of relocating to major cities such as San Francisco, Los Angeles, Denver, Dallas, and Chicago as part of a federal program operated by the Bureau of Indian Affairs. Like Oklahoma City, these places had been dramatically transformed by World War II. This created some opportunity for Native people to work in major metropolitan centers, but the limits of belonging became apparent during downturns in local economies or racism on the part of local residents who didn't want any minority people moving into their neighborhoods, including even First Americans.

Like every city in America, Oklahoma City has always been an Indigenous place, and not only because of the capital's proximity to thirty-nine tribal nations. It grew with Native American people, and not apart from them. That Jesse also referred to the city as a "six-gun broken-bottled town" perhaps added a chapter to his blues musician mythology by exaggerating the Wild West themes of his upbringing. But if he employed some creative license, there was a fundamental truth to his characterization. In any case, we can understand why the diverse world of music, where people regularly reinvented themselves, became a refuge for Jesse Ed Davis. But before setting out with a guitar and his grandfather's Los Angeles address in hand, he first rose through the ranks of great musicians within Oklahoma.[49]

One day in August 1963, some of Eddie's friends went to see "The King of the Jukebox," rockabilly star and future country music hitmaker Conway Twitty, at Springlake. Filing through a few thousand people, they looked up at the stage and saw nineteen-year-old Eddie Davis strapped into a Gibson ES-345 guitar, playing with the band. They were shocked, but not surprised.[50]

Four

... BUT YOU CAN'T TAKE OKLAHOMA OUT OF THE BOY

J ESSE ED DAVIS LOVED the song "Bacon Fat." He played a version of Andre Williams's 1955 original during the early '60s with his first serious group, the Continentals. In 1969, he recorded the Levon Helm and Robbie Robertson arrangement of the tune with Taj Mahal for the *Giant Step* album. "Oh baby, aw honey, why you bacon fat?" Taj pleads before sending it over to "*Mister Davis!!!*" Jesse replies with one of his best guitar solos, a composition that builds gradually but cuts clean through with a masterful touch.

Jesse recorded it again as a rowdy horn-popping number with altered lyrics for his third solo album, *Keep Me Comin'* (1973). It was a staple in his solo band setlist throughout the '70s, and he played it with the Grafitti Band during the eighties. More so than any other song, no matter where his career took him, it remained central in his repertoire. On the surface, it's a jolly and bluesy stomper, about a new dance, but drenched in innuendo. At a deeper level, it's a song about home.

In OKC, the song became associated with a salad. At Hardy's Steakhouse, chef Bernard Smith served a concoction called "Shore Patrol Salad," named for a World War II Navy shore patrolman stationed at the

OKC courthouse who dined at Hardy's and complained that he missed the wilted greens that formed his salads back home. Chef Smith made a bed of cold lettuce, showered it with garlic salt, and smothered it with smoking-hot bacon grease and bacon crumbs.[1]

Hardy's was *the* place to eat when important people came to town. Eddie Davis would spy Conway Twitty or Levon and the Hawks there after hours, recovering from a live gig with a steak and a bowl of soggy lettuce. Before they became Bob Dylan's Band, the Hawks regularly featured "Bacon Fat" in their live set, and it became customary for the group to sing the tune when ordering a Shore Patrol Salad at Hardy's after a set at the Onyx Club. When Eddie's first serious groups started making a little bread, they celebrated at Hardy's too. That's what the successful groups did.[2]

Still, "Bacon Fat" was more than a salad or a song. It held real meaning for Jesse. "While I was down in, uh, Tennessee," it goes, "all my friends was glad to see me." After first spotting friends walking along the railroad track, the song's narrator observes cotton pickers coming in from the fields. When Jesse cut it for *Keep Me Comin'*, he changed the opening lyric to "While I was back in OKC," and the railroad track became Reno Street, referring to OKC's notorious vice district. Then "Diddly whomp" became "lickety bomp," as Jesse made it his own. At its core, and especially in Jesse's rendition, it's a song about going back home and seeing how people are still dancing. This idea held real meaning for Jesse, both in Oklahoma City and over in Kiowa and Comanche country.[3]

The friends Jesse Ed Davis made and the partnerships he cultivated playing music in Oklahoma and beyond during high school and college would sustain him for many years. Some of his early bandmates became lifelong pals and later tried in their own ways to help Jesse when he needed support from old friends. An astonishing number of them became successful in their own careers, at times working with Jesse on albums he produced in California, including his own. He didn't have to return to Oklahoma to see old friends. He was surrounded by them in Los Angeles, and then he met even more Okies when he got there.

Jesse was always amused by the fact that he had to go all the way to California to encounter the Tulsa crew led by Leon Russell. But then Tulsa, less than two hours down the road, might as well have been a thousand miles from Oklahoma City. With California farther still, Jesse started at home and built a career from the ground up. He and his collaborators made a community, and that community became mobile and eventually merged with other like-minded musicians from Los Angeles to London and beyond. Jesse's central spirit of community and collaboration made him attractive to many of the most prominent musicians of his era and defined his experiences for the remainder of his life and career.

ONE AFTERNOON IN 1959, an aspiring teenage musician named John Selk was playing guitar in Oklahoma City's Larsen Music. This was not an uncommon occurrence. Any number of musicians young and old could be found there picking guitars. It was a hub for musicians hoping to bump into others looking to form a band. John Selk already had a group, the Continentals, playing bass with his drummer pal John Ware. They were looking to reconfigure their lineup after parting ways with their unreliable singer and keyboardist Jerry Fisher, who would later front the hit group Blood, Sweat, and Tears.[4]

Selk noticed an American Indian kid watching him play. This went on for a while before the silence broke. "Hey, you play pretty good. Do you mind if I play with you?" "No," Selk consented. The kid grabbed a guitar off the wall and immediately made Selk's jaw drop. After exchanging phone numbers, Selk hurried home to call Ware. "Man, I met this Indian kid today that plays his ass off. . . . His name is Eddie Davis." "Call him," Ware instructed. Eddie Davis answered. He was interested.

To experience Eddie himself, Ware brought him to a regular gig at the YMCA Camp Ione just outside of town. It didn't go well. Eddie played a totally different kind of music and didn't gel. The Camp Ione group performed crisp country-swing versions of rock and roll tunes. Eddie's sound played loose by comparison—more soulful and less precise, more organic than technical, a trait that persisted. Ware loved it, but the others pulled him aside and protested: "Don't bring him back anymore. He's an Indian and he's a sloppy player."

Ware quit the gig and went to Eddie's house to hear him play some more and to inspect his record collection. Ware's mother was happy to learn her son formed a group with Eddie Davis because her own friend collected Bus's artwork. But first Eddie needed encouragement. He was guarded and full of self-doubt. "'Aloof' is in the dictionary next to a picture of Eddie," Ware quips. Nevertheless, Eddie and the two Johns began rehearsing together every chance they had, though rehearsal was often more a matter of listening to Bus's records—Joe Pass, Wes Montgomery—than playing their instruments. Soon, this group gelled.[5]

Before going any further, the Continentals needed a new singer. With a certain sound in mind, Ware wanted a Black vocalist. Visiting the Colored Musicians Union in search of a match, they gave him a number for "Mama" Summers's son Carl. The timing was perfect. Charismatic Carl Summers, thirteen years old, could sing every radio hit of the day, and he was bored in his current group that kept him in the background when he longed to be in front.

"Call me Rogel . . . Carl Rogel," Summers insisted over the phone. Agreeing to that request, Ware recruited Rogel for a sock hop at Northwest Classen High School. Rogel appeared with no rehearsal. The group scanned their setlist, determined a key for each number, and hit the stage. Rogel may have been the first Black kid inside Northwest Classen. Somehow it all worked. The audience went wild and the Continentals landed more gigs, appearing in school cafeterias, at sock hops, and at one high school auditorium gig that featured over one thousand students—a serious feat for a local band of teenagers.

When Ware, Selk, and Eddie Davis graduated high school, the Continentals were just getting started. Selk would drive up to Oklahoma City and bring Rogel, still finishing high school, down to Norman for practice and gigs. They soon developed a reputation as one of the best young bands in Oklahoma. The core group gradually picked up rotating members who would fill in for someone who couldn't make a gig—or randomly to expand the lineup with keyboards and horns. When joined by a horn section, the Continentals could stretch to seven or eight members. This fluid system reflected the big-band music Jesse Davis loved. He continued employing this model in the 1970s when he formed his own solo groups. Working the club circuit in California, he nurtured his foundational Count Basie lessons and the big arrangements and sound of the New Orleans jazz 78s his parents used to play at night. We also hear the vibrant New Orleans spirit preserved in Jesse's solo albums, especially 1973's *Keep Me Comin'*, with its jubilant horns, funky rhythms, and festive atmosphere.

The Continentals mastered many styles. When Larry Hollis joined on saxophone, they covered more challenging artists, such as Rahsaan Roland Kirk. Eddie loved Kirk, the radical jazz musician who could play three saxophones simultaneously with infinite breath. Kirk was an important figure in the 1960s Black revolutionary jazz movement, singing about "Volunteered Slavery," in tune with history while exploring new musical paradigms. This wasn't standard high school sock hop stuff or music for squares. I was only slightly surprised when I listened to a mixtape of Jesse's favorite songs and heard Kirk's "The Inflated Tear."

The Continentals were good enough to become a popular group without relying on popular covers. They did play popular songs such as Chubby Checker's "The Twist," Hank Ballard and the Midnighters' "Let's Go, Let's Go, Let's Go," and the Isley Brothers' "Shout," but the crowd had to wait for them between original arrangements of Ray Charles, Freddie King, and Jimmy Reed blues numbers, including "Baby What You Want Me to Do?" that were undanceable, unfamiliar to audiences, or both.

At the University of Oklahoma, various fraternities hired the band to play college parties and river bottom shows. The latter were quite literally giant parties in dry riverbeds on the outskirts of Norman. Organizers would lay out a giant tarp for the band to stage their gear on and bring generators to power the equipment. The setlist veered into vulgarity at these gigs. University students, even in socially conservative Oklahoma, loved the overt sexual innuendo of "Baby Let Me Bang Your

Box" and other numbers from Doug Clark and the Hot Nuts' novelty albums—*Homecoming, On Campus, Rush Week*—released appropriately by the Gross Records label.

The group's versatility earned them different types of gigs. They might pack OKC's Peppermint Lounge on 10th Street with three hundred fans or headline Purple Passion parties at OU's Beta House, decorated floor to ceiling in purple for the event. On one occasion, Eddie was a bit too passionate about "the purple stuff," a guaranteed-hangover blend of grape juice and grain alcohol. "He passed out under the dining table and could not be resuscitated," Ware recalls. Eddie's future music partner, Moon Martin, who later wrote the hit "Bad Case of Loving You (Doctor, Doctor)," first saw Eddie Davis there and filled in for him on a song or two when Eddie was incapacitated. "I was kind of the last man standing," Martin said.[6]

Before long, the Continentals were hooking a U-Haul to a sedan and hitting the road for shows from Tulsa all the way to Dallas and Odessa, Texas. Nothing, however, matched the excitement of their first weekend stand in 1963 at Ronnie Hawkins's legendary Rockwood Supper Club out on Highway 71 in Fayetteville, Arkansas. All the top national and regional groups, including the Hawks and Conway Twitty, played there. This was real validation of the Continentals' talent. To the group, it might as well have been Carnegie Hall.[7]

The Continentals first mingled with Ronnie and the Hawks after Springlake Amusement Park gigs. This was before the Hawks left Ronnie Hawkins and became both Bob Dylan's electric backing band and a Hall of Fame group in their own right as the Band. The otherwise Canadian group, plus drummer Levon Helm from Arkansas, were popular in pockets of Canada and the United States, and especially in Oklahoma, where they were bona fide stars to Eddie Davis and company.

Initially, "Indian Ed," as they called him, was the kid who watched every local Hawks show from the front row. "The Hawks really impressed me with their musicianship and their musical dignity and integrity," Jesse later stressed. Guitarist Robbie Robertson often looked down to see teenage Eddie Davis staring at his fingers as they worked the fretboard. "I could tell in a second that this guy was a guitar enthusiast," Robertson noted, "just by the look in his eyes." Raised on the kind of Cowboys versus Indians dramas typical among American kids in the twentieth century, Helm sometimes wondered if the Hawks would "get out alive" if audiences in Indian Country didn't like them. The notion of menacing Natives is an old trope in settler imaginations, but the Hawks did occasionally encounter some hostility. At gigs in Tahlequah and Pawhuska, capitals of the Cherokee and Osage Nations, members of the audiences stole the band's gear. The promoters refused to intervene. "You gotta go out there and talk to your people," Hawkins ordered Robertson, who, despite being Mohawk and Cayuga from Ontario's Six Nations Reserve, was no interlocutor. "They don't give a shit about a Mohawk from Canada!" he pleaded. He was an outsider. "Where the fuck is Indian Ed when we need him?" Robertson grumbled.[8]

Eddie Davis and John Ware were such big Hawks fans they once drove Ware's '64 Impala all the way to Toronto in a gambit to hang with the band at their home base. Only when they reached the Le Coq d'Or club, where the Hawks had a weeklong gig, did they learn they weren't old enough to enter. Helm, now leading the group as a singing drummer, pulled some strings and directed Eddie and John to stand to the side of the stage. If a waitress approached, they were instructed to say they were only there to watch and learn. And they did, absorbing the Hawks up close and personal for a week. But to their disappointment, the Hawks didn't want to hang out. They preferred being with family and girlfriends at home. "We were like vultures," Ware says, blushing. Relocating to a cheap hotel, they hatched a plan to salvage the trip. They headed for New York City, where they hit the streets, seeing as much music as they could. At a small bar, they caught the Staple Singers, with Pops Staples at the lip of the stage guiding young Mavis. Then at Joey Dee and the Starliters' Peppermint Lounge, they witnessed an amazing young guitarist named Jimi Hendrix.[9]

Back home, as the Continentals' profile grew, so did Eddie and Carl Rogel's unique bond, fastened by shared experiences. On one level, Carl could relate to Eddie as a racialized person. In the 1950s and '60s, Native people were in some respects treated like Black people. But Carl's mother was specifically a Chickasaw freedperson. Did they talk about Jesse's

Indigenous ancestry? "Didn't have to," Rogel laughs. "Jesse was a picture of what you'd call an American Indian." One of the few people during this period who referred to Jesse by his birth name, Carl related to the poor treatment his friend received for being Indian, and how it gave him a certain edge. "He had a way of expressing himself," Rogel recalls. "There was nothing you could say in which you could outtalk him. . . . He didn't have a lot to say to outside people."[10]

Jesse also looked out for the younger Carl and tried to shield him from racism. When they stopped at a diner before a WKY Radio teen hop in Ponca City, Oklahoma, the waitress brought a tray of drinks to the table before informing the group that Carl and Eddie would have to eat in the kitchen. The dining room was for white people only. "White?" Jesse begged, pretending he didn't hear. "Yeah," she replied. Eddie grabbed his glass of milk, poured it all over the counter, and asked: "How do you like this white?"[11]

Rogel's role in the band was controversial in a nation still battling segregation. Of course, Rogel was no stranger to the subject. He led a youth council within the National Conference of Christians and Jews, which worked hand in hand with the NAACP. After hearing about how Frank Sinatra refused to play New York City's Copacabana unless a Black person could attend, Rogel leveraged the idea in OKC, telling club owners he wouldn't play unless there could be at least three Black people in the venue. At the popular Esquire Club, he effectively began an integration movement.[12]

At showtime, Rogel could win people over. Unfortunately, venues sometimes didn't give the Continentals a chance after seeing the singer. In Dallas, the group had to sneak Rogel into hotel rooms. Sometimes Jesse's presence was just as problematic in a time and place marked by violent race relations. "[Oklahoma] was just not a healthy place to grow up in some ways," Ware regrets. But then, even in Oklahoma, not everyone realized Jesse Davis was Native. People often asked about the "Hawaiian guy."[13]

Appearing with a Black singer and two white guys on bass and drums, Jesse was already in the precise configuration he would be five years later with Taj Mahal. While the Taj Mahal band deserves greater recognition as one of only a few successful interracial groups of the 1960s, alongside the Paul Butterfield Blues Band and Sly and the Family Stone, Jesse and the Continentals had already achieved that distinction before he left Oklahoma. There was no other group like the Continentals in the area at that time. On a grander scale, they were ten years ahead of eventual trends that reshaped popular artists and audiences. "We looked like television in the 1970s," Ware says as he describes their diverse group.[14]

The group's diversity wasn't by design. They cared about civil rights, but their band wasn't a vehicle for any cause. "We weren't paying attention to what color anybody was," Selk reflects. Jesse and Carl Rogel didn't want to focus on differences between people. Among musicians, they could forget that they were different. " 'Do you know that you're colored?' " Rogel remembers the manager at the Onyx Club asking him. This was supposed to be fun. It wasn't yet a matter of envisioning a professional career in music. Selk was determined to be an airline pilot, while Jesse still imagined a future as an English teacher. Ware was so convinced of college's importance that he left for school in California while planning to rejoin the group for summer dates when he visited home. It was then that the Continentals became Jesse's group.

AT COLLEGE IN NORMAN, Eddie Davis was too absorbed with music to attempt to rival his parents' illustrious reputations in the campus community. Eddie was recognizable, but more for his presence outside classrooms than inside them. He could often be found sitting outside playing guitar all day. In the dorm room Eddie shared with John Selk, listening to Aretha Franklin and Elmore James was a greater priority than studying for class. For Eddie, music was an irrepressible obsession that gradually overwhelmed his interest in an English degree. It was also a refuge from the sting of rejection and an alternative language for expressing his humanity. Eddie signaled pride in being Native American. At the same time, he struck people almost as more of a spiritual brother to B.B. King and other Black bluesmen. He could easily defy expectations.[15]

Notwithstanding, Eddie's college experience got off to a painful start when all the fraternities denied him because he was Native American.

"That kind of stuff happened all the time," John Selk recalls. Eddie went to Kappa Sigma, where he should have been a legacy recruit based on his father having been a member, but the fraternity had no interest in considering him. They refused to even rush Eddie Davis. So racially exclusive were they that they refused John Selk, too, simply because he shared a dorm room with his Native American friend.[16]

Eddie learned to counter racism with his guitar and wit. When someone kept honking and trying to intimidate Eddie one day as he crossed the street to Campus Corner, he launched his stack of books high into the air and pretended to be deeply shaken, taking what seemed like five minutes to pick them up, stopping traffic while the light changed colors. On another occasion, at a restaurant on the same Campus Corner, a waitress who always gave Eddie a hard time had to clean up chunks of beef after she said something offensive to him. Having heard enough, Eddie pretended to projectile vomit, using a can of stew he smuggled in his coat.[17]

Drummer Erik Dalton saw a similar side of Eddie. Before starting at OU, he had already heard about "this crazy Indian guy" from Oklahoma City. On the first day of classes, he was second to arrive for his English course. Across the large classroom, one student sat inside a roped-off section of desks. Dalton sat down beside him, unsure where he was supposed to sit. They looked at each other, but didn't talk. Minutes later a group of big guys followed the professor into the room. "What are *you* doing here?" he quizzed, before explaining the section was reserved for the football team. "Please move," the professor instructed. "No," the first student didn't hesitate to reply. Dalton dug in too until the professor surrendered. After class, Dalton learned that his partner in the resistance was none other than the guitar player friends told him to find.

Ed Davis, as friends began calling him, continued to make good on that first impression. Not unlike Jimi Hendrix, Davis was much less of a brooding character than the one conjured by popular memory and his fate. Like Hendrix, Ed Davis was a prankster. Dalton, who knew both musicians, suggests that Davis and Hendrix exhibited twin personalities. "You didn't take Eddie too seriously until he picked up that guitar." Their friendship flourished through music. If they missed a lot of class, they also saw a lot of great music, including the Hawks, Jerry

Lee Lewis, Ike and Tina Turner, and more. Sometimes Ed filled in on guitar with Dalton's group the Disciples, mostly playing Freddie King covers. They remained friends after moving separately to Los Angeles, where Ed would produce an album for Southwind, a group that evolved from the Disciples.[18]

When Ed Davis wasn't playing or listening to music, he was teaching it. While enrolled at OU, he picked up a gig as a guitar instructor at Mike Richey's guitar shop on Campus Corner. An impressive number of future successful musicians all taught there simultaneously. Ed's own bandmate John Selk went on to play with Donovan, Walter Egan, and the Everly Brothers. Moon Martin would enjoy success as a songwriter and solo artist. The great fiddler Byron Berline taught at Richey's before landing a gig with Dillard & Clark, the country rock group that featured ex-Byrd Gene Clark on vocals and guitar. Later, in California, Ed Davis and Gene Clark became best friends. The music business already seemed a small world before Ed ever left for LA, where it got smaller.

While teaching guitar, Ed Davis continued developing his own technique, exploring different styles and sounds. With the Continentals, he achieved a fuzz tone by playing through a cheap Standel transistor amp that he overdrove to produce the effect. Ed even tried putting banjo strings on his guitar to see how it would sound. Then, blues guitarist Lonnie Mack's signature vibrato, extracted from a 1950s Magnatone amplifier, gave Ed the idea of trying to play through a rotating Leslie speaker. He became one of the first guitarists to use this effect.[19]

Ed Davis also first attempted slide guitar during freshman year at OU. He sat in his dorm room for hours playing along to an Elmore James record. Ed began showing people his technique when working at Richey's. At first a little sloppy, he made up for it with a soulful and emotional tone. Indeed, Ed didn't yet know the benefits of playing slide guitar in open E or G tuning and instead came up with his own approach of simply tuning his G string to G sharp. "I turn everything up to ten," Ed once explained about his sound. But that was only half of it.[20]

Ed Davis's distinctive tone came from a blend of competing forces: playing through an incredibly loud amplifier, but with an incredibly light touch, almost caressing his guitar strings. His earliest guitar heroes included Chuck Berry, Jimmy Reed, Freddie King, and Elmore James, but jazzier players such as Charlie Christian, Wes Montgomery, Django Reinhardt, and Joe Pass encouraged a certain degree of sensitivity in his playing that transcended the rock and roll school of guitar.[21]

Joe Pass made an especially pronounced impression on Ed Davis. The jazz guitarist who backed Ella Fitzgerald exhibited a masterful finesse in his playing and a sympathetic approach to his place in a song's arrangement and mix. He taught nine principal rules for tasteful guitar playing:

> *Lay the melody up high.*
> *You don't need a chord for every note.*
> *Don't overdo reharmonization.*
> *Add different alterations or colors to chords (rather than
>   heavy reharmonization).*
> *Prioritize strong voice movements between chords.*
> *Exhibit motion and movement in chords.*
> *Do not play fills that go nowhere.*
> *Don't play the bass note, chords, and melody all the time.
>   Instead, cycle between all three.*
> *Keep it easy for yourself.*

All nine rules are evident in Davis's playing. Such strategies separated him from his peers, precisely by playing a guitar style designed to *not* stand out. Very early, Jesse Ed Davis learned speed, intensity, and volume could become a distraction. He was more interested in touch and soul.[22]

Joe Pass also struggled with heroin addiction. After moving from Pennsylvania to New York City for steady gigs in the 1940s, he became hooked on the drug that compromised, and sometimes ended, the careers of so many great jazz musicians. Then, a yearlong schedule of gigs at a network of strip clubs in New Orleans, where virtually every drug was easily available, sent him into a complete nervous breakdown. In 1974, when drugs were becoming a more prominent feature of Jesse's life and experience in the music business, Pass reflected on his relationship with hard drugs and their impact on his life:

It's just part of the environment and still is. . . . I thought that was the way to go, and I went from one thing to another and that's how I got started. I got heavily involved and people were saying, 'You'd better cool it, you'd better stop.' But . . . I couldn't hear anything they said. Everybody, people close to me, my family; I didn't hear them; you never do.

Pass was one of the greats, but greatness took a toll on him and people around him. "[Staying] high was my first priority; playing was second; girls were third," he once said. "But the first thing really took all my energy." Pass's music made an impression on Jesse. It's difficult to know if the cautionary tale did too.[23]

Ultimately, Jesse Ed Davis's approach to guitar was an expression of his own philosophy, physicality, and, to some degree, his Indigeneity. Beyond mastering the pentatonic scale, he was compelling as a Native guitarist who heard musical kinship in Black musicians from New Orleans. "And he takes it to the white boys, I'm talking about the English, who really, really hungered for that music," Carl Rogel suggests. "I think that's why everybody wanted him." Ed's sound also came from his center. The fact that he closed his eyes tightly when he sang might have been more than a musical charm. It's typical among Indigenous singers to close one's eyes tightly while performing. It's partly a reflection of how music honors the Creator. Taken together, Ed's talent, and the human force behind it, could be downright intimidating. To some of his Continentals bandmates, Ed was like a teacher, a judge, and a bandmate all rolled into one. To Ed, there was nothing especially complicated about what he did. "I just play the notes that sound good," he once said. "I just play what I like to hear—that's all."[24]

COUNTLESS HOURS LISTENING to music, playing music, and teaching music prepared Ed Davis for his first major professional opportunity. The same hitmaking Conway Twitty who had been a hero to Davis for many years now needed someone to replace Al Bruno, one of Ed's "first real idols on guitar," as he put it. Bruno used to teach Ed guitar licks backstage. That proved useful when Ed assumed Bruno's position.[25]

Ed Davis first appeared with Conway Twitty in Oklahoma City on August 30, 1963, at Springlake Amusement Park—the venue where he used to watch Twitty from the front row. The band included "Big" Joe Lewis on bass, Tommy "Porkchop" Markham on drums, Denzil "Dumpy" Rice on keyboards, and two saxophonists. Playing with the popular Conway Twitty was a remarkable achievement for eighteen-year-old Ed Davis. Twitty had a number one hit in "It's Only Make Believe" and a devoted audience.[26] Moreover, playing with a star came with special perks, including fancy tailored suits, which Ed wore with pride. The gig came with keys to fancy cars, too. One winter, Twitty loaned Ed his brand-new Cadillac Fleetwood. Ed drove his fiancée Mary Carol around the city to see Christmas displays and show off the car. The couple glowed like the warm lights all around them.[27]

In either 1964 or 1965, Jesse Ed Davis made his first television appearance. On WKY-TV's *Country Social*, he joined a cast of musicians backing Conway Twitty on "Walk Me to the Door" and "Lonely Blue Boy," the Country Social Girls on "I'll Lose My Mind Before I'm Over You," and Bud Mathis on a version of Tennessee Ernie Ford's "Blackberry Boogie." Mathis was both the television showrunner and co-owner of Mathis Brothers' discount furniture store. "We got them fire blazin' prices at Mathis Brothers Fur . . . ni . . . ture," the show sponsor's anthem went. Ed Davis appears nervous, or tired, when he rubs his eye before Mathis begins his number, but when they kick in, he's all smiles in a dark suit and skinny tie, tapping his toe and picking his cherry red Gibson ES-345 with confidence. Mathis hacks his way through a solo while Ed, the better player, manages the basic rhythm part. In "Lonely Blue Boy" with Twitty, Ed finally cuts loose, clearly thrilled to be there.[28]

Ed embraced the opportunity to further expand his guitar skills with Twitty teaching him country guitar licks and turning him on to Chet Atkins. Before joining the rockabilly star, Ed hadn't been away from home much, only slightly exaggerating when he said, "I'd never been out of Oklahoma City in my life." That changed quickly. With Twitty, he played everywhere from the Navajo Civic Center in Window Rock,

Arizona, to small midwestern towns like Clear Lake, Iowa, and Moline, Illinois. With Twitty, Ed appeared on television, traveled around playing music for enthusiastic audiences, and shared concert bills with the Hawks, a favorite band alongside the one he joined. Even when it wasn't glamorous—some nights, the group slept six to a hotel room in remote places—Ed thought he was on top of the world.[29]

Ed experienced not only the end of Twitty's rockabilly period but also ruptures in music culture and American culture more broadly. The civil rights movement, Vietnam, Students for a Democratic Society, the Student Non-Violent Coordinating Committee, and more were important features of the world around Ed. "You could almost see the kids changing from day to day," Twitty noticed. "They were beginning to realize that they had strong influence as a group." The social, cultural, and political contexts would only continue transforming with the National Organization for Women, the Weathermen, the Brown Berets, the Black Panthers, the American Indian Movement, and more on the horizon.[30]

While Twitty loved the music these shifting currents inspired, he wasn't as radical as the young people who comprised his audiences. "They weren't afraid to do almost anything right out in the open—things we never dreamed about doing in our day," he said, worrying that the revolutionary impulse could change things too quickly and consequentially, in a way that might even result in young people being hurt. Twitty moved in a different direction, joining the ranks of country music, which demonstrated its own dramatic transformations during the era but nevertheless felt more like home to an artist trying to find comfortable footing. This directional shift corresponded with his recent move to Oklahoma City, which he considered a "big country town."[31]

Jesse Ed Davis's memory was sometimes foggy on the facts of his career. He wasn't averse to peppering his stories with a little mythology, always partly rooted in reality. It wasn't malicious. He played many gigs and sessions with many artists, and at times his memory may have been beset by substances. Above all, he was a great fan of rock and roll, and he liked to tell good stories about it. The Conway Twitty chapter was no exception. Jesse claimed to have begun playing with him when he was either sixteen or eighteen. The latter is true, and it's probably also true when Jesse said he first met Twitty when he was seventeen. He told a story about being on the Tulsa turnpike with Twitty when smoke began billowing out the back of their vehicle. The band escaped in the nick of time and watched it burn from the side of the road. It's a true story. It happened four miles south of Onawa, Iowa. Flames shot up from the car and the group evacuated just seconds before watching it blow up. But this happened in August 1961, before Ed joined the group, when he was sixteen years old, still in high school, and still learning to play guitar.[32]

A second Twitty road story proved too good to be true. Jesse talked about sharing a bill with the Hawks in Friars Point, Mississippi, where Twitty's parents lived. After the gig, Ed and Hawks guitarist Robbie Robertson went searching Helena, Arkansas, just across the river, for the legendary Sonny Boy Williamson, who lived there and broadcast his blues on the *King Biscuit Time* radio program that reached across the Mississippi Delta. To their amazement, Ed and Robbie found him. Ed noticed Williamson spitting into a coffee can all night, assuming it was tobacco juice, only to later find that it was blood from the bout of tuberculosis that killed him a couple months later. It's an engrossing story, but Ed wasn't there for it, Robertson insists. It was only the Hawks, including Robertson and Levon Helm, who found Sonny Boy that night. Ed likely heard the story from Levon, who discussed it in great detail in his autobiography. Why appropriate Levon's story? For the blues credibility. Jesse wanted to be there too.[33]

The end of Ed Davis's tenure with Twitty is an equally compelling story. Given his vivid grasp of the details, I believe it. In June 1965, he went with Twitty to Somers Point, New Jersey, across the Great Egg Harbor Bay from Ocean City, to play Tony Mart's beach club. The Hawks were on the bill too. This gave Ed a chance to get to know them a little better, and if one version of events is correct, then Bob Dylan dropped by that weekend to scout the Hawks before inviting them to become his new band.[34]

Tony Mart's featured two go-go dancers, Christine Christiana and Gail Patterson, seven drink bars, twenty cash registers, and forty bartenders and bouncers. "We had a ball there," Ed recalled. Following an exuberant set by the Hawks, Twitty and company opened with a traditional version of the Irish standard "Danny Boy" before launching into their rock and roll numbers and a string of Elvis Presley tunes. Though the crowd was smaller this time, those in attendance danced with their usual enthusiasm.[35]

Twitty's set featured a brand of rock and roll reaching back to the late 1950s. While his approach would soon be eclipsed, Twitty wasn't too far removed from a musical era dominated by the type of big bands, once rebellious in their own place and time, that Eddie Davis loved as a kid. But the big bands were now disappearing. Twitty, Ed, and the rest of the group were reminded of it when they repeatedly saw old posters in concert venues advertising groups that no longer played there or continued to exist at all. For Twitty it was "a strange feeling to watch great music like that die." He didn't know his talented young guitarist would later help bring it back to life. Part of John Lennon's, George Harrison's, Ringo Starr's, Bob Dylan's, and others' attraction to Jesse was in the fact that he knew the music from that bygone era, and he could play it perfectly.[36]

A rival performer who appeared across from Tony Mart's at the Bay Shores club reflected the musical changing of the guard underway everywhere. New bands were beginning to perform in jeans and t-shirts, letting their hair grow and challenging popular conventions. This included the Bay Shores headliner Tito Mambo, aka Tony Fresca, who arrived at gigs inside a coffin transported by a hearse. Mambo's pallbearer bandmates, the Messiahs of Soul, paraded the coffin through a parting sea of fervent fans to the stage where Mambo rose like Lazarus during the opening number and stepped out looking like Jesus His Holy Self—long hair, beard, and robe, shepherding his flock of hippie disciples with a Stratocaster. Over at Tony Mart's, the suit-clad Conway Twitty and his Oklahoma Revue—"the last of the gentlemen"—were tossing out Elvis tunes to their loyal but diminishing crowd. Jesse Ed Davis was there, as both witness and participant.[37]

Soon, fearing the well was running dry, Twitty took the next exit to a career in country music. Facing his own uncertain future, Ed Davis knew Uncle Sam would send him to Vietnam if he didn't improve his grades in college. Later in Los Angeles, after his mentor Conway

Twitty pulled into the country music station, Ed Davis would charge
headlong into those same radical transformations that caused Twitty to
change course.

WHEN NOT ON THE ROAD with Twitty, Ed Davis continued leading
the Continentals, applying his new professional lessons to his old group.
He scored the Continentals a manager in the form of his Twitty bandmate Big Joe Lewis and a booking agent in Hattie Ruth Sallee from
the American Federation of Musicians. As bandleader, Ed handled the
group's weekly affairs, organized rehearsals, directed the live set, and
collected the cash after a gig. During Thanksgiving 1963, John Ware
visited home from California to find Ed had rechristened the group,
partly because there was another outfit using the name Continentals.
They were now Joe Banana and the Bunch, named after a Sicilian crime
boss from Brooklyn who was making national news after disappearing during a mafia war. Ed recruited his father to help build a trailer
with shelving and semipermanent racks the group could use to haul
their speaker columns and instruments on the road. Bus added his artist
touch, painting Joe Banana and the Bunch graphics on the side of the
trailer: "Their Sound Has Great A-Peel!"

In 1965, Ed took Joe Banana and the Bunch into Gene Sullivan's
small three-track studio to cut a single. Sullivan performed on *Louisiana
Hayride*, a radio show broadcast from Shreveport that helped break Elvis
Presley. He had ties to publishing companies in Nashville, where his song
"When My Blue Moon Turns to Gold Again" made him enough money
to build a studio that doubled as a makeshift home in Oklahoma City's
Capitol Hill district. Alongside Norman Petty's studio in New Mexico,
Sullivan's succeeded as the only other professional music recording studio between California and Nashville. Bands from all over the Midwest
and Southern Plains recorded there, and Nashville labels sent over new
bands to make affordable jukebox fodder or cheap demos before booking
costlier studio time in Music City. Sullivan's studio operated on a budget,
but it boasted legitimate Ampex tape machines and could get the job
done, turning out some real gems.[38]

Before getting started, the bunch needed to change its name again. This was serious business, and their name was a joke. Now going by the New Breed, they cut two songs composed by "J. Edwin Davis" for the Tennessean Bobby Boyd's OKC-based Boyd Records Inc, which later released a record by another Kiowa-Comanche artist, the dual psychedelic rocker and standup comedian Paul Littlechief and his group the Uprising. For this important occasion, the New Breed featured Mike Boyle on bass, Roger Edwards on vocals, Warren Sherman on drums, John Selk on guitar, Larry Hollis on saxophone, and Ed on guitar. "It was typical inexperienced guys in a funky little studio in Oklahoma City," Selk recalls. Still, the two songs they recorded mark Jesse Ed Davis's first-ever professional recording session, featuring his first-ever production and writing credits.[39]

Recorded live with no overdubs, the New Breed's A-side was "Just Another Bird-Dog," a 4/4 foot-stomper with soulful horns, a lead vocal delivered with enough zeal to distort the microphone, and a slinky Ed Davis guitar solo. The lyrics are typical teenage angst about a guy trying to rescue his girl from the clutches of a bad boy. That other guy is not true, Ed's lyrics warn. "He's trying to push all of his lies into your life / he thinks he can win." The pre-chorus rises with desperation: "Won't you listen to me? / Oh, can't you see? / He's trying to put the hurt on you!" Then a dramatic pause before the chorus: "He's just another bird dog!"[40]

The flipside, "You'll Be There," is a sad crooner ballad. "All my friends, I will leave / Many dear hearts I will break," Ed's words confess, before insisting it will all be worth it. It's difficult not to hear his lyrics as a forecast of his approaching future, when he would wave goodbye to his friends in Oklahoma, breaking his engagement with Mary Carol, trying to convince himself she'd still be waiting if he returned. "It just wasn't meant to be," Mary Carol realized.[41]

Though now an old-fashioned sentiment, there was once a music story cliché that captured the thrilling experience of a musician hearing themselves on the radio for the first time. Maybe you pull your car over in amazement and savor the moment, or yell at some passerby: "Hey! That's me!" I once experienced this with my own music. Jesse Ed Davis first heard himself on the radio in 1965 when "Just Another Bird Dog"

achieved regional airplay. The song earned the band a little celebrity at
OU, where friends and classmates loved it.

The group continued playing as either Joe Banana or the New Breed
with rotating membership according to time of year. They worked the
Springlake, Wedgewood, and Frontier City amusement parks, music
clubs, high schools, country clubs, frat parties, river bottoms, and the
storied Cimarron Ballroom in Tulsa while continuing to venture out to
Arkansas and north Texas. Meanwhile, they expanded their repertoire,
making room for everything from their own version of Percy Faith's
"Theme from *A Summer Place*" to Ed Davis's ripping guitar jams on
Muddy Waters's "She's Nineteen Years Old."[42]

As the rotating outfit trekked around the region for gigs, it began
spinning its wheels literally as well as metaphorically. For some members, the end of college was approaching, and professional careers, families, and traditional adulthood were calling. Not everyone wanted a
future in music, or believed one was possible. Ed Davis stood out in
this respect. "Eddie was driven by his music," recalls Mike Boyle, who
wasn't surprised when his friend made the big time. "He created an
aura about him."[43]

BACK AT SCHOOL, Ed Davis still majored in English and occasionally
went to class. He hadn't improved much on his inauspicious start in
fall 1962, when he earned Cs, Ds, and Fs in classes including English
Composition, General Anthropology, and Foundations of Air Power.
He didn't fare much better going forward. Mostly earning grades of D,
the only time Ed did better than a grade of C was when he scored a B
in Marriage and Family Relationships.[44]

Ed did love some classes, even if his grades didn't reflect it. He took
two US History courses with Professor Donald Berthrong, a World War
II veteran like Ed's father. Berthrong researched Native American history and became a foundational scholar in the field. His work was part
of an early movement that turned prevailing narratives on their head,
describing settlers who took Native land not as pioneers but as invaders.
Interacting with Indigenous people in Oklahoma, Berthrong learned to

take them seriously: "[Y]ou develop this understanding and empathy as to what the other person is about. And you discover very quickly that they are human."[45]

Berthrong specifically wrote about Ed Davis's Southern Cheyenne ancestors and the Washita Massacre he would sometimes mention in his future music career. Given Berthrong's expertise, he would have been as enlightened and sensitive a professor as any Native student could reasonably hope to find at a public university in the early 1960s. Later, in 1985, when asked for book recommendations for learning about Native people, Jesse didn't hesitate in recommending Berthrong's *The Southern Cheyennes*, published in 1963, the year Jesse had class with him.[46]

With the benefit of hindsight, it's apparent that Professor Berthrong got one important thing wrong in his work. In the 1960s, most all historians made this mistake. He described Native people in crisis and Native culture in decline—the infamous "disappearing Indian" myth:

> The days of freedom were ended. The warpath, the buffalo hunt, the thrill of horse raids were all in the past. Rations, schools, Christianity, and the cultivation of land were unsatisfactory substitutes, but the Southern Cheyennes were powerless to contest the superior force of the white man. Stripped of their reservation . . . the Cheyennes declined as disease, despair, and lethargy took their toll. The Southern Cheyennes clung stubbornly to their institutions until finally, in the 1930s, some recognition of their culture was granted by the United States' government.[47]

It's an earlier version of the pernicious *Bury My Heart at Wounded Knee* narrative that hit the bestseller list in 1969. The noble victims trope was ubiquitous for decades, much to Native peoples' detriment. Berthrong's assessment caricatures Native Americans' lives in the past and present while contradicting everything that explained Ed Davis's appearance in his own classroom.

In fairness to Berthrong, just taking Native people seriously as historical subjects was a progressive proposition in the early 1960s. Here was a professor capable of treating Ed Davis as human and valuable, not in spite of his Indigeneity, but partly because of it. And to his credit, Berthrong grew as an individual and scholar, too. Later in life, he stressed his interest in the subject as being about more than the mythology of Native people. He became interested in stories that didn't end with military defeat and confinement on reservations. "We have to take the same group of people and show how they maintained their tribalism and beliefs, survived despite the enormous pressures placed upon them for acculturation and assimilation," Berthrong wrote. Native American student Ed Davis would advance from Professor Berthrong's history classes and live one of those stories to an extraordinary degree.[48]

Taking fall semester 1963 off, possibly on academic probation, Ed focused on his work with Conway Twitty and the Continentals. In November 1964, he briefly withdrew altogether. He was back in summer 1965, but continued struggling into the fall. It wasn't just music that occupied his time and energy. In October, having moved on from Twitty, trying to improve his coursework, and determined to avoid Vietnam, he enlisted in the Oklahoma National Guard, becoming Private Jesse Edwin Davis III in the Photography Section, Charlie Company, 145th Signal Battalion out of Oklahoma City. This communications position resembled his father's role with the US Navy in World War II, although, unlike his father, Ed Davis joined the guard as a means toward avoiding war during an expanding draft. "Mama said, 'Son, baby, what about your schoolbooks' / 'Baby, baby, what about the draft?'" Jesse Ed Davis sang in "Washita Love Child," assuming his mother's voice, before adopting the perspective of his father, who promises Jesse's music will carry him over any obstacles along the path. It's easy to sympathize with Mamacita not wanting to lose her only child to the Vietnam War.[49]

Alas, Ed Davis didn't fare much better with the guard than with his classes at OU. During an annual training weekend at Fort Chaffee, Arkansas, famous to Ed as the base where Elvis Presley had his sideburns shaved after enlisting for service in 1958, Ed fell on an obstacle course and injured his head. In February 1966, he again withdrew from five courses at OU. In October 1966, he formally separated from the Oklahoma National Guard. Neither college nor the military was working for him. But music did, and he began wondering why he should continue wasting time with anything else.[50]

SOMETHING EXTRAORDINARY HAPPENED in Oklahoma during the 1960s, with so many talented and successful musicians emerging at once. Just within Jesse Ed Davis's high school and college groups, Mike Brewer achieved fame with "One Toke Over the Line" in his Brewer & Shipley duo; Carl Rogel fronted one version of "Yakety Yak" hitmakers the Coasters, studied with soul legend Barry White, cut solo records for Stax, and wrote for Motown; Bill Maxwell became a prominent rock and jazz drummer, session musician, and music producer for film and television; John Ware went on to a major career drumming for Linda Ronstadt, Mike Nesmith, and Emmylou Harris; and John Selk, who several years later would return from Vietnam, crash in Jesse Davis's converted garage in Marina del Rey, and play guitar on ex-Byrd Gene Clark's *White Light* with Davis in the producer's chair, made a career backing Linda Ronstadt, Donovan, the Everly Brothers, and Walter Egan. Finally, Jerry Fisher, who left the Continentals when Eddie Davis joined, would one day sing with Blood, Sweat, and Tears. Those are only the greatest hits, and that's without considering the musicians who trekked out of Tulsa in Leon Russell's caravan.

Was something in the water? Maybe, or the wind, or the red clay, or the way Oklahoma's harsh environment breeds character. Or, even if Oklahoma isn't exactly a Southern state, it reflects Southern culture. Young Okie musicians' fascination with Southern blues musicians extended from it. It wasn't uncommon for carloads of friends to drive down to New Orleans on weekends and witness firsthand the music they adored at home on their turntables.[51]

Perhaps more important than Oklahoma's relationship to Southern culture are its own unique features that extend from its profound historical diversity. Black Towns, Indigenous Nations, and Southern white folks have all shaped the sound of Oklahoma. At the center, Oklahoma City boasted a revered symphony orchestra and several vibrant music venues. To play in Oklahoma, one had to be able to play *everything*. The more diverse the audience, the more diverse the material. A first set might be quieter jazz music, before a louder second set filled with rock and roll and rhythm and blues. Okie musicians were known for being reliable in the studio and not getting high. They took live gigs seriously and delivered solid performances. That same Christian sobriety char- acteristic of people here sometimes benefited young musicians looking for professional opportunities. This all added up to one basic principle. "If you weren't good, you weren't going to play," Continentals drummer Bill Maxwell concludes.[52]

Jesse Ed Davis would later explicitly identify his music with the Oklahoma landscape. He launches his second solo album, *Ululu* (1972), with a second autobiographical tune, sort of a darker sibling to his debut album's "Washita Love Child." Borrowing a lyric from a J. J. Cale song, Jesse swears he "Ain't no Beatle / Ain't no Rolling Stone"—two groups from Britain. Who is he, then? "I'm just a red dirt boogie brother all the time!" he wails with both his voice and guitar. Alongside Jim Kelt- ner's superb drumming, Jesse delivers his own ripping solo. Though the album's cast is large, he doesn't lean on Eric Clapton or any other guest guitarist this time.

With "Red Dirt Boogie, Brother," Jesse Davis became one of the first to use "red dirt" as a music reference. Red Dirt music, historically rooted in Stillwater, home of Oklahoma State University, is a sister genre to the Tulsa sound. But it's even more difficult to define in terms of sonics. It might be that Red Dirt is as much about a shared culture as a sound. Still, there are some irreducible features, including the influence of West- ern swing descended from Bob Wills, and an emphasis on humor, some- times ribald, carried on down from the Cherokee multimedia star Will Rogers. And obviously, to anyone familiar with Oklahoma's landscape, Red Dirt referenced the soil, and in this way connects back to legendary folk singer-songwriter Woody Guthrie. Comparing Jesse to Oklahoma itself, Little Feat keyboardist Bill Payne suggests, "In your imagination, you think it's vacant like in the way Jesse was quiet, but it's not, it's filled with a lot of subtleties." Blending the influences of Oklahoma City, Still- water, and Tulsa with Dixieland jazz, various subgenres of rhythm and blues, rock and roll, folk, and country, as well as the California counter-

cultural scene where he established his professional career, Jesse created
a sound all his own. He would do this a second time in the 1980s when
he began playing with John Trudell and the Grafitti Band, creating a
new style of music even more difficult to define.[53]

The meaning of "Red Dirt Boogie, Brother" is as layered as the earth
it references. When Jesse claims he "ain't no Okie from Muskogee," it
isn't exactly true. He was from Oklahoma and he was a Mvskoke Creek
person. Instead, he was suggesting that he's not like the Okie simultaneously championed and ridiculed in Merle Haggard's famous tune about
people who "don't make no party out of lovin'" and "still wave Old Glory
down at the courthouse." When Jesse sings about red dirt, he means
both the distinct color of the iron-rich soil found here and the home of
Indigenous people—*Oklahoma* itself is a Choctaw word that translates
as "place of red people." When Jesse Ed Davis sang about who he was
and where he came from, he referred to people, place, and history.[54]

Growing up in Oklahoma, Ed Davis quickly gained experience as a
musician playing in diverse settings with a diverse range of artists. He
went on tours, worked in a professional studio, and appeared on television. He formed bands and joined bands. He backed artists and led
groups. Two of his songs were published. He was achieving great things
and succeeded on his own terms. His parents wanted him to finish his
degree, but otherwise supported his music ambitions. He was almost
prepared for a greater journey. He only needed one thing: a new guitar.

In 1970, Jesse told a story about a lonesome Fender Telecaster that
hung in a music store window for years, calling to him when he was
a kid. He often visited the shop and played it, dreaming about it. He
saved for it, and finally bought it in 1961 or '62. "It was brand new when
I got it," he stressed. The story was slightly different when he told it a
second time. In the alternate version, it was 1960 and his father bought
it for him. These stories are endearing. The truth is a bit less romantic.[55]

Ed had a friend named Rick White who played guitar in a group
called the Jades, which shared drummer Bill Maxwell with the Continentals. White was a great fan of Ed Davis, and Ed turned White on
to the Hawks. In summer 1965, White bought a Telecaster and Super
Reverb amplifier, because that's what Hawks guitarist Robertson used.

But White couldn't bond with the new guitar. He found an enthusiastic trade partner in Ed Davis, who wanted to put down his jazzy
semi-hollow-body Gibson ES-345 and pick up a more versatile guitar.
The Telecaster's brighter and clearer single-coil pickups were a better
option for the type of country, rock, and blues picking he was exploring.
Because the Gibson was worth much more than the Telecaster, White
threw his Super Reverb amp in to balance the trade. The Telecaster
became Jesse Ed Davis's signature guitar. When he told stories about
how he acquired his first Telecaster, he was reaching his professional
peak. Perhaps he just wanted a better guitar origin story. In the end,
the story didn't matter as much as the fact that he now had the proper
tool to set out for stardom.[56]

IT'S SURPRISINGLY DIFFICULT to determine exactly when Ed Davis
left Oklahoma for California. Ed himself sometimes placed it as early
as 1965, but that's impossible given evidence at hand, and he was often
blurry on these sorts of details. Some recall him leaving in 1966; others think it was 1967. If it were 1966, then it had to be late fall or early
winter. He withdrew from classes at OU for the last time in February
'66, and received his discharge from the Oklahoma National Guard in
October '66. It could simply be that Ed went back and forth to California
a couple times, as one friend remembers.[57]

In any case, when exactly Ed left isn't as interesting and inspiring as
his story about how he left. He was back in class at OU, still trying to
become an English teacher. But he couldn't focus. He couldn't stop the
music in his head. His every thought was set to a soundtrack, and then
at night he dreamed about music too. "I'd just sit in English and just
look out the window and just be thinking guitar riffs in my head all day
long," he recalled. "Not just guitar, sometimes I'd get whole symphonies
going in my head." No longer able to resist:

Right in the middle of class one day, I walked out. Went down to
the administration building and dropped out of school, packed up
all my stuff from the dorm and drove home, which is about twenty

miles. Hung around for a couple of days and in a week, I was in Los Angeles. I didn't know anybody, not one soul.[58]

He was again slightly exaggerating. He knew Levon Helm, who had stepped away from the Hawks tour with Bob Dylan and helped Ed get established in Los Angeles by connecting him with the "Oklahoma Mafia," session pro Leon Russell's Tulsa gang camping out in the Hollywood Hills at a place called Skyhill. "I had to go to California to meet guys from Oklahoma who grew up 90 miles away from me," Jesse acknowledged. And he knew his grandfather, with whom he initially lived in Silver Lake. And he knew his music and Oklahoma Guard friend Joe Royer, whose 1966 Corvette Joe and Ed pointed down Route 66 toward the Golden Coast. Old friends would see Ed again, sometimes on the cover of his solo albums.

Venturing from Hollywood and New York City to London and Paris, Jesse never forgot home. From the porch of his future apartment in Venice, he enjoyed firing his Ruger .22 into the ocean while shouting in his Okie drawl, "You can take the boy out of Oklahoma, but you can't take Oklahoma out of the boy!"[59]

On the way out of Oklahoma City, Joe Royer and Ed Davis saw their guitar player friend Joe Bob Nelson. "Hey, you wanna come with us to Los Angeles?" Ed asked. "What are you going to do out there?" Nelson replied, rejecting the invitation. "I need to go make my mark," Ed Davis declared.[60]

Five

TURNED ON IN TINSELTOWN

L os angeles was as far from Oklahoma as Route 66 could take Ed Davis. There the highway ends at the Santa Monica Pier, which extends 1,600 feet over the beach and first waves of the Pacific Ocean. Arriving in late 1966, Ed would not be an overnight sensation. He remembered that he only made $6 by the end of the year. Surviving on hospitality at his grandfather Bill Davis's place in diverse Silver Lake, Ed needed to find his people.[1]

He was hardly the only Native American person from Oklahoma when he got there. LA had become home to one of the largest Native populations in the United States. From 1952 to 1972, the Bureau of Indian Affairs moved roughly one hundred thousand Native American people, one-fifth of the total population, from rural Indian Country to a limited range of major cities in the Midwest and West. Native people who went on relocation typically trained as welders, hairdressers, and other gendered occupations, often competing against each other for few openings in professions that were suffering with the nation's gradual shift toward a service economy. Ed did not migrate through the program. Instead he set his course alongside over one hundred thousand Native people who moved to cities through their own means during the same period.

Native people newly arrived in Los Angeles often confronted racism in schooling, housing, job markets, and policing. Some struggled with the distance from their people and land. They depended on each other and built community, working together to improve social prospects for Indigenous people. They gradually recast Los Angeles as an Indigenous place, as it had once been. Some made a living playing Indian as canoe ride operators in Disneyland's Indian Village. Others managed to blend into the Los Angeles socioeconomic sector, gradually cultivating a new Native American professional class that included doctors, lawyers, professors, politicians, actors, and more. Some later became leaders in their tribal communities, like Cherokee chief Wilma Mankiller, who grew up in San Francisco. Ed Davis was more than a participant in this dynamic generation. He proved that Indigenous people could even become rock stars.

But although Ed would be reminded along the way that he was different as an American Indian person, he also sometimes must have felt different relative to other Native people. He didn't fit the era's caricatured profile of an urban Indian, dislocated in a bustling metropolis. His Kiowa family had moved to Oklahoma City in 1932, twenty years prior to the urban relocation program. He didn't come from the rez. He came from cities, where he had lettered in football in a middle-class high school, attended a major university, toured regionally with the Continentals and nationally with Conway Twitty. This all occurred before he moved to Los Angeles, where Okies had long journeyed to make their dreams come true. But Ed didn't have to go to California to discover himself. Metaphorically speaking, he already had. "California was a great place for me to get my things together," he said. "I got into a much more happening thing for me. I was just really happy."[2]

BEYOND HIS GRANDFATHER'S HOUSE, the closest thing to a relocation services agency Ed found in LA was Skyhill, at the foot of the Hollywood Hills. More than a makeshift studio, the funky grass-green two-story house, accented with pink and aqua carpets, sheltered a mutual aid society for a coterie of Okie musicians—a "hippie commune bona fide," Skyhill leader Leon Russell called it. Pianos filled the rooms at awkward angles. Music and smoke filled the air, day and night, weekends and holidays. If you got lost, you could follow a microphone cord like a trail map.[3]

Jesse's sponsor in this scene was his old pal from the Hawks, Levon Helm, who was looking for some peace and quiet after quitting Bob Dylan's 1965 electric tour. Levon could no longer endure intolerant fans who now booed at every concert, convinced their folk-music hero Bob Dylan had been abducted by a pop star sporting Wayfarers, a leather jacket, and an electric guitar. Before long, Ed Davis would play with another new version of Dylan.

Levon took Ed to meet Skyhill honcho Leon Russell, who was already a legend among Okie musicians. Ed was immediately impressed by the young studio veteran's striking pompadour; for his part, Ed was only just beginning to let his hair down. More importantly, Leon's résumé was long. Top Hollywood producers first began recruiting the teenage phenom for his idiosyncratic piano chops, which partly stemmed from paralysis in his right arm due to a spinal injury at birth. Leon's talent also reflected the teachings of a piano instructor he coincidentally shared with Ed's mother years earlier in Oklahoma. Before long, Leon was a first-call session cat, landing on records by everyone from Frank Sinatra to the Byrds. He became a feature member of the ace studio gang known as the Wrecking Crew, playing glorious piano on the longing Darlene Love classic "Christmas (Baby Please Come Home)," the signature Beach Boys tune "California Girls," and so many more famous songs he eventually lost track. Elton John later cited Leon Russell as his greatest influence.

At Skyhill, Leon was both transitioning to the producer's chair and launching a solo career that would be defined by his spellbinding "A Song for You," a modern standard. Leon's larger "nest of Okies" included J. J. Cale, Carl Radle, Jim Karstein, Jim Keltner, Roger Tillison, Gary "Colonel" Sanders, and Junior Markham, as well as Tennessean Bobby Whitlock and Texans Bobby Keys and Marc Benno. Many of these musicians went on to remarkable successes of their own, playing with Eric Clapton, George Harrison, Bob Dylan, the Rolling Stones, the Doors, and more.[4]

Though Ed was a new face, especially as an OKC musician mostly in the company of Tulsans, he quickly gravitated to Skyhill's center. Teenage guitarist Marc Benno was quietly mesmerized and intimidated by the whole scene, especially Ed. "I felt like I was surrounded by royalty," he says, "And in fact, I was." Steve Miller Band keyboardist Ben Sidran observed something similar:

> I went with Ed to Leon Russell's place once, and it was something like out of a fantasy. It reminded me of San Francisco in the late sixties where you had these scenes and the dynamics of what was going on weren't clear, the relationships between the men and the women weren't clear, and it was definitely communal, and Leon was some sort of guru. I think Ed . . . he didn't aspire to being a guru, but he was certainly familiar with the court. He could work his way through that.

Future Harrison and Clapton collaborator Bobby Whitlock likewise kept quiet after moving in from Memphis. He focused on learning everything he could from Ed Davis, who had a certain stature about him. "Everyone loved and respected him," Whitlock remembers.[5]

As many as twenty-five people might crash in the four-bedroom house at one time. Few paid rent, rendering the domestic situation congested and unpredictable. Most of the time, Ed could be found camped out on a couch in the living room. In addition to the regular squatters, random guests ranging from Gram Parsons to Pat Boone showed up any given day. Drummer Jim Karstein described it as "trains coming in and out of a station."[6]

Just keeping track of who was who could be a challenge unto itself. Most of the Skyhill gang began referring to Ed as "Indian Ed." Singer Bonnie Bramlett later recognized how it was inappropriate. She and others hope Ed knew it was affectionate, if misguided. It probably wasn't what Ed had in mind when he sought a serious music career that transcended tokenism. More than that, Leon insisted they couldn't keep calling him Ed Davis. Everyone became paranoid when they heard that name. The other Ed Davis was chief of the LAPD. He was famous for leading the Robert F. Kennedy assassination case and for taking down Charles Manson, and infamous for regularly raiding LGBTQ+ establishments and cracking down on pesky longhairs, once sending officers to a Pink Floyd concert, where they arrested 511 people for cannabis possession.[7]

Before long, Ed began playing rhythm, lead, and slide guitar with a rotating cast of Skyhill musicians led by Cherokee harmonica player Jimmy "Junior" Markham. When Levon Helm brokered an introduction, he warned Markham that Ed didn't talk much. This was true. Ed didn't speak the entire first day he spent jamming with Markham. Under various names—the Tulsa Rhythm Revue, the Jimmy Markham Quintet, the Jimmy Markham Sextet, and so on—whoever was available among roughly a dozen Okies and a few honorary Okies met up to play Jimmy Reed, Lightnin' Hopkins, Howlin' Wolf, and Hank Ballard covers. They worked clubs in Santa Monica, Silver Lake, North Hollywood, and beyond, from the happening Whisky a Go Go to the shabby Peacock Alley, typically for ten bucks a gig and free beer. Virtually everyone associated with Skyhill passed through the group at some point. At a club in North Watts, Ed experienced the type of racial tension he tried to escape in Oklahoma. During a set break, some of the Tulsa Revue guys got in a fight with Black patrons who didn't like white musicians invading their stage. Ed leapt into action defending his bandmates, like he did for Carl Rogel back in Oklahoma, but this time with the race dynamics inverted.[8]

While the gigs were up and down, Ed began earning new professional recording opportunities. He joined a configuration of Markham's group alongside J. J. Cale, Marc Benno, and Bill Boatman to cut 45 rpm singles—"Black Cherry," "Operator Operator," "Gonna Send You Back to Georgia"—for a deal Markham had with the independent Uptown label. These were Ed's first professional recordings since the single he produced with the New Breed back in Oklahoma. Unfortunately, the Markham singles sank.[9]

Other opportunities didn't fare much better. Leon recruited Ed for some early sessions he produced for the emerging Delaney & Bonnie Bramlett tandem, who would subsequently partner with Eric Clapton and George Harrison. Though the recordings only saw release on an obscure British label, Ed got to play alongside some of the great Wrecking Crew session pros who worked for Phil Spector, the Beach Boys, the Righteous Brothers, and more. Likewise, the Leon Russell and Marc Benno Asylum Choir albums Ed appeared on are interesting artifacts of their time, but they too went mostly unheard until Leon's subsequent star turn.

Back at Skyhill, Ed began impressing his cohort with his developing slide guitar technique. He picked up some new tricks after seeing Muddy Waters at the Whisky and learning the benefits of retuning his guitar to open G, D, or E. In autumn 1967, he sat in for a recording session Markham produced for a new group calling themselves the Flying Burrito Brothers. They were led by Ian Dunlop, who had just left the International Submarine Band, in which he played alongside Gram Parsons. They cut a version of the old Sleepy John Estes number "Divin' Duck Blues" with Ed employing a small slide on the tip of his left pinky, another approach he learned from Muddy Waters. This allowed him to seamlessly switch between slide and standard fretting in the same song. Ed's playing was brilliant, but the group fell apart, the tapes went missing, and Parsons, otherwise uninvolved with this earlier incarnation, adopted the name for an altogether different country rock group.[10]

It may be that Jesse was so disappointed in his early session opportunities that he imagined successes that didn't happen. Jesse claimed to play on Gary Lewis and the Playboys' top-ten hits "Everybody Loves a Clown" and "She's Just My Style," but neither is possible. They were recorded in 1965, before Jesse went to California, and Jesse's close friend Jim Keltner, who drummed in the Playboys, insists those claims are absolutely false. "He certainly didn't need to inflate his already amazing credits," a baffled Keltner suggests. If Jesse's memory was merely foggy, and he did play on some other Lewis tune, many of which were indeed produced by Leon Russell, then Lewis himself doesn't remember it either: "If he played on any of my songs, I never knew it."[11]

Most folks gathered at Skyhill eventually headed in new directions. This was due to shifting ambitions or just a desire for new scenery, to say nothing of more space. Many didn't go far, ending up right back in a communal domestic setting down the road in Sherman Oaks. They christened their new house the Plantation, not a nostalgic gesture to Old South culture but a nevertheless inadvisable reference to the struggling musicians' feelings that they were working like slaves in the music business. Leon's old drummer pal from Tulsa, Gary Sanders, rented the place after marrying a mother of two children who understandably didn't want to sleep on the floor at Skyhill.

Beyond the Plantation, as many as twenty more Okies spread throughout the neighborhood. Jesse first took a room upstairs at the Plantation, before relocating around the corner with bass player Gary Gilmore. Another bassist, Carl Radle, lived at the end of the block, and Okie affiliates Delaney and Bonnie Bramlett lived a few streets over, where their keyboardist Bobby Whitlock slept on their couch. At the Plantation, visitors included everyone from Gram Parsons to Eric Clapton. Their fluid music relationships reflected the way things had been back in Tulsa and Oklahoma City, and more recently, Skyhill. Everyone knew the same songs. There were no great rivalries and no one was possessive. People were free to play with whomever, whenever.[12]

That's not to suggest there were never disturbances at the Plantation. One night a drunk Junior Markham, looking like Elvis Presley, stormed through the house wielding a knife, waking everyone in search of his girlfriend. He finally found her in drummer Chuck Blackwell's bed. Gary Sanders tried to get the situation under control, pleading that "women are for loving, not fighting." When that failed, Sanders brandished a gun and began firing at Markham, hoping Markham would drop the knife. "Oh, Oklahoma's lonesome cowboys are turned on in Tinsel Town," Leon Russell sang about the affair.[13]

Modest successes, minor missteps, and occasional brushes with death characterized life and work at Skyhill and the Plantation. The daily shuffle was also literal. Ed and other musicians comprising the Oklahoma Mafia began developing a new sound, borrowing from an old one. For some, it was only later when they realized, or someone convinced them, that they had created the Tulsa sound. Others could never agree on what it meant, or if such a thing actually existed. "That was like a dust cloud that came up behind them after they began getting recognized," says Ian Dunlop, evoking a Dust Bowl metaphor. There certainly was something peculiar and appealing about all of these Okies playing together. It was audible and visible in their music, language, social and professional network, and historical significance.

That is to say, the Tulsa sound is real. It extends from the city itself, once known alternately as the "Oil Capital of the World" and the "Indian Capital of the World." It's where Cain's Ballroom house band Bob Wills and the Texas Playboys rocked and rolled a little more than the standard country swing groups of their time. The sound blends country, rock and roll, gospel, and jazz with a blues music core that's a little more friendly and melodic than the rival version south of the Red River. Reflecting the cultural diversity of its namesake, it would seem the Tulsa sound could only be made in Tulsa, except it wasn't. It was made in the Hollywood Hills. If the Bakersfield sound in country music grew from an earlier series of Okie migrations to California, the Tulsa sound signaled the arrival of a new generation, but now more counterculture than country.[14]

The sound is most pronounced in the unique feel Tulsa drummers Jim Keltner, Jim Karstein, Chuck Blackwell, and Gary Sanders achieved when playing a shuffle that didn't sound like it was in such a hurry. We can also hear it in Jesse Ed Davis's easily recognizable rhythm guitar playing. His groove doesn't just reflect his Oklahoma home; it also reflects Oklahoma as Indian Country. The shuffle comes from Native people and their traditional dances. It comes from the ground. What then would a Tulsa sound be absent a Native American contributor?[15]

Asked to define the Tulsa sound, Leon Russell demurred. "A lot of people have been through Tulsa. *Charlie Parker went through Tulsa.*" Several minutes later, apparently still thinking about it, Leon suddenly circled back to the Tulsa sound, calling it the "Oklahoma beat." He began tapping his cane on a wooden table inside Tulsa's legendary Cain's Ballroom, where the Tulsa sound and Oklahoma beat had been playing for decades. "DUM-dum-dum-dum / DUM-dum-dum-dum / DUM-dum-dum-dum." It's the old Hollywood American Indian drumbeat, heard in countless films when Indian adversaries are approaching. "If I had to say what is the Oklahoma beat, that would be it," Leon decides, hearing whatever is exceptional about Oklahoma music not just in a sound but in the rhythm of Indigenous people's drums.[16]

On another level, the Tulsa sound was more about community than music. It began with a colloquial language, reflected in slang, sayings, and other verbal shorthand wherein the Okie accent worked like glue. A network formed from the simple fact of everyone living together and dating within the same circle. This produced an almost telepathic effect when they played music together. They could finish not only each other's sentences but also each other's melodies, riffs, and fills. "I think somebody kind of misnomered that into a sound," Jim Karstein was convinced, "because as far as an actual musical sound, I've never been able to put my finger on it anyway."[17]

Those paying attention realized it wasn't a coincidence that these musicians were all from Oklahoma. But if the Tulsa sound is more recognized in hindsight, it's partly because it wouldn't have made sense to call it that in the late 1960s. Many within the larger coterie didn't go to California to market their Okie roots; they went there to escape them. At the time, Californians were still capable of great hostility toward migrant Okies, dating back to the Dust Bowl crisis and Great Depression that sent poor migrants searching for opportunity. Remembering how his Okie accent was a liability in his California high school, Jim Keltner stresses, "I wanted to remove it as much as I could and as quickly as I could."[18]

Before long, the Tulsa sound and Skyhill gang became hip and started appearing on hits. When dark vibes began to overtake the coastal counterculture, folks started searching for something authentically new or old, and something rebelliously rural. The mystic Van Morrison migrated from Belfast to Manhattan to Boston to Woodstock before finally securing refuge in Marin County, California. Bob Dylan headed for Woodstock and immersed himself in rustic fatherhood. Across the Atlantic, Fairport Convention, the Incredible String Band, Vashti Bunyan, and others retreated to communal living in the countryside. Ronnie Lane formed an old-timey traveling circus based in the Welsh countryside at a farm called Fishpool. The former Hawks, now

called the Band, including Skyhill recruiter Levon Helm and Ed Davis's
early guitar hero Robbie Robertson, had become so enviable in their
bucolic county fair splendor that both Eric Clapton and George Harrison
asked to join their group but couldn't get in.

The red dirt Okies congregating at Skyhill and the Plantation offered
an accessible and perhaps more authentic alternative. Dylan, Clapton,
and Harrison all thought so. "That influence and that music is still
alive," stresses Bobby Whitlock, who emerged from Skyhill by way of
Memphis, before landing on Harrison's *All Things Must Pass* and Clapton's *Derek and the Dominoes*. "It's forever a sensation, the Tulsa sound."[19]

ONE NIGHT IN 1967, promising blues singer Taj Mahal cut through a
contradictory blend of bikers and suburbanites sipping beer and wine at
the Topanga Corral tucked in the Santa Monica Mountains. Taj had a
record contract with Columbia and he needed a band. He got a tip on a
young guitar player who was turning heads, but it came with a warning:
"Now, he's an Indian." "Yeah, *and the problem is?*" Taj pressed. Snaking
his way toward the stage, a guitar sound washed over him like a ray of
light. "Oh, hell yeah!" Taj said to himself. Before the song finished, he
was certain this was his guy. Ed Davis thought so too, describing the
beginning of their music partnership as "love at first sight."[20]

Ed Davis and Taj Mahal quickly became more than bandmates.
Ed called Taj "Captain," and Taj referred to Ed as the "Indian Agent."
Beyond his principal position on guitar, Ed also played organ and piano,
arranged horns, handwrote album liner notes, and functioned as music
director. Taj appreciated how Ed didn't merely copy Freddie King and
B.B. King like most guitar players coming up. Taj instead recognized
the breadth of Ed's talent and penchant for always playing something
interesting. Above all, Ed Davis had a deep knowledge of the blues that
rivaled the collection constantly playing in Taj's photographic memory.
Taj wanted to put a new spin on old music, and Ed was perfect for
the project.[21]

It took a while for Taj and Ed's group to take shape. When Gary
Gilmore drove Ed to the airport for a gig in San Francisco, Taj was

sitting on the curb, crestfallen. The bass player quit, he announced. Ed didn't hesitate: "Gary plays bass!" During the flight, the reconfigured group studied the setlist. While Gilmore held his own at the gig, Ed was unhappy with Sandy Konikoff's drumming, and dismissed him when they got back to LA, though the two remained friends and worked together again. Jim Karstein, Bill Boatman, and Gary Sanders all filled in before Taj and Ed found their ideal drummer.[22]

Oklahoman Chuck "Brother" Blackwell had toured with the Everly Brothers and Jerry Lee Lewis and had played in the house band Shindogs for the short-lived music variety TV show *Shindig!* He was also familiar as a lady killer who crashed at the Plantation. With Blackwell, the classic lineup was set: three Okies backing Taj. Blackwell considered this arrangement "the sweetest brotherhood" he experienced in his life. The three albums the solidified Taj Mahal lineup made together—*Taj Mahal, The Natch'l Blues*, and *Giant Step*—earned a durable reputation as some of the greatest and most influential works in the blues rock genre.[23]

Making the first Taj Mahal record, Ed was cool and confident. "We played neck and neck on that," Taj recalls. When developing song ideas, Ed typically sat in a chair holding his Telecaster and staring into the distance, under some kind of spell, as though his power came from somewhere beyond him. Long minutes might pass before he suddenly returned to his body with instructions for the drums, bass, horns, and keys. The group marveled at Ed's talent, including effortless transitions between rhythm and lead play and call-and-response vocal and guitar interplay. The dynamic between Ed and Taj was more of an unspoken bond, but Taj still learned something valuable from Ed, who approached each song as a blank canvas. Ed could arrange an entire song in his head. "He was *incredible*," Taj stresses.[24]

The band worked quickly in the studio. Rarely attempting more than three takes, they aimed for a fresh and direct sound that could be reproduced live. Though most songs began with Taj's harmonica riffs, each member contributed something essential, especially given the audio space in their no-nonsense approach to album production. Ed's versatility is apparent across all three records, from his infectious rhythm pattern for

"She Caught the Katy," weeping horn arrangement for "You Don't Miss Your Water," funky organ on "Give Your Woman What She Wants," and rollicking piano on the trucker anthem "Six Days on the Road." An additional distinctive quality emerged from the group's avoidance of standard keys that permeated popular music in the late 1960s. Where a typical group might play in the key of A, the Taj Mahal band played in B flat, like the blues bands of old.

From the group's second album *The Natch'l Blues*, "The Cuckoo" towers as one of the best hard blues cuts from the genre's emergent era. The song is in fact a centuries-old British folk tune the group refashioned into a hard blues number. The song soars between Ed Davis's twin guitar parts that sing back and forth to each other from the left to right speakers before he steers the band into a wicked unison refrain where the bottom drops, forming a deep valley. It's as heavy a groove as anything Led Zeppelin was laying down when they shared concert bills with Taj Mahal at the time. "The first album that got my attention and just destroyed me was *The Natch'l Blues*," says the Cars guitarist Elliot Easton. "And then *Giant Step*. Those two were like bibles to me."[25]

The group's collaborative talent can best be heard on *Giant Step*'s aching "Farther on Down the Road." Credited to all four members, the song came together when Taj arrived a couple hours late to the studio one night and heard a tune building from Ed's guitar. "What is that?" Taj asked, stopped in his tracks. "Oh, it's just something we've been working up," Ed replied. "Really? I'll be right back." Twenty minutes later Taj returned with lyrics born from the sensation Ed's guitar elicited. The song was a departure for the band and they loved it. Ed Davis was so proud of it he would later record it again for his second solo album, *Ululu*, and he kept it in his live set for the rest of his life.[26]

By all accounts, Taj Mahal and the Great Plains Boogie Band, as they christened themselves, was a sensational live group. Like the Grateful Dead, the Allman Brothers, and Little Feat, they were best experienced communally. Whereas much of the prevailing counterculture music of the late 1960s inspired focused, mouth-agape attention from concert-goers' seats, Taj and company's music inspired dancing and sweating. Above all, this was soul music. "You couldn't play behind Taj without giving 110 percent," Gilmore suggests. Their fans responded with equal fervor.[27]

The Natch'l Blues and *Giant Step* cracked the Billboard top 200. Each record eventually outperformed the previous one in sales and airplay, but the climb was gradual. The band worked hard to build an audience through touring, which resulted in local FM stations learning about them. They played over 150 dates in 1969 alone. You can practically hear Taj's mind race over a mental map when he concludes the only places they didn't play were North Dakota, South Dakota, and Las Vegas. Working clubs, colleges, theaters, parks, amphitheaters, and beyond, both as headliners and support, the group shared imaginative and diverse bills with Led Zeppelin, Jefferson Airplane, the Grateful Dead, Janis Joplin, Jimi Hendrix, Country Joe and the Fish, Mother Earth, Genesis, Otis Redding, the Doors, Big Mama Thornton, the Velvet Underground, the Byrds, Cream, and more.

Locally, the group played all over town, but most often could be heard at the Palomino, Topanga Corral, and Ash Grove. In the late '60s, the Palomino was still a country music club that once proudly featured Merle Haggard and Johnny Cash. At first, rednecks routinely threatened the shaggy musicians who invaded their venue, until groups like the Flying Burrito Brothers helped broker a peace. The Topanga Corral, where Taj and Ed first met, was a funky scene featuring an eclectic blend of artists. Out on the dance floor, patrons could gaze up at a giant painting of a naked couple entitled *Pisces Dancing*. Immortalized as the inspiration for the Doors' popular tune "Roadhouse Blues," the club eventually burned down, twice. The Ash Grove was a hipper affair, where audiences occupied imported church pews and freely smoked reefer in the back. Owner Ed Pearl founded the club in 1958 to promote a blacklisted Pete Seeger after a canceled gig at UCLA. From there, Muddy Waters and Lightnin' Hopkins brought further renown to the club as it grew into an anti–Vietnam War protest center.[28]

Beyond LA County, Taj Mahal crisscrossed the country in a Dodge van purchased from the International Submarine Band. In between tours, the band would crash in any number of a network of friendly homes throughout Topanga Canyon. People would compete with each other for the right to host the band. "It was an honor to have the great Jesse Ed Davis stay with you," insists Sweet Mama Janisse, the namesake of one of Taj Mahal's best tunes. If their records sold modestly, the band basked in gushing praise from famous musicians who regularly ventured backstage to share their love for the group.[29]

Traveling with the band, earning the respect of his peers, Ed Davis's life was in motion. There is perhaps no better place for a young musician to contemplate rapid changes and boundless horizons than a seat next to friends in a touring van, traversing shifting landscapes, where hours pass through your reflection in the window, simultaneously creating kaleidoscopic vistas and memories.

The band certainly landed in some colorful places. At the Space-Out in LA's Barnsdall Park, dancers cavorted in a thirty-foot-high, one-hundred-foot-long air balloon, or "people tunnel," that vibrated to the music, before rolling down a grassy hill. Each attendee was guaranteed a free bag of pure air, supposedly unadulterated by the city's oppressive smog. The Taj Mahal band took the stage sometime between a coordinated pigeon release and a People Arranging Contest.[30]

In August 1969, Taj Mahal and the Grateful Dead co-headlined the Bullfrog 2 Festival, a sort of mini-Woodstock in the woodsy Oregon countryside. Like the more famous festival held in upstate New York a couple weeks earlier, the Bullfrog organizers were forced in the eleventh hour to find new staging grounds for the concert. Local backlash prevailed when the county district attorney led a successful contest against the festival agreement, convinced the community would suffer "narcotics, intercourse in the open, and parking on private property," among other infractions. The event officially became Bullfrog 3 when local farmer Melvina Pelletier rescued it by offering her grand pasture for the festival. Why? She liked the music. "My old lady's bones have limbered up a little bit—in my mind that is." As for concerns about rampant debauchery, Pelletier couldn't foresee it. Besides, she said, "I wouldn't recognize a cigarette with marijuana in it if I tripped over it."[31]

In another unpredictable situation, in spring 1969, the Taj Mahal band had to cancel a date in Fort Lauderdale. Doors singer Jim Morrison had been arrested in Miami on accusations of public drunkenness and indecency, or, as Ed described it at the time, "When Jim Morrison jacked off onstage he freaked the whole state of Florida out!!" Word from ahead was that the cops were going to arrest and beat every hippie they could get their hands on over Easter holiday. "Oh, Jesus Christ. I thought it was just us!" Doors guitarist Robby Krieger laughs at this.[32]

Among the whirl of live dates, a few concerts stand out. At the 1968 Newport Folk Festival, Taj Mahal played alongside many of their heroes, including B.B. King and Mississippi Fred McDowell. Opening for Led Zeppelin at the Fillmore West in 1969, the band received a standing ovation, uncommon for an opening act. There was also Cincinnati's Black Dome, or the "Fillmore Midwest," where Taj Mahal broke attendance records. The venue held nine hundred people when completely packed. Over a two-night headlining stand in May 1969, over two thousand concertgoers packed in even tighter. Local news sang praise of the group that "includes a full-blooded Indian on guitar and two former Oklahoma cowboys on bass and drums." It was then that the group really grasped the effect they had on live audiences. Fifty years later, Taj can still feel the heat of the oversold venue: "The people were enjoying the hell out of that music. I was like, 'Wow, they get it!'"[33]

Onstage, Taj Mahal and the Great Plains Boogie Band was visually striking in Western wear that looked ridiculous on other artists. "Who's this brother with the cowboy hat and boots on, and then Jesse, Indian Ed?" bassist Bill Rich wondered before later replacing Gilmore in the band. But the clothing wasn't a gimmick. It was a reflection of the band's purpose. Taj dressed as a cowboy to honor Black cowboys' overlooked importance in histories of the US West. And with Indian Ed on guitar, they had rare but requisite Native representation. "Black, Red, and White from the U.S. soil. Plugged in that deep?" Taj muses. The band appeared revolutionary during turbulent times. In fact, their appearance might be what held them back. Loyal fans embraced the group's diverse profile. But others recoiled at an interracial cross-section of American people performing together. It wasn't just that Columbia Records didn't know how to market them; the country wasn't ready for, in Taj's words, "two white guys, a Comanche Indian, and a Black cat."

Though some of their music had roots in the fifteenth century, they were too forward thinking.[34]

Fighting upstream, the band recognized where they could fit, or not fit, within the era's fraught race relations amid a growing militancy among people who had become frustrated by the glacial pace of change. Ed and Taj had both attended college at a time when violent race conflicts devastated communities across the country. The two bandmates represented different peoples who mutually lacked access to power within postwar globalizing of industrial capitalism. Black and Indigenous people still, perhaps more than ever, depended on the arts as a platform for broadcasting their place and potential in the world. Both Taj and Ed had experienced racial conflicts firsthand. They no longer wanted any part of it. Through music, they could deliver a different message and bring opposing forces together. Opening for Jefferson Airplane in Salt Lake City, Taj shouted into his microphone: "I DON'T NEED BLACK POWER OR WHITE POWER, 'CUZ BABY I'VE GOT BLUES POWER!"[35]

For all their deserved recognition and cultural importance, Sly and the Family Stone, one of Ed Davis's favorite groups, was not the only interracial rock band active in the 1960s. Where Sly and his crew appeared fabulous and free, the Taj Mahal group was serious and tough. Ed's beaming smile belied the fact that you didn't want to mess with these guys. Indeed, it was Ed who acted as group guardian. One way he "played Indian" was by embracing old Hollywood stereotypes as a defense strategy. Whenever anyone cracked jokes about the group's long hair or masculinity, Ed's smile turned into a scowl, "like Geronimo," Gilmore remembers. "Jesse didn't take no crap off anyone," Blackwell echoed. After finishing their first set during a gig in Boston, the band was walking across the room when a local biker stepped on Ed's foot. "Hey man, aren't you going to apologize?" he protested. Suddenly they were exchanging punches and wrestling on the floor. Ed emerged victorious, albeit with a fat lip and swollen eye. When the second set began, the biker was gone and Ed Davis played the best guitar his bandmates had ever heard.[36]

Despite his outward confidence, Ed displayed a mixture of pride and trepidation about being Indian Ed. He wanted to be Indigenous without becoming a novelty act. "He didn't want to be a mascot," suggested fellow Indigenous musician Robbie Robertson. Ed was careful about wearing his Indigeneity on his sleeve, but he couldn't help but wear it on his face. In pictures, his hair gets longer by the year, and he gradually accumulates more jewelry and beads. Ed discussed his relative comfort or discomfort with Taj, explaining how being visibly Native stirred mixed emotions, especially in light of his parents' experiences in forced assimilation programs. It still felt dangerous to be Indian in white society, Ed told Taj. But while Taj was a brother of color, he couldn't completely relate to Ed's perspective. "Black people didn't have to go through that indoctrination," Taj realized. "Pull down your bow and arrow and come over here and put on these jeans, and a crew cut." But knowing that the blues have always belonged to Indigenous people, Taj helped convince Ed that, maybe more than anyone else, he belonged out there playing their music.[37]

Jesse's Indigenous identity certainly mattered when the band played in Indian Country. In the late 1960s, hippies descended on Taos, New Mexico, with painted Volkswagen buses, yoga studios, and health food stores. There was real tension between the hippies and the local Pueblo people, who resented uninvited guests, except on this occasion. When the band returned from dinner before a gig in Taos, the promoter looked like a ghost. At first worried no one bought tickets, the band instead found the venue packed with young Pueblo kids who filled the first five rows. The elders had met and decided to support a venture into town together for the concert. It was rare to see a Native brother on a major music stage. Indeed, it was an event.[38]

Ed's caution about emphasizing his Native identity made sense in a counterculture environment that fetishized Indigenous cultural motifs that were typically inaccurate and relatively removed from Indigenous peoples' contemporary worlds. In Oklahoma, Ed had felt "always a little weird anyway, being an Indian." Now, in California, he was surrounded by middle-class suburban kids erecting tipis in their backyards and giving each other Indian names. Within Ed's music peer group, Neil Young donned a fringed buckskin shirt and Tim Buckley rambled in knee-high moccasins. "We're all buying Indian clothes / wearing Indian shoes," went Leon Russell and Marc Benno's song "Indian Style," which featured Ed on guitar. In that context, the most radically or authentically Indian thing Indian Ed could do was *not* dress in buckskin.

In head shops and record stores, Sitting Bull often stared back at hippies from posters advertising underground events, as if the Lakota holy man himself endorsed rock concerts from his place in the Great Mystery. Ed must have seen these images, and perhaps he related to Sitting Bull better than anyone around him. During the 1880s, Sitting Bull, the most famous Native American in the world, recycled, autographed, and sold his own image as a side gig while touring with a group of Native American performers supporting Buffalo Bill. This was a matter of controlling the dissemination of one's own Indigenous likeness and any profit it garnered. And that would have made sense to Ed Davis.[39]

On the road, with the right people, Ed occasionally shared Indigenous culture. Soulful singer Tracy Nelson, whose group Mother Earth went on a package tour with Taj Mahal, experienced this once in Boston. Despite growing up in Wisconsin, where there are eleven federally recognized Native nations, Nelson had never met a Native American person. "He was just gorgeous, and I'm sure that every woman that ever came across him would say the same thing," she chuckles. Ed at first seemed brooding and remote, but a few dates into the tour he loosened up. Ed took Nelson to the roof of the Lenox Hotel to witness a solar eclipse, which, he explained, represents the time when the great frog swallowed the sun. Now they must scare away the frog in order to rescue the sun by yelling loudly and banging anything that made noise. Nelson convinced him to skip that part, as they had snuck onto the roof without permission. She didn't know this was actually a Cherokee cultural tradition, and Ed wasn't Cherokee. That was beside the point. "It was so romantic and emotional," she recalls. "I think he knew that that aspect of his personality was really attractive to women. . . . He charmed the pants off me. I don't mean that literally."[40]

While many women were drawn to Ed Davis's dark and handsome features, he wasn't in the market for a girlfriend. In 1967, just as work with Taj was ramping up, a "golden sun goddess" shined a beam of light through Ed's heart. Patti Daley was a California girl. Everyone adored her. Everyone still asks about her. Friends liken her to a mythical fairy, or a glamorous 1940s Hollywood star. The latter characterization was animated in Patti's hobby of collecting old clothing from the nearby studios. She could pull off the slinky dresses she found at auctions. With Patti, not only had Ed moved to Tinseltown; he even scored his own starlet.[41]

For Ed, falling in love with Patti didn't just create partnership. It also required him to become a parent. In September 1966, prior to meeting Ed, Patti and her then-husband Robert Noriega had a son, named Billy. The following year, Patti saw Ed playing at the Ash Grove with Taj Mahal. Her experience was similar to Taj first seeing Ed onstage. She was spellbound. "I was totally taken, heart and soul," she described the encounter. This wasn't a problem for Patti and Robert. They knew their marriage wasn't working. Patti rarely saw Robert, who was attempting his own career in music. There were no hard feelings when Patti took Billy to begin a life with Ed. In fact, Robert was a big Taj Mahal fan, too, and continued attending the group's gigs. "I always knew the score from the time I could remember," Bill reflects. "I had two dads." Ed embraced Billy as his own son, referring to him as such, and he asked Patti to tell people he was the father. Patti obliged, wanting them to function like a real family. "[Billy] was the blond little boy," singer Bonnie Bramlett recalls, "and he would sit on Ed's shoulder like a little parrot, and Ed absolutely adored that kid."[42]

The new family stayed connected while Ed was on tour. Sometimes Patti would take leave from her job at a hospital and meet the band on the road. In between physical reunions, Ed and Patti practiced an epistolary romance. "Oh baby I need you so much!! I love you so much! I can't wait until May to be in your loving arms again, where I belong forever," Patti wrote in one letter. "Hurry home to me & Billy," she pleaded in another. "I dream of you night and day." Ed was happy when he began earning enough money to send home to his sweetheart. "Here's your weekly allotment from your Aborigine," he wrote Patti from Philadelphia.[43]

Having found his place with Taj Mahal, playing some of the best music of his life, recording for Columbia Records, sponsored by Fender guitars, becoming a guitar hero, making a living, traveling the country as a twenty-something in the exhilarating 1960s, and making a family with Patti and Billy, Ed must have wondered if his life could get any better. Then he met the Beatles and the Stones.

NO GIG LOOMS LARGER in Taj Mahal lore than one staged in London just before Christmas 1968. Back in Los Angeles that November, Taj Mahal opened for original "Hound Dog" singer Big Mama Thornton at the famed Whisky a Go Go on Sunset Strip. During their set, Taj looked down at a crowd gathered in front of the stage. To his surprise, he saw Mick Jagger, Keith Richards, and Brian Jones dancing with a troupe of women.

The popular British musicians loved old blues music. England was in the midst of an American blues revival so fervent that Howlin' Wolf, Albert King, Buddy Guy, Muddy Waters, and other blues statesmen were appearing across the pond on the morning news. After their set, the Taj Mahal band received raves when introducing itself at the booth where the Stones held court. Thinking nothing would come of it, Taj encouraged Mick and Keith to reach out if they ever saw an opportunity to enlist their services. Shortly thereafter, Taj and company received eight plane tickets and an invitation to join *The Rolling Stones Rock and Roll Circus* concert and film event, soon beginning production across the Atlantic. "They made us really feel royal and special," Taj revels. "And there was nothing that they had that they didn't share with us. They really went out and put on the dog, all the way around."[44]

Because the Taj Mahal band did not have time to prepare work visas, their involvement in the Circus had to be discreet. They claimed to be tourists, despite boarding their flight with two guitars, a snare drum, and cymbals. The Stones sent a limo to collect them at the airport and bring them to the Londonderry Hotel, where they found gear set up for a jam and an anxious audience in the Stones, the Who, and John Lennon. After Taj Mahal played a couple tunes, Keith Richards tapped Gary Gilmore on the shoulder and pointed to Ed: "Mind if I take your bass? I need to play with that cat." Various configurations of musicians proceeded to play for hours. Later that night, Jagger invited the band over for a gathering at his estate. Chuck Blackwell toted a suitcase packed with obscure rhythm and blues 45 rpms in anticipation of DJing a wild party. Instead, Jagger served tea and launched into a lengthy lecture on the history of Stonehenge. The next day the Taj group went to a sound-stage to shoot their part in the film, everyone still jet-lagged and suffering December colds. It was the first time any of them had been overseas. "It was such a whirlwind," Gilmore says.[45]

Unlike Jagger's tea party, the *Rock and Roll Circus* was indeed wild, replete with fire eaters and flying trapeze artists. The Who played their lengthy new "A Quick One," previewing where they'd go next with *Tommy* (1969). The emerging Jethro Tull made an appearance, as did an ad-hoc supergroup called Dirty Mac, comprised of John Lennon, Keith Richards, Eric Clapton, and Mitch Mitchell, performing a ripping version of the Beatles' "Yer Blues," with Yoko Ono stirring underneath a black shroud in front of Keith's amplifier. The Stones closed the festival with tunes from their new *Beggars Banquet* (1968) and a preview of "You Can't Always Get What You Want." Rapidly withdrawing into a void of drug despondency, Stones guitarist Brian Jones delivered one of his last shining moments playing slide guitar on "No Expectations."

For their part, the contrastingly unadorned and unassuming Taj Mahal band tore through stellar performances of "Corrina," "Leaving Trunk," "Checkin' Up on My Baby," and an especially powerful "Ain't That a Lot of Love." Perhaps captured at their peak, Taj Mahal and the Great Plains Boogie Band stole the show. Taj considers the event a pinnacle in his career. Writing home to Patti, Ed was elated: "What a gas!!! Honey you should just be with me. You're so beautiful you would knock everyone completely out of sight. I miss you and Billy so much."[46]

Backstage at the Circus, Ed grabbed his guitar and occupied a chair. He was less interested in mingling than making more music. He also noticed how he and John Lennon had been awkwardly eyeing each other throughout the day. Ed chuckled at the way people were "fawning" over Lennon everywhere he went. In truth, Ed was excited to meet Lennon too, but Ed's approach was to not approach at all. "We didn't speak for hours that first day," Ed said. Finally, when he began picking "Mystery Train," popularized by his hero Elvis Presley, the door burst open. John Lennon charged in and grabbed a guitar. After the pair played a few tunes together, still without speaking, Lennon flinched first. Introducing himself, he mentioned how, when the spotlight hit Ed's face just right, he looked "very Indian and beautiful." Then they jumped back into Elvis and Carl Perkins numbers for what seemed like hours. "We were communing on a higher plane," Ed said about their meeting. "We were like the perfect foils for each other. It was true love."[47]

Ed Davis and John Lennon instantly formed a strong bond rooted in the rock and roll tunes stored in their fingertips. Ed admired Lennon's intelligence, calling him "one of the brightest people I've ever known. Incredibly talented, and a relentless person." Ed also considered Lennon an underappreciated guitarist, championing Lennon's inventiveness and melodic sense. The final day, December 12, while filming continued, Ed danced and sat in the audience with his new pals John Lennon and Yoko Ono, wearing what Ed described as Ku Klux Klan outfits. They are better described as silly looking yellow capes and pointed hats—like something someone saw in an acid trip.[48]

The *Rock and Roll Circus* proved triumphant for the Taj Mahal band and for Ed Davis in particular. He didn't just meet John Lennon; he also met future collaborators George Harrison, Ringo Starr, and Eric Clapton. Ed was on top of the world. "I'm going to pat myself on the back some more: (Heh Heh!!)," he wrote Patti, reporting that the Stones were so impressed they "couldn't say enough." "Patt, this whole experience has been so fantastically rewarding and personally satisfying. . . . I really miss you hon'. I think of you and Billy all day long. I can't wait to get back to you. . . . Your Ed."[49]

The event should have launched Taj Mahal to wider acclaim. But the Stones supposedly hated their own set, with some claiming the Who's and Taj Mahal's performances overshadowed the stars of the show. That didn't surprise Ed. He remembered how Stones guitarist Brian Jones struggled, requiring the band to film several takes. The headlining band put so much effort into the visual part, down to Jagger's bare painted chest, but neglected the music, which Ed considered "real abysmal."[50]

Apart from a few special screenings, the Stones stuck the film in their vault. Finally releasing it commercially in 1996, the Stones flew Taj, Gary Gilmore, and Chuck Blackwell out to New York City for a big premiere and gave them the red carpet treatment. Ed Davis, a star at the original event, both onstage and backstage, should have been there too.[51]

BACK IN THE STATES, Taj Mahal and the Great Plains Boogie Band continued recording and touring, while beginning to worry they were on a plateau. The Stones' disappointing decision to shelve the *Rock and Roll Circus* slowed the band's momentum. They now seemed stuck in the role of opening act. In summer 1968, Creedence Clearwater Revival opened for Taj Mahal. Six months later, roles reversed. The band was also bewildered by Columbia's failure to help push their catchy single "Corrina" into the top forty, given FM radio's support. The lack of focused support the band experienced with Columbia was typical for smaller bands on big labels.

A little effort would have made a difference, especially after the group made a video for the song that aired nationally on *Something Else*. The short-lived television variety program featured different groups lip-syncing to their hits in various settings. The Taj Mahal band filmed their scene in New Orleans, on the Mississippi in bright daylight, occupying various vessels withering in a ship graveyard. The band, and Ed's hair, sway in the breeze in perfect rhythm with the trees. Just up the river, forty years earlier, Charlie McCoy and Bo Carter popularized the old folk song "Corrina" with their early recorded version. Taj and Ed composed their own arrangement of the song, whose origins are so murky we might as well credit the river as the writer. Picking guitars there on the bayou, the mouth of so much music that filled Ed's home growing up, singing across the water that carried that music deeper into the country, Taj and Ed played the blues where Black and Indigenous people long ago invented the genre.[52]

In December 1969, between several dates with Crosby, Stills, Nash & Young, Taj and company dropped by Pacific Recording in San Mateo to record a version of Bob Dylan's "I Pity the Poor Immigrant" and the traditional number "Jacob's Ladder." The recordings captured Ed Davis near the height of his talent. Beyond his reliably brilliant guitar parts, we hear his deft piano playing, and by extension, his mother's. But then the band fell apart. Blackwell left first, opting for a gig with Leon Russell. Soon after, Gilmore left too, convinced it was time for a change. Blackwell went on to great success with Leon, and later returned to Oklahoma, where he became a stained-glass maker. Gilmore moved back to Tulsa, bought a livestock ranch, and occasionally played with guitarist J. J. Cale. There were no hard feelings. In fact, Gilmore soon promoted a packed show for a new Taj Mahal lineup at the Party Barn on the outskirts of Tulsa—a gig Taj still remembers for the large audience of Native American fans who packed the venue.[53]

In early 1970, Ed too began wondering about moving on. He might have perceived it an omen when someone broke into the Taj Mahal van in New York City and stole the hand-painted Telecaster he played at the *Rock and Roll Circus*. At the same time, Ed had the persistent adulation of the British rock stars associated with the *Rock and Roll Circus* on his mind, especially after the Stones had reached out the previous year to gauge his interest in replacing Brian Jones. "Rumblings across the water, the Stones want my services," he wrote Patti from New York City in April 1969. "Lennon & McCartney and company also would like to make use of my many and varied talents. Glyn Johns and several top English producers and pop people are just waiting for me to split with Taj. It looks like I'll be set if I ever do." But Ed felt loyal to Taj. "I can't see it right now," he told Patti. "I can only see you when I close my eyes."[54]

Ed and Taj carried on. In February 1970, the duo went to Miami and cut four songs with the legendary Dixie Flyers, who backed Aretha Franklin. Two classic songs emerged from the session: "Sweet Mama Janisse" and "Tomorrow May Not Be Your Day." Back in California, Ed and Taj brought Jim Karstein back on drums and recruited a new bass player in Bill Rich. They first saw Rich playing with Buddy Miles at the Whisky on a night when Jimi Hendrix appeared, to rapturous excitement, as a special guest. The show made such an impression on

Ed that he later wrote an essay about it. "How do I get somebody like you to play with me?" Taj asked Rich after the smashing set. "Maybe you just ask him," Rich replied.[55]

In early spring 1970, the group ducked into the studio in San Mateo again to record "Oh Susanna" and "Chevrolet," which appeared the following year on *Happy Just to Be Like I Am* (1971). Jesse helped Bill Rich learn the material. "He was very professional, liked to have the music down, everybody knowing their parts," Rich recalls. In March, the band headed east for a series of shows in New York and Ottawa. They rented a house in the picturesque New York hamlet Phoenicia, using it as a home base while shuttling to gigs around the northeast in a car pulling a U-Haul. Ed brought his new family along, refusing to go back on the road without them. "They were a happy family," Bill Rich noticed. The group also picked up a keyboard player in John Simon, who had recently produced landmark albums for Janis Joplin, Leonard Cohen, and the Band. From there, the group journeyed across the Atlantic for a second time, embarking on a tour of England and mainland Europe for the remainder of spring 1970.[56]

The Taj Mahal band arrived in London on April 14, playing dates with Johnny Winter, Traffic, and a mesmerizing show at the Royal Albert Hall with Santana. Then they were off to Sweden, Denmark, and the groovy German Internationales Essener Pop and Blues Festival for a crowd of ten thousand European hippies, and finally, dates in Paris and Amsterdam before returning to England for several more engagements. "It was amazing," Bill Rich remembers of his first trip to Europe. "Here I am, 21, just fresh out of Omaha, Nebraska. . . . For a midwestern boy, that stuff was blowing my mind."[57]

Musically, the band was outstanding at these gigs. Financially, the tour was a failure. Under a bad contract, the dates lacked adequate promotion and suffered low attendance. At various stops, angry promoters threatened the band, and in Bournemouth, England, one disgruntled promoter hired some goons to blow up the Taj Mahal tour bus with explosives. The band's road manager caught them in the act, averting disaster and possible death.

Years of traveling were catching up with the band. They needed a break. But in a greater sense, the music industry was turning dark. The drugs were changing. People were getting hurt and sometimes dying. When the tour concluded in London, Taj, worried this could be his fate, accepted an invitation to meet a friend in Ibiza. Disregarding a two-week break in the work schedule, he stayed for several months. "I spent last summer on an island, in the Mediterranean Sea," he sang about his time there. "The sunshine was so bright, yes you know it burned me down to my soul."[58]

Ed was finally ready for a change. When the tour wrapped, he told Taj he was going to explore a solo career. "I knew I was lucky to be working with him," Taj understood, "and that he was able to play with these other guys. . . . He figured he was out there, people knew his name, he might as well go put something out himself." Had they stayed together, Taj hoped to record the next album in Nashville, where they might achieve a cleaner sound. They also dreamed of collaborating with musicians in Africa. The results would have been brilliant.[59]

As with Blackwell and Gilmore, there were no hard feelings. Ed professed his desire to grow musically, and this depended on his ability to play with new musicians. The repetition wasn't fun for him anymore, and he felt he had been drifting away since the beginning of the year. But that didn't make the break any easier. Looking back three years later, he confessed, "I wasn't ready."[60]

ED DAVIS SECURED a lasting legacy with Taj Mahal. He became a guitar hero, in league with Robbie Robertson, Robby Krieger, Ry Cooder, and Mike Bloomfield, but with a sound unmistakably his own and instantly recognizable. Moreover, with Taj Mahal, Ed codirected an influential group that achieved something greater than the music they produced. They managed not just artistic excellence, but also historical significance. During this chapter, Ed became not just a guitar hero but a visibly Native American one.

Ed's music peers loved the clarity, purity, and soul in his playing. Rarely did he flavor his sound with guitar effects, preferring the clean tone of an otherwise temperamental Fender Telecaster plugged into a

Fender Bassman amplifier. For now, his only foray into the emerging guitar effects trend was the use of a rotating Leslie speaker, primarily employed to produce vibrato for organs, an idea he borrowed from keyboardist Booker T. Jones. "My thing's pretty smooth in reference to most of your younger guitar players today," Ed distinguished himself. "They like to scream and do the wah-wah thing."[61]

Ed insisted on playing for the song, rather than over or against it. His goal was to complement the song, rather than steal it. He rarely recorded overdubs and played few takes. "I went to see Taj Mahal and the original quartet, and I must tell you, that band was floating on clouds," says drummer Gary Mallaber, who played on several Van Morrison classics. "My jaw was dropped, because of the type of moves that they were playing and how smooth it was. The first guy I noticed was [Ed]. His rhythm playing and what he was doing was just magic." Guitarist Marc Benno, who played with the Doors, shares a similar description. "It was like butter. . . . It was just jaw-dropping to me." Ed made such an impression on Benno that the latter thought, "This is what I want to do. I want to play the kind music that Ed Davis is playing." It was the blues.[62]

If Ed's sound made him a favorite among guitar enthusiasts, then his slide guitar playing made him significant in the history of rock music. "I had heard some old Black guys playing it, but I had never heard it the way Ed Davis played. . . . That's where Duane got his shit from," notes keyboardist Bobby Whitlock, referring to Allman Brothers guitarist Duane Allman. "It was Ed Davis. That's the true deal." Whitlock personally experienced Ed's influence on Duane, working with the latter on Eric Clapton's "Layla," which features Duane Allman's gorgeous slide guitar in the song's coda.[63]

Gregg and Duane Allman were working out in Los Angeles at the end of the '6os, trying to launch music careers across the continent from their home in Georgia. There are different versions of the story about Duane first hearing Jesse Ed Davis, but when he did, it forever changed his and his brother's fortunes. According to Gregg Allman, it was Duane's birthday, November 20, 1967, when his brother was suffering a bad cold and a sprain from a horse-riding accident. Duane blamed the accident on Gregg, who left a bottle of Coricidin cold relief and a copy of the first Taj Mahal album at Duane's door, rang the bell, and ran off. Later that night, Duane wasn't angry anymore when he called Gregg: "Get over here, babybrah quick. Quick, man!" When Gregg arrived, Duane kissed him and said, "Man, that record you brought me is out of sight. There's a guy called Jesse Ed Davis on there, this Indian dude, and he plays guitar with a damn wine bottle. Dig this." Gregg continued:

> And then I looked on the table and all these little red pills, the Cori-cidin pills, were on the table. He had washed the label off that pill bottle, poured all the pills out. He put on that Taj Mahal record, with Jesse Ed Davis playing slide on "Statesboro Blues," and started playing along with it. When I'd left those pills by his door, he hadn't known how to play slide. From the moment that Duane put that Coricidin bottle on his ring finger, he was just a natural.

Duane continued playing along with Ed Davis's guitar part for hours, resetting the turntable over and over again. Soon, the Allman Brothers Band began featuring the Taj Mahal arrangement of "Statesboro Blues" in their set. Meanwhile, Duane Allman became widely regarded as per-haps the greatest slide guitarist in popular music history. Beginning with Jesse Ed Davis's influence, Duane Allman "entered a new musical universe," Gregg said. And for Ed Davis it began back in Oklahoma, sitting in a dorm room playing along to Elmore James records, resetting the turntable over and over again.[64]

Ed Davis's influence didn't end there. Elliot Easton, guitarist for the hitmaking group the Cars, experienced a similar infatuation with Ed's remarkable guitar playing. As a teenager, Easton raced home from school each day, ate a snack, and sat down with a guitar and his Taj Mahal records, studying each note. Then he did his homework, ate din-ner, and went back to learning Ed's guitar parts into the night. "That Taj Mahal lineup was one of *the* great American rock and roll bands," Easton proclaims. "That rhythm section, I'll put up with Booker T. and the MGs, in terms of the economy, pure funky, playing the air and spaces, not being busy, just laying down a pocket so deep." Easton credits Jesse's solo on "Six Days on the Road" with directly inspiring his solo on the Cars' hit "My Best Friend's Girl." Ed's future frequent session guitar partner Danny Kortchmar experienced a similar rapturous relationship with the early Taj Mahal albums. "The real deal, if you want to know about Eddie and his playing, is that *Natch'l Blues* album," he raves. "I must've listened to it five hundred times, over and over and over again." First hearing Ed's work with Taj Mahal, The Minus 5 founder and R.E.M. multi-instrumentalist Scott McCaughey "fell under the spell" of Jesse Ed Davis. Seeing Ed with Taj in 1970 at the Santa Clara County Fairgrounds, McCaughey felt like a "junior Frankenstein" being truly jolted alive for the first time by Ed's electric performance. "I tried to follow his exploits relentlessly," McCaughey says about his lifelong fandom. "Guys like Jesse Ed were the signpost for me," Little Feat founding keyboardist Bill Payne says, "in terms of what was possible, where the bar was being set, and who he was playing with." Even the Beatles chimed in when they sent the Taj Mahal band a signed letter declaring their love for *The Natch'l Blues*.[65]

On yet another scale, Ed Davis had emerged as a key player among Oklahoma musicians who were now making serious advances in the music business, appearing on hit records and collaborating with the biggest music stars of the day. These Okie musicians represented a true counterculture within the larger iteration that increasingly became commercialized through reproduction. The Okies exemplified an earlier incarnation of outlaw music that morphed into the Americana music genre. To a young Bonnie Raitt, Jesse was one of the "mythical figures."[66]

The Oklahoma Mafia and Tulsa sound didn't only influence the California music counterculture. It also became transatlantic. Top British musicians were drawn to the Okies. They loved the music, which featured an endearing simplicity. "It was pure rock and roll. *E-A-B. C-F-G*," Bobby Whitlock stresses. Moreover, artists such as Eric Clapton and the Beatles craved the camaraderie. Despite a certain closeness born from relentless external pressure, the Beatles didn't quite enjoy the kind of easy fraternity exhibited by the Okie gang. The fame took a toll on the love. On the road with Delaney & Bonnie, Clapton piled into a station wagon with everyone else. Clapton, John Lennon, George Harrison, Keith Richards, and other British rock aristocrats embraced the Okie musicians as peers. "We were all equals," Bobby Whitlock stresses. "The same was true for Ed Davis. He was an equal."[67]

The Taj Mahal chapter of Ed's life had ended unceremoniously. But he'd see Taj again, and his stature among his peers appeared capable of sustaining a career move. With Billy on his shoulder, Patti on one arm, and an analog tape of recordings for his first solo album under the other, Ed launched headlong into the 1970s.

Six

¡JESSE DAVIS!

IN MAY 1970, Ed Davis was in London with everywhere and nowhere to go. Having received Ed's resignation, Taj was on a plane to Spain. Professionally and artistically, Ed's prospects appeared boundless. The most popular musicians of his generation sought his company and his talent. But personally, he had nowhere to go. Patti and Billy were with him. Though Los Angeles ostensibly remained their home, they had no current residence there. "I was in England, flat broke, no gig, and just a couple of people I made friends with," Ed said. He therefore welcomed an invitation to stay at Eric Clapton's Hurtwood Edge Estate in Surrey. If Ed lacked a coherent plan, his impressive résumé and friends in high places carried him.

One afternoon brainstorming together in the kitchen, Clapton said, "How about an Ed Davis album?" Minutes later, he handed Ed the phone. It was legendary Atlantic Records producer Jerry Wexler, who popularized the term "rhythm and blues" and shepherded the careers of Aretha Franklin, Ray Charles, and other artists in Ed's pantheon of musicians. "Would you like to make an album for ATCO?" Wexler asked. They quickly sketched contract terms over the phone with no paperwork. Find a studio and get to work, Wexler instructed, and cash would be released upon delivery of an album. Within one month in summer 1970, Ed went from no work and an uncertain future to a major album and production deal with one of the most powerful moguls in the music industry. Ed was ready to come into his own. This was reflected in one final name change. Ed became Jesse.[1]

While Ed began putting his songs and recording plan together, he and Patti became close with Clapton and other new friends, including George Harrison, George's wife and Clapton's secret muse Pattie Boyd, and Beatles assistant Chris O'Dell, the latter an Okie like Ed. On one level, easygoing Ed and Patti Daley fit right in. Ed especially benefited from her outward charm and the adoration she reflected back on Ed. But in the world of rock wives and girlfriends, Patti stood out as a devoted mother in a setting where few other women had children, and those who did were often apart from them. Ed and Patti prioritized their new family. That commitment and challenge could easily become strained within the rock scene and lifestyle.

For now, Ed and Patti achieved a rhythm and harmony that impressed their music friends, though there were hints of how things might go wrong for the couple. Pattie Boyd felt great affection for Ed, but she worried about alcohol's exaggerated effect on him during parties at her and George's estate when Ed sometimes overindulged. He acknowledged it, explaining to Boyd that he was more susceptible to it as a Native person. To Ed and Patti's other new friend Chris O'Dell, Ed seemed to suffer from depression, something O'Dell better recognizes in hindsight as a professional therapist. "There was an aloneness to him," O'Dell observed. His new friends struggled to express their concerns. In their circle, it wasn't hip to ask prying questions about personal backgrounds, or, for that matter, drug and alcohol consumption. In a music culture milieu where people traditionally sought escape and reinvention, if Ed seemed private about some things, so did everyone else. "You went with the flow; you didn't question it," O'Dell notes. "There were always crowds around, and a lot of drugs."[2]

With dates booked at London's Olympic Studio, Clapton helped enlist Beatles and Stones engineer Glyn Johns to guide Ed's first recording sessions as a solo artist. Johns needed no introduction to the "phenomenal Native American guitar player." He already knew him from his work on the Stones' *Rock and Roll Circus* in 1968. From there, Johns helped recruit a sizable pool of musicians for the project. Various configurations recorded live, minimizing overdubs, cutting two to four songs per day. At the end of each session, Ed personally walked around with a mysterious briefcase full of cash and paid the players. "Everything came just the old-fashioned way everybody used to record," recalled drummer Alan White, who lent his talent to Jesse during a break from his regular gig with John Lennon. White and the other musicians appreciated the creative freedom Ed encouraged. If Ed could be vulnerable in certain social settings, he exhibited complete confidence in the studio, performing the role of producer for the first time since he cut a single with his old college band back in Oklahoma. "He seemed to be pretty much in control," White described Ed. "He knew what he wanted to do. . . . He was a very cool, calm character." Throughout the London sessions, people came and went, many just to hear what this Native American guy was putting down. The loose and communal atmosphere would continue to characterize Ed's studio work and aim as an artist.[3]

Some of these British musicians weren't too dissimilar from their American counterparts in that they'd seen Indian characters depicted in John Wayne films, but had never met an Indigenous person in real life. For his recording partners, the jewelry and large black cowboy hat Ed wore during the sessions only punctuated Ed's Native identity. On one occasion he explicitly appealed to his background through a strange exercise that resulted in a good laugh, maybe at his collaborators' expense. Wrapping the sessions in London, Ed called everyone out to the studio floor, asking them to sit down cross-legged for an Indian chant. "Miah hohne bah na nah," he began reciting, for what seemed like half an hour. Everyone, including Clapton, enthusiastically chanted along, eyes closed tight, when Ed suddenly busted up laughing. "I'm just fucking with you!!! We're not doing an Indian chant!!!" What then were they singing? Something about a banana. Only Ed thought it was funny. "But that was Jesse," keyboardist Ben Sidran sighs.[4]

At the end of May 1970, Ed, Patti, and Billy returned to Los Angeles, where Ed restarted work on his solo debut. Pausing only to join Leon Russell's group for a massive concert with the Who at Anaheim Stadium, Ed further expanded his team of music contributors, now recruiting many of his old friends, including Delaney Bramlett, John Ware, Gram Parsons, and Sandy Konikoff, as well as former Taj Mahal bandmates Chuck Blackwell, Bill Rich, and John Simon. Ed also embellished his sound with a coterie of horn players and backing vocalists, including "The Magnificent" Merry Clayton. Finally returning the favor for Ed's appearances in the studio and live, Leon Russell contributed distinctive piano chops. Ed was initially thrilled with the results. "I just know my album is gonna knock you out because it's just like I like it!" he wrote to Jerry Wexler at the end of July, making plans to hand deliver his master tapes. In fact, he was eager to begin work on the next one. "I've got enough material for two more right now," he declared.[5]

Not unlike many music artists, Ed eventually soured on his first album, wondering if he was sacrificing quality of music for quantity of musicians. "That's a really strange effort," he described his debut only one year after its release.

> I tell you, man, making your own album is really hard. It's like all of a sudden here's this record that's out and it's got your name on it and your picture and everybody says, "That's how Ed Davis plays. This is his music." But it's really not. It's just the way it was that night in the studio. I wish more people were hip to that.

In the end, he claimed to only like three songs from his debut album. The rest he considered the product of a "brain enema." He elaborated, "All these ideas I'd been saving up through the years just all of a sudden plopped out. Some of them are rather dated. Some of them are stolen. Some of them are borrowed."[6]

Yet even Ed agreed that the album's autobiographical tune "Washita Love Child" is unimpeachable. "Reno Street Incident" also remained a favorite of his, and a staple feature of his live set. Discussing the song, he compared Oklahoma City's Reno Street to New York City's Bowery slums, noting the blend of Bible missions and brothels, including one where Ed, at that time Eddie, first "got laid, man. It's about losing my cherry to this wonderful woman named Helen." It's one example of the album's energetic and often suggestive sense of humor. It's a great tune, though probably not as autobiographical as "Washita Love Child," Ed's notes on the tune notwithstanding.[7]

Ed was particularly proud of "Every Night Is Saturday Night"—his manifesto, stretching past seven minutes with horn blasts and an accelerating tempo evoking a New Orleans street party. "That sure was a Saturday sounding night," Ed beamed. "I didn't tell them to speed up. The horns were overdubbed. . . . When it got to the sped-up part, I didn't tell them that was happening. I said, 'Don't stop. Play all the way to the end.' They kept giving me weird glances back through the glass." The rest of the album is filled out with odes to Patti, including "Golden Sun Goddess," and a few cover tunes. On Pam Polland's "Tulsa County," Ed introduced a slight variation in the second verse lyrics that gestured to his Kiowa home: "In Anadarko, you said you needed my assistance / When I showed up, there was no way to go."[8]

Ed claimed to have enough material for two more albums, and in fact some tunes for his second album were cut alongside those for his first. But he was not a seasoned songwriter, despite securing complete artistic control and the creation of his own production company, contract features rare for new artists. His talent as a songwriter was only just emerging. This is evident in the numerous cover tunes, many unreleased, he recorded for his first two albums for ATCO. These include the Jimmie Rodgers classic "Looking for a New Mama," the rock and roll standard "Kansas City," Leon Russell's "Dixie Lullaby," Dylan's "Love Minus Zero" and "Blowin' in the Wind," Taj Mahal's "Tomorrow May Not Be Your Day," Smokey Robinson's "Tracks of My Tears," a second Van Morrison cover in "Caravan," and a version of Jimi Hendrix's "Little Wing" with Eric Clapton on guitar. Though these tunes failed to make the albums, they form a map of Ed's musical paths, from rock and roll, country, blues, and folk to Motown, Leon, Dylan, and Taj.

In any case, Ed delivered his solo debut with excitement, partly because he finally got paid, though it wasn't much. ATCO gave him $200 for each of the five songs he wrote. "We sure need it!" he exclaimed in a letter to his label.[9] When the album hit shops in January 1971, reviews were as mixed as Ed's own. "Some record albums sneak into town and then out again before you even realize they've arrived," the *Rolling Stone*'s review began. "This new disc by Jesse Edwin 'Indian Ed' Davis may be one of those, so listen up quick." The reviewer dismisses some tunes as "slight," while suggesting others "might make you clap your hands and stomp your feet." Here the "raucous and raunchy" "Reno Street Incident" and Indigenous anthem "Washita Love Child" are highlights, with the latter's guitar solo, played by Clapton, described as a "stunning and technically original guitar solo that'll curl the hair on top of your head and the socks down around your ankles." Discussing "Every Night Is Saturday Night," the review captures the general sound and spirit of Ed's music: "Take your garden-variety good-time music, add some Salvation Army brass, a passel of backwoods dancehall enthusiasm, and a gang of funky-drunken friends & neighbors—and you got it, a rock n roll Saturday night that'll keep you boogiein' for a week." Possibly intended as a compliment, the reviewer refers to Ed's "distinctly Leon Russellish voice."[10]

Actually, the Leon comparison dogged Ed's entire solo career. Despite admiration and affection for his Okie pal, Ed resented it. It happened again in a British review of the "Every Night Is Saturday Night" single, which noted Ed's "odd non-singing voices that become easier to accept, the more we hear. (Dr John probably started the current vogue; Leon Russell may well finish it.)" A kinder, though factually incorrect, review of Ed's work on a B.B. King album referred to a "crazy Oklahoma Cherokee who sounds like Leon Russell's brother." Meanwhile, Ed maintained that he intended for his vocals to approximate guitar parts. To those who suggested that he borrowed Leon's vocal style, he said, "That's a misconception. Leon sounds like me." Either way, Ed did credit Leon with teaching him how to be a lead singer, if not how to sing. Leon encouraged him to lean into his voice and project with confidence. Singing with great conviction can compensate for less conventional vocal qualities, Leon revealed. The raw emotive and tonal character provide unique appeal.[11]

Not so much behind the music as in front of it, perhaps the greatest triumph in Ed Davis's solo debut can be found in the name boldly emblazoned on front: *¡JESSE DAVIS!* Here he newly announces himself to the world, using a new name, his birthname and his father's name. From now on, symbolic of his emergence as a solo artist, he would be Jesse. To achieve this rebirth, he sent his label illustrated instructions, including an approximation of the painting his father created, a back cover photo of Jesse on Venice Beach, and exact directions on arranging and cropping the images. The packaging reflected Jesse's vision right down to the forest green background, standard ATCO liner notes placement and font, and the title "with exclamation points in white large pt. Indian style or old-time poster block letters."[12]

The album cover's ¡JESSE DAVIS! title framed a vibrant work of art. For his painting, Jesse Edwin Davis II was paid $500, about half of what Jesse earned. "I'm really proud of that," Jesse said. "Because, it's the first artwork he's done in about ten years. He hasn't painted in a long time. Buy it just for the cover. In case you can't see it over the radio, on the cover is a painting of an Indian man smoking a peace pipe, and he looks very, very stoned." Jesse may have reinforced widespread false beliefs among hippies that Native people smoked grass in calumets, but he never claimed to speak for any Indian but himself. The young Indian man on the cover is only supposed to be him.[13]

The front and back covers for ¡JESSE DAVIS! are mirror images, one serious and one satire, capturing a young Native person facing their future. On the front an Indian man with long black hair falling around his shirtless shoulders and torso sits cross-legged, drawing a puff from a pipe, a red streak across his eye. It's a literal and figurative profile. And that's a black-and-white photo of the real Jesse on the back cover, sitting cross-legged on Venice Beach about fifty yards from his front door, smoking a salami in a tie-dye t-shirt and cutoff jean shorts. These countervailing images of Indigenous Jesse captured him not only facing his possible futures but also inhabiting his present with a seriousness of purpose rooted in the past and a sarcasm that could shield him from any vulnerability inherent to his mission and presentation as an Indigenous artist.

If you hold the album in your hands and flip it back and forth, the images become one; Jesse becomes Jesse, alternatingly looking ahead and looking back at you. Taj Mahal remembers seeing it for the first time.

"His first album was like, bam . . . *Native*. No matter what you're going to hear on the inside, this is who he is. That was powerful. . . . He pulled it off," Taj said. In front of a garage door across from the alley behind their new beach house in Los Angeles, Jesse, Patti, and Billy posed for a series of promotional photos. In one image, if you look very closely, Jesse's outfit is anchored by a belt buckle featuring the Love's truck stop logo, from Oklahoma. In others, Jesse strums a Martin 000-28, almost certainly his father's Martin acoustic guitar that he used to sneak from the closet as a kid back in Oklahoma City when he dreamed about a career in music. Now, his dream had come true.[14]

JESSE LAUNCHED HIS solo career at the head of a decade most everyone around him seemed anxious to commence. The shifting social context, signaled by the end of the '60s, encouraged a certain cultural retrenchment and tribalism. Some people felt desperate in a seemingly corrosive social climate. Others sought new modes of living and imagining their place in the world. People regularly misquoted Gandhi, imploring themselves and others to "Be the Change You Want to See in the World," declaring that the real revolution begins within. These were the sentiments of many Californians who had been through hell in the City of Angels.

Jesse experienced real proximity to events that marked the turbulent end of the decade. At Altamont in December 1969, his friends in the Rolling Stones, Grateful Dead, and Flying Burrito Brothers were on hand for the figurative "Day the Sixties Died," when Meredith Hunter died at the end of a Hells Angels biker's knife after waving a gun in the air a couple rows in front of the exasperated Rolling Stones. Earlier that year, the Stones had considered Jesse for their vacant lead guitar spot, now filled by a young Mick Taylor. Back in LA, everyone was already aghast at the terrifying Manson murders and many hadn't yet emotionally recovered from the 1968 assassination of Bobby Kennedy, fatally shot only hours after greeting supporters in Venice, where Jesse and his family now lived.

Jesse, Patti, and Billy sought refuge in their new beachside rambler.

No more than thirty steps from the beach, the house sat on the border of Venice and Marina del Rey, at the southern end of a sprawling bohemian community, long famous as an art colony, writer's retreat, and haven for drug culture. In music lore, this is where the Doors formed in the 1960s and Jane's Addiction formed in the 1980s. Located at 20 Hurricane Street, Jesse's place became known as the Hurricane House. It's an apt and irresistible metaphor. Life there was a whirlwind. Thrilling but treacherous, everything moved fast. Jesse escaped tornado country only to get caught in a hurricane on the coast.

Jesse's beachside manor granted him social cachet within his music circles. Everyone wanted to be by the ocean, so the Hurricane House became a hub of operations where famous musicians regularly visited. Jesse's personal assistant Pete Waddington recalls one day when Jesse told him to answer a knock at the door. It was famed Animals singer Eric Burdon. Pete and Jesse were listening to Burdon on the stereo at that precise moment. It was Burdon's classic tune "We Gotta Get Out of This Place"—an anthem among Vietnam veterans like Waddington, who was stunned and confused.[15]

Sometimes visitors came bearing gifts to share—Gregg Allman with a baby food jar of cocaine, Gram Parsons with a giant rock of snow that ruined a Thanksgiving dinner Patti prepared. "The scene in that house was 24/7," keyboardist Ben Sidran muses. "There were always musicians falling by and craziness going on. I mean, you can imagine, LA in '71. . . . It was Mad Dogs and Englishmen time." Sometimes there would even be a member of the Fab Four sitting on the living room couch. "When I walked in, I thought 'Oh God, I'm seeing one of the Beatles,'" Marc Benno remembers about encountering George Harrison there. "I was enamored with the Beatles, and I think they were enamored with Ed."[16]

A steady stream of friends crashed in the garage, forming ad hoc additions to the family. Jesse spread a rug across the garage floor and draped a large orange and white parachute from the ceiling, down along the walls, like a tipi. Jim Karstein stayed there for three years, longer than anyone else. Records circulated between Jesse's stacks inside and Karstein's out in the garage. They had enough between them to open a record store. Other garage inhabitants included Chris O'Dell and drummers Gary Mallaber and Sandy Konikoff, who joined Jesse's live band for various durations. And there was Jesse's old Continentals bandmate from Oklahoma, John Selk, who experienced culture shock when he showed up in Venice in January 1971 on his way home from a tour in Vietnam. Deciding to stay, he had to adjust quickly. "Get your axe," Jesse ordered. "You're going to play on a Gene Clark album." The Hurricane House could seem like a never-ending party, with shades drawn during daytime and music at night. Despite the heavy foot traffic, the place was immaculate. Jesse and Patti both insisted on it. "You could eat off the floor there," Sandy Konikoff notes. "The house was so clean."[7]

If Jesse had his way, they would all live in Santa Monica, but they couldn't afford it. Jesse instead made the Hurricane House into a funky home with a communal atmosphere that reflected his Indigenous cultural emphasis on hospitality. No matter how much he struggled at times, or how often his friends were the ones helping him when he was down, Jesse tried to support those around him. Throughout the rest of his life, he prided himself on being a music business and Los Angeles entrepôt for anyone who needed a hand, regularly inviting everyone from hustling California musicians to old Kiowa friends and relatives from back home to stay with him. He liked having a lot of people around, even if he sometimes seemed alone among them.[18]

Meanwhile, bobbing in the waves of rock stars rolling into the Hurricane House was Jesse's family of three and their dog Abernathy. It helped that Patti was a quintessential beach girl. To Jesse she was the physical embodiment of California itself, happiest in a bikini with her toes in the sand. Jesse gave her the nickname Lulu, for her middle name Louise, and later named his second solo album after his habit of saying "Ooh, Lulu" when her beauty captured him. "Eyes of ocean green yet cosmic blue / hair of golden sunshine rays," Jesse sang about her in his breezy "Golden Sun Goddess." When Jesse's old Continentals bandmate Carl Rogel came to visit, he was both captivated and amused by Patti's effect. "Wow," Rogel said to Jesse, "you got a woman and a guru too?" Patti was good for Jesse, all of his old friends noticed. Jesse equally adored Billy, encouraging use of the name Bill Davis in formal matters and endowing Billy with his own set of affectionate nicknames: Bad Bill and Billy the Kid. With Patti's support and Billy in tow, Jesse seemed to bring his professional and his personal lives into alignment.[19]

For the rest of her years, Patti held onto a small blank card displaying a watercolor painting of a red sailboat and a white sailboat swaying together in the seafoam breakers near Santa Monica Pier some sunny day. The image and note within captured Jesse's love for his family. In his exquisite hand, inside he wrote,

—THREE OF US—
18 SEPTEMBER, 1971
SANTA MONICA PIER

"Lord it was just us three," Jesse sang in "Washita Love Child" about the trio he, his father, and his mother formed upon his birth in Oklahoma. Now he was reproducing that dynamic with Patti and Billy. In more ways than one, he really had become "Jesse."[20]

By day, Jesse got a lot of work done out there by the beach. When friends visited, Patti might meet them at the door and whisper, "Shhhh. . . . He's working at the piano," and motion for an impromptu walk along the beach where they could hear Jesse's notes drifting out over the sea. Depending on Jesse's mood, friends might be allowed to stay and listen. "When I'm talking about Jesse at that house on the Marina Peninsula, I'm sitting there with him," bassist Bob Glaub reminisces. "I can just see the piano. He used to love to play piano." Throughout the day, Jesse practiced an adventurous approach to making music. His guitar was always set up and plugged in. He bounced between it and his upright piano, composing songs he imagined in his head. He regularly instructed his personal assistant Pete Waddington to procure random instruments—banjo, cello, French horn—and taught himself to play them. When Jesse wasn't working on his own music, the radio, turntable, or cassette player were constantly on. Jesse especially liked cassettes, and loved making mixtapes for Patti and his friends. "I just remember a lot of music," Bill stresses about being a kid at the beach house. "A lot of musicians. Music was the focus of the Hurricane House."[21]

The first thing visitors saw when dropping by was the framed original painting Bus, or Papa D, as Billy called him, made for Jesse's first album. Nearby hung an autographed 8×10 of Duane Allman signed by the man himself: "Jesse: Thanks for the licks in Statesboro!" Hundreds of motel keys that Jesse took as souvenirs from his days on the road with Taj hung here and there around the house, as did products of Jesse's leatherworking hobby. The title of backgammon champion was a high honor in the Hurricane House; on the coffee table rested a homemade backgammon board that Jesse made from a mirror and electrical tape. Gauzy light from an assortment of lamps glowed through Patti's multicolored scarves. Motown, Stax, Freddie King, Albert King, Pat Martino, Howard Roberts, Wes Montgomery, Bucky Pizzarelli, and more from Jesse's formidable record collection transmitted from the turntable. Occasionally, Jesse held band rehearsals in the small living room, with Jim Karstein practicing on Billy's child-sized drum kit. Jesse often sat on his couch for hours playing acoustic guitar, sometimes serenading friends with the official Hurricane House anthem—"Walk Right In" by the Rooftop Singers. "Walk right in, sit right down / Daddy, let your mind roll on."[22]

The beach looked different then. There was just sand, water, and an oil rig pumping oil, the latter a lingering impression of Venice's status as an oil field earlier in the century, the industry that made Hollywood. Next door at 24½ Hurricane Street lived Vietnam veteran Ron Kovic, who hosted Veterans Movement meetings while writing his bestselling memoir, *Born on the Fourth of July* (1976). On nights when Patti didn't make dinner for Jesse, Billy, and the garage lodgers, various combinations of people walked ten minutes up Speedway to Jesse and George Harrison's favorite restaurant, the Crab Shell. A bit farther north stood the burned-out Pacific Ocean Park, languishing in Disneyland's shadow.[23]

No one enjoyed greater stature at the Hurricane House than Jesse's parents and grandmother. Everyone loved Mamacita. "She's just this little round heart full of love and light and a warm smile," Bill remembers her at the time. She was the type who went to visit someone and became the hostess when they got there. She loved Jesse's music pals, sharing her frybread recipe with Patti's girlfriends, giving the Waddingtons a Kiowa blanket for a wedding gift. Jesse's friends reciprocated. During one visit, Mamacita and Papa D couldn't get their travelers checks to process. Delaney Bramlett stepped in and loaned them enough money to complete their visit and return home. Jesse's music friends marveled at giant Papa D. He liked walking over to the beach and feeling the sand on his bare feet while he stared over the Pacific Ocean. Far across, he had once fought in the Second World War. At night, after the sun set, Mamacita and Papa D loved staying up with Jesse and the gang, spinning records, pouring drinks, dancing. Everyone saw Jesse in them.[24]

Jesse's cousin, more like a brother, Russell Saunkeah, came to live with Jesse at the Hurricane House for a few years before heading back to Oklahoma in 1974 when he became uncomfortable with Jesse's escalating drug use. Taj reconnected with Jesse, too. His appearances were like having more family on hand. One special visit included Jesse's greatest guest of honor, his Kiowa grandmother Anna. Having not seen her grandson Eddie in years, she was enamored with his long black hair. She told all his friends that it reminded her of the old days.

In the eye of the Hurricane House, Jesse worked at being a father to Billy. Sometimes he struggled. Friends thought he was hard on Billy, who doesn't disagree. Jesse's discipline took different forms, Billy learned:

> I just remember thinking as a kid, "Oh, good. He's going to be gone for a while. I don't have to be on the edge or on pins and needles around him." Because I always had to act a certain way. Had to perform. My mom told me that he was trying to build the perfect kid. Trying to raise the perfect kid. I just remember getting in trouble all the time over shit I didn't really understand. Don't chew with your mouth full. Use this fork and not that fork, that kind of crap. He was really strict about that kind of stuff. I think that comes down to however his father raised him. Like it or not, we all become our fathers in some way.

What hurt Billy most was his seeming inability to satisfy Jesse's expectations for learning musical instruments. Billy loved playing his little four-piece Pearl drum kit. It was the John Lennon–style Rickenbacker guitar and Pignose amp Jesse bought Billy that provoked Jesse's impatience and ire. Although Jesse scheduled daily practices, "The Virgo in him made any progress not good enough," Bill suggests. (Bill is also a Virgo.) It was as if Jesse didn't realize he was the great Jesse Ed Davis, and a kid can't just pick up a guitar and play like him. "I always loved the music," Bill says. "I just didn't like playing it anymore after he made it a chore to do. Which is really sad because I got a love for music in me." Jesse wanted so badly for Billy to be his true son. Through his guitar, Billy could become a real part of Jesse. Instead, Jesse pulled him too close and pushed him away.[25]

Like any kid feeling unable to please their father, Billy sometimes courted trouble, partly for the attention it might bring. In such instances, Jesse's temper could ruin the immense love he was capable of practicing as a father. Billy and a friend liked to play with matches and fire—though they never intended to set an apartment building ablaze as they did one afternoon. Fire trucks roared onto the scene and extinguished the flames before anyone was hurt. Jesse and Patti were liable for several thousand dollars in damage, which they couldn't afford at the time, as Jesse's first album hadn't exactly rocketed up the charts, and he was hustling bread from session contracts. John Lennon and George Harrison's bassist Klaus Voormann was at the house that day. He observed Jesse's overwhelming anger. When the fire marshal came over to discuss the matter, Jesse directed him toward Billy. "What did you say to him?" Voormann asked Jesse. "I told him to talk to the kid." After everyone had left, Jesse's anger boiled over. Patti had to get between Jesse and her son. After many years of reflecting on Jesse's physical anger and through discussions with his mother, Bill came to understand it, even if he struggled to forgive it: "Jesse was really . . . the way I was scared of Jesse was the way he was of his dad. . . . So [Jesse] had to deal with that."[26]

One Halloween, Jesse dressed Billy as an Indian—fringe leather jacket, beaded necklace, black wig, red headband, and war paint. Billy innocently pretended to be an Indian like the ones he saw in cartoons. "Hi, me wantum to be your friend." Jesse responded with a slap, revealing the irrepressible effect mockery of Native people had on him, even coming from his five-year-old son, even after *he* was the one who dressed

Billy in faux Indian attire. "Do I motherfucking talk like that, mother-fucker?" It's possible Billy had become a proxy for all the kids who bullied Jesse with cultural stereotypes growing up in Oklahoma City. But Billy wasn't them, and Jesse was no longer there. Still the pain persisted, and Jesse made Billy feel it. "I never made that mistake ever again," Bill reflects. "I just didn't know any better at that age."

Decades later, after learning that he has Blackfeet ancestry, Bill's greatest regret is that he and Jesse didn't know that back then, when he was "Billy the Kid." Bill wishes they could have bonded over it, imagining how it could have been a bridge between them, a step toward a meaningful father-and-son connection that Billy's Rickenbacker guitar could not provide. "I would like to see Jesse's reaction to me being part Indian," he says.

It's a relief learning Bill cherishes many memories too, including yearning memories of the colorful canal festivals he attended with Jesse. In the early '70s, Venice could still be a dangerous place. By day it was a scene of multicultural and countercultural splendor, where people were free to be themselves. To people suffering some sort of social or cultural marginalization, Venice could be paradise. But Venice boasted the lowest average rent prices on the west side of Los Angeles for a reason. As late as the 1950s, the beach couldn't be used because of oil contamination while a persistent stench emanating from the canals gave the place a reputation for being a slum. At night violent gangs roamed the canals, subverting the community's playful daytime vibe. "Cops in cars, topless bars," sang Venice icon Jim Morrison, summarizing the nightlife in a song about a Los Angeles woman he never saw "so alone."[27]

The Venice Canal Festivals provided an opportunity for everyone in the neighborhood to come together for nightlong parties and get to know each other. In 1969, the festivals began organically through word of mouth and flyers stapled to telephone poles. No one quite anticipated how far the communal enthusiasm would spread. Thousands of people opened their homes, including their refrigerators and bathrooms, to thousands of strangers. People gathered in houses and backyards, on front porches, streets, and beaches, grilling food, sharing stuffed grape leaves, lemonade, cake, beer, and reefer joints, displaying paintings, sculptures, clothing, crafts, and jewelry, and jamming together in makeshift bands. Jesse and Billy loved the canal festivals—Venice's "Birthday Party"—especially because they annually corresponded with their own Virgo birthday month of September.[28]

The festivals regularly attracted over ten thousand people from beyond the community. Women sold kisses for 50¢, while ragtag regiments of mimes, fire eaters, and contortionists paraded through the streets. Nearby, a giant papier mâché "canal monster" swam through the waterways to raise support for single mothers. Eventually, inevitably, the city sought to capitalize on the popular event. Officials began charging for permits that dramatically diminished available space and created parking and transportation nightmares. Meanwhile, housing development plans spiked rent rates around the community. Police presence increased, as did police brutality. In 1975, festival organizers finally held a funeral for their grand event, replete with a coffin led through the streets by a biker named Happy Jack, who carried a staff mounted with a plastic skull. A troupe of belly dancers trailed behind in mourning. In retrospect, the festivals, spanning from 1969 to 1975, reflected Jesse's own personal and professional arc throughout that period, from festive fun and games to a gradual state of struggle and misfortune.[29]

IN VENICE, Jesse could blend in if he wanted to, or express his Indigeneity in a more tolerant environment. But then, Indigenous people are often treated as exotic folk in even the most diverse settings, and hippies were certainly not averse to appropriating imagined versions of Indigenous culture. Jesse was searching for something different. While people everywhere romanticized American Indians, Jesse romanticized blues musicians. We hear it most in "Reno Street Incident," his ode to a world of shingle shacks, red lights, and music blasting through juke joint windows. Playing against ongoing federal efforts to assimilate Indigenous people into mainstream American society and culture, as well as persistent Indian myths and legends that inspired the encompassing counterculture, Jesse continued his transformation into an authentic blues artist.

Jesse's solo career unfurled during a time when new Native leaders such as John Trudell, Dennis Banks, and Russell Means entered mainstream media consciousness demanding sovereignty rights and self-determination. Despite some dismissing them as "media chiefs," they invoked great leaders from the previous century—Crazy Horse, Sitting Bull, Geronimo—when they occupied Alcatraz Island in 1969 and the Bureau of Indian Affairs building in Washington in 1972 and exchanged gunfire with US Marshals at Wounded Knee, South Dakota, in 1973, almost one hundred years after as many as three hundred Lakota people were murdered there by the US 7th Cavalry in 1890.

Jesse's only explicit gesture to the movement for Indigenous people's sovereignty rights was a cover of Leon Russell's "Alcatraz." In an amazing coincidence, the lyrics in the final verse refer to a "local chief on the radio" who's "got some hungry mouths to feed." That was John Trudell, host of *Radio Free Alcatraz*, who would become Jesse's future music partner. The song is from the perspective of an Indigenous person taking the island. "I like to think Leon wrote this song for me," Jesse said. At least through song, he briefly placed himself in the political zeitgeist. Jesse inhabits the tune with fervor, but he was otherwise more interested in plugging into a guitar amplifier than plugging into tribal activism.[30]

Jesse nevertheless received acknowledgment within the Native community as an important artist who contributed to popular music. A 1973 issue of *Navajo Times* that focused on XIT, the intertribal rock band from Albuquerque, discussed the Indigenous artists who paved the way for XIT's success. Beginning with hybrid Native-English language songs that emerged in the late 1940s, through Reg Begay, Phillip Whiteman, Cheyenne Dave, Patrick Sky, and others, the story arrived at Jesse, the "Oklahoma Comanche." From there, the feature discussed Jesse's Indigenous contemporaries, including Floyd Westerman, who would later appear live numerous times with Jesse and John Trudell's Grafitti Band. In this company, Jesse was a part of a legacy, one among a handful of Native artists who were being seen and heard in the dynamic 1960s–70s musical landscape.[31]

Indianness could certainly be marketable, especially when Indigenous matters were making headline news. Before Jesse recorded guitar for her album *Stars*, Cher had a number-one hit with a song called "Half Breed" that reflected her conflicted experiences stemming from her mother's claim of Cherokee ancestry. The song depicts the two-worlds trope, in which Native people are helplessly caught between two cultures, belonging in neither, a theme typically intensified if the person in question isn't "full blood." "Half breed, she's no good they warned / Both sides were against me since the day I was born." It's another song about an Indigenous person's life as tragedy, written during a time when some young Native American people were beginning to argue that colonizers wielded blood quantum as a weapon to divide and conquer Indigenous people. Being Indigenous wasn't about blood, they argued, it was about kin, place, and belonging.

When John Lennon appeared with Yoko on *The Dick Cavett Show* in 1971, he betrayed an elementary knowledge of Native issues, though he demonstrated the courage to introduce the subject on national television. "What are American people doing for Indians?" he begged Cavett, before suddenly veering into tragic legends of Mayan, Incan, and Aztec peoples. After Cavett reminded Lennon there are American Indians facing real problems in the present, Lennon turned to the audience: "You didn't know he was an Indian freak, did you?" Lennon proceeded to describe contemporary Native people as "illiterate, uneducated, not looked after. . . . It's pretty rough for them, isn't it?"

These were generalizations and stereotypes that may have reflected real crises in parts of Indian Country but far too often led to a demoralizing fixation on Indigenous poverty. For John Lennon, who would soon initiate a musical partnership with Jesse, the facts of Jesse's life and experiences could provide an alternative example of Indigenous life and consciousness in the 1970s. At least Lennon grasped some fundamental truths about Native American people and North American history in his efficient summary of the past: "They made so much money out of the Indians. First, they took the land, and then they made movies about them taking the land. It's a bit mean, you know?" The audience erupts with laughter, but Lennon was trying to shame them. How could Jesse enter such conversations and arenas, where ignorance always foiled good intentions? Jesse didn't want to be a villain, like in the old Western pictures John Lennon loved, and he didn't want to be a victim in progressive historical pageants. Jesse understood there were other options.

Looking back, Jesse's drummer Gary Mallaber wishes he had tried to get to know something about Jesse's background as a Native person. "Because I could always see kind of a faraway look in his eye, and we were not capable of really talking about ten feet under the surface. I wish we did," he said. When Mallaber played with Van Morrison, he never hesitated to ask Van about growing up in Belfast or the inspirations and ideas behind Van's music. On the other hand, Jesse might have struggled to convey how being Native felt for him in that place and time. When he did open up, it was typically through humor. In the end, cultural identity and personal backgrounds often seemed secondary. Mallaber's partnership with Jesse first extended from music that "got in our blood, that's the only thing that drove me and that's the only thing that drove him and that's what I saw. And there we were, you know, like the movie *Close Encounters*, staring at Devil's Tower."[32]

Sometimes when friends did acknowledge Jesse's Native identity, it quickly, if innocently, became heated. On one occasion, a friend was sitting in Jesse's kitchen in the Hurricane House, where Jesse was grilling food. Something caught on fire, with smoke filling the kitchen and billowing out the window. "Whaddaya doing, Ed, sending smoke signals?" his friend quipped. Jesse, expressionless, unconcerned with the fire, turned and dictated, "No racial slurs." For Jesse, the humor was only acceptable when it came from him. He used to tease Pete Waddington, for example, calling him "immigrant" and "foreigner."[33]

When Jesse lowered his guard, he talked about how he was harassed as a kid and how hard it was for him growing up in Oklahoma City. As with his experiences playing with Carl Rogel back in Oklahoma and Taj Mahal more recently, Jesse could better relate to other musicians of color, including Jesse's Puerto Rican percussionist Bobby Torres. Jesse taught Torres the Kiowa creation story and quite seriously told Torres that his people worshipped the sun. Maybe he wasn't just messing with unsolicited religious messengers when he invited them into his home and told them the same. Torres's experiences as a Puerto Rican kid growing up in New York helped him bond with Jesse and facilitated a mutual sympathy and respect. Jesse mentioned how his approach to racism had evolved to a point of trying to not "give a shit about it." Torres understood. "We just fit, you know? He looked so fucking cool, with his long hair, but I never really thought about him being Native American. When you hear some guy who's a motherfucker, you don't give a fuck where he's from, you just like to play with him."[34]

JESSE'S FIRST SOLO ALBUM had only just arrived in record shops when he was hard at work on his next effort. When George Harrison dropped by the Hurricane House one afternoon in summer 1971 for a visit, Jesse mentioned that he still needed one more song to complete the album he was calling *Ululu*. That's when, as Jesse put it, "George laid the 'Sue Me, Sue You Blues' on me, which is about his friends the Fab Four." Jesse quickly hit the studio with it and released it before George cut it for his own next album, *Living in the Material World* (1973). Meanwhile, George mentioned his upcoming concert plan to Jesse. It would be a benefit for Bangladesh, which was economically distressed after the US government compelled the country to eradicate its hemp plants, destroying the soil and causing a famine.[35]

After learning the concert had sold out in minutes, Jesse asked: "How about an extra ticket?" George didn't hesitate. In August, Jesse and Patti flew to New York, expecting only to attend the concert. Then, Jesse elaborated,

> The day before, at the most important rehearsal, Eric Clapton turned up very ill, with the flu and a temperature of 104 degrees. Everyone was sure he wasn't going to be able to make it. Since I was right there in the room, I was the logical choice for a replacement. The day of the concert, Eric did manage to stagger onto the stage and hold his guitar. He was very under the weather, but it did cause me to play the concert, and it was incredible, unfathomable. . . . It was extreme bliss, all those wonderful musicians. I was standing right in front of Ringo Starr. His bass drum was booting me in the back. . . . Of course there was George waving his arms, scared to death.[36]

It was a smashing success. "Mission accomplished," Billy Preston described the event. "It was a miracle really," Ravi Shankar agreed. A year later, a live album and feature film provided music fans all around the country an opportunity to experience it. There was Jesse, shoulder to shoulder with some of the greatest artists of his time.[37]

Returning home to Los Angeles, Jesse prepared *Ululu* for release. Although he had more time to put this one together, he again worked quickly, perhaps too quickly. He continued searching for a particular sound and style, reflected in the album's performers and performances, as well as its disjointed track list. The album is similar to *¡JESSE DAVIS!* in its tone, presentation, large cast of musical guests, and dependency on cover tunes to fill two sides. Some of the basic tracks were leftovers from unfinished sessions Jesse produced for Gram Parsons. Most of these tracks never saw release, possibly due to an argument over money.[38]

After Jesse's first album failed to run up the charts, ATCO ordered him to enlist a coproducer, someone who could evaluate Jesse's ideas and help keep things on track. Jesse chose an up-and-coming producer named Albhy Galuten. Galuten would go on to invent the drum loop and helm the soundtracks for *Grease* and *Saturday Night Fever*, two of the biggest-selling albums of all time. Jesse first met Galuten in February 1970 at Criteria Studios in Miami while cutting tracks with Taj Mahal for a project that didn't advance. Galuten suspected that Jesse chose a relatively new producer with the idea he could push him around and avoid label interference. But that was never necessary. The two hit it off and together they headed to Miami to complete the album.[39]

The Miami portion of the project was largely a matter of sorting out a mess of tracks Jesse started back in Los Angeles. In Miami, they focused on recording Jesse's vocal parts. Far removed from the Hollywood scene, Miami provided a relaxing environment conducive to getting work done. The studio was connected to a living area and came with a team of assistants who rented cars, brought food, and kept an accurate list of the types of cigarettes everyone preferred. But even in such an inspired setting, where Jesse's hero Aretha Franklin made records, Jesse struggled to find his singing voice and became frustrated with the results. He lacked confidence and couldn't "get his voice to do what his ears could hear," Galuten explains.⁴⁰

As with his first album, Jesse eventually became disappointed with *Ululu*. Still, it remains a favorite among many of his fans. His version of "Sue Me, Sue You Blues," with its loose and soulful guitar solo, quite possibly surpasses George Harrison's version. "Red Dirt Boogie, Brother" became Jesse's second signature autobiographical tune, and it featured in his setlist years thereafter. His take on the Band's "Strawberry Wine" grooves along merrily, and "My Captain" is an aching tribute to his old partner Taj Mahal:

> When I played with Taj all those years that's what I called him all the time. It was a great team with Gary Gilmore and Chuck Blackwell. We really rocked and rolled. We played all over the country. We didn't have many record sales, I don't think, but we had a huge following on the strength of our personal appearances. We had a rock-solid, super-tight band and we were the envy of a lot of the folks. . . . About "My Captain," one more thing I'd like to point out is that, if the words seem a little melancholy, it's that Taj and I, since we're not playing together anymore, we have very little to say to each other, and it's just kind of sad. Taj, if you heard that tune man, I love you, okay?

Finally, "Ululu" is an atmospheric tribute to Patti. "Sweet Lulu, if two could become one it's you and I," Jesse sings.⁴¹

Jesse's idea for the album cover was a dramatic black-and-white photo Cheryl Waddington took of him performing live. When they asked the label for a few hundred dollars in exchange for the image, assuming it would be an incidental drop in the bucket, the label balked and dispatched the photographer team of Tom Wilkes and Barry Feinstein, who designed covers for Joe Cocker's *Mad Dogs and Englishmen*, George Harrison's *All Things Must Pass*, the Flying Burrito Brothers' *The Gilded Palace of Sin*, Neil Young's *Harvest*, *The Concert for Bangladesh*, and more. They came up short with the *Ululu* cover shot—an unremarkable picture of Jesse, dwarfed by a giant colorized Aztec Brewing Company logo painted on a brick wall. It isn't clear whether the dull, tan-colored cover was trying harder to sell JESSE ED DAVIS / ULULU, in small font at the top, or the more "famous A.B.C. Beer."[42]

Jesse was perhaps proudest of the album's stellar cast of musical guests, including Leon Russell, Donald "Duck" Dunn, Jim Keltner, and Dr. John. In fact, Jesse did a great Dr. John impersonation: *"Jessaaaaay, er ah, whyyy don't you hand me that jernt? I wants to Beauregard it, cuz I wants to dig myself."* Jesse nailed the malapropism and Dr. John's Cajun accent on the ol' "Don't Bogart that joint" doper's etiquette. "Humphrey Beauregard!" Jesse loved it.[43]

But Jesse reserved his strongest praise for drummer Jim Keltner. "He's one of my very, very favorite persons in the whole world," Jesse said about his pal Jimmy. The two practically became a package duo as Keltner played on more sessions with Jesse than any other musician. The mighty rhythm section they formed, often with rotating bassists Carl Radle, Klaus Voormann, and Duck Dunn, graced many of the greatest albums of the 1970s, including records by Albert Collins, Albert King, Booker T. Jones and Priscilla Coolidge, Harry Nilsson, Leon Russell, Joe Cocker, John Lennon, George Harrison, Ringo Starr, and more. "The first time I played with him, I felt my playing improved, and that my playing sounded real for the first time," Keltner recalls. "He had such a strong groove." Upon initially meeting, Keltner was intimidated because Okie bassist Carl Radle kept stressing that Jesse was a "full-blood Indian," not something to take lightly, Keltner thought. "I had great respect for him right off the bat. Because, being from Oklahoma, the Indian thing was not romanced at all. Unfortunately, it was like you can imagine." Keltner quickly realized he had nothing to worry about: "I couldn't do anything wrong when I played with Jesse."[44]

Ululu's reviews were as mixed as they had been for the first album. Critics continued praising Jesse's guitar playing and his music's exuberant atmosphere, while complaining about his vocals and lack of focus. "Davis' vocal work is not particularly good, but his voice is effective within its own limits, and Davis is smart enough not to try and transcend these limits," one critic granted.[45] A reviewer for the *Montreal*

Star was less impressed: "After a few phrases from Davis, I wondered, 'Now, who would want to sound like Leon Russell?'" before continuing, "Oh, everything's technically perfect on this record, but the music's not at all spirited. If anything, it drags." Compared to Leon Russell, the reviewer concludes, "Davis doesn't stand a chance as imitator."[46] Meanwhile, *Rolling Stone* praised Jesse's second album, putting it ahead of Jesse's debut "not because of the prestigious back-up musicians" but because the album "seems to show off his talents in a more personal light than anything else he has done so far."[47]

Other media coverage fastened Jesse to his identity as a Native American artist, though the observations were often cheap and offensive. A regrettable article in *Punk Magazine* made a game of comparing popular pro wrestlers to popular rock musicians. "Little Beaver was a lot heavier than Jesse Ed Davis even if he didn't play guitar for Bob Dylan," the writer waxed. Setting aside the rather forced comparison, Little Beaver, a legendary little person wrestler who went on to star in WrestleMania III at Detroit's Pontiac Silverdome, was French-Canadian. He marketed himself as Native, but he was not. Jesse primarily did the opposite. Equally curious, a review of *Ululu* from a Midwestern newspaper characterized Jesse as a "short, raven-haired, dark-skinned guitar player." Never mind that Jesse was six feet tall. The reviewer went on to describe Jesse as an "expressive and tender guitar player," though they didn't think he was as good as Clapton. But that seemed beside the point in a review more eager to focus on his Indigenous identity and appearance. "He's an American, and wears his dark skin proudly," the piece continues, "slipping in references to it occasionally in his songs." But apart from Jesse's cover of Leon's "Alcatraz," *Ululu* does not reference Jesse's Indigeneity.[48]

Interestingly, in a review for Indigenous group Redbone's 1972 *Message from a Drum*, released the same year as *Ululu*, one critic wonders why there's no room for "superstar Indians" in rock music. "One reason," they suggested, "might be that people have been bludgeoned to death by the enormous tragedy that the Indian has suffered at our hands and that we are powerless to correct, both because of the cultural toll it has taken and because the effects at this point seem irreversible." The

writer then highlights Jesse as a Native artist allegedly guilty of "infus-
ing most of their material with the suffering mournful chants they've
known all their lives." Apparently, lyrics about the plight of Native
Americans, somewhat ubiquitous at the time, were acceptable as long
as they were delivered by non-Native artists. Was the point that there
were no superstar Indians because all the Indian musicians talked about
being Indian? To the reviewer's question, perhaps more Native musicians hadn't become superstars because the media was so determined to
caricature and diminish them. Audiences seemed to like them just fine
when they had the chance to speak and sing for themselves.[49]

With two albums now on the shelves, Jesse began putting more effort
into promoting them. He played numerous gigs around Los Angeles and
occasionally ventured out of town for random engagements. This was
made possible by a series of ad hoc band lineups that reflected both his
performances back in Oklahoma City, where he led a rotating roster of
musicians that could range from four to ten members, and his experience
with the large Concert for Bangladesh ensemble. "I think playing for all
those people at Madison Square Garden on the concert for Bangladesh
was such a rush, man," Jesse said. "All the cooperation amongst the
artists and all the really high feelings that happened that day is what
convinced me to get my own band and go play in front of people."[50]

Supporting his first two albums, Jesse's revolving lineups included
Ben Sidran, Jim Karstein, Gary Mallaber, John Selk, Bobby Torres,
Sandy Konikoff, bassist Wolfgang Melz, keyboardist Jim Gordon (not
to be confused with the drummer by the same name), Flying Burrito
Chris Ethridge, and Muscle Shoals keyboardist Spooner Oldham. Jesse's
group regularly included a horn section comprised of saxophonist Jerry
Jumonville, trumpeter Gary Barone, and trombonist Jock Ellis, who
played from head charts and followed Jesse's commitment to musical
improvisation. At the end of each gig, Jesse ordered Pete Waddington
to divide the money, sometimes as little as ten bucks per bandmember.
"You don't take any money and I don't take any money and divide up
the rest," Jesse instructed.[51]

Similar to Leon Russell, Eric Clapton, George Harrison, and a few
others, Jesse established his own crew of musicians who were loyal to

him. If they all had other gigs, they could still be thought of as Jesse's guys. The common denominator was a devoted love and knowledge of the foundational rock and roll records from the 1950s. One night in 1972, the band got into a serious debate when someone asked drummer Gary Mallaber his pick for the greatest shuffle ever committed to tape. "Well, it's got to be 'Honky Tonk (Part 1 and Part 2)' by the Bill Doggett Quartet," Mallaber didn't hesitate. Jesse fell out of his chair. That was his answer too, and it might have been when he got the idea to enlist Doggett's sax player Clifford Scott to play on his next solo album.[52]

The Jesse Davis band worked the old Taj Mahal stables, the Ash Grove and Topanga Corral, as well as the Whisky a Go Go on Sunset and the Troubadour on Santa Monica Boulevard, the latter venue hosting more hitmaking musicians on a typical Monday night than any other place in the world. In fact, a significant share of Jesse's audience—sometimes one hundred people, sometimes ten, sometimes more people in the band than the audience—was comprised of fellow musicians. Everyone heard about Jesse and wanted to see him play. Jackson Browne remembers how Jesse often played his best licks with his back to the audience, as though he didn't want to reveal his secrets.[53]

Though Jesse was at the height of his musical talent, backed by some stellar bandmates, he struggled to assume the position of frontman and lead vocalist. Going back to his Oklahoma groups, he always had someone else to play that part. Jesse came across as laconic and withdrawn. Critics pounced. "If his Ash Grove performance is any indication, it's the role of solid supporter rather than central figure that suits him best," the *Los Angeles Times* suggested. "Part of the problem can be traced to his halfhearted singing, which is usually inaudible and, when it does reach the ear, rather expressionless." Accusing Jesse's group of "lumbering in a directionless fashion," the reviewer thought more guitar solos would create a focal point, suggesting that Jesse's few big lead guitar spots mostly just teased his audience. The reviewer ultimately rejected Jesse and company's performance as a Delaney & Bonnie imitation, absent any real excitement.[54]

A review of Jesse's set opening for the Steve Miller Band at the Santa Monica Civic Center was kinder. "As soon as we entered the auditorium, our olfactory systems were assailed by the pungent odor of Killer Weed," it begins, "and I got an immediate contact high that told me this would be a great concert." While the review suggested that Jesse's band was probably better suited for a club, it acknowledged the audience's fervent reception. And, rare in Jesse Ed Davis media coverage, this critic loved his singing: "Davis' laid back easy manner and clear solid voice is at once relaxing and exciting."[55]

In January 1971, Jesse accepted a feature spot opening for Big Brother and the Holding Company at the El Monte Legion Stadium. On this occasion, he enlisted two drummers—Jim Karstein and Gary Mallaber. This worked well in "The Pink Elephant," as the venue was known for its massive size and pink paint. The El Monte Legion Stadium was designed as a school district complex, though it never actually served that purpose. Some of Jesse's heroes—Fats Domino, Sam Cooke, Ray Charles, Ike and Tina, and his own former bandleader Conway Twitty—had performed there. Just outside of Los Angeles city limits, the El Monte was proudly integrated, initially one of the only major venues that would book Black artists when others denied them. Black, Chicano, white, and Native American people arrived from around the region to fill the stadium while popular DJ Art Laboe promoted the concerts and appeared as the emcee. Today the old venue is a post office.

Lacking an agent and any coherent touring plan, Jesse and his band sometimes ended up in strange, seemingly arbitrary places. In December 1971, Jesse flew to posh Palm Beach, Florida, with a down-home band featuring drummer Jim Karstein, Skyhill harmonica player Junior Markham, Flying Burrito bassist Chris Ethridge, and the great Muscle Shoals keyboardist Spooner Oldham. At the invitation of Jesse's label boss Jerry Wexler, the group of three Okies, an Alabaman, and a Mississippian performed at a Breakers Hotel wedding reception for an audience of famous actors and aristocrats. Film producer, Delaney & Bonnie manager, and heir to the Dixie Cup fortune Alan Pariser married Lady Patricia Pelham-Clinton-Hope, daughter of the Duke and Duchess of New Castle. Jesse had previously played in the courts of metaphorical British rock royalty, but he was now performing for literal British royalty. One attendee, however, scoffed at Jesse's band, with their "props like long hair, biblical sandals and babies strapped to their backs. Cute." Every musician has stories about strange gigs in strange places. The 9th Duke of Newcastle-under-Lyne getting down to "Red Dirt Boogie, Brother" certainly makes for a good one.[56]

Also in 1971, Jesse and company flew to Seattle for a successful three-night residency at a local club. At the hotel, after each gig, the band gathered to drink beers and listen to Karstein's old 45s on his portable children's record player. From there, Jesse and company were scheduled to play a joint out in Bellingham. Arriving at the venue, they saw a warehouse with bullet holes in the wall. "I'm not going in there," Jesse protested, sensing bad vibes. They left without a word and went straight to the Seattle airport, where they had about twelve hours to kill, so everyone took acid.

Karstein was offended, not on behalf of the venue but because of his commitment to the gig. You play the gig, Karstein believed, period. He had been a friend and bandmate to Jesse for five years, first with Taj Mahal and then with Jesse as a solo artist. Now he began doubting whether there was a future with Jesse. "It seemed like, he was kinda waiting for them to come to him, rather than for him to get out and actually hustle his own act," Karstein reasoned. "I wasn't too crazy about playing in that place, either, but we had gone all that way, was right outside the thing, and then we had to sit in the airport until 10 o'clock that night. I would've just as soon set up and played, making our twenty bucks or whatever." Keyboardist Ben Sidran also wondered about Jesse's strategy, or if he even had one. "It didn't seem to me that too many decisions were being made at all, by anybody," he recalls. "He hired you, so play the song. That was it. Do what you did, and then we're gonna go back here and get high."[57]

All told, ATCO spent $180,000 on Jesse's first two solo albums. "He spent a fortune on me," Jesse said about Jerry Wexler. Much of it went toward hours of studio time and the elaborate cast of musicians who populated Jesse's album notes. Jesse was often over budget on studio sessions because he spent so much time fighting with his vocals. One time he played something new for Pete Waddington and asked what he thought. "Wow, that's really good. It's got a lot of feeling, like Leon." Jesse was embarrassed. Pete quickly realized he had insulted his boss with the Leon comparison. In any case, Jesse's records took a loss, selling only in the "high hundreds," Jesse once quipped. Maybe he wasn't kidding.[58]

Regularly hitting the road would have helped sell Jesse's albums while engendering radio play. Jesse had ample experience from his days criss-crossing the country with Taj Mahal and Conway Twitty, and he had numerous popular music friends who could have taken him out as an opening act. There was serious talk of a tour with Elton John in 1971. Jesse's "Glide Band," as he planned to call them, would have featured two drummers in Sandy Konikoff and Gary Mallaber. But the tour plan fell apart. Jesse would have benefited from a manager, but he initially recoiled at the idea, preferring self-determination. But then Jesse didn't demonstrate a great business acumen. "He just didn't have his business shit together at all," Jesse's bassist Bob Glaub realized. "It just seemed like that wasn't in his wheelhouse."[59]

Jesse was recording for a major record label and working with some of the best musicians in the business, but that didn't guarantee a reg-ular cash flow. As exciting as life was at the Hurricane House, there were some lean days and weeks. On calls with friends, Patti occasion-ally mentioned how they were out of food. Bill remembers subsisting on Top Ramen instant noodles. It didn't help that Jesse and Patti some-times spent frivolously, not so much an act of financial irresponsibility as a reflection of their youthful artist ethos. Jesse had to hustle. It was never easy for him, even as he reached the top. His music characterized his experience entering and navigating the music business now on his terms. "Keep Me Comin'," "Keep a-Movin'," "Keep Steppin'," he cried.

In June 1972, with Jackson Browne's "Doctor My Eyes" featuring Jesse's signature guitar solo sitting in the top ten, Jesse was so broke he had to borrow money from his old high school friend Mike Smith to buy a plane ticket to Oklahoma City for their ten-year high school reunion. That didn't preclude Jesse and Patti from making a royal entrance at the reunion. They rolled up in a rented white convertible, with Jesse sporting two-toned wingtip Oxfords, designer shades, and a fabulous white suit, not unlike the one George wore at the Bangladesh concert. Patti, with beach blonde curls that fell atop an aquamarine dress, practically resembled a mermaid from the Pacific Ocean. The alumni committee enlisted Jesse to perform at the event. He was so proud of what he achieved and who he had become.[60]

With his records in stores but his future with ATCO as a solo artist uncertain, Jesse increasingly depended on his work as a producer for other artists and his growing reputation as a top session musician, now earning triple scale through the musicians' union. There would be one more shot at a solo career, and a new opportunity to again play the role of lead guitarist and principal collaborator for another artist—this time, for arguably the biggest rock star in the world. Each path—producer, session musician, solo artist—featured its own benefits and pitfalls. The mutually reinforcing tension between them would partly prevent Jesse from getting very far in any one direction. Meanwhile, increasingly perilous consumption of drugs, and an increasing dependence on them, began damaging his physical and mental health. Soon it began also taking a toll on his family of three.

Seven

THE CIRCUS COMES TO TOWN

R EFLECTING ON the arc of his career, Jesse once said, "One day, the circus just left town." That referred to both the people he played with and the music they made: the performers and the act. But Jesse's statement doesn't indicate whether the circus *had* to move on, as a consequence of natural cycles in the popular music industry, or if the circus chose to leave him behind. In another sense, the circus meant the spectacle of rock stardom. Rock and roll could be a dangerous job, filled with occupational hazards, as it traveled from town to town and people ran away with it. The life could be hard on people like Jesse, who sometimes exhibited self-sabotage, exacerbated by addiction, or vice versa. The circus took as much as it gave, but Jesse was experienced, now having worked seriously in the music business for ten years, backing Conway Twitty, Taj Mahal, Bob Dylan, George Harrison, and more. He knew the game and he embraced all it required and encompassed. Overcome by the thrill of it all, he decided it was worth it.

From 1971 through 1975, Jesse's schedule was filled. He worked practically every major studio in Los Angeles, launched and relaunched his solo career, produced both new and veteran artists, worked stages from clubs to arenas, and played with the most popular musicians of his time, including Dylan, the Beatles, the Stones, the Allmans, and more. Indeed, sensational rock and roll stories can overshadow the fact that Jesse worked incredibly hard. His was a labor-intensive occupation. Appearing on more than one hundred albums and singles in his career, much of that work in a roughly five-year period, he simultaneously advanced his solo project.

Jesse achieved this distinction as a Native American person who labored in Hollywood like his Seminole-Mvskoke grandfather had— like the thousands of Native people who moved to Los Angeles for work and social opportunities, and like the numerous Indigenous people who helped create the Hollywood industry from its inception, as actors, producers, technicians, and more.

During the early 1970s, Jesse became one of a small but influential coterie of Native American artists who achieved the highest levels of music business success. What set him apart even within select company was how he thrived in multiple roles. He was literally and figuratively a producer, heard and seen from album to stage. He performed at a time when Native people, young and old, were demanding and exercising treaty rights and self-determination and were practicing new methods of social, political, and cultural visibility and adaptability, especially in the arts, through film, radio, literature, and song. As an Indigenous music hero, Jesse both experienced and embodied these trends.

JESSE'S SESSION WORK was financially lucrative. It also afforded him notoriety as a professional musician. It took special skill to gain distinction as a session musician. Those who did were not middling musicians who couldn't do anything else but often the opposite: musicians who were so talented and adaptable that they were constantly in demand. They had to play proficiently in a wide variety of styles, under great pressure, but with great technique. They needed to be both creative and improvisational, while simultaneously capable of quickly meeting a producer's or artist's alternatingly specific and cryptic demands. Above all, they depended on a strong sense of humor and camaraderie to preserve their sanity. "There is a real underreporting and undercrediting of those session musicians from the 1960s and 70s," Mike Nesmith, guitarist and writer for the Monkees, stressed. "These are the greatest musicians in the world. Period. Jesse Ed Davis deserves the attention."[1]

Jesse quickly rose through the ranks of the American Federation of Musicians Local 47—Los Angeles to become a first-call guitarist making triple union scale. In fact, he reached a level that put him in an elite group that even defies the term of "session musician." "No, no. He's not one of those guys," Jackson Browne insists. Jesse was more than an industrious plug-and-play machine. He was similar to his peer Ry Cooder in that, if either got the impression they were on hand to play anything other than genuine music from the soul, they'd take their guitar and disappear undetected. "Jesse didn't do sessions," Browne says. "He played music."[2]

If Jesse perceived an injustice of any nature, artistically or personally, he wasn't afraid to speak his mind and surrender his pay. One music partner recalls Jesse working in the studio with Stephen Stills, who was cutting his first solo album. When Stills wouldn't stop hitting on singer Rita Coolidge, Jesse told him to cool it and focus on the music. Stills sent the producer over to inform Jesse that he was not in charge of any aspect of the session. Jesse laughed, packed up, and left without another word.

Jesse and guitarist Danny "Kootch" Kortchmar worked together so frequently they eventually started getting booked as a duo. Neither was afraid to argue with producers and engineers. When put together, they were a formidable tandem. When one producer tried telling them how to play a certain groove, Kootch scoffed, "So, you mean the absence of a groove?" Jesse loved that retort and often repeated it as shorthand for a bad music environment or idea. "He and I were specialty guys that had a certain sound and when called on dates we were called upon to be ourselves," Kootch says. They didn't consider it an insult to be called a session musician, but they knew they were more valuable than someone merely hired to play something someone else dictated. "You wouldn't sit down and nitpick what you want Jesse Ed to play," their frequent drum partner Russ Kunkel recalls. "You would give him as many tracks as he wanted."[3]

Stringing high-profile sessions together, Jesse occasionally had money coming in faster than he could manage it. He would have benefited from an accountant, but he hated the idea. It wasn't uncommon to see him walking around with upward of ten thousand dollars crammed into his jeans' pockets. Making triple scale, or three times the standard musicians' union rate, was the mark of greatness in the session world. Sometimes Jesse would exceed it with bonuses. In 1972, a triple-scale three-hour session could pay $700. In some instances, if Jesse had to cancel one session to play another, he could earn $500 for just a half-hour of work. The cash was a reflection of Jesse's coveted talent, but it was also a reflection of the demands on his time, as his schedule determined his rate just as much as his talent did. Producers would occasionally have to outbid each other for Jesse's services.[4]

The session appearances could be exhausting. Neighbors noticed Jesse speeding in and out of the Hurricane House alley in Patti's Porsche with his large amplifier precariously strapped to its modest luggage rack and his guitar tossed in the backseat without a case. Jesse might work three to four sessions per day, six to seven days per week. His personal assistant Pete Waddington always scheduled his boss one hour early because he was perpetually running one hour behind. The grueling nature of the work encouraged a sort of mutual aid society among the elite session players. "If somebody was going through any kind of shit in their life, guys were there to talk, and be supportive, and hang with them, so it went beyond the music," bassist Lee Sklar explains. "Everybody spent a lot of time together away from the studio, too." It was a rare money-making venture that seemed devoid of competition and grounded in creativity and community.[5]

ONE OF JESSE's greatest career and artistic opportunities emerged when he was "lucky enough to be in on the Bob Dylan–Leon Russell experiment," he put it. The March 1971 Blue Rock Studio session in New York's Greenwich Village was born out of Leon Russell's desire to hear Dylan play with a band again after years of solo exercises. Leon had heard about Dylan's amazing talent for crafting songs on the spot while making *Nashville Skyline*. Dylan was apprehensive. "When I get even two or three more people, it's just crazy—it goes haywire," he complained. "Well, how about me bring a little rhythm section up to you?" Leon persisted. "And what I'd like to do is, I'll give 'em the changes. And then I wanna watch you write the songs, to those changes." When Dylan finally relented, Jesse couldn't believe what he witnessed. "We came into the studio and Dylan didn't even have a pencil or paper. We began playing 'Rock of Ages' and 'Gospel Hymn' and it turned into Dylan's 'When I Paint My Masterpiece.' "[6]

Leon could have brought anyone with him. Dylan could have demanded anyone. They would have come. That Leon picked Jesse says a volume about Jesse's talent and Leon's confidence in him. "Well, he was unusual—a very unusual player," Leon said about Jesse—a compliment to be sure. "It didn't get any better than playing with Leon Russell, Carl Radle, and Jesse Ed Davis," Jim Keltner insists, wishing that core group would have continued working together. "I just know that I never, never got that feeling again, ever, with anybody, and I played with all the best in the world."[7]

It's a thrill hearing Dylan play with the team Leon christened the Tulsa Tops. Before joining Dylan in New York, the group recorded some Dylan tunes in Los Angeles in January 1971, both as a warm-up for the studio date and as an early birthday present for Dylan. Their covers of "She Belongs to Me," "It's All Over Now, Baby Blue," "Love Minus Zero," and "A Hard Rain's A-Gonna Fall," are all stamped with the Tulsa sound. Reactivated in New York, the group was still cooking. Dylan exclusively sang during these sessions, surrendering musical directorship to Leon, who counted off the tunes.

More than any other song, "When I Paint My Masterpiece" showcases Dylan's peerless lyrical talent as he leaps through centuries to report stirring scenes from ancient Rome. Jesse's slinky guitar weaves through Keltner's deft brushwork, Radle's rhythmic bass, and Leon's bouncy piano. Across multiple takes, the song developed in real time as the music transformed with the lyrics, including an unreleased fourth take with a brilliant Jesse outro guitar lick. They painted a masterpiece indeed, with each member coloring Dylan's evocative sketch.[8]

The rousing "Watching the River Flow," released as a single, is even more impressive. Dylan's lyrics refer to the actual songwriting challenge

George Harrison, Klaus Voormann, Jesse Ed Davis (age 26),
and Eric Clapton at the Concert for Bangladesh, 1971. *(Associated Press)*

George Harrison, John Trudell, Bob Dylan, and Jesse Ed Davis (age 42)
at the Palomino Club, 1987. Photo by Abe Perlstein. *(Abe Perlstein)*

Jesse's Comanche
great-great-grandfather Tah-
pui ("To Scout on Foot").
*(Kansas State Historical
Society)*

Jesse's great-great-grandmother
Alice Brown Davis, first female chief of
the Seminole Nation in Indian Territory.
(Seminole Nation Museum)

Anna Poolaw, Jasper Saunkeah, and Jasper Saunkeah Jr., July 6, 1938. Photo by Alphia O. Hart. *(The Gateway to Oklahoma History, Oklahoma Historical Society)*

Jesse Edwin Davis II, William Graham Davis, and Madison Berkley Davis, 1942. *(Courtesy of Richenda Davis Bates)*

Jesse Edwin Davis II, 1966. Fifteen years earlier, his art professor erroneously predicted Davis would become "completely absorbed in" the "White man's world." *(Courtesy of Philbrook Museum Archive)*

Jesse Edwin Davis III (age 5), Vivian Davis, and Jesse Edwin Davis II, 1949. *(Courtesy of The Oklahoman)*

CHEYENNE DOG SOLDIER

Cheyenne Dog Soldier by Jesse Edwin Davis II, 1959, tempera. *(The Arthur and Shifra Silberman Collection, National Cowboy and Western Heritage Museum)*

Eddie Davis (age 10) and his cousin Mary Helen Deer (first and second from right), St. Luke's Methodist Church, Oklahoma City, 1954. *(Courtesy of Mary Helen Deer)*

Eddie Davis (age 12, third row, sixth from left),
Carol Furr (first row, third from left), 1956. *(Courtesy of Carol Furr)*

Eddie Davis, football lettermen senior yearbook photo, 1962. *(Courtesy of Michael Smith)*

*EDDIE DAVIS
Wt. 174
Ht. 5'10"

Continentals/Joe Banana & the Bunch/New Breed. Front row: Roger Edwards, Mike Boyle, Chris Frederickson; second row: Larry Hollis, Ed Davis, Warren Sherman. *(Courtesy of Roger Edwards)*

Early Continentals lineup (Ted Kalman, Eddie Davis, Rex Kennard, John Ware) in a '61 Corvette. *(Courtesy of John Ware)*

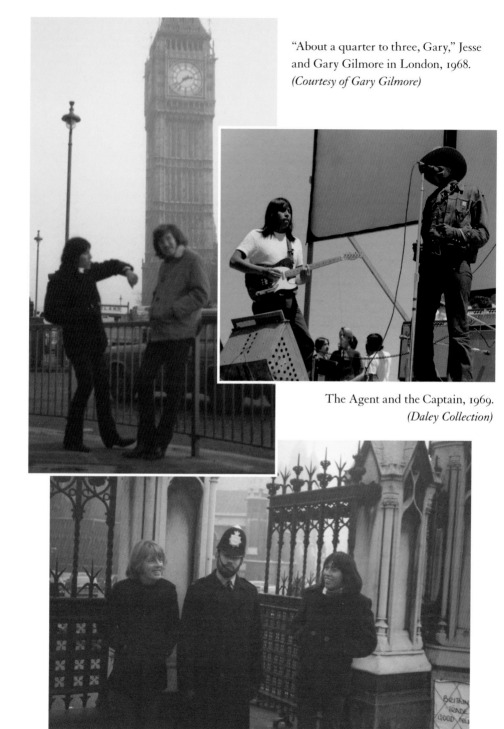

"About a quarter to three, Gary," Jesse and Gary Gilmore in London, 1968. *(Courtesy of Gary Gilmore)*

The Agent and the Captain, 1969. *(Daley Collection)*

Chuck Blackwell, Bobby, and Jesse in London, 1968. Photo by Gary Gilmore. *(Courtesy of Gary Gilmore)*

Jesse and Billy, circa 1971. *(Daley Collection)*

Billy opening his birthday gift from John Lennon, a complete box of Beatles and solo Beatle albums. The Rickenbacker guitar Jesse bought Billy stands nearby. *(Daley Collection)*

Jesse and Patti, Northeast High School Ten-Year Reunion, Oklahoma City, 1972. *(Daley Collection)*

The proposed cover image for *Keep Me Comin'* that Jesse rejected. Painting by Wayne McLoughlin. *(Courtesy of Mona Maiman)*

Jesse was proud of his headlining gig promoting *Keep Me Comin'* in 1973. He kept this photo with him for years, and took it to Hawaii as one of very few possessions. Left to right: Jesse, John Herron ("Jerry Lee Domino"), Bob Glaub, David "Buzzy" Buchanan (drums), Jerry Jumonville, Jock Ellis, Gary Barone, Ray Eckstein. Santa Monica City College Amphitheatre, 1973. Photo by Howard Tsukamoto. *(Courtesy of John Granito)*

Ronnie Wood, Rod Stewart, and Jesse getting loose before a Faces show, 1975. *(Daley Collection)*

Jesse in his dark Venice Beach apartment, circa 1976–77. *(Daley Collection)*

Jesse at Ming Lowe's in Palm Desert, circa 1977, ready to undergo heroin addiction treatment. His short hair may have been a mournful gesture to his father's recent passing, as is customary in Kiowa culture. Photo by Ming Lowe. *(Courtesy of Ming Lowe)*

Tantalayo and Jesse, wedding ceremony in Oklahoma City,
August 1980. Photo by Gary Gilmore. *(Courtesy of Gary Gilmore)*

Jesse and Kelly, circa 1986. Photo by Jackie Warledo.
(Courtesy of Dave Tahchawwickah)

Working hard on Gene Clark's *White Light* album with Jesse in the producer's chair at Village Recorder, Los Angeles, 1971. Left to right: Jesse, Joe Zagarino, Carlie Clark, Chris Ethridge, Gene Clark. Photo by Cheryl Waddington. *(Courtesy of Cheryl Waddington)*

Grafitti Band, the Palace Theater, Los Angeles, February 5, 1987. Left to right: Jesse, Mark Shark, Bob Tsukamoto, Jim Ehinger, Gary Ray, John Trudell. Photo by Abe Perlstein. *(Abe Perlstein)*

"Jesse, Waving Goodbye, Throwing Love out the Window, with Holes in His Arms." Painting by Ming Lowe. *(Courtesy of Ming Lowe)*

Jesse goofing around before a gig at the Palomino, 1987.
Photo by Tim Garon. *(Courtesy of Laura Garon)*

Bill Davis Noriega with the author in the alley behind 20 Hurricane Street, Marina del Rey, where Billy, Patti, and Jesse took promo pictures for Jesse's first solo album in 1970. Photo by Tammy Dunkley-Nikolov, August 2022.

underway in front of his dual audience and band of Okies. "What's the matter with me?" he pleads in frustration, having promised to write a song on the spot. "I don't have much to say." Actually, he says plenty. So does Jesse, who was silent between takes but spoke forcefully through his guitar, beginning the song with a whining slide lick that scampers down the fretboard while Dylan reports on the scene in the studio.

The song began as a swinging 4/4 rocker, marked by fuzzier versions of Jesse's solos and Keltner's syncopated ride cymbal riffs. Initial attempts focus on the group's fondness for a false ending that they struggle to execute. "You can just let me and Ed pick it up after the break," Leon finally says, not wanting to offend. That problem resolved, they continue panning for gold through several more takes, each featuring a completely different Jesse Davis opening guitar hook and feature guitar solo, played both with and without a slide. Like Dylan, Jesse rarely played a song the same way twice and preferred improvising his parts. Meanwhile, Dylan tries different lyrics: "Yesterday on the street I saw somebody who'd forgotten how to smile," he sings. "Seems like when everything turns out right there'll always be someone to cry." Even better: "People disagreeing over just about everything, seems so hard to take / makes you almost think that everything in History is just one big ol' mistake," Dylan preaches, this time with even greater verve in his voice.

With the lyrics taking shape, the song seemed stuck. Dylan appeared exhausted. Like Jesse, he wasn't partial to endless experiments in the studio. "I'll do one more time," he warns. Either oblivious or recognizing his last chance, Leon leans into the microphone: "Can we do one as a shuffle?" "Yeah!" Bob exclaims with a burst of new energy. It's a revelation before it ends. This take became the released version. "I think that's it, for my money," Dylan informs the band as they cheer in agreement. Jesse's approving laugh finally enters the space cleared by his guitar.

The session also produced numerous unreleased covers of American music classics, including "Spanish Harlem," "That Lucky Old Sun," Josh White's haunting "Blood Red River," Leadbelly's "I'm Alabama Bound," and "I'm a Ladies Man," featuring a rare example of Jesse's splendid country picking probably rooted in old rounds with Conway Twitty. The best of the bunch is a swaggering rendition of "I'd Just Be

Fool Enough (to Fall)." Heavier than the Johnny Cash version, it's one of Dylan's greatest turns. Mystifyingly, it remains unreleased.

It must have been just as exciting for Dylan as it was for the band on hand. Both "When I Paint My Masterpiece" and "Watching the River Flow" still feature in Dylan's setlist over fifty years later, signaling his enduring pride in these numbers. Though these two Blue Rock session originals continued evolving through live performances, they could only have emerged from that particular session, written with that particular group, everyone's contribution essential, including Jesse's. In fact, Keltner still largely attributes those recordings' success to the partner he misses so much. "That groove that we played, that shuffle, you could not go wrong with Leon and Carl, but when you put Jesse in there with it, it just became the thing that . . . I could've played that sleeping. I mean, it just was so easy, man. Jesse was the shuffle king." Renowned slide guitarist Bonnie Raitt certainly noticed Jesse's playing with Dylan. For her, that's when Jesse first came into view. Hearing "Watching the River Flow," she immediately thought, "Who the heck is that?" and went searching for an answer.[9]

A second obvious contender for Jesse's greatest session work can be heard in Jackson Browne's first top-ten hit, "Doctor My Eyes." It contains Jesse's signature guitar solo, the one most often cited by fans, fellow musicians, and journalists. Some go further, calling it one of the greatest guitar solos in the classic rock canon. It captures everything that was so impressive about Jesse's musicianship, evident in the tone, composition, and personality of his performance. It recalls some of his best work with Taj Mahal, but with even greater confidence and idiosyncratic style. No one since has played that solo quite as memorably. Jackson Browne, who credits Jesse with making "Doctor My Eyes" a rock tune and a hit, doubts anyone really can. Jesse's solo is inimitable and sublime.

The story behind Jesse's appearance on the song is equally compelling. Jackson met Jesse a few years prior when both were auditioning for Pamela Polland's band. Neither got the gig, but Jackson didn't forget Jesse, especially his imposing physical stature. Jesse measured six feet tall, but to Jackson and drummer Russ Kunkel, he seemed much taller when he arrived at their session in 1972, like a gentle giant. "I thought he was just magical," Kunkel says. "He was so striking," Jackson agrees, still picturing that day:

> To have him playing the music that he was playing, in the middle of all of this sort of revival of interest in Native Americans, the whole hippie counter-culture involvement with Native American culture. . . . But then, in many ways, he had more confluence or connection with what we thought of as southern. Jesse Ed was just so vibrantly, cinematically Indian. But, when he spoke, he spoke with that deep *Oklahoma* . . . really deep Oklahoma accent.[10]

Jackson had a song called "Nightingale" cued up for Jesse to contribute a part. Jesse took a seat in the control room, listened one time, and objected. "I don't want to play on that." It made Jackson doubt the song so much he ended up giving it to the Eagles to record. Then Jackson instructed the engineer to load a different song. Jackson himself was unsure about this one. Maybe Jesse could help bring it to life. It was in a skeletal state, just Jackson's piano and scratch vocal, Lee Sklar's bass, and Russ Kunkel's congas. Kunkel later overdubbed drums. "Okay, yeah, I'll do that," Jesse said when the song ended. He strolled into the tracking room, plugged his Telecaster into a small Fender Vibro Champ tube amp, ideal for running quickly between sessions, and cranked it to maximum volume. "That's just these two instruments," Jackson notes, referring to Jesse and his guitar, "you put them together and it's magic."[11]

Amazingly, Jesse's lead guitar on the final version of "Doctor My Eyes" was his first and only time playing it. One take, without even a complete rehearsal. Of course, the solo is brilliant, but there's more. Notice Jesse's sweet and subtle licks in the second verse as he begins dancing into the shuffle. Then the grand entry at the 1:42 mark as Jesse comes stepping and singing to the beat of Kunkel's congas, giving it a tribal feel. One final run through the chorus and Jesse returns with a few more moves. It's beautiful and free, evoking his past as a young powwow dancer. "It was really performance driven," bassist Sklar recalls. "It's a really quirky solo when you listen to it." The song fades with Jesse's solo playing into the forever. Jesse was indeed magical.[12]

"Holy crap," Kunkel exclaimed in the studio when Jesse's guitar stopped. Everyone was thrilled. If that was Jesse's first run through it, imagine where he might take it with a few more attempts. "You ready for another one?" engineer Richard Orshoff asked through Jesse's headphones. "No. That's it," Jesse declined. "That's it?" Orshoff replied, puzzled. "Yeah man. I got another session. I gotta go!" Jackson looked around the control room in disbelief. "Here's a guy that was on his way somewhere else who threw this off in one pass," Jackson says. "That's what makes everybody stop and pause for a minute and realize that this wasn't something that he worked at. . . . He was just so spontaneously plugged in to something magical, it didn't require work on his part."[13]

Jesse was unplugging his gear when Orshoff came in begging to try one more idea. Could Jesse add a second guitar part, maybe trying an old trick? If he could touch the tip of his guitar headstock on the amplifier to produce feedback, that would be great. Jackson remembers the disdain in Jesse's expression, as if he were saying, "You fucking tourist." Jesse had tried his entire career to *not* be the guy who performs cheap tricks. "For you, I'll do it." Jesse smiled. "Run the tape."[14]

Jackson deleted the feedback part, though it might have been too late. It could be what soured Jesse on the song. In typical Jesse fashion, he claimed he didn't like his part for the FM radio staple. It wasn't his best work, he suggested, and he felt rushed. Everyone else recalled the opposite. It was Jesse who was in a hurry to be somewhere else. Bassist Lee Sklar may agree that Jesse's exceptional solo on the song doesn't define his work: "I think he went far deeper than that." But the soul and performance of Jesse's solo are unimpeachable. Perhaps his dissatisfaction was an example of his self-sabotaging ways. Always determined to lay back in a musical setting, sometimes to the point of turning his back to the audience, did Jesse shine too brightly?[15]

THROUGHOUT THE EARLY 1970s, while launching and relaunching his solo career, Jesse continued guesting on albums by strangers, friends, and occasionally his heroes. His schedule was full, his assignments were rewarding and diverse, and his playing was remarkable. Highlights from this period include work on two Arlo Guthrie albums, a Steve Miller Band album playing alongside his own bandmates Ben Sidran and Gary Mallaber, perhaps his most wicked groove on Joe Cocker's "Black-Eyed Blues," searing slide guitar on Cocker's "High Time We Went," and a masterful acoustic slide guitar duel with British folk musician Bert Jansch on "Open Up the Watergate." "[Jesse] wasn't the only slide player around," recalled Monkees guitarist Mike Nesmith, who produced the Jansch album, "but he had an authenticity to him."[16]

Farther from the beaten path, you can hear Jesse on his Skyhill pal Marc Benno's *Minnows*, playing lead on the pensive "Speak Your Mind." "He wasn't just playing blues licks or something," Benno says. "If it was an original song, he would find a melodic line that would fit perfectly in the song." Jesse's originality is evident on jazz luminary Charles Lloyd's inventive "Rusty Toy" from Lloyd's avant-garde *Warm Waters* (1971). It's one of the most intriguing entries in Jesse's catalog, and an important occasion when jazz-loving Jesse collaborated with a bona fide jazz master. "Jesse served the music well," Lloyd remembers, stressing Jesse's determination to play for the song, and not for his ego.[17]

Most significant, Jesse began appearing on records by artists who populated his own record collection, including some of the most esteemed blues musicians of all time. In the early '70s, many veteran bluesmen sought to reach white rock and roll fans who loved groups like Led Zeppelin that borrowed heavily from foundational blues music. To some degree, the popular rock acts owed their audience to the elder blues statesmen. Younger blues guitarists like Jesse were happy to support such commercial endeavors, wherein they could gain opportunities to play with idols such as Lightnin' Hopkins, John Lee Hooker, Albert King, and others. One critic went so far as to suggest that Jesse helped "Iceman" Albert Collins, another master of the Telecaster, "rekindle his fervour."[18]

When Jesse arrived at a B.B. King session for *L.A. Midnight* (1972), it was about an hour past the album's namesake. King was relaxing in the chair, tie undone, when he saw Jesse enter across the room. His whole face and body lit up. *"Mr. Jesse Ed Davis!"* King announced, before anxiously plugging Jesse into a guitar and instructing his band to prepare for more recording. Parked next to legendary "Tutti Frutti" drummer Earl Palmer, Jesse and fellow hotshot guitarist Joe Walsh dueled with the eminent King on several cuts from this overlooked gem of an album.[19]

One of the other "Three Kings" of blues guitar gave Jesse a different reception. From the minute Jesse plugged in for Albert King's *Lovejoy*, the "Velvet Bulldozer," as King was known, began plowing into Jesse with insults. The album took Jesse back to Leon's Skyhill Studio, where King and his Flying V guitar arrived in a tense and cantankerous mood. Leon and Jim Keltner had played with Albert King before. Maybe they could form a buffer. Alas, King condemned the shuffle Jesse played. Breaking tradition, Jesse gave in and tried to play what King wanted. Yet each time Jesse got the beat down, King asked for something different. Jesse finally snapped. *"Man, I can play any kind of shuffle you want!"* he barked. After listing a dozen or so signature shuffles, Jesse yelled, "Hell, I can play a Louis Prima shuffle!" At this left-field reference to the New Orleans trumpeter Jesse loved growing up, everyone, including King, couldn't help but bust up laughing. Jesse was angry and serious, but he broke the ice. "Jesse stood his ground, toe to toe with the great Albert King, and I loved watching that!" Jim Keltner says, still laughing about it, before concluding, "But the thing is, Albert knew that Jesse was a bad son of a gun."[20]

Jesse continued earning respect all around town. When they bumped into each other coming off the elevator at the Hyatt House, Little Richard shouted at him, *"Damn Jesse! How you doing?! You almost look as good as I do!"* Then, one night in the studio, another hero of Jesse's apologized profusely when his session ran into Jesse's time slot. When Sly Stone and his infinite entourage finally made their exit, Sly begged Jesse's forgiveness with a big bag of cocaine and then paid for Jesse's studio time.[21]

In studios, drugs were sometimes currency, but sometimes they commandeered the sessions. During overnight recording marathons, players might become ensnared in a Seussian maze of microphone cables that seemed to have no ends and no beginnings. They'd give up and try again the next night. Guitarist Robby Krieger is certain that, after the Doors disbanded, he played his first-ever session alongside Jesse for a wealthy Japanese artist. He remembers how Jesse mentored him in the new setting, teaching him the music and how to function as a session pro. The only thing is, Krieger cannot recall the actual artist or album. "Who knows if it ever came out," he ponders. "It was a weird thing."[22]

As effortlessly as he cruised between parties and studios, Jesse frequently appeared as a live guest with various artists. In June 1972, back in Oklahoma for his high school reunion, he took the stage backing J. J. Cale and Freddie King at the Tulsa Fairgrounds, where a massive crowd had gathered for the Leon Russell Show. In September 1973, Jesse sat in with the Allman Brothers Band at the LA Forum, opening their second set with "Southbound" and "Statesboro Blues," the latter song an homage to Jesse's formative influence on Duane Allman, who had recently died in a motorcycle accident. Allmans' guitarist Dickey Betts, in partnership with his Ojibwe wife Sandy Bluesky Wabegijig, organized this concert as a benefit for the North American Indian Foundation and its mission to protect Indigenous religions and promote cultural renewal. It's an early example of Jesse's career explicitly crossing paths with the period's prevailing modes and goals of Indigenous activism—formal activist organizations broadcasting cultural and political persistence through mainstream media and popular entertainment.[23]

Jesse produced other artists through his Washita Productions company that was an extension of his ATCO contract. The artistic aspects of producing came naturally to Jesse, but the business dimensions did not. His work as a producer reflected his work as a guitarist in that he approached the position with a care and restraint that encouraged an organic feel, free of clutter, with room to breathe. Jesse's best work in this can be heard on Gene Clark's *White Light* (1971).

One particular production story captures Jesse in all his glory. In 1970, some of his old friends from Oklahoma blew into town with their group Southwind. Jesse took drummer Erik Dalton to meet his new Okie friends and to see Delaney & Bonnie perform at Carolina Lanes, a combination bowling alley and strip club by the airport. Jesse mentioned his (at the time) new production company and soon Southwind hit Sunset Sound to cut a record with Jesse in charge. A few weeks into the project, approaching the finish line, the band showed up at the studio on schedule, but the gates were locked and the parking lot empty. Just before giving up, they spotted a box sitting by the curb. In it were their master tapes. Jesse had gone into the studio alone, added slide guitar across the album, mixed it, and stuck a note on the tapes: "Here's the final album—hope you love it!"

Southwind's record label boss Bob Krasner was livid. Jesse didn't seem to mind. Arriving in a fancy suit, Jesse appeared for a meeting at Krasner's office. Krasner, fresh from a Rolling Stones project, a big cross dangling around his neck, waltzed into his small office to find it overflowing with Jesse and the band. Before Krasner was in his seat, Jesse launched in: "I want my $20,000 for producing the record." "We never got the proofs on that," Krasner snapped. "I'm not paying you!'" After a few more words, Krasner suddenly leaped over his desk and the two wrestled each other to the little floor space that remained. "It's the president of the record company and Ed Davis and we don't know what to do!" Dalton laughs, before stressing, "It wasn't funny at the time." The record never saw release, though Southwind singer Jim Pulte, as a solo act, went on to make another album with Jesse producing. "This is before Jesse played with Dylan, Lennon, Harrison, and others," I remind Dalton. "Why did he think he had the license or stature to finish your tapes without your approval and then fight the record label?" "I know, I know, I know," Dalton intones. "But that's what was so wonderful about him."[24]

Things went a little better in 1971, when Jesse produced an album for Roger Tillison, whom he had known for years through the Hollywood Okie gang. "One of the great undiscovered artists," Jesse said about Tillison, whose song "Rock and Roll Gypsies" Jesse covered on his first solo album. *Roger Tillison's Album* should be a classic. Jesse, Bill Rich, and Jim Keltner swing hard on the strutting standout "Just Before the Break of Day." This was another instance of Jesse using his talent and connections to support his friends' music and help advance their professional opportunities. Through no fault of Jesse's, however, Tillison sabotaged it. With the dramatically overbudget album stalled in the ATCO release schedule, Tillison took his advance payment for the album, bought a jar of pills, threw a party on the roof of a hotel, and then split home to Oklahoma, where he resumed his career as a construction worker.[25]

By 1974, Jesse too was growing tired of the music business game. He was burned out on studio work, having done so much of it he couldn't accurately recall his discography. If you went for a ride with him, he would claim to have played on every song that came on the radio, several friends suggest, right down to "All I Want for Christmas (Is My Two Front Teeth)." Friends couldn't tell when he was joking. It seemed he *had* played with everyone.[26]

While studio work earned Jesse significant income and a reputation as one of the best guitarists in the profession, it became a drain on Jesse's own creativity and solo career. "I realized I wasn't a musician anymore," he said in 1973. "I was like a jukebox. I was like a color on someone's palette just to plug in and turn off at their will." He began thinking he was making "wallpaper music." "Let's say you have three hours to cut a tune," he elaborated, "this doesn't leave you with any time to develop the song or think of something much better to play." He was relentlessly pulled in different directions, and often struggled with the limitations of each. He never fully committed to a particular path, because he wouldn't or couldn't. When he tried, matters beyond his control spoiled his effort.[27]

WORRIED HIS TALENTS WERE languishing, Jesse was met with a new course toward developing his solo career. Despite generally hating the business folks, he secured a new manager in Joel Maiman, associated with Leon Russell and Shelter Records. Maiman helped score Jesse a contract with major label Epic Records in New York City. The deal was only for one album guaranteed, but it was a chance to make another record under his own name after working so extensively for others. In a stroke of serendipity, Jesse simultaneously found some admiring new allies and bandmates right within his neighborhood.[28]

On Ironside Street, directly across the back alley from Jesse's place on Hurricane, lived a troupe of young friends and musicians who jammed in their garage while dreaming of music stardom. The group of late teenagers and early twentysomethings included bassist Bob Tsukamoto and multi-instrumentalist Ricky Eckstein, who hung around their older musician brothers Howard and Ray, respectively. Another bass-playing friend, Bob Glaub, who would later achieve an illustrious career with Jackson Browne, Stevie Nicks, Warren Zevon, and more, was over so often he practically lived there too. Ray Eckstein's girlfriend Kelly and a drummer named Gary Ray rounded out their regular gang. To their surprise, they soon realized a rock star lived one street over. "We were in awe of him," remembers Gary Ray, whose first-ever concert featured Jesse with Taj Mahal at the Shrine Auditorium in 1969.[29]

Bob Glaub also recognized Jesse from Taj Mahal gigs at the Ash Grove. He was a big fan. "I could not take my eyes off Jesse," Glaub says. "He was so unique looking. I knew right away that he was Native American. There was a regal look about him. . . . He didn't slouch, but he always had one foot out, big head of hair, pretty well dressed." Glaub had learned bass guitar by playing along with Taj Mahal albums, and he increasingly began seeing Jesse's name on records he loved. The Bangladesh film, more than anything, inspired Glaub to attempt a life in music. And now the Native American guy in the film was living across the street. But they were all too intimidated to approach him.[30]

One day Jesse heard them rehearsing in their single-car garage, where they had egg crates nailed to the wall to muffle their volume. He knocked on their door. "Can I jam with you guys?" They jumped at the chance. Before Jesse departed, he invited the gang to come over and hang out anytime they wanted. Unsure if Jesse was serious, only Glaub embraced the offer. They fast became friends, with Jesse taking the young bass guitarist under his wing. Long nights passed hanging out in Jesse's living room, smoking joints, and listening to Jesse's collection of obscure soul records. Glaub soaked in Jesse's stories about being on the road with Taj Mahal. If the mood struck, Jesse might tell stories about his Native American ancestors. Glaub felt privileged. He had never met a Native American person before. Through these conversations, it became clear that Jesse adored his father, as both an artist and a man, but also that he was intimidated by his father, convinced he could never live up to his example.[31]

Jesse's friendship with his young admirer eventually resulted in a recording opportunity, Glaub's first. One night in late 1972, Jesse called from the studio where he was beginning work on his new album for

Epic. He was clashing with the current bass player, to the point of physical tantrums. "What are you doing right now?" Jesse asked Glaub.
"Nothing much." "Get your bass and come down to Paramount Studios.
We're making an album and we need you." Glaub was overwhelmed and
elated. "He could've called anyone in town . . . he just took a chance on
me," he says. Glaub's only real experience to that point was a gig with
a lounge act in the Lake Tahoe mob scene. Now he was in the studio
with Jesse and Jim Keltner, two of the top session musicians in the world.
Glaub plugged into Jesse's Fender Bassman, lit a cigarette, and, with a
shaky right hand, held on for dear life as the trio launched into Jesse's
rousing instrumental romp, "Natural Anthem."[32]

Jesse was just as excited as Glaub. In Jesse's estimation, his first two
solo albums had been commercial and professional failures. He blamed
this outcome on his refusal to promote any particular image of himself,
as a rock star or as a distinctly Native American artist. "When you have
to work within all the restrictions that you have to make a record commercial, you have to watch out for all kinds of rules," Jesse said at the
time. "Don't make it over three minutes, and it has to be catchy, and you
have to dance to it. I might not even want to play anything like that. But
right away I had to try and direct myself to play that kind of shit. Sometimes it gets to be too much of a weight." With this new project, Jesse
wanted to achieve his own sound. "Any of the 200 people that bought
my first two albums should be able to tell this one's mine," he promised.[33]

In early spring 1973, after Jesse and Patti attended a signing party
hosted by Jesse's new label in New York City, Gregg Allman dropped
by the hotel to gift Jesse a silver and turquoise bracelet in honor of the
latter's influence on his late brother Duane. Mick Jagger visited, too, and
gained an impromptu guitar lesson when Jesse sat on the bed with him
and taught him some licks. Jesse was finally poised for a big break.[34]

Back in Los Angeles, Jesse worked quickly to finish the record. His
studio lineup included bass, drums, keyboards, backing vocalists, a robust
horn section, and a new cowriter in the form of a singer from Detroit
who called himself Johnny Angel. Despite its size, this was actually a
smaller cast than those that supported Jesse's first two albums. With
Jesse handling all of the guitar parts himself, the core group recorded

the basic tracks for the album in five days, keeping with Jesse's typical approach in the studio. Then Jesse spent several months trying to get the sound right. His determination to be more direct with this album was reflected in his initial plan to record the material live in concert.

In many ways, Jesse succeeded. *Keep Me Comin'* is superior to his first two albums in its sonic qualities. It features Jesse's best songs and most coherent presentation. "I think it's my best effort so far," Jesse concluded. "I'm really proud of it." Patti loved it too. She thought the material was "fresh and original. Jesse's musical personality had emerged at the time." She remembered Jesse being very happy with it, feeling that he achieved his vision as an artist. The three formal instrumental tracks were "pure Jesse," she noted. Percussionist Bobby Torres considers the title track his proudest moment. I tell him the song was featured in acclaimed Seminole-Mvskoke director Sterlin Harjo's film *Mekko* (2015). "Wow." Torres pauses, having had no idea. "This is fucking me up, man."[35]

Keep Me Comin' reveals Jesse not only at another musical summit but also at the pinnacle of his relationship with Patti. We can hear it in the title track, a song Jesse cowrote with his new collaborator Johnny Angel. For me, it's Jesse's greatest song, and it could have been a hit. In the first verse, Jesse sets the scene, singing about some timeless morning in Venice, lost in a dream beside his love. Later he sings about how Patti delivered him from his demons: "Blues once fell all around / my sweet love you brought me up from down."

Epic Records promoted Jesse's new release with publicity photos by the esteemed photographer Jim Marshall, some featuring Jesse and Patti goofing around, giving each other bunny ears, capturing the album's relaxed spirit. Promotional buttons announced "ED'S IN TOWN." The album's insert highlighted Jesse's impressive résumé as a studio musician. The music within reasserted Jesse's place as a solo artist. The album credits include the dedication "For Joe," gesturing to Joe Zagarino, who had been immortalized in the Rolling Stones song "Torn and Frayed" and who engineered every album Jesse had produced to that point. Zag had been battling an addiction to heroin that took his life on New Year's Day 1973, when Jesse was making plans for *Keep*

Me Comin'. "His body just gave out," Pete Waddington says. "He was another victim of tragic ends, though an incredible talent," remembers Bobby Whitlock. "It seemed like that was a domino effect. It seemed to be the way things were at the time."[36]

Unfortunately, some great PR photos and a modest run of buttons were no match for the damage Jesse did to his own album and career relaunch when he insisted on a controversial cover concept. Well before the album's release, Jesse's new managers Joel and Mona Maiman brought a painting by an artist friend to Jesse and proposed it for the album cover. Depicting Native American people, it would again market Jesse as a Native artist, like his first album. But that may have been the problem. Jesse hated it. "'Ching Ching China Boy' was real," Mona says about Jesse's response to the painting, referring to Jesse's song on *Keep Me Comin'* about the racism he experienced as a kid. "Being Native was painful for Jesse," Mona began to understand. "Part of him wanted to get away from it by becoming a rock star." The proposed painting is evocative, but it depicts Indigenous people disappearing, at odds with the album's message and Jesse's life at that time. Or maybe Jesse didn't like it because his first album already featured a Native image, one created by his own father. In any case, Joel Maiman had promised complete artistic control and he allowed Jesse to pitch an alternative concept.[37]

Jesse's vision for the *Keep Me Comin'* cover reveals how increasingly erratic and sometimes reckless in his behavior he was becoming, even at the top of his game. The image Jesse arranged depicted him with arms folded above a concho belt, in front of a sexually explicit collage of *Penthouse* centerfolds, tempered only by minimal airbrushing. At best, it inadvisably reflected Jesse's love for risqué humor, not unlike that of his friend John Lennon, who often sent letters and cards to people made from pictures torn from pornographic magazines. It also signaled Jesse's affection for the raunchy blues tradition. At worst, Jesse's cover concept was deeply offensive. Both Patti and Mona were aghast, trying in vain to convince Jesse it was misogynistic. Jesse dug in. It wasn't a "sexual thing," he later insisted, but if the album's title and title track spoke to something more sophisticated, the album cover's background images speak for themselves. What was he thinking? This is when Jesse "started to get really strange," Bobby Torres regrets. "He was really getting out there," agrees Pete Waddington, who was approaching the end of his partnership with Jesse. Having always been happy to carry Jesse's guitar, Pete was now becoming anxious about carrying Jesse's drugs.[38]

The immediate problem with the cover for Jesse's definitive album was that music retailers refused to carry it. Jesse feigned confusion when he found out. The whole thing was his idea, but he pretended the record label's art department did it without his knowledge. When a label staffer informed Jesse they were going to rerelease it with a new cover, Jesse punched a hole in the wall. "I got a boxer's fracture in my right hand," his guitar-playing hand, he lamented, though he convinced the doctor to leave thumb and forefinger openings in the cast so he could still grasp a guitar pick. "I had put my heart and soul in this record, and they returned them all without even trying to put them on the shelf," he later complained. But that wasn't exactly true. Either way, Jesse's relationship with his new label crumbled and *Keep Me Comin'* failed to get a rerelease with an appropriate cover. The few copies one can still find for a relatively considerable price are from the initial run that were mostly returned.[39]

Nevertheless, promotional copies that reached music critics were mostly met with acclaim. One reviewer praised the instrumentals while complaining that "Davis isn't cut out for lead vocals." But most others acknowledged *Keep Me Comin'* as Jesse's best album yet. "It's really his first tight, exciting and smooth recording—the previous outings were premature," offered one review. Referring to Jesse as "the Oklahoma Mafia's favorite son," another review highlighted Jesse's version of the classic "Bacon Fat," which he previously played with Taj Mahal. Despite Jesse's reluctance to issue his new album with a painting of a Native American person, one reviewer regrettably led with a cheap quip about Jesse's Indigeneity, describing him as the "Oklahoma Indian friend of Leon Russell," as though Leon was the Lone Ranger and Jesse was Tonto. Even after completing his finest work, Jesse still struggled to escape Leon's shadow.[40]

To promote the album, Jesse brought Jim Karstein, Bob Glaub, and Ray Eckstein with him for a few gigs in Buffalo and Rochester, New

York, and Aspen, Colorado. Once again indicating weak promotional strategies, they didn't actually play New York City, the biggest market in North America, despite being in New York, where the label was based. Then, for the gig in Colorado, they bewilderingly didn't book any shows on the long drive out or the way back. Still, Buffalo media raved about Jesse's set opening for the Paul Butterfield Blues Band, suggesting he was finally "destined for recognition and fame," with a partly inaccurate emphasis on how "the Indian from Tulsa" smiled a lot when he played.[41]

Finally, in a more creative attempt at album promotion, hot on the heels of Jesse's album release fiasco, he appeared as a special guest judge, billed as a "Rock Star," for a high school talent show at the Long Beach auditorium. In addition to raising money for Long Beach Schools music programs, it was an endearing reflection of Jesse's status in the music community.[42]

BY THE END OF 1973, with session dates still controlling Jesse's calendar, it had become apparent that his latest solo album, the one he was most proud of, was being met with more indifference among the buying public, at least in the few places where they could actually find it. Still determined to reduce his reliance on studio work as a session musician, Jesse began reconsidering the appeal of membership in a group, where he could play a lead role supporting another artist, similar to his success with Taj Mahal. That fall, there was serious talk about forming a band with Rolling Stones pianist Nicky Hopkins, drummer Jim Keltner, and bassist Steve Thompson—the latter played on the London sessions for Jesse's first album. They would be an entire band of popular session musicians striking out on their own. "Both Jesse and Jim are interested in joining up with me as they, like me, are getting fed up of hopping from one band to another all the time," Hopkins said. "And it's important for me to get musicians who have been through it all." Nicky and Jesse would be co-frontmen, sharing vocal duties. Unfortunately, the band didn't come together.[43]

In spring 1974, Jesse embraced a band opportunity when British bluesman John Mayall invited him to join his group. In the late 1960s,

Mayall's Bluesbreakers had, in rapid succession, featured three of the most prominent guitarists of the classic rock era: Eric Clapton, Fleetwood Mac's Peter Green, and the Rolling Stones' Mick Taylor. Jesse was already a known commodity, but Mayall's imprimatur could elevate him as one of the greatest guitarists in the business while also providing a steady gig.

The plan was for Jesse to join Mayall for a tour of England and continental Europe in April 1974. A date at London's Royal Albert Hall would be recorded for a live album announcing Jesse's membership in the group. Jesse was supposed to begin rehearsals with Mayall and his band in March, but he showed up in poor condition from increasing drug abuse, asked for his advance, spent it, and failed to appear for practice. After British music media had already announced the new lineup, including Jesse, Mayall broke his leg in a swimming pool accident and canceled the tour, foreclosing any chance for Jesse at redemption. When Mayall returned that fall, it was with guitarist Randy Resnick in Jesse's place. Even in an industry characterized by ubiquitous drug consumption, Jesse's growing dependence was becoming a liability. Meanwhile, an overlapping opportunity to join a band with one of the biggest music stars of the century was also underway. This may be why Jesse didn't take the Mayall gig more seriously. This other path might be his last great chance at prolonged success. This time, he would not destroy it. To some degree, it would instead destroy him.[44]

Jesse's professional collaboration with John Lennon almost began back in 1972, when John and Yoko considered inviting Jesse, Jim Keltner, Nicky Hopkins, and Klaus Voormann to permanently compose the protean Elephant's Memory group that backed John and Yoko live. "And that would have been a great band, but it meant that every time I wanted to do something, I would have had to call them from all over the damn world!" Lennon worried. In late 1973, he changed his mind, and assembled those same musicians to form his new regular backing group.[45]

In that short time, much had changed in John Lennon's life. Hoping it might improve their now faltering marriage, Yoko instructed John to disappear in Los Angeles for a while with their plucky personal assistant, May Pang. Yoko encouraged John to have an affair with Pang, who had been a dutiful employee, caring for John and obeying Yoko. To John and May's surprise, they accidentally and genuinely fell in love. Their romance formed the heart of what became known as Lennon's "Lost Weekend." Jesse became one of John's closest friends throughout the whirlwind experience.

Lennon liked visiting Jesse at the Hurricane House. The former Beatle enjoyed walking along Venice Beach and signing autographs when he wasn't sufficiently blending in. It was a quiet professional and artistic strength of Jesse's that he was at ease around celebrities of John Lennon and George Harrison's stature. Jesse knew something about being confronted with strangers' awkward and incessant predictions and predeterminations. As an Indigenous person, he could sympathize with social and cultural objectification. It allowed Jesse to form a genuine partnership with Lennon, rooted in their mutual love for early rock and roll music. John respected Jesse because Jesse knew how to play all the old music John cherished. Jesse had long thought Lennon a genius and he learned to love him like a brother. "It was a perfect fit," May Pang recalls.

At night, Lennon hit the town with May and the boys. Forming a drinking club called the Hollywood Vampires, they frequently claimed a room at the top of the star-studded Rainbow Bar and Grill on Sunset. Lennon reveled in a new freedom previously prohibited in the confines of Beatlemania. In LA, he exorcised pent-up emotions in unpredictable and sometimes dangerous displays that could range from catharsis to tantrum. "He had a dark side," Jesse's assistant Jim Catalano remembered about Lennon, "and it came out at night." Jesse was part of those experiences, sometimes to the point of following John into the void. It may have been therapeutic for both, but it put great stress on those around them. May Pang remembers how Jesse and John could bring out the worst in each other when they overindulged. "I loved Jesse, and I loved him as a person," she stresses. "But I also saw the other side of him." Jesse could be demanding, but Lennon would never say no to Jesse. And from Jesse, Lennon received the same.[46]

The most outrageous example of Jesse and John going over the edge occurred on January 12, 1974. Their night of mischief began at the campy Lost on Larrabee Restaurant on Santa Monica Boulevard and ended with police rifles pointed at them in a destroyed apartment in West Hollywood. Obsessed with Ann Peebles's hit "I Can't Stand the Rain," John invited Jesse and Patti to join him and May for Peebles's performance at the Troubadour. Jesse enlisted Jim Catalano as designated driver. At dinner before the gig, Lennon set the tone when he emerged from the bathroom with a Kotex pad taped to his head. Jesse thought it was hilarious, but the rest of the party tried to ignore it, as not to encourage John's behavior. At the Troubadour, a delighted Peebles dedicated a song to Lennon, who, with the pad still stuck to his forehead, responded by yelling sexual obscenities at Peebles before security removed him.[47]

Everyone piled into Catalano's car. He set a course for the home of Harold Seider, John's lawyer, where John and May were staying. On the way, John suddenly began screaming while attempting to throw May's jewelry out the window. Then he tried kicking out the windows. When Catalano ordered him to stop, John threatened, "One more word out of you and I'm going to take your fucking eyes out." Upon reaching Seider's place, Jesse helped John trash the place, smashing gold records, lamps, chandeliers, and tables. At that point, Yoko called, escalating John's tantrum, as he swung the base of the phone around, breaking more stuff. "It was like Keith Moon or something," Catalano thought in disbelief. Inevitably, John and Jesse began wrestling each other on the floor. May and Patti were distraught. Catalano asked if he should take a picture.

When things calmed down for a moment, May hurried upstairs to use the bathroom. Suddenly she heard Patti screaming, "OH MY GOD! YOU KILLED HIM! HE'S DEAD! HE'S DEAD!" May ran downstairs, grabbed Patti, and beseeched her to stop. John yelled, "HE'S NOT DEAD!" referring to Jesse. But John wasn't exactly sure. He ran to the fridge, grabbed a carton of orange juice, and shook it vigorously, ostensibly to blend the pulp. Then he poured it over Jesse's face. Jesse bolted up, eyes burning from the citric acid: "WHAT HAPPENED?!!!"

There are two versions of what had just happened. In Jesse's, they began wrestling again, John kissed Jesse, Jesse bit John's tongue, and then John smashed an ashtray over Jesse's head. In May's account, while she was upstairs, John went to the fridge to grab a sixteen-ounce bottle of

Coke. Jesse crawled over on all fours like a dog and bit John in the ribs (May remembers the deep teeth marks). John then smashed the Coke bottle over Jesse's head, at which point Patti screamed and May came running downstairs. At a minimum, we know Jesse bit John and John knocked Jesse out with a blunt object. Distraught, May sent John upstairs while Catalano and Patti lifted Jesse onto a couch.

Seconds later, LAPD pounded on the door. "OPEN UP!!!" Jesse remembered the context: "They're looking for Charles Manson, you know?" Somehow, "We sobered up real quick." May opened the door to six shotguns and flashlights directed at her face. "I could have been blown away," she realizes. "Do you know how many nightmares I have going back into that thought, what could have happened?" In swarmed the LAPD, leather boots and all. Against the odds, the unit included an Apache Indian sheriff. He marched straight up to Jesse. "Aren't you Jesse Ed Davis?" he asked. "Never mind that I look ridiculous like that sitting there," Jesse recalled. "He's proud to see another Indian in such distinguished company. He starts giving me the fan treatment, and I was barely coherent." What a picture to imagine Jesse meeting a fellow Native and fawning fan while orange juice dripped from his hair. Meanwhile, John nervously emerged from upstairs. One cop ran his flashlight over John's face and realized he had caught a Beatle in his beam. "Can I ask you one question?" the officer requested. "Sure, anything you want." "Are the Beatles ever going to get back together?" John thought for a moment, and replied, "You never know."

The next morning, everyone realized how lucky they were, especially because there were drugs in the house, and federal officials were known to be looking for any excuse to kick John out of the country. When John came downstairs, he gestured to Catalano: "Hey Jim, how's it going?" seemingly oblivious to everything that had occurred. "It was one of the highlights of my life," Catalano quipped. Jesse slept in the back of the car that night, waking the next morning with a serious headache and the pillow that Patti gave him stuck to his head from the OJ. "Oh, what a night," Jesse sighed.

Was this some kind of exercise in toxic masculinity, with John and Jesse trying to upstage each other? To May, it seemed more childish than masculine—just boys being boys. "What started [John] off that night?" Jesse later reflected. "Vodka. You hear all kinds of stories about Indians and alcohol, you know, getting violent. I'm not really a shit-stirring instigator. I sort of follow along," he confessed. "I never get violent when I'm drunk, unless John decided he wanted to tear something up when I was with him, and then, 'Shit, sure, let's tear it up!' But it never occurred to me to do those sorts of things."

Jesse claimed John could be manipulative, sometimes to an endearing degree. For example, he'd intentionally do a poor job ironing his shirt in order to coerce Jesse's assistance. "Give me the goddamn iron and I'll do it for you!" Jesse would finally intervene. It's the comprehensible if inadvisable behavior of someone who for many years had teams of people attending to his every need, great and small. Jesse accommodated John's outlandish behavior, understanding that it stemmed from the constraints John, now thirty-three years old, had experienced as a Beatle. "I had been on the road and I had seen probably a lot more than he had seen," Jesse reasoned. "Because when he was on the road he could never leave and go out and do things. He tried to live vicariously through a lot of experiences." It seems counterintuitive. Surely if anyone could destroy a hotel room with impunity, it would have been the most popular rock group in the world. But the Beatles couldn't function that way. They didn't have that kind of freedom. They had been all around the globe, but often only saw it through windows. It wouldn't be wise to trash their hotel room when they were stuck in it.

John appreciated this quality in Jesse. He could be an accomplice to someone who desperately wanted to be in a regular band and throw television sets out the window like normal rock stars. Jesse loved John, and was either too intimidated to say no or too willing to help his friend work through his emotional challenges. "He sort of did that to see if I would get into it like he thought it was going to be," Jesse explained. "He thought, 'If I smash the chandelier, what will Jesse do?' Will he tell me to calm down, or will he jump in it with me?' And at that particular time, I jumped in it with him."[48]

That night at Seider's place, John was also acting out because his ex-wife Cynthia did not bring their son Julian over for a visit at the promised time. A credit to May Pang's influence, John was in the process of meaningfully connecting with his first son for the first time. When Julian showed up the next day instead, John secured private access for Julian, Cynthia, May, Jesse, Patti, and Billy at Disneyland outside of regular hours. "You have to understand this was the first time John had seen his first wife in years," May stresses. "And it's not Yoko with him; it's me. I think at that point, because we had Billy out with us, that there wasn't that big drama." Jesse and John stayed sober, though they did stop for a photo Billy took of them pretending to offer a cigar store Indian statuette a toot of cocaine. For all involved it was a memorable excursion, one of the sweetest days of their lives. John reveled in the "It's a Small World" ride and kept singing the song for days after. "That was a fun time," May remembers, "a real family thing." It was a glimpse of how family life and music stardom could more easily coexist in John and Jesse's world.[49]

IN FALL 1973, partly stemming from a contested obligation to a music publisher, John Lennon began working on an album of rock and roll standards for what would become *Rock 'n' Roll*, featuring Lennon's core group consisting of Jesse, Keltner, Nicky Hopkins, and Klaus Voormann, augmented by somewhere around thirty additional musicians, some uncredited, tasked with achieving producer Phil Spector's famous Wall of Sound recording technique that layered instruments across the sonic spectrum, creating an echoing and exhilarating effect. By enlisting Spector to helm the project, John could feel more like a regular member of the band. At the same time, using an overlapping group of musicians that Ringo and George also used on their solo albums helped John stay connected to the Beatles.[50]

Unfortunately, Phil Spector wasn't going to mediate any conflicts or turn the temperature down on John and Jesse's antics. Spector was more dangerous and disruptive than anyone, especially given his obsession with guns, including the one he visibly stationed on the studio mixing console. "Every night it was something else," May Pang recalls. "Every night he was a different personality. One night he was a doctor. The next night he was a karate expert. [I laugh.] I know you're laughing, but I was a 22–23-year-old trying to hold down the fort." Jesse thought Spector, the eccentric, and later murderous, former teen producer phenom, was "hilarious. It must have been hard for Phil to be a has-been at age nineteen."[51]

One night, Jesse's Allman Brothers drummer friend Butch Trucks came to visit the studio. Soon Spector started screaming somewhat incoherently. Then the screaming turned into vague taunts, gradually evolving into passive-aggressive comments about the Allman Brothers Band. Trucks now realized the whole charade was directed at him. Finally he had enough:

> I stood up and told him to take that piece of shit he was working on and shove it up his ass. I was heading back home to some sanity. John looked at me and apologized for the scene and I went to kick open the door that was a pull door. Then tried to rip it open (ever try and rip open an airtight studio door?). I finally walked into the hallway with my leg and arm hurting like hell and there was Jesse. He had been one of the first to leave. I told him I was going back in that studio to punch out that little jerk and Jesse told me that would be a bad idea since the big dude in the back corner was a 28-degree black belt with guns and knives.

Jesse escorted the enraged Trucks down the hall where they found refuge listening to Joni Mitchell working on her magnificent album *Court and Spark*. Jesse saved the day. It was the type of gesture friends loved about him.[52]

Not seeing release until 1975, Lennon's *Rock 'n' Roll* hit the top ten, but its reputation suffered, partly because of the undesirable legal circumstances that forced Lennon to make the album. Now increasingly experiencing a reevaluation, however, it contains many gems. Jesse was the perfect choice for lead guitar. His great accompaniment skills, elaborate studio experience, and intimate knowledge of foundational rock and roll music made him an essential contributor. His slide guitar solo on Lennon's hit version of "Stand by Me" is one of the most impressive moments in Jesse's entire recorded legacy.

While intermittently advancing work on *Rock 'n' Roll*, Lennon launched two more projects, this time from the producer's chair: Harry Nilsson's *Pussy Cats* (1974) and a second new solo album, this one comprised of original material. Jesse was thrilled to join so many friends on the Nilsson project, including Keltner, Voormann, Ringo, Bobby Keys, Keith Moon, Danny Kortchmar, and more. "[Nilsson] just sang so fucking great," Jesse evangelized. "He would sing a phrase for so long and pull it out of the fire, and went beyond anything you could imagine. His melodic sense was just phenomenal." Jesse cited Nilsson's "That Is All" from a subsequent album as one of the most beautiful songs he had ever heard, and remembered how his accompanying guitar part was, in his words, "dripping melodically all the way through it." It was one of his proudest moments.[53]

In terms of their music, Jesse thought Lennon and Nilsson's competitive friendship brought out the best in each other, but where their behavior was concerned, he confessed that the three of them together also encouraged the worst in each other, including a second incident involving an ejection from the Troubadour in March 1974. Later, in 1986, working as an addiction counselor, Jesse reflected on his work with Lennon and Nilsson. By then he understood what those years had been about. Maybe they courted conflict, he thought, or just a "spanking." There was "some great guilt involved in all three of our personalities," he figured. But by that point he had learned a lot about himself, he suggested, and learned a lot about how guilt encourages conflict and confrontation.[54]

To establish a home base away from the studio, Lennon and Nilsson rented a house at 625 Pacific Coast Highway, overlooking the beach in Santa Monica. It had a salacious reputation as a place where President Kennedy rendezvoused with Marilyn Monroe in 1961. The splendid pad's legacy would only grow. In addition to Lennon's crew, numerous other prominent musicians regularly visited, including Keith Moon, Eric Clapton, and, notably, Paul McCartney. In fact, Paul's visit resulted in the last photos ever taken of the old Beatle bandmates together, as they chatted privately on the patio while the sun was setting. Likewise, on one afternoon at a nearby studio, Jesse, Stevie Wonder, and a few others joined John and Paul for a lengthy jam session that would mark the final time the former Beatles partners played music together.[55]

When not recording, the gang of musicians grew closer as friends and bandmates. If anyone wanted to raise hell, then they would at least be together and contained within one place. Just as often, the beach house became a retreat, sometimes even family-oriented with Billy, Julian, Paul and Linda McCartney's kids, and other children in the mix. Ringo, Jesse, John, and Harry, especially, loved playing rock and roll charades and music trivia late into the night. "Who played saxophone on the intro to the Del-Vikings' "Whispering Bells?'" someone would call out. "SAM THE MAN TAYLOR!" someone else would yell. Building on the Davis family tradition, they also played endless games of backgammon. Bill cherishes a memory of beating Ringo out of exactly $64 after rolling seven doubles in a row.[56]

Where occasional hijinks were concerned, John had been prodding Jesse to help him obtain and try peyote. An unfortunate exercise of Indigenous cultural appropriation on John's part, it was improper for John and Jesse to use the sacrament in recreational fashion, outside of the proper ceremonial context and administration. But Jesse was game, perhaps as an extension of his commitment to helping John indulge his wildest impulses. He didn't regret it. In fact, he claimed it was the single best time he ever had with John. On Palm Sunday 1974, with everyone else away and a quiet beach house, Jesse procured four buttons for John, May, Patti, and himself from "an old Indian . . . a real spiritual, mystical kind of guy," he put it, and ground them up into avocado sandwiches. May declined. John and Jesse dove in. Throughout the alternatingly sunny and drizzly day by the pool, John followed Jesse around, repeating two words: "Good medicine." Jesse thought this was hilarious. It only became awkward when Paul, Linda, and their kids suddenly appeared for an unscheduled visit. Jesse and Patti would see them again under more normal circumstances in 1975 when they boarded the *Queen Mary* for Paul and Linda's *Venus and Mars* album release party.[57]

Though Jesse and John's adventures and misadventures had been mostly harmless, McCartney later recalled his simultaneous amusement and dismay over his old partner's social environment: "It was a bit strange, John and I, seeing each other at that time." As Paul put it, he encountered John working alongside "three beautiful total alcohol nutters," Jesse, Nilsson, and Keith Moon. Yet the beach abode's location was "perfect." The first time McCartney visited, Nilsson offered him elephant tranquilizer. "Is it fun?" Paul asked. "No," Nilsson admitted. "[John] was a teenager again. It was everything he always wanted to do in Liverpool," McCartney recalled. "He was just being his old Liverpool self, just a wild, wild boy. . . . Spector was there letting his gun off. . . . I mean, those are not sessions I would want to be at." Paul remembered feeling heartbroken one day at the beach house when all the kids were together. John turned to Paul and asked for advice on how to play with children. John didn't know. He had no experience with it.[58]

Nevertheless, Jesse's partnership with Lennon opened up new opportunities in the business. One hub of activity was the Jim Keltner Fan Club, organized by George Harrison, who made buttons announcing its existence. Why the Jim Keltner Fan Club? All the musicians loved him. They formed a loose collective including Jesse, Lennon, Ringo, Jagger, Nilsson, Stevie Wonder, Bill Wyman, Jack Bruce, Billy Preston, Bobby Keys, Gene Clark, Marc Benno, and others who gathered at the famed Los Angeles Record Plant for private jams that allowed them to relax away from outsiders' interruptions and expectations. No recording was allowed when the club met on Saturday nights, playing everything from Bobby Freeman's classic "Do You Want to Dance?" to the Beatles' "Yesterday."[59]

Keith Moon's birthday party at the Beverly Wilshire also featured an impressive cast of Los Angeles musicians, including Jesse, Nilsson, Micky Dolenz, and Nickey Barclay from the underacknowledged all-women rock group Fanny. Late in the evening, Beach Boy Brian Wilson arrived in a bathrobe. Suddenly, a second person sprang from underneath Wilson's egregiously informal attire. It was Rod Stewart, conversely donning a suit. At around one in the morning, Jesse grabbed a guitar and joined others in a rendition of the Beach Boys' "Don't Worry Baby." Had Jesse picked up a copy of the *LA Free Press* that carried the story on page six, then he also might have noticed an adjacent story about the previous year's violent Wounded Knee occupation in South Dakota, where two people died in a clash between Native American activists and federal agents.[60]

Some of the parties Jesse began frequenting were downright disturbing, especially to uninitiated friends from back home. These were the days when Keith Moon often dressed in Nazi regalia, impersonating Hitler. Having not seen Jesse in years, Jesse's close friend and neighbor from Oklahoma City, Carol Furr, was excited to visit him in Los Angeles. Proud of his success and anxious to grant his old friend a glimpse of his new world, Jesse invited Carol to a party in the Hollywood Hills. Perhaps Jesse didn't know what to expect. When they got inside, he strangely kept instructing Carol on where to stand, and then suddenly moved her into a different room, telling her to stay there and not look at the TV in the adjacent room. "I didn't want you to see the film," he told her when they soon left. "Why, what was it? Pornography?" "No, it was a snuff film." Carol realized then that Jesse had entered a world far from Oklahoma. She appreciated the brotherly protection Jesse offered in the moment, but she worried about him in that setting.[61]

Beyond the studios and parties, Jesse experienced some frightening reminders that his fast life could suddenly stop. One day, Patti was driving her Porsche with Jesse in the passenger seat and Billy lying in his standard spot on the deck below the rear window. Patti lost control of the car and wrapped it around a telephone pole. Billy wasn't responsive and Patti panicked, convinced he was dead. Mercifully, he had only been knocked unconscious, while Patti and Jesse miraculously avoided serious injury. Only the car was destroyed, but the fear remained.[62]

For Jesse, sobering reminders of mortality came from many directions. In August 1974, while working in New York with Lennon, he received news of another music partner's terrible demise, this only a year after Joe Zagarino's and Gram Parsons's drug overdoses. Jesse learned there had been an after-hours robbery at the All-American Burger Shop back in Los Angeles. Three employees were conducting cleanup when two armed men accosted them. After grabbing $500 from the cash register, they instructed the manager to open the safe. But he couldn't; it functioned on a timed system. The perpetrators shot him. It was Jesse's keyboard player from the Ironside Street gang, Ray Eckstein. He died at the scene. He was twenty-two.[63]

Everyone was deeply shaken. "I'll never forget Jimmy Karstein practically holding me up at Ray's funeral," Bob Glaub remembers. Going forward, Jesse would visit Ray and his brother Ricky's mother on every Mother's Day and anniversary of Ray's passing. They would drink tea or coffee and console each other. "Jesse was a real stand-up guy," Glaub says. "That probably helped Ray's mom. They became really good friends." During later years, when Jesse was unhealthy, if Ricky called the house and Jesse was over, Ricky would remind his mother to not give Jesse money. "Ricky, I'm fine, don't worry about me!" she insisted. Ricky was later relieved when he learned that Jesse in fact never asked his mother for money. They only talked about Ray. "And he did that until the end of his life," Ricky remembers about Jesse's visits.[64]

LASTING ROUGHLY EIGHTEEN MONTHS, Lennon's "Lost Weekend" featured plenty of escapades, some funny, some frightening. But often lost in the wild tales is the fact that Lennon and his stellar cast of musicians completed a lot of work. They were a professional musical unit and Lennon was serious about his role as producer on Nilsson's *Pussy Cats* and his own new solo album project called *Walls and Bridges*. The title is appropriate. It's a personal album about open and closed circuits in relationships, including the one John had with himself.

Though partying was encouraged while making *Pussy Cats*, recording for *Walls and Bridges* commenced under a no-drugs policy. "Listen, I don't care. Whatever you want to take. But let's not do it during the session," Lennon instructed. "We couldn't even get a beer during *Walls and Bridges*," Jesse moaned. Worried he was ruining his career, Lennon needed to deliver a convincing studio statement. He did not lack focus, as some have argued. Jesse realized how, for John, failing as a musician was "worse than dying. He did feel he had an image to live up to."[65]

Album rehearsals began at music publisher Morris Levy's Sunnyview Farm in the tiny town of Ghent, in upstate Columbia County, New

York. Interestingly, Levy was the same person threatening to sue Lennon over a songwriting disagreement that obligated Lennon to make the still incomplete *Rock 'n' Roll* album. The plan was for Lennon to record songs for which Levy owned the publishing rights. As far as Levy was concerned, this would settle the dispute. To Jesse, Levy's Sunnyview estate "looked like the fucking state capitol." Breakfasts were big communal feasts preceding a round of rehearsals until lunchtime, after which various combinations of folks walked in the woods, watched the cows, took boat rides, and played backgammon and cards. Then a communal dinner, before rehearsals continued deep into the night. Along with Keltner, Hopkins, and Voormann, Jesse enjoyed the experience not as a temporary session musician but as a member of a fully and formally contracted band backing John Lennon, making four times the money session work earned him back in LA. Jesse was in a legitimate band again for the first time since playing with Taj Mahal. For now, it marked a new benchmark in Jesse's unpredictable musical career.[66]

When the group relocated to New York City in August 1974 for a professional studio recording, a *Rolling Stone* reporter dropped by at around 3 a.m. Everyone was tired from both the grueling recording and vexing context as Lennon faced reawakened threats of deportation over a bogus dope charge dating back to London in 1968. Jim Keltner professed his exhaustion and the typically tranquil Klaus Voormann was beginning to lose his patience. "Even Indian Ed (Jesse Davis) was starting to droop and you know what an ox he is," the reporter observed. John was running the band into the ground, working overtime to finish the album, trying to get everything right. Jesse by contrast preferred working quickly in the studio. He wasn't used to this. Lennon was a "slavedriver," Jesse told the reporter.[67]

The relentless approach produced impressive results. Jesse's guitar features throughout, including the first number-one hit he appeared on, "Whatever Gets You Thru the Night," with special guest Elton John on piano and vocals. Jesse's melodic and milky guitar enhances captivating numbers such as "Old Dirt Road" and the enduringly popular "Dream #9," another top-ten hit and fan favorite. Talking about his contribution to the latter, Jesse said, "That was me doing my slide guitar imitation of

George Harrison. . . . I tried to play like 'My Sweet Lord.' I have total respect for George's musicianship. I think he's one of the greatest." Klaus Voormann, who played bass on "My Sweet Lord" and *Walls and Bridges*, remembers how Jesse installed an oversized volume knob on his guitar, maybe two inches tall, and conducted riveting volume swells with it, creating a unique tonal effect. "There's some great guitar playing on there with a beautiful touch," Voormann says. "He wasn't playing heavy rock and roll stuff, which he could have done too. He had a very, very personal type of guitar playing."[68]

There's been plenty of debate over the unintelligible phrase Lennon sings in "Dream #9." Jesse claimed that Lennon asked for some Native American words he could sing. Supposedly, Jesse took the opportunity to prank Lennon, feeding him fabricated words that crudely approximated a reference to women's anatomy. Lennon used it, not realizing Jesse was kidding. "John loved it!" Jesse insisted. It's as plausible an explanation for the bit as any other. Jesse had previously pranked people using Native language, or some imitation of it. Likewise, Lennon often invented words for his songs and frequently indulged in sexual innuendo.[69]

The album's external packaging was just as interesting, including an essay on the history of the Lennon surname, random asides about witnessing a UFO, a pronouncement that "possession is nine-tenths of the problem," and even references to Native American people. The colorful sketch of two Native Americans galloping on horseback through a canyon Lennon drew when he was eleven couldn't have been inspired by Jesse, but its inclusion on the album may have been. Jesse could also be responsible for Native American people being on Lennon's mind when he christened his horn section the "Little Big Horns." Similar to his request for Jesse to find peyote, Lennon's understanding of Native people and Native culture seemed superficial, much like that of virtually everyone else in the twentieth century. But Lennon also must have recognized how Jesse's presence and performance in the upper echelons of the music business could disarm old stereotypes and assumptions.

Although a lot of fun and hard work went into making the chart-topping *Walls and Bridges*, Jesse and Klaus Voormann were unhappy with the finished product. They thought the engineer who conducted the final mix sucked the life out of the lead guitar and bass tracks by using too many limiters and compressors. "He got really pissed off. . . . Jesse got real angry about it, furious," Voormann recalls. But then, Jesse never seemed to like any of his work. He later warmed up to it, or at least decided to forgive the album's sound, when he introduced it to friends as one of his foremost achievements. Interestingly, Lennon initially denounced the album too. May Pang concludes that it was simply necessary to denounce something from their relationship when Lennon eventually returned to Yoko.[70]

When 1975 arrived, disco and punk rock were rapidly disrupting the music business as the former shot up the charts and the latter questioned the integrity of what had come before. President Ford had pardoned Nixon for Watergate, and Native people landed a major policy victory with congressional orders concerning education and political self-determination. Meanwhile, Lennon suddenly and permanently returned to New York, first with May Pang, and then, unceremoniously, with Yoko. He sent Jesse, Jim Keltner, and Klaus Voormann each a letter explaining he would make his next album with different musicians there, while promising to eventually reunite the *Walls and Bridges* group and possibly take them on tour. It was at least a kinder breakup than the one May Pang experienced. Actually, Keltner was relieved: "That made me very happy, because I had hopes that we would see John again, one day when we were all more sober, more mature." Jesse's response was different, one of "deep sadness," Keltner remembers. "Jesse put all his eggs in that basket." While his experience with John had further boosted Jesse's profile, now he felt abandoned, left only with a couple albums he didn't initially like, the dissolution of a group he thought would enjoy a long future together, and a consolation prize in the form of a 1955 Lyra guitar Lennon signed to him: "To Jesse With Love From Yer John Lennon '75."[71]

What now? Back to the studio session treadmill? Yet another new attempt at launching a solo career? Perhaps another opportunity to join an established artist or group would materialize. The year 1975 would be a deeply challenging one for Jesse as he tried negotiating these possibilities, especially as he began to lose footing on the high-wire act.

Eight

WHERE AM I NOW
(WHEN I NEED ME)

I N 1975, Jesse was reeling from the end of his partnership with John Lennon, but his career wasn't dead. Quite the opposite. His résumé now featured several top-ten and top-twenty records and singles, including appearances on albums by three of the Beatles—John, George, and Ringo. Jesse's reputation was immense. If he could keep it together, he could go anywhere.

And Jesse now had a serious shot at joining the self-proclaimed "greatest rock n roll band in the world." The Rolling Stones' interest in Jesse dated back to the 1968 *Rock and Roll Circus*. In 1973, when Keith Richards was on the hook for a drug bust and possible prison time, Mick Jagger was prepared to call Jesse, with whom he had recently worked in the studio on a cover of Willie Dixon's "Too Many Cooks" that John Lennon produced. "I think Keith's going down," Jagger predicted. "But it's alright. I've got Jesse Ed Davis with his bags packed in LA. He can be on the next plane." Taj Mahal remembers "a whole segment where . . . Mick Jagger says, quite plainly, if Keith had to really spend some time away from the band, the next call was to Jesse Davis."[1]

Richards dodged jail time, but in 1975 there was new potential for Jesse to become a Stone. The group's virtuoso guitarist Mick Taylor left in late 1974, partly out of fear for his life as drugs were taking a toll. With Jesse in the running, Jagger, Richards, and Charlie Watts went to see his solo set at the Topanga Corral in Los Angeles. "They loved him," recalled drummer Jim Karstein, who was backing Jesse that night. Alas, Jesse wasn't the only guitarist under consideration. Ron Wood began looking like the frontrunner, which became a foregone conclusion when he joined the Stones on tour in June 1975. But then another marquee opportunity fell in Jesse's lap. He received an invitation to join the other rowdy and wasted troupe of British blues rockers: the Faces, Ronnie Wood's primary gig.[2]

Jesse had completed long tours with Taj Mahal and appeared on some big stages, but as a hitmaking arena act, Rod Stewart and the Faces were operating at a level heretofore unknown to Jesse. "Where Am I Now (When I Need Me)," a song from Jesse's most recent solo album asked. By the end of the year, that question had come to dominate his life. Then, over the next couple of years, he would practically disappear altogether. Perhaps a fitting analog, Jesse, Patti, and Billy moved out of the Hurricane House before Jesse's big tour with the Faces. Jesse had been fighting their landlord for years, protesting the spiking rent rates. For now, the future was beside the point. Jesse had a limo waiting to take him to fame and fortune.

JOINING THE FACES was an irresistible proposition. With frontman Rod Stewart's recent chart-topping turn as a solo artist, the band had become true stars in America and beyond, playing for crowds eclipsing fifty thousand at some dates as a group at the forefront of the industry shift to large stadium tours. Though Jesse was disappointed in not getting the Stones gig, he could have done worse than the Faces for a consolation prize. His solo career had been met with little national fanfare. He was burned out on session work. He had been playing professionally for fifteen years, made three solo albums, produced records for other artists, toured the United States and Europe, played on a list of sessions longer and more diverse than he could accurately recall, and he was still struggling to make ends meet. He couldn't afford not to accept the gig.

It was important to Jesse to be more than a hired hand, and the Faces promised him more than that. Jesse was a "highly-respected session guitarist who is now a permanent member of the Faces," Stewart announced to media. Drummer Kenney Jones operated with a similar understanding. "If the Faces would have stayed together, I'm convinced he would've been playing with us still. Because he fit in great with us," Jones believes. Jesse relished membership in a top group, and he was earning a significant payday and having the time of his life, especially with some chaps who shared his bawdy sense of humor. This was another big break for Jesse, one sometimes overshadowed by what happens next in the story.[3]

The addition of Jesse created some tension among bandmates, as different members took credit, and Jesse unwittingly became an object of the group's ongoing internal conflicts. Rod Stewart, Kenney Jones, and keyboardist Ian McLagan recall Stewart ushering Jesse into the mix shortly after Jesse's contributions to Stewart's new *Atlantic Crossing* (1975) album. Stewart decided a second guitarist was needed to augment their sound, alongside a twelve-piece string section. Though Stewart had a new solo album, the Faces as a band lacked new material. Stewart thought they should at least spruce up their live set with some new features. Jesse could enhance the sound and allow Ronnie Wood greater freedom and creativity as a lead player. Why Jesse? "Christ, he's just so good we had to ask him to play with us," Stewart put it.[4]

Stressing a different element, McLagan claimed Stewart orchestrated the addition of Jesse to spite Wood, who was coming off a tour, more of an audition, with the Rolling Stones, where he played with a second guitarist. At a media session before the tour began, Stewart said, "The only thing that's got me worried is that we're going to walk out there in front of hundreds of thousands of people and Woody's going to start playing the chords to 'Brown Sugar.'" The jab was obviously intended as payback: Wood had agreed to an extension of Rolling Stones tour dates that caused the Faces to cancel their first two scheduled shows in Florida, where tickets were already on sale, and instead open the tour in North Carolina. McLagan initially regretted Stewart's move, thinking it embarrassed Wood. "There was a lot of tension in the house and we hadn't even started rehearsing, but there was worse to come," McLagan recalled.[5]

Patti expressed suspicion and hesitation about Jesse joining the Faces. She explained it as a matter of Wood wanting Jesse in so he could orchestrate his exit and become a Rolling Stone without damaging his current group's viability. In this interpretation, at least Wood had the courtesy to train his replacement and give Jesse a break as runner-up for the Stones gig. There may be some truth in this. To wit, Wood claimed it was him, and not Stewart, who brought Jesse into the group, and that Stewart first wanted Steve Cropper if they were going to add a guitarist. "I said 'No—Jesse Ed Davis,'" Wood explained at the time. "I love Steve Cropper, but Jesse had a lot more weight to lose, and he'll do that on the road. And he's got a lot more rocks to get off." I won't pretend to decipher Wood's rock star speak. In any case, perhaps the reality was in the middle. Stewart introduced the idea and Wood saw an opportunity in it.[6]

Jesse was either oblivious to these unfolding dramas or confident enough that he would win people over and the band would ultimately prevail. He also had some security in a budding musical partnership with Rod Stewart that had recently resulted in a cowrite and some of the most impressive studio work of his career. Even if he could foresee the band faltering, he had no reason to think he wouldn't at least continue with Stewart.

The group gathered for tour rehearsals in July 1975 at 461 Ocean Boulevard in Golden Beach, Florida, immortalized in classic rock as the house Eric Clapton lived in while making his album named after the address. Jesse was in town early, helping Stewart finish *Atlantic Crossing* at Criteria Studio.[7] After the cancellation of the Florida dates due to Wood's absence, rehearsals shifted to Asheville, North Carolina, where the band practiced with a local twelve-piece string section by day and partied at the Great Smokies Hilton by night. After opening night in Asheville on August 19, the band hit the road for what was supposed to be a world tour, sometimes playing two shows per day.[8]

If things were miserable in the band, it didn't show, not even backstage. It was common knowledge by August that Wood was permanently taking the Stones gig and this would be his farewell to the Faces. The group rallied and treated the tour like a farewell party. Onstage, Jesse looked, danced, and played like a star. He held his own in a powerful group at the height of its popularity, if not the peak of its creativity. Once he adjusted to the group's rhythmic sensibilities, he made valuable contributions to the sound, delivering his distinctive rhythm chops and occasionally exchanging searing lead licks with Wood. And it wasn't lost on concertgoers that the man playing guitar on stage left was an American Indian. In solidarity, Brit Ronnie Wood began tying a bone choker around his neck like Jesse.

The Faces' live set opened with Rod Stewart and gang strutting onstage through a tinsel-curtained archway to the sound of David Rose's seductive instrumental classic "The Stripper" blasting through the PA system. "Appearing to have on more makeup than a traveling Avon sales-person," one concert reviewer wrote about Stewart, "he was dressed in a black and white stripe kimono-type outfit with a red sash around his waist." Also donning a fifteen-foot orange scarf, Stewart performed som-ersaults onstage and kicked around a soccer ball as a gesture to his origi-nal teenage ambition. Meanwhile, local string players from each stop took to the stage in tuxedos and gowns, applying violins and cellos to covers of Sam Cooke's "Bring It On Home to Me" and "You Send Me" and Jimi Hendrix's "Angel," while an overhead rotating mirror ball showered the crowd in diamonds of light. The show climaxed with Stewart's hit "Mag-gie May" highlighting Jesse's melodic sensibility before Jesse and Wood exchanged dueling slide guitar on the Faces classic "Stay with Me."[9]

Jesse's versatility, forged in Oklahoma and refined through tours with Taj Mahal and several years of session and solo work, was an asset to the Faces. Drummer Kenney Jones formed both a musical and a per-sonal bond with him. He appreciated how Jesse introduced a country music feel to some of the Faces' material, powered by guitar upstrokes, reflecting Jesse's Oklahoma roots and training with Conway Twitty. In return, Jones helped Jesse make his Chuck Berry downstrokes a little more pronounced for the Faces' harder rock material. Jesse and Jones became a swinging rhythm section, enhanced by a blossoming friend-ship. "When he was onstage, he made you feel so welcome and you could bounce off his smile and his great vibes," Jones says.[10]

Offstage, Jones appreciated getting to know a Native American per-son for the first time. He grew up playing Cowboys versus Indians in

England, where young kids growing up in the shadow of World War II romanticized stories of the American Wild West and the cowboy heroes who roamed it. Jones's initial experience with Jesse was filtered through those films. But Jesse quickly became real to him, and so did the numerous Native people who asked to meet Jesse throughout the tour. "Other Indians would come and see Jesse and so I thought a lot about Native Americans on most of our tour, through different parts of America," Jones reflects. With Jesse, he felt he was being introduced to the true American people for the first time.[11]

Jones also indulged in Jesse's elaborate pranks. After spending an afternoon floating around in the ocean on an inflatable mattress, legs dangling in the water, getting burnt to a crisp, Jones came inside for dinner and turned on the news. A shark had bitten some guy's leg off only about a half mile down from where he was lazing in the water. "Lucky I've got my two legs," he thought. Jones told Jesse, who insisted that they go see the first-ever summer blockbuster, *Jaws*. During the opening sequence's horrific shark attack, Jones "jumped fuckin' miles in the air." Having already seen the film, waiting for Jones's reaction, Jesse died laughing.[12]

Despite his initial reluctance, McLagan also grew to love Jesse. "A Native American, he was a brilliant guitarist and a character, and I warmed to him immediately," he said. "I knew his guitar playing from Taj Mahal's first two incredible albums . . . and John Lennon's version of 'Stand by Me.' But having met him, I discovered a gentle man who had a sly rascally side that particularly appealed to Ronnie and me." Jesse could be a bit rambunctious in his adjustment to rock stardom— but this only made him a better fit for the Faces. Decadence and hotel hijinks were de rigueur, and the Faces could drink anyone under the table. Jesse threw television sets out the window with everyone else, but that was novice stuff. Ripping every door off their hinges with fire axes at the Water Tower Hotel in Chicago was more creative. In Honolulu, the band destroyed "I Am Woman" singer Helen Reddy's room after Reddy and her husband, who had the next reservation for the suite Rod Stewart occupied, complained that the group wasn't departing quickly enough. Allegedly, Reddy's husband sucker punched Stewart in the lobby.[13]

They went even bigger in Florida. At the Lakeland Holiday Inn, where Stewart was desperately ill, the band grew tired of waiting several hours for a breakfast delivery that eventually bled into lunch. Jesse offered the closed hotel bar $200 for a bottle of booze to pass the time. When the bar said no, McLagan began hammering the walls. The rest of the band and some fans then proceeded to fill the swimming pool with furniture. When police sent in a riot squad, the Faces feigned ignorance, telling management they were leaving because the hotel was too noisy from the police and the kids throwing stuff in the swimming pool. Lakeland police nevertheless made an example of the group, arresting Rod Stewart the next morning, despite the ailing singer being the only one who hadn't participated. Stewart later expressed regret for what he considered exaggerated stories of drunken debauchery, or at least any suggestion that band behavior diminished their performance and fans' concert experience.[14]

When Jesse's friends saw him on the tour, they were surprised by how much he bought into the rock star glamour and attitude, wearing crushed velvet pants and almost as much makeup as Stewart. Almost ten years after moving to Los Angeles, it seemed Jesse had finally gone Hollywood. "He saw the big stage and he wanted on it, and as far as how good those guys played, I think he played better," Taj Mahal said. On August 28, Jesse blew into Oklahoma City with the Faces, playing the part of hometown kid done good. But friends were dismayed by his strutting behavior. Jesse's old friend Rick White, who once traded guitars with Jesse before the latter first moved to LA, now saw him roll up at the music shop in fancy car and fur coat. He seemed a thousand miles from the Jesse he remembered from ten years ago. That night, Larry Hollis rode in a limo with Jesse and Mamacita to Oklahoma City's fifteen thousand–capacity Myriad Convention Center to watch his old Continentals bandmate play guitar. He almost didn't recognize his friend prancing around stage. Jesse was still playing some iteration of the blues, but to Hollis the glam element was a fake version of the music he and Jesse played growing up. After the tour, Jesse's solo band drummer Gary Ray recalls, the rock star behavior continued: "He was kind of a different guy." The transformation was embodied in a lavish white Corvette Jesse bought from *Godfather* actor James Caan. It would soon be a waste of cash.[15]

Jesse betrayed a competing sense of achievement and regret when reflecting on his tenure with the Faces. He made great money playing for big crowds, weaving an impressive guitar blend with Ronnie Wood. "You could hire yourself for $1,000 a day to these rich acts on the road," Jesse recalled. He always treated music as a communal experience and a celebration. The Faces provided that to a degree he never imagined. But in putting a price on himself, he might have been expressing some remorse for buying into the machine.[16]

At the same time, thousands of Faces fans may not have known his name, but they saw a Native American musician belonging on that big stage playing rock and roll. "One night when we were in Arizona," Ian McLagan recalled, "another Indian and his wife came back to the hotel after the show and presented Jesse with an eagle feather. This was a great honour, and even owning an eagle feather is illegal, so Jesse took it from him with humility. The guy's comment was: 'It's good to know one of our people has a steady job.' "[17]

The tour finally ground to a halt in Minneapolis on November 1, 1975. The band had canceled the next leg, and everyone pointed fingers. McLagan blamed Stewart for hogging the spotlight. Wood also blamed Stewart, claiming the latter's relationship with Swedish model Britt Ekland alienated Stewart from the group. Wood also agreed that Stewart had been dominating the band while simultaneously threatening to quit. Peacemaker Kenney Jones blamed Wood and Stewart equally. He thought the group was still a great live act, but he had long begun resenting how so many of the songs they recorded were leftovers from Stewart's, and more recently, Wood's solo albums.[18]

During the press conference in December announcing the band's breakup, Stewart blamed Wood's new position with the Stones. A year later, during an interview with *Crawdaddy*, Stewart suddenly veered into the subject, now rejecting the idea that Wood's Stones gig was a factor:

The Faces breaking up had nothing to do with Woody playing with the Stones. Ian McLagan and I couldn't get on any longer. I still believe Woody's loyalties would have been with the boys. Mac and I were the crux of the whole issue. I wanted to take the band further than a five-piece. That's why we took Jesse Ed Davis and the strings on the road for our last tour. Mac wanted to keep it as a five-piece on the bare boards. We had endless arguments. It took a lot of deciding to finally quit the group.

Jesse would continue working with Stewart as a member of his solo band. If he felt like a pawn in his bandmates' game, he certainly didn't show it when he gifted Wood the TV Yellow Les Paul Special guitar he played on the tour.[19]

BOTH THEN AND NOW, the greater tragedy wasn't that Jesse lost the Faces gig; it was that he lost his girl. Billy and Patti had joined Jesse on the road. Billy luxuriated in the proximity to rock stardom: "By the time Rod Stewart came along I was truly in my element." He rode in limos with Jesse, ordered room service, and made cash on the side selling Rod Stewart's toothbrush and hairbrush to groupies—a minor heist compared to the first tour date in North Carolina, where someone stole Stewart's entire wardrobe locker from backstage.[20]

Patti and Billy flew out to Hawaii for the Faces tour date in Honolulu in early September. They instantly fell in love with the place. Hawaii was paradise, especially for Californians who experienced the islands as their own version of a western frontier and golden coast where they could escape and reinvent themselves. Patti and Billy didn't want to leave. In fact, Patti had quietly become unhappy. While Jesse's tenure with the Faces marked some of his greatest professional success, it corresponded with a troubling and accelerating affair with alcohol and heroin. Patti understandably became distressed.

There in a beachside bungalow at the Hilton Hawaiian Village, Patti searched her feelings and decided to leave Jesse. After the Honolulu concert, she informed him she was staying behind with Billy and taking some time away from the circus. Jesse journeyed back to the mainland to continue the tour without her. Billy protested. Approaching his ninth birthday, he was growing up fast in the music environment and he loved it. Now they were going to leave it all behind? Patti told him he could continue living with her or go stay with his biological father. Either way, they needed a break from Jesse. "I'm not sending you off in that circus," she said. "I hated her for it," Bill remembers. "Mom wanted to just grow vegetables and live out on the beach at Lanikai."[21]

Friends had recognized for some time that Patti was in an increasingly unhealthy relationship. It was apparent that Jesse's dalliances with harder drugs were becoming an addiction. When the Faces rolled into New York in October, Jesse rang May Pang. She thought they were only getting together to catch up before Jesse asked her to take him to the East Village to pick something up. They entered an apartment building on St. Mark's Place. It was like going to the doctor, with people rotating in and out. "As we're approaching, someone was coming out, and he looked like another rock star," Pang recalls. "Who the hell knows. The two of them looked at each other, and Jesse said, 'He looks familiar.'" It was a strange scene in the apartment, where a cat was lying in a frying pan. Two weeks later, Pang got a chill when reading the newspaper. After a deal gone bad, someone shot the drug-dealing couple who lived in the apartment. Jesse's developing addiction was becoming downright dangerous.[22]

Back in Hawaii, Patti eventually made friends with a group calling themselves the Source Family. They had only recently relocated from Los Angeles and had lost their leader in a hang-gliding accident. Their talk of holistic health and higher consciousness, macrobiotic food and futons appealed to Patti, though she preserved some distance, wise from the world she had just escaped. Billy headed back to California to reunite with his birth father. For his recent birthday, he received the ultimate present, a reminder of that circus his mother made him leave behind. John Lennon sent a big box containing vinyl copies of every single Beatles album and every Beatles member's solo album. "That was my treasure," he says.[23]

NOW BACK IN Los Angeles alone, Jesse took an apartment on Ocean Front Walk at Venice Beach. Sometimes failing to show up for gigs, he pawned guitars to pay rent and score heroin. Friends came to visit, but he wouldn't come out of the bedroom, where he preferred lying in the dark with the blinds drawn all day. "Too fucked up to deal with, and there was nothing I could do," Jesse's close friend and assistant Jim Catalano regretted. "I loved him but you can't change people." Jesse's guitar-playing acquaintance Gary Vogensen called to invite Jesse to a session with Frank Zappa. "I don't think about music unless I'm working," Jesse said in a stroke of mystifying logic, before declining.[24]

Though Jesse's condition was concerning, it wasn't exceptional, not in his world. If he stood out, it was more for his extremities than his proclivities. "He had a little crazy streak," drummer Jim Keltner confesses. "He seemed to always be in some kind of trouble." That substance abuse was pervasive in the 1960s and '70s music business, from backstage out across the audience, is well understood, to the point of becoming a trope. It wasn't much different before then either, when jazz giants like Jesse's hero Charlie Parker tangled with heroin. "We're talking about very dark drug years," Keltner elaborates. "Those years were very, very steeped in drugs. Everybody was very into drugs—the musicians, the business people, everybody. It wasn't unusual at the time, but it was very destructive." In that context, people were often left to fend for themselves. For some, drugs were merely a problem. For Jesse, it was developing into a legitimate disease and should have been treated as such. Make no mistake, friends tried.

Still, there were flashes of Jesse's determination to advance his career even as his health declined. During 1975 and '76, he received continuing, if diminishing, invitations to demonstrate his talent as a session musician. In 1975, he played guitar on some of the stronger material from George Harrison's latest album, *Extra Texture*, including the "While My Guitar Gently Weeps" sequel "This Guitar (Can't Keep from Crying)." He also appeared on albums by Ringo Starr, Cher, Neil Diamond, David Cassidy, Tracy Nelson, three more albums with Harry Nilsson, and more.

Examples of Jesse's most exquisite musicianship emerged during this otherwise dark period. His work on tracks such as "The Ballad of Jennifer Lee" and "Cordelia" from David Blue's *Cupid's Arrow* (1976) is simply brilliant. He blends perfectly within an arrangement of masterful musicians, including old pals Levon Helm and Duck Dunn, and the skilled David Lindley, who contributed mandolin, fiddle, and lap steel guitar. Their interplay on "Cordelia" is stunning, with Jesse's descending guitar figure setting the song's melodic spine. It demonstrates Jesse's exemplary talent for hearing the essence of a song and strengthening it.

Elsewhere, Jesse shined on Van Dyke Parks's *Clang of the Yankee Reaper* (1976). "He brought great luster to my effort," Parks affirms. Jesse also plays dexterous slide guitar on Eric Clapton's appropriately titled "Hello Old Friend" from the top-ten album *No Reason to Cry* (1976). This coincided with an all-star jam at Clapton's birthday party in March 1976. Jesse joined Robbie Robertson, Ronnie Wood, and Clapton on guitar while Van Morrison delivered blues standards and Billy Preston belted out Ray Charles tunes. When the all-nighter reached roughly 8 a.m., Bob Dylan showed up, grabbed the microphone, and began making up songs on the spot, including four songs roasting each of the four Beatles.[25]

Around this time, possibly taking a step toward another solo album, Jesse invited *Keep Me Comin'* drummer and bassist Jim Keltner and Bob Glaub to join him in the studio for a new song he wrote called "Keep a-Movin'." The song features Glaub's characteristically fluid bass work and Keltner's typically funky and musical drumming. Jesse's guitar tracks, both acoustic and electric, feature in the mix, but the song's signature sound was something entirely new, at least coming from him. An enthusiastic foray into synthesizers, almost to the point of prog rock, dominates before Jesse, returning to more familiar terrain, drops in a ripping electric guitar solo and shouts "SMOKE THAT GUITAR!!!" Still unreleased, the song didn't lead to a new album, but its place in Jesse's story indicates a moment when things might have gone in new musical directions. Jesse would later return to keyboards for his work with John Trudell in the 1980s. He even recycled the drum break from "Keep a-Movin'" for "Bringing Back the Time" on Jesse and Trudell's *Heart Jump Bouquet* (1987).[26]

One of Jesse's greatest studio achievements resulted from his work on two Rod Stewart albums that hit the top ten in the US and number one in the UK. Jesse contributed guitar across *Atlantic Crossing* (1975), including the song he cowrote with Stewart, "Alright for an Hour," featuring Jesse's frantic and funky strumming. Jesse especially shines on the "slow side," where "I Don't Want to Talk About It" and "It's Not the Spotlight" foreground his softer touch on acoustic guitar. Though it receives less mention than his bluesy electric highlights, Jesse was an outstanding acoustic guitar player, having begun on the instrument when he used to sneak his father's Martin from the closet.

One of Jesse's greatest recorded moments can be heard in his gorgeous, appropriately seductive acoustic guitar on Stewart's "Tonight's the Night" from *A Night on the Town* (1976). Jesse got Bob Glaub on the session as bassist. They arrived at Cherokee Studios to play alongside one of the greatest session musicians ever, Stax Records guitarist Steve Cropper, who backed Otis Redding, Booker T. Jones, Wilson Pickett, and other legends. Cropper, "the Colonel," rightly pulled rank and occupied the lead guitar position. This left guitarist Pete Carr and Jesse to take up rhythm tracks—one electric, one acoustic. Jesse chose the latter, punctuating Cropper's slinky lead licks with glistening acoustic guitar figures befitting the song's sultry sound. Here we really hear Jesse's sweetness and sensitivity, skills that set him apart in a town that would soon be struck by lightning guitarists. If Cropper's guitar provides the song's body language, then Jesse's guitar delivers a kiss. "It was a very romantic period for me," Stewart noted. The song hit number one, remains a staple in Stewart's set today, and continues to play everywhere from radio stations to grocery stores.[27]

Unfortunately, Jesse's partnership with Stewart was slipping away. Jesse called his friend Walter Trout for a ride to a Stewart session in 1976. "Bring some dope," Jesse instructed. Walter reached Jesse's place and delivered the bad news: "I don't have any heroin. I'm out." "Well, I've got to get some before the session." They drove to five or six places, searching for heroin, and then the heavy sedative Doriden, wasting hours while finding nothing. Jesse was supposed to be at the Stewart session by 8 p.m. He and Walter arrived at 11:30. There was a sign on the door saying, "Jesse: We got another guitar player. Go home." That marked the unceremonious end to Jesse's chart-topping partnership with Stewart, who had given Jesse plenty of chances. Now Stewart prefers remembering his old bandmate at his best: "I witnessed Jesse's singular talent up close when he joined the Faces for our whirlwind final tour and contributed his signature guitar to my albums *Atlantic Crossing* and *A Night on the Town*."[28]

With Rod Stewart and the Faces in the rearview, Jesse formed a new solo group. Bassist Bob Glaub and drummer Gary Ray carried over from the previous lineup. Jesse thought he couldn't or shouldn't replace his late keyboardist, Bob and Gary's best friend, Ray Eckstein. Instead, Jesse searched for a second guitarist, perhaps to re-create some of the magic from his work with Ron Wood. Indeed, it seemed apparent to everyone that Jesse was so enamored with his Faces experience that he was now determined to reproduce it with his solo group, right down to the hair, makeup, and clothing. This was most evident in the singer Jesse recruited to front his band.

John Angelos, better known by his stage name "Johnny Angel," came from Detroit, where he briefly sang lead vocals in Ted Nugent's Amboy Dukes. He had some talent as a writer, evidenced by his collaborations with Jesse on the *Keep Me Comin'* album. Angel danced like Mick Jagger and delivered the look and the raspy sound, if not range, of the more popular "blue-eyed" blues rock singers of the era—Steve Marriott, Van Morrison, Frankie Miller, and, above all, Rod Stewart. Bob and Gary were skeptical, partly because they thought the group was better with Jesse in front singing his own songs. But Jesse had always lacked confidence in his singing and talent for fronting a group. That couldn't have been any easier after three solo albums that went nowhere.

Finally, Jesse met his new guitar player at a party in the Hollywood Hills. Walter Trout came out from New Jersey. Shortly after showing up in LA, Trout found himself in a relationship with a woman who also happened to be one of the biggest drug dealers in town. "I was living with the female version of Tony Montana," Trout puts it. At the party, Trout recognized Jesse Ed Davis across the room. He couldn't believe it. He was one of Jesse's many self-proclaimed "biggest fans" who studied all of Jesse's work with Taj Mahal. "I was big eyes; I was starstruck," Trout recalls. Hearing Jesse was looking for a guitar player, he gave Jesse a bump of some of the finest cocaine around, asked for an audition, and promised, "You let me come and play a song with you and I'll bring more of that stuff." It wasn't as imprudent as it sounds. At the time, many music partnerships were formed that way. Walter has deep regrets, but if Jesse wasn't already into heavy drugs, then Walter's guarantee wouldn't have been worth much to Jesse in the first place.

Trout showed up at their rehearsal spot in Marina del Rey, plugged into a Fender amp, and began warming up. Jesse stopped him immediately. "The first thing you gotta do: turn off that fucking reverb." Despite this initial rocky start, Jesse took a liking to Trout, and not just because of the drug connection. With a complete lineup intact, Jesse informed the group they would now be called Boy. The name revealed Jesse's current state of mind. "Boy" was a common slang term for heroin, while "girl" referred to cocaine. For all intents and purposes, they were going to call their band Heroin. Trout protested. "Nobody gives a shit about Boy, but if you call it the Jesse Ed Davis Band, you're gonna have guitar players lining up out the door," he argued. Glaub too was dismayed. "Well, that was life in a band with three junkies," he sighs.

The group's focus on the wrong themes began showing when they appeared live. Gigs started to seem more like an excuse to get high than to play great music. "It was a total junkie concept [Jesse] was getting off on," drummer Gary Ray describes it. The music began changing too, incorporating elements of both the prevailing punk scene and T. Rex–style glam rock. This wasn't the sound the modest but loyal Jesse Davis fanbase wanted. A reviewer from the *Los Angeles Times* wasn't impressed when they caught Boy opening for the Doors' keyboardist Ray Manzarek at the Starwood. "Jesse Ed Davis's group Boy reflects the usual session-guitarist's flaw—plenty of talent but little vision." The reviewer then described Johnny Angel as a "striking James Dean Gene Vincent presence," but one whose singing "simply goes from Stewart to Jagger to Bowie and back again."[29]

While Trout was no angel, he became distressed about the state of the band's health and affairs. Unlike Bob and Gary, he loved Johnny Angel's singing, but he was otherwise terrified of their frontman. "He was a madman," Trout says. "If Bob Glaub thought I was a madman, he was looking in the wrong direction because Johnny Angelos was almost frightening to hang out with. Like, I got to get away from this dude or I'm not gonna survive the night, you know?"[30]

Trout eventually convinced Jesse to enter treatment with him at a methadone clinic in Redondo Beach. Each day, they drove over and received a cup of orange juice with a gradually diminishing dose, until one day they were drinking pure juice. For Trout, it worked. He had been thinking about what he would do if it did. He told his girlfriend he had a gig that night, loaded his Stratocaster and amp into his car, and left town, leaving everything else behind, including Boy. He went on to play with Canned Heat, John Mayall, and his own award-winning Walter Trout Band, which continues today, even after Trout survived a liver transplant.

Years later, Trout went to a Taj Mahal gig and saw Jesse walking down the aisle. He ran up to his old partner. "Jesse! Hey man, it's me! Walter!" Skipping the pleasantries, Jesse replied, "Where is she?" Trout was confused before finally realizing Jesse was referring to his drug-dealing ex-girlfriend. Trout had long moved on. Jesse seemed completely oblivious to the fact that it had been over five years since they drank their last cup of orange juice together. Only then did Trout know the treatment didn't work for Jesse. "It was very sad," he says.[31]

DURING ONE OF HIS occasional better days, Jesse began seeing a new romantic partner named Ming Lowe, a talented painter who loved Jesse dearly. During the 1970s, she was something of a rock star muse. Almost by accident, she began hosting large gatherings of artists, musicians, poets, and other creative people at her home in the desert that functioned like a hippie salon. After impassioned but volatile relationships with Paul Butterfield, the Velvet Underground's Sterling Morrison, and Big Brother and the Holding Company's James Gurley, she met Jesse, who immediately insisted that they be together. In fact, the two had briefly met in 1968 at a Taj Mahal show, when Jesse seemed quiet and shy, and only smoked a little dope. Sometime in 1976, Ming moved into Jesse's oceanfront apartment and tried to help him. "Jesse was full of love," she remembers him today. "He was a good man." But she couldn't save him.

At the beginning of their romance, Ming marveled at Jesse's artistic passion and appreciated his literary intelligence, always remembering how Jesse taught her the word "copacetic." Jesse took Ming and Harry Nilsson for a ride on a boat he borrowed from Marjoe Gortner, a famous television evangelist who studied Mick Jagger's moves and used rock and roll themes to help the rock and roll generation get high on Jesus. A film featuring his traveling tent shows managed to win an Academy Award. More interesting, Marjoe had recently starred in a wacky film called *Acapulco Gold* (1976) about a heroin smuggling scheme between Hawaii and Los Angeles. The boat Jesse, Ming, and Nilsson took out was the boat from the film. Ming's experience with rock stars benefited her in this context. She was almost willfully unimpressed, which made her more attractive to Jesse.

Less glamorous was the night Jesse, driving drunk, crashed the new Corvette he had bought from James Caan. He wound up with the turn signal stuck in his arm. As old pictures of Patti blew around the Pacific Coast Highway, Jesse staggered to a payphone and called Ming, begging her to go with him to the police station and support a stolen car story. He was terrified of a DUI and, never forgoing a hustle, he hoped to collect the insurance money. Ming reluctantly agreed, putting her neck on the line for Jesse, as other friends often did, out of an inextinguishable sense of obligation to him. She told the police Jesse was away with her in Palm Desert at the time of the crash. To Ming's amazement, the scheme worked. Or, deep down, she knew it would work. Jesse had that kind of effect on people.

Jesse told Ming he wanted fame. He wanted greatness. He wanted fans and wanted to be loved as a musician. But he struggled with putting himself out front. He wasn't comfortable with it. He was always modest in that way. Many of his friends and colleagues observed the same, emphasizing how often he lay back in his playing when others would grab the spotlight. Gary Vogensen describes the first time he saw Jesse live, appearing with Mike Bloomfield at the Fillmore West in the late 1960s. Bloomfield kept trying to pass a solo spot over to Jesse, but Jesse wouldn't take it. Likewise, if you listen to Jesse sitting in with the Rolling Stones at the Los Angeles Forum on the *L.A. Friday (Live 1975)* album, you'll need a relatively sophisticated ear to pick him out of the mix behind Keith Richards and Ron Wood in their lengthy rendition of "Sympathy for the Devil." They brought Jesse out as a special guest in front of eighteen thousand people, but Jesse was more content to weave his guitar with Keith and Woody, blending inconspicuously into their collective sound. That's what made Jesse great.

In his solo career, Jesse surrounded himself with a coterie of musicians, some rather famous, who allowed him to be part of an ensemble, within which he played a surprisingly negligible number of guitar solos, even inviting Eric Clapton to play lead on his first album's centerpiece "Washita Love Child." With his more defined sound on his third album *Keep Me Comin'*, Jesse wisely sang lead vocals but then hired his writing partner John Angelos to front his live band. In his final act, Jesse was happiest putting music to John Trudell's words and producing the Grafitti Band. "He wasn't into the dog and pony show," his Grafitti Bandmate Mark Shark insists. His career is the culmination of a long series of wanting the embrace of fame but refusing the spotlight. Even when he played live, he often turned inward, or even backward, obscuring how he played some of his licks. When he faced the crowd, he leaned his head back and got lost in the groove with his eyes closed. As a musician, Jesse demonstrated an alternating determination to both stand out and blend in. As Ming puts it, "He was there, but he was not there. He was everywhere, but he wasn't."[32]

In 1977, Jesse went to Ming's studio in Palm Desert determined to kick heroin and get his career back on track. Under her careful and sympathetic watch, he endured agonizing withdrawal, spending most of the time, what seemed like years, in Ming's icy bathtub. It was actually just three days before Jesse told her he couldn't take it anymore. He needed to go back to Los Angeles, score, and stop the pain. She understood and appreciated his honesty.

Jesse accidentally left a small bindle of China White at Ming's place. The curiosity was overwhelming, not because she wanted to dive into heroin addiction but because she wanted to understand its incomprehensible power over someone she loved. She put the tiniest amount she could collect on her fingertip and raised it to her nose. Minutes later, she rushed to the bathroom, vomited, and then lay on her bed. When it took effect, she knew she was still alive, but felt like she was dead. It wasn't ecstatic, orgasmic, or transcendent. She was now only more confused. Though Jesse and Ming remained close friends, it was clear to Ming that they couldn't have a future together. She knew she couldn't possibly withstand his disease and had already learned she couldn't help him defeat it.

Ming holds on to better impressions. Above all, Jesse was a joker. She can still hear his laughter, one of his defining features. It's as memorable as the pain she endured from loving Jesse, which she once immortalized in a painting she titled "Jesse, Waving Goodbye, Throwing Love out the Window, with Holes in His Arms." Ming's stunning portrait of Jesse depicts him waving goodbye, not to Ming, but to heroin. The painting's wish didn't come true.

Other friends and colleagues who interacted with Jesse in this condition struggled to help. Musicians of Jesse's era were frequently caught up in their own maelstrom of addiction. By 1975, various icons from Jesse's scene, including Jimi Hendrix, Jim Morrison, Janis Joplin, and Tim Buckley had already died from it. Many around Jesse were managing their own drug issues. Things moved so fast that people could not get an accurate read on someone's situation. "I drove Jesse to a methadone clinic," remembers Sandy Konikoff, Jesse's drummer friend dating back to the early Taj Mahal days. "He was reading a book the whole time with sunglasses on. I put it all together then."[33]

When Jesse visited home at Christmastime in 1976, he met his ex-fiancée Mary Carol Kaspereit in Oklahoma City, not to rekindle romance but to see an old friend and go Christmas shopping. "I noticed that there was something wrong when I picked him up," she recalls. "He had gotten a little wild." When they went shopping, Jesse was uncharacteristically rude to the store clerks. Then, the underlying problem became explicit when they went for dinner at Magic Pan. Jesse pulled out a hypodermic needle right in the middle of the crowded restaurant.

Mary Carol had just begun work as a high school teacher. Jesse's behavior frightened her.[34]

Jesse's addiction was so dangerous it began threatening people close to him. Jim Catalano understandably panicked when Jesse snuck heroin into a line of cocaine they were sharing. It destroyed their friendship and professional relationship. But Jim worried more about Jesse. "It was more that he was endangering himself," he recalled. Jim rightly understood what Jesse was up against. "He was overwhelmed by a disease. He didn't see the whole picture." Jim finally left for Santa Fe, where he focused on his career as a painter.[35]

If Jesse was already struggling in early 1977, then a phone call he received from home completely cast him into darkness. Shortly before Catalano split, Jesse attended a session Phil Spector was producing for Leonard Cohen's *Death of a Ladies' Man* album. Bob Dylan, in the midst of his divorce from his first wife Sara, drinking straight from a whisky bottle, had reconnected with Jesse, and invited his old friend to hang at the studio.[36] Bob had the poet Allen Ginsberg with him. They hadn't come to record, but suddenly they were singing together on Cohen's bawdy "Don't Go Home with Your Hard-On." Then Jesse strapped in for an impromptu guitar track. Spector either loved or hated it, no one was sure. He repeatedly yelled from the control room, "THIS IS PUNK ROCK, MOTHERFUCKER!" An amused Leonard Cohen poured Cuervo. The phone rang. Someone passed the phone to Jesse. He listened for a second, hung up, and broke down. His father had died. The music stopped. Bob put his arm around Jesse and led him outside, where they took a long walk together in the early morning hour. Bob may have been the only person in Jesse's life, apart from his mother far away in Oklahoma, with enough power over Jesse to pick him up in that moment.[37]

At Jesse Edwin Davis II's funeral reception, Jesse greeted people outside the front door in a flamboyant green suit. Realizing Jess Davis Sr. was only fifty-four, Mary Carol Kaspereit was shocked. Not long after, Jesse called to explain his father's fate. After being rushed to St. Anthony's, Jess had died from heart failure during a bout of delirium tremens. It didn't make sense to Mary Carol. She remembers there being liquor in the Davis home, but that was typical. If Bus had been a heavy drinker, he hid the extent of its effects.[38]

IN THE WAKE OF his father's death, Jesse entered a black hole of declining emotional and physical health. On at least one occasion, his rock star connections afforded him a little health care. John and Yoko sent him to see their doctor Yuan Bain Hong in San Francisco. Dr. Hong was a Chinese herbalist and acupuncturist. John saw him in 1972 for help with methamphetamine addiction and he later sent Harry Nilsson to him too. Jesse thought the alternative treatment helped, noting that he at least didn't experience the awful side effects that accompanied other approaches. Chinese acupuncturists have been dealing with opium addiction for thousands of years, he reasoned, "So it makes sense."[39]

In August 1977, returning from a visit with Dr. Hong, Jesse went down to San Diego to stay with his manager friends Joel and Mona Maiman, trying to nurture his own support system with trusted people. Mona recalls the strange treatment Jesse was undergoing, specifically a tea made of crushed insects that he had been instructed to drink. Jesse was standing at her stove boiling bugs in water when a news bulletin interrupted the TV program. Elvis Presley had died. Earlier that year, Jesse lost his father. Now he lost his first great music hero. The shock and sorrow were too much. He drank his tea and got up to leave. On the way out the door, he turned and told Mona and Joel the truth: he was going up to North County to score. They couldn't stop him.

With the arrival of winter in late 1977 came a possible new lease on a music career from an old friend, one with enough clout to put Jesse back in the business. Bob Dylan was planning to take a twelve-piece group on a world tour beginning in February 1978. He tasked his bandleader Rob Stoner with bringing in a good blend of talent. Stoner recruited several Los Angeles players, but Dylan wasn't digging any of them. One day, Stoner showed up at the rehearsal space in Santa Monica surprised to see Jesse Ed Davis playing guitar. Losing patience with Stoner's parade of hopefuls, Dylan had finally made his own pick for the coveted lead guitar spot. Stoner loved the idea, but there was a problem. Jesse kept playing his way around the lead spots, preferring to play rhythm, as he often did on big stages with the Stones, the Faces, and the Concert for Bangladesh.

This was Jesse's shot at nailing down the lead guitar chair. Worried, Stoner pulled Jesse aside. "What are you doing?" Stoner pleaded. "You're letting this slip away." "Bob asked me to just play rhythm," Jesse replied. Stoner wasn't surprised given Dylan's mercurial nature, but they already had three people playing rhythm chords, and they didn't need that from Jesse. Returning from a break in rehearsals, Stoner told Jesse to ignore Bob's advice and show what he could do from the lead position, but Jesse refused. It isn't clear why Dylan instructed Jesse to play rhythm during his search for a lead guitarist, but it's clear Jesse was loyal to Dylan's desire. In the end, it probably wasn't a deciding factor, Stoner suggests. What likely mattered more was that Jesse was obviously strung out, and probably not in shape for a rigorous world tour.[40]

Jesse wasn't new to Hollywood and the music industry when he got on a bus with the Faces in 1975. His growing dependence on drugs to soothe his pain, depression, anxieties, and to soften professional misfortunes also predated 1975. Various people who were close to him provide different accounts of how heroin first got into him. It was during a party at Keith Moon's house in Malibu, one insists. "Ed was a leader, but he was also a follower when people would invite him over," they add. No, it was with Keith Richards in New York City, another source is certain. No, it was during the Faces tour. It's their fault, one popular narrative goes. The competing accounts may suggest that, like his father, Jesse was at first keeping the extent of his use hidden.

That Jesse's relationship with heroin worsened during the Faces tour is indisputable, but he had been experimenting with it before 1975. He had squandered the John Mayall gig in 1974. That same year, Jesse's adoring cousin Russ Saunkeah, who by then had been living with Jesse at the Hurricane House for two years, became worried enough to move back home, not wanting to get caught on the wrong road. One close friend clearly recalls Jesse visiting them at a music club in Malibu no later than 1974, and possibly as early as 1972, seeking help locating heroin. "It took me weeks to get my mind around the whole thing," they remember. "Ed was an equal opportunity substance abuser, man, but so was everybody around him," another friend concludes. "I don't know exactly what he was all consuming, but I know he was consuming whatever came his way, from the time I met him [in 1970]."[41]

Does pinpointing Jesse's first time with "the boy" matter? There were famous heroin users in every direction. Jesse was close with many of them. When I ask his friend and frequent studio collaborator, bassist Lee Sklar, about the temptation to blame any one person for Jesse's addiction, he doesn't hesitate: "That's bullshit." He continues,

> I'm sure, being Native American, there's baggage he had to live with that transcended anything we could ever imagine. He might be able to bury it when working with you, but when he went back to his hotel room and was on his own, who knows what kind of demons he might've had that just are a part of being who he was. I've lost a lot of people in this business over the years. . . . If you're looking for answers and you choose heroin, the odds are you're going to go down pretty fast, and it's not going to be anything anybody can help you with.

Sklar loved Jesse. To him and others, Jesse's problems were not rooted in his disease. It was the other way around. Those close to him understood he suffered from private or undiagnosed pain. They just didn't know how to stop it, or if they really could.[42]

Beyond John and Yoko paying for Jesse's trips to Dr. Hong, Jesse didn't have the type of expansive support system that surrounded someone like Keith Richards. The Rolling Stones had lawyers and cash. They had people on their payroll. They were an elaborate business entity. Rock stars at that level didn't have to meet their dealers. They didn't touch the money. They could take drugs with impunity. Jesse moved in those circles, but he was not Keith Richards. He operated on a much smaller scale, mostly hustling a career.[43]

Jesse's problem was twofold. First, taking drugs was a ubiquitous social practice. They were currency and gifts. It wasn't uncommon for someone in the industry to be paid with drugs. Many artists appealed to them for access to altered states of introspection, extroversion, consciousness, subconsciousness, and unconsciousness. If Jesse wanted them, he could find them. More often the harder part was affording them. Second, and more importantly, drugs were medication for the disease of addiction. We should just as appropriately think of those suffering from drug addiction as being like patients suffering from cancer. Jesse was an addict. He became sick. Not using drugs became a daily struggle for him. Drugs ease that pain. And the shame from using them creates more pain. The pain becomes cyclical. It's natural to want someone to blame when we lose a loved one to addiction, but it's futile. Jesse's disease was bigger than any one perpetrator, and it was bigger than Jesse himself.[44]

IN 1978, somewhere in the United States, a Dakota person named John Trudell, who led the 1969 Alcatraz protest that Jesse once sang about in "Alcatraz," was walking across the country with other American Indian activists to Washington. They comprised the Longest Walk, which symbolized Indigenous people's forced removals from their ancestral lands while drawing attention to treaty rights. "I knew I was an Indian in my head, but I didn't know I was an Indian in my heart," one participant said. Along the way, now in his position as national spokesman for the American Indian Movement, Trudell delivered media interviews and more of the powerful rhetoric that made him a leader back in San Francisco. He and other Indigenous people were hip to the ideas behind settler colonialism well before scholars developed the term. "They called us Indian. And then they called us heathens, savages, hostile. They called us renegades. . . . Now they call us militant, communist, but they never, ever called us the People," Trudell said. His words didn't sound different from those he would one day speak in a musical venture known as Grafitti Man.[45]

Meanwhile, back in Los Angeles, Jesse kicked off 1978 with an increasingly rare studio session, guesting on his old friend Ben Sidran's *A Little Kiss in the Night*. Surprisingly, Jesse then made a trip to Oklahoma in February and March for a series of dates at Tulsa's Paradise Club, backed by his old friend Junior Markham on harmonica and his old Taj Mahal bandmates Gary Gilmore on bass and Chuck Blackwell and Jim Karstein rotating on drums.

Finally, Jesse started thinking about Patti again, or he never stopped. He did what any number of poor fools longing for a lost love did in those situations: he made Patti a mixtape. He put his heart into it, clearly attempting to rekindle her affections. The A-side, titled "Ululu," began with Jesse's tribute of the same name to Patti, before advancing to Aretha Franklin's "You and Me" and a further series of songs that imagined reunited love, including Patti's favorite song "Wild World" by Cat Stevens and Jesse's own version of "Farther on Down the Road." The anguished B-side, titled "Remember Christmas," took its name from the poignant Harry Nilsson song included within: "Remember is a place from long ago . . . Remember life is never as it seems." For Jesse, the future lay in his past with Patti. First, he sent his mixtape letter across the ocean to Hawaii. Then he got on a plane.

Nine

WAS IT JUST A DREAM?

THE VIEW FROM Jesse's hillside abode on Koohoo Place in Kailua was both sobering and intoxicating. He could begin each day with a breathtaking ocean panorama, framed by swaying palm trees, filled with glowing aquamarine waves that wrap around the seabird Nā Mokulua islets in the distance. White sand forms Lanikai Beach on the windward side of O'ahu, where the rolling tide that relentlessly reshapes the shore is an irresistible metaphor for Jesse's chapter in Hawaii. If Los Angeles is a long way from Oklahoma, then Lanikai Beach is otherworldly. It's postcard material to an almost perilous degree. "Hawaii held a special place in [Jesse]'s heart, a place of healing," his soon-to-be first wife Tantalayo recalled.[1]

Jesse's ambitions were clear, though they transformed during his brief time here, as he moved in and out of relationships and residences. In Hawaii's diverse environment, he could blend in even easier than in Los Angeles. But Jesse wasn't here to get away. He was here to recover something. His first objective was to resuscitate his romance with Patti, his "Golden Sun Goddess," who sought refuge in Hawaii. When Jesse proved incapable of rescuing their relationship, he tried a different path with her friend Tantalayo, who was herself searching for new purpose and belonging. In the care of both women, Jesse hoped to repair himself and find relief from addiction.

Hawaii was paradise to Patti. She fell in love with it when Jesse played Honolulu on the Faces tour in 1975. She was a beach girl at heart, and here she could keep what she loved about Los Angeles while escaping a life that had become too overwhelming and at times too frightening. She juggled jobs at a jewelry store, a frozen smoothie joint, and a bikini shop, made new friends, looked inward, and wondered if some time away in Hawaii could revive her relationship with Jesse, or if she and Jesse could continue to have a relationship at all.

Jesse finished the Faces tour in 1975, witnessed the group's dissolution just when he had settled in, and watched his session invitations diminish. He had little left to lose in Los Angeles. In Hawaii, he had everything, namely Patti, to regain. When they reunited, they kept different addresses, splitting time between Honolulu and Kailua, separated thirty minutes by the Pali Highway tunnels connecting the leeward and windward sides of O'ahu. On the slopes of Diamond Head Circle in the capital, Jesse initially stayed in an estate built and owned by the Hollywood actress and pin-up model Lana Turner, with a swimming pool designed by Tarzan actor Johnny Weissmuller. Jesse's new manager Leroy Jenkins, a former radio DJ and owner of the Acoustic Workshop chain of Hawaiian Hi-Fi shops, rented the place for his new artist. Jesse's old friend and Rolling Stones pianist Nicky Hopkins, frequently smiling but rarely speaking, kind of like Jesse at the beginning of the decade, often crashed there and relaxed by the pool. In this setting Jesse could imagine he was still a rock star, only on an extended vacation. The effect was both good and bad.[2]

Sometimes Jesse would take Kalākaua Avenue from Honolulu out to Mākālei Beach, which wraps around the Diamond Head crater. He could often be found at a cement picnic table on a shady expanse of grass, reading books. At the beach, Jesse sought peace from what he personally characterized as a Jekyll versus Hyde struggle within him. But it wasn't entirely a matter of good versus evil. He could just as often betray a disarming conflict between revelatory genius and an "Aw, shucks" vulnerability, friends from Hawaii recall. "When Jesse was sober, he had a glow around him. . . . He radiated emotional intelligence," says Mike Piranha. "I could see why the best of the best wanted to be around him." When Piranha marveled at Jesse's ability to read a tome in one day at the beach, Jesse replied, "I like being around myself when I'm sober."[3]

Friends remember that Jesse was also better when he was around Patti. By day, they could be any ordinary couple, passing long afternoons at the beach, occasionally with Patti calling in sick to work so they could stay a little longer. They sometimes went swimming in nostalgia at the Hilton, where they stayed with Billy in 1975 while Jesse was on tour with the Faces. Other days they'd go shopping and grab a pizza or catch a movie—*The Deer Hunter, Alien, Manhattan, Midnight Express, Monty Python's Life of Brian*. Some nights they stayed together in one of their separate "hobbit holes," Patti called them. "Jesse is looking good," Patti noticed. Abandoning California, they were possibly falling in love again.

Nights were still filled with music. They saw Dolly Parton at Honolulu's Blaisdell Center and David Bromberg, whose 1975 album *Midnight on the Water* featured Jesse's guitar. At an Elvin Bishop gig, Jesse took the stage for a guest spot. They also went to see Roger McGuinn, Chris Hillman, and Gene Clark's partial Byrds reunion. This might have been when Jesse's old pal and music partner Gene started thinking about moving to Hawaii.[4]

In January 1980, Kris Kristofferson and Willie Nelson flew in for a concert in Honolulu. One of Jesse's guitar heroes, Grady Martin, was playing with Willie, and Jesse's roving bandmate from early '70s Los Angeles, Chris Ethridge, was on bass. Before their set, Ethridge noted Jesse's presence. "Have him come up and play," Willie enthused. Willie took the stage in his typical gray t-shirt and faded jeans, but this time distinguished by haku and maile lei. During a break halfway through Willie's set, Jesse strode onstage with a Telecaster. From the circular balcony directly behind the stage, a group of ten or so Native American people loudly cheered, one yelling, "Hey Indian! HEY INDIAN! Yá át tééh!" Jesse looked around, then up, waved, and joined in on the next number with the biggest smile on his face. So much for Hawaii as a place where he could blend in. He loved the recognition.[5]

On a smaller scale with a smaller budget, Jesse nurtured his professional career while on retreat in Hawaii. This chapter of Jesse's life has understandably been mischaracterized as one of professional dormancy and decline, but Jesse was actually quite active. He worked to advance his career away from the spotlight, preferring recovery in the shadows. It couldn't have been easy. He was still committed to a career in music, employing the same three strategies from his most successful years in Hollywood: producing other artists, working as a session guitarist, and developing his own projects both live and in the studio.

A local progressive rock guitarist named Daniel Jones called it a "life-changing experience" when he met Jesse in Honolulu in 1979. It began with a crush on Patti. "You're cute, but I have a boyfriend," she told Daniel when he finally asked her out. When she revealed his name, he couldn't believe it. He had all of Jesse Ed Davis's records, and all the Taj Mahal records with Jesse too. Minutes later, Jesse drove up in an old Volkswagen. Patti said she just met his biggest fan. "Tell him to get in," Jesse responded. Like most everyone else who encountered Jesse, the first thing Daniel noticed was his smile, beaming with big, white teeth. They were off to Mama Mia Pizza, where Jesse basked in Daniel's fan questions about his career and a story about sitting for hours with *Keep Me Comin'*, trying to learn Jesse's guitar part on the instrumental opener "Big Dipper." Where had this fan recognition been? Jesse wondered aloud. Next, the trio headed to Puck's Pub, where Jesse planned to guest with a band he was considering producing. The next thing Daniel knew, he was onstage too, playing two Allman Brothers classics, "Whipping Post" and "Statesboro Blues," the latter of course a Taj Mahal and Jesse Ed Davis classic. "That was Jesse," Daniel recalls. "Spontaneous." Being with Jesse meant being prepared for anything.[6]

Jesse decided to pass on the group at Puck's, and instead began embracing the eighteen-year-old Daniel as a protégé, not unlike how he brought along younger musicians back in Marina del Rey. Jesse set up a demo session at Commercial Recorders in Honolulu, where he called in some favors to get Daniel's group, the David Flowers Band, some free studio time late at night. "We couldn't do anything for him," Daniel recalls. "It wasn't to advance his career. He was just a big-hearted man."

After a series of preproduction meetings, the group went into the studio for five nights. Jesse taught Daniel how to get things done, but he also exhibited a hands-off production style, preferring to instead cultivate an environment where the band could comfortably be itself. "He let you try and find your way and only intervened if something was really going off the rails," Daniel remembers. He also gave Daniel some performance tips, especially when making a setlist, insisting it should be like an ocean, with a tide coming in and out, or like getting laid. Not much came of the demos they made, apart from memories of being young and working with a music hero. Drugs were certainly part of the experience, and that included heroin, but Jesse was nonetheless in good spirits.[7]

That same year, 1979, Jesse took a group of Chicago transplants under his wing, the Piranha Brothers. Patti loved them. "They'll make it big!" she guaranteed. Jesse and Mike Piranha had met at Lucky Pierre's, central in the college neighborhood club scene. Like Daniel Jones, Piranha couldn't contain his fandom as he sang Jesse's "Doctor My Eyes" guitar solo to him. They became fast friends. Piranha appreciated Jesse's dynamic personality, which ranged from reckless adventurer prone to ribald humor to a musical tactician exhibiting relentless desire for greatness. "He made me understand that fame isn't something that I read about—that I could at least shoot for it," Piranha describes Jesse's inspiration. "Then when fame didn't matter to me anymore, his musicianship powered me through my playing as a professional musician my whole life. He was so real." Piranha pauses, then, "He was also jump-off-the-roof-with-an-umbrella guy."[8]

Jesse adopted the Piranha Brothers as a means of getting back on track in the record business. Cocaine flowed freely, but that was typical. While those around him experienced Jesse's polar extremities, Jesse himself demonstrated a sense of seriousness and purpose in his music production. He produced two songs for the Piranha Brothers in Honolulu and then flew the band to Los Angeles to mix them at the Record Plant. They occupied waterbeds in the studio's lodging quarters, with beer vending machines outside their door, and dined with famous actors and music industry folks. This was exciting stuff for young musicians trying to make it. "The songs weren't very good," Piranha later said, "[but] the time we had doing them was."[9]

In addition to producing new talent, Jesse pursued new opportunities as a session musician, which required him to jet back and forth to the mainland. Though the invitations were less prestigious than they had been five years before, they were more peculiar. In 1978, he accepted one of the more dubious assignments of his career in providing a soundtrack for the bonkers film *Cocaine Cowboys* (1979), about a rock and roll band that smuggled cocaine from Colombia to fund its fledgling ambitions. The plot was a partly true portrayal of the leading man Tom Sullivan's real life.

Sullivan was something of a mysterious superstar in Andy Warhol's world and the Studio 54 scene in New York City. Sometime, somewhere in South America, he got hurt and addicted to morphine, which led to a heroin addiction. He somehow became the head of a drug smuggling ring in Florida, quietly earning millions. Heading to New York, he visited the same heroin dealer as John and Yoko and enjoyed a prominent benefactor in Margaret Trudeau, spouse of the prime minister of Canada Pierre Trudeau and mother of Justin Trudeau. Margaret partied at Studio 54.[10]

Despite having no acting or singing experience, Sullivan decided he could be a movie star and portray a hustling rock singer. He partnered with Tom Forcade, the founder of *High Times* magazine, who helped produce *Cocaine Cowboys* before he died from a self-inflicted shotgun wound prior to the film's completion. Sullivan put up enough money to bring the legitimate actor Jack Palance on board; talked Andy Warhol into letting him shoot the film at Warhol's estate in Montauk, New York; and even convinced Warhol to make a rather incoherent cameo in the rather incomprehensible film.

The music was only slightly better. It isn't clear how Jesse became involved with the project, but in October 1978, he was in charge at a studio in Los Angeles arranging music for the film and producing the band. When the film's screenwriter Victor Bockris visited the studio, it was apparent the band was hooked on junk. "They were happy and excited," Bockris remembers, "but they were talking and walking the way junkies do. . . . My memory of the music in the film is just dreadful." Sometime later the band lip-synced the film's titular song at a house in Los Angeles. Jesse's old Taj Mahal bandmate Chuck Blackwell played the group's shirtless drummer, but Jesse didn't appear in the film. He possibly had a falling out with Tom Sullivan, who insisted on complete control despite complete ineptitude. In any case, the film bombed. "The director couldn't direct, and the actors couldn't act," Bockris chides. Summing up what went wrong, he concludes, "Heroin destroys your life, and takes away your soul, leaves you in awful shape with no money."[11]

In 1979, a second session assignment in Los Angeles was less farcical. British songwriter Paul Kennerley had no album deal, no publishing deal, and really no contacts at all in the music business. But he had one powerful fan in Beatles engineer Glyn Johns, who helmed Kennerley's first album, *White Mansions* (1978), a concept album about the American Civil War. While finishing that album, Kennerley picked up a Time-Life *Gunfighters* book from the set advertised on television each Sunday. He became enthralled with Jesse James and began writing his next album about the legendary outlaw. Realizing he couldn't write another album like this from the bus stop in the London rain, he set out for America to make *The Legend of Jesse James*.

Eric Clapton featured on Kennerley's previous album and was set to appear on this next one, another soundtrack for a hypothetical stage or film production. But Clapton quit at the last minute, leaving Kennerley in a bind. "Don't worry, I'll get someone," Johns promised, immediately thinking of Jesse Davis, whose London sessions Johns engineered for Jesse's first album. Eight years after the Concert for Bangladesh, Jesse was again set to fill Clapton's vacancy on guitar.

The *Jesse James* band all stayed in a Hollywood mansion with a swimming pool, chef, and maid. Deep friendships emerged among everyone living together, but Jesse, who opted for a motel and getting a ride back and forth to the sessions, missed out. The band worked for just over two weeks, exclusively recording live, with all the musicians playing together in one room. Jesse didn't rehearse or really learn the music at all. Instead, he set up right next to drummer Levon Helm, who still referred to his old pal as "Indian Ed," and improvised, responding to Levon's drums, "like an Olympic gymnast," Kennerley describes Jesse, who was generally "gleeful" and "obviously a little stoned."[12]

While Jesse couldn't be found after hours at the mansion with everyone else, he was reliably present in the studio, predictably occupying the same chair, holding a Fender Stratocaster, almost always on time—an about-face from days when he sometimes missed studio assignments altogether. That isn't to say his physical presence always prevented conscious absence—Jesse was prone to nodding off. Still, he demonstrated an amazing ability to "come out of a cloud" and play brilliantly when called upon, before predictably slumping back down into his chair when finished. Given that the concept album's feature character is named Jesse, Emmylou Harris, who vocally portrayed Jesse James's mother Zerelda, often sang or spoke the main character's name into her microphone. Each time, Jesse sat up like a sunbeam, thinking he was needed, ready to deliver. It was endearing, if concerning.

Whatever Jesse's limitations, Glyn Johns was thrilled to work on Jesse's lead guitar parts, especially because he never needed to bump the volume fader up or down on Jesse's track—Jesse played perfectly. Johns regretted that the album didn't gain wider recognition, considering the project one of his career favorites. Kennerley too remembers Jesse being "the star of the whole thing." When the LA sessions concluded, Johns and Kennerley took the tapes to Nashville for a Johnny Cash lead vocal overdub on "Help Him, Jesus." Cash, having arrived straight from a hunting trip, still donning his camouflage gear, quickly ducked into a room before reappearing in his obligatory black attire, like a superhero minister. Grabbing a pair of headphones, he took his spot in front of a microphone, and began rehearsing his vocals. "Wait. Stop the tape," he ordered. "Who is that playing guitar?" asked the astonished Man in Black. It was Jesse.[13]

Jesse's addictions couldn't entirely spoil his talent, but back in Hawaii, they once again sabotaged his attempt at a relationship with Patti. One day in October 1979, Patti had waited over an hour for Jesse to pick her up from work when she finally noticed he was passed out in a car across the street. She tried stirring him, but in his stupor, he became violent. "I still feel a numb feeling in the heart & soul," Patti wrote to herself that night, trying to process the pain.[14]

The tide was rolling out. In the fall, Jesse was scheduled to tour Japan. Patti kept the dates—October 28 through November 7—in her journal, but there's no evidence Jesse went through with the tour. Matters further spiraled in mid-November when Jesse was in a terrible car accident, not his first, that landed him in the intensive care unit for three days. Patti realized their lives quite literally couldn't go on like this. In January 1980, Jesse sent a letter addressed to the juice bar where she worked. "Honey, you'll never love me if I don't change my ways," he wrote in his handsome hand. "You know I love you very much. It is a mighty struggle just to cool it. Please help me."[15]

ROLLING BACK IN with the tide was a new love interest who used the professional name Tantalayo. Patti first befriended her on the beach and introduced her to Jesse in 1979. Soon it seemed that if anyone could break Patti's spell, it might be Tantalayo. She was enchanting—an archetypal muse like Patti, but in a different fashion. Like Patti and Jesse, she was a wandering spirit currently seeking new direction and greater purpose after a recent ebb in her own dramatic experiences.[16]

Born Rosemarie Saenz in East Los Angeles in 1955, Tantalayo endured a tumultuous childhood, especially given her parents' trouble with the law. She partly filled this void with a claim to Seminole ancestry through her mother Betty Achee, whose family came from Florida and Louisiana. Though she knew stories about being Seminole, she lacked the immediate community that could make that claim meaningful. In the meantime, Tantalayo found belonging elsewhere. She became a member of the Source Family, a communal group, some say cult, of young people, some of them children of important people in Hollywood. They followed the teachings of a man named Jim Baker, who called himself Father Yod or YaHoWha. Father Yod was a fabulist, self-made spiritual guru, and aspiring Hollywood stuntman—to his credit, he was incredibly strong—who bore an uncanny resemblance to music producer guru Rick Rubin. Yod's Family believed in the Age of Aquarius that supposedly brought about an era of monumental and transformative evolutions in humanity, society, and consciousness. In 1969, their first revolution would be with food, as they opened the popular organic vegetarian Source Restaurant on the Sunset Strip, where John Lennon enjoyed a meal and Woody Allen ordered a "plate of mashed yeast" in *Annie Hall*.

Tantalayo ascended to the privileged position of one of Father Yod's fourteen wives, alongside Isis, Prism, Venus, Galaxy, and others. Finally securing family, support, sustenance, and love, Tantalayo embraced Yod's teachings and added to the group's entertainment pool by playing the character of an exotic tribal dancer, sometimes performing with the family band Ya Ho Wha 13. In 1975, the Source Family ran afoul of the City of Los Angeles and sought new shores in Hawaii. Tantalayo moved with the Family, but the Family soon broke apart. Yod had never attempted hang-gliding in the past, but he was certain he could get the hang of it midair and tried one morning in August. To no one's surprise, he crashed. Refusing medical attention, determined to demonstrate his Holy power, he left his earthly body nine hours later. The group soon experienced its "Great Diaspora," some splintering into rival groups, some returning to the mainland, and some cast adrift.[17]

Patti met Tantalayo and other remaining Source people at the beach. They welcomed Patti to the point of giving her a Source Sister name, Ariel. Patti's consciousness was kind and cosmic enough to play along from a distance, but she didn't become a devoted member of the group. Perhaps more at stake for Patti was their mutual Source friend Laura Garon's impression that Patti imagined Tantalayo as both a way out of her relationship with Jesse and a possible future for Jesse. Tantalayo branded herself a singer and a healer. Maybe she could help him.[18]

The Source Family featured a rotating cast of members who tried to be rock musicians—even Father Yod occasionally strapped on a double-neck guitar. But whereas some like Jesse's future close friend Tim Garon demonstrated genuine talent, most were pretending. Much of the music is awful, though some outsider music aficionados, including John and Yoko's son Sean Lennon, disagree. Tantalayo had been around musicians making records, but Jesse Ed Davis was a legitimate talent who had played with Bob Dylan and John Lennon. Tantalayo hoped to launch a career while Jesse hoped to rescue his own. "She had stars in her eyes," recalls Gary Ray, who drummed for her and Jesse. At first it worked. Jesse submitted to Tantalayo's power, affection, and care as the promise of their musical partnership turned romantic. He even made gestures to Tantalayo's spiritual beliefs, on one occasion signing a letter, "Beloved Tantalayo, in Yahowa Forever, I Love You, JED."[19]

In August 1980, they were married in Oklahoma City in a traditional Kiowa ceremony, conducted in Kiowa language, at Martin Park Nature Center, where the community really turned out, all smiles, despite sweating through their formal clothing in the oppressive heat. Jesse's mother, who arrived in a Thunderbird convertible, stood at her son's side. Jesse's Kiowa cousin Russell Saunkeah served as best man. Vows were administered by Mt. Scott Kiowa Methodist Church pastor Lenora Pauahty, an Indigenous pastor from Jesse's Kiowa family who, in a side gig, recorded and released traditional Indian music through his American Indian Soundchiefs Corporation. Jesse and Tantalayo dressed in ceremonial buckskin, with Jesse donning a magnificent headdress. As is customary in Kiowa culture, Tantalayo wore clothing representing Jesse's family, specifically the same dress and beaded headband Jesse's grandmother Anna Poolaw wore in her wedding to Jasper Saunkeah. Jesse was marrying an Indian girl. Everything seemed beautiful.[20]

THE COMMITMENT TO a new life that Jesse and Tantalayo vowed in August 1980 was shot down that December.

That fall the couple began recording a version of John Lennon's "Mucho Mungo," a song inspired by Jesse and first known as "Mucho Macho." John started the song back in 1973. A portion of it was combined with another tune on Harry Nilsson's *Pussy Cats* album, featuring Jesse on guitar. Lennon later finished the song and sent a demo copy to Jesse, under the new title "Mucho Jesse." In his own home-recorded version, John sang about the power and peace in Jesse's eyes and face. Jesse was so proud of it.[21]

Jesse last saw John in January 1976, when Lennon's lawyer Jay Bergen flew Jesse to New York to be a witness in Lennon's defense against a record business lawsuit introduced by Roulette Records' Morris Levy. Jesse canceled two weeks of studio work to be there. Only a week prior, Beatles road manager and band assistant extraordinaire Mal Evans descended into a violent and psychotic state in his Beverly Hills home with a gun. When cops pleaded with him to drop his weapon, he allegedly pointed it at them, and they shot and killed him instantly. The beloved Mal's terrible death deeply shook the Beatles' circle.

Jesse struggled with the news when Harry Nilsson called. Mal had helped look after Jesse, too. He always appreciated how Mal went over to Harold Seider's house and cleaned everything up the day after Jesse and John had their brawl that left Jesse unconscious. Jesse remembered how the lovable gent used to get drunk and say how unloved he felt, that people only cared about him in relationship to the Beatles. Contemplating Mal's bouts of depression, Jesse recalled his friend saying no one loved him for just being Mal. But that wasn't true. Mal's death broke Jesse's heart.[22]

Two days after Jesse arrived in New York for Lennon's trial, Ronnie Wood phoned him at the Drake Hotel, where he was staying. Ronnie was in town with the Rolling Stones making *Black and Blue*. Did Jesse want to come hang with Ronnie and Mick Jagger? "Yeah, yeah man. . . . Cool. Sure," Jesse replied. Lennon's lawyer Bergen pleaded with Jesse to not get too wild before testifying on Lennon's behalf in two more days. "No problem," Jesse assured him. "I'll be cool. Don't worry." Jesse hit the streets, ending up at an Ara Gallant fashion shoot where he and Jagger knew they would find the company of attractive women. "We'd go over there and pretend to see Ara, and try to drag two of his models out the door," Jesse described his and Jagger's escapade. When Bergen returned the next day to check on him, Jesse had changed hotel rooms, explaining that he brought two Puerto Rican girls back with him and the hotel manager wouldn't let him have three people stay in his current room. They had moved him into a suite. Two years later, the Rolling Stones had a hit with "Miss You," including Jagger's lyric about getting a call from a friend with "some Puerto Rican girls that's just dyin' to meet you!" The next day at the hotel, Ronnie Wood called again, and Bergen again pleaded with Jesse to take it easy, reminding him of the court appearance in the morning.

When the date arrived, John, Yoko, Bergen, and guitarist Eddie Mottau waited for Jesse to show up at Bergen's office. They were finally giving up and heading for the door when the elevator opened and out spilled a fabulous, if bleary-eyed, Jesse Ed Davis in a long fur coat, green suit, and black tie. He had just returned from a night out with Woody, changed his clothes, and was ready to go. Shockingly on point in the courtroom, Jesse assuaged any worries, effortlessly defending John, charming the courtroom in his examination and cross-examination while Yoko knitted from her seat in the audience. "You don't need a lead sheet to play 'Tutti Frutti,'" Jesse chided the prosecution during a pivotal moment. Jesse was brilliant. He set the stage for John's testimony and ultimately successful defense. "That was great, really great," John cheered afterward. "You were both terrific, weren't they Yoko?" John asked, referring to Jesse and Mottau. "Yes, they were," Yoko confirmed. As for Jesse's green suit, he repurposed it the following year at a more somber affair—his father's funeral.[23]

Jesse and John Lennon remained in touch after Jesse moved to Hawaii. Having initially been devastated by the termination of his musical partnership with John, he appreciated that John still checked in and helped with things when he could. One day in 1980, Mike Piranha was at Jesse's place when Jesse called him into the kitchen, picked up the wall phone, and began dialing a number. Piranha began rolling a joint while Jesse walked into an adjacent room, uncoiling the phone cord. He quickly returned: "I want you to say hello to someone." Jesse handed the phone to Mike. "It's John Lennon," he silently mouthed. "I wasn't prepared to deal with as much as a pizza delivery guy at that point in the party, let alone speak properly to the most famous musician in the world," Piranha muses. Twenty seconds later he handed the phone back, and overheard Jesse, now back in the next room, ask for five thousand dollars. "Call Harry [Nilsson]," John instructed, "he's always bragging about how much money he's got." "I did call Harry and got my loan,"

Jesse confessed, "and I did pay him back." Jesse and John spoke by phone again in early December 1980. John mentioned that he had recently fired his bodyguards.

Jesse Ed Davis might be the only person who knew and ever spoke face-to-face with both John Lennon and a man named Mark David Chapman. The latter was head of security at the Monte Vista condo where Mike Piranha lived and Jesse frequented. No one could come or go without signing in with Chapman at the gate. Mark David Chapman had long been obsessed with John Lennon. A devoted Beatles fan, he grew upset with John's music, offended by the lyrics to "Imagine" and "God." He eventually decided to go find Lennon in New York City, determined to discuss the matter. Before leaving Honolulu, Chapman bought a .38 Special at the J&S Sales gun shop. "GUNS 7 DAYS A WEEK!" the shop advertised. "It was right in this little mini-mall complex that I used to go to all the time," Jesse recalled. "At the time I was in Hawaii I had a real erratic income." He was alluding to how he sometimes went to the same shopping complex to pawn guitars for cash.[24]

Just before 11 p.m. on December 8, 1980, John and Yoko returned from a recording session to the Dakota building on Manhattan's Upper West Side, where they lived. The couple exited their limousine and headed for the entrance when Chapman fired his gun five times, hitting Lennon four times in the back, killing him. "Everything went black," Jim Keltner described that night.

I'M JUST OLD ENOUGH for John Lennon's death to have had a profound impact on me when it happened. It's my earliest flashbulb memory, as they are sometimes called, and my earliest memory of an event that generated mass mourning on a transcendent human scale. I was four years old. I remember our television showing people weeping while holding a vigil in New York's Central Park. It was my first realization that people from everywhere could share one feeling.

Jesse and many of John's other friends happened to be together that night in Los Angeles. Specific accounts differ, but trying to parse the details and determine what's true and what was an extension of confusion and pain seems beside the point. "It didn't make any sense," Jim Keltner reflects. He was with Jesse at a session Harry Nilsson was producing for Sylvester Stallone's brother Frank. "All I remember is no one said a word," Keltner continues, "and Jesse called for a car to pick him up. And when it arrived it was a *limo*. . . . It was the last time I saw Jesse."

If Jesse didn't literally die that night like John, to Keltner he figuratively did. "The next horrible thing after John was, they found Jesse . . . And, you know . . . I immediately thought 'Okay,' Jesse said, 'John went? Fuck it. I'm gone too. . . .' I have a feeling he gave up." Keltner remembers Lennon's plan at the time of his death was to re-form his solo band with Jesse, Keltner, and Klaus Voormann. That Jesse could have reunited with Lennon in the new decade, when he was most in need of a career restart, only to lose him, must have been crushing. "[John] loved us," Voormann says, then pauses. "I know that."[25]

Tantalayo recalled being with Jesse in the studio that night, but for a different session, to work on the bridge of her and Jesse's version of "Mucho Mungo." Someone called the studio and told Jesse John had been killed. That was "the night the rock and roll circus left town," Tantalayo wrote years later, repeating Jesse's favorite metaphor. "Jesse's heart was on the floor, as was Jesse," she continued.[26]

Jesse's longtime drummer Gary Ray doesn't recall Tantalayo being there or a limo coming to pick Jesse up. It was him, he is certain, who drove Jesse to the Frank Stallone session and drove him home. Jesse was living with Gary at the time, both with and without Tantalayo, reflecting the newlyweds' volatile relationship. Gary recalls the night vividly. Jim Keltner was Gary's hero, and he tried to sit by him and watch him drum before the engineer kicked him out of the recording room. Ringo Starr called the studio to tell everyone the news. Nilsson took a vote on whether they should continue. They voted yes, in honor of John.[27]

In Jesse's own recollection, it was Beach Boys writer and musician Van Dyke Parks who delivered the news. They were working in the studio with Nilsson, Keltner, Voormann, and Bobby Keys, cutting tracks for the Frank Stallone project Nilsson was producing. Van Dyke made a run to the liquor store. When he returned, Jesse remembered,

> He was just white as a sheet, and he was shaking, and I said "What's the matter with you, man, are you sick?" "You won't believe what I just heard over the radio in the liquor store." Now these were guys that all played on John's records. It was his band. And Parks said, "They shot John on a street in New York." And I said, "Who shot John?!" And he said, "I don't know. Let's go listen to the radio." The word went around the studio like electricity, and we all crowded around the lobby and turned the radio on. And every station, all you could hear was John Lennon music. We couldn't find out what the hell happened. We tried every place. AM. FM. Finally, we found an all-news stations with bulletins. Harry went berserk and started smashing his fist against the wall. I stopped him.

Jesse's memory of that night was tear-stained and blurry, inevitably, like everyone else's. Klaus Voormann was confused when I tried asking him about that night. He wasn't there; he was back in Germany. As is sometimes the case in examples of the Rashomon effect, it might be that Jesse's feelings are more important than the facts. He convinced everyone to finish the session because John would have wanted them to play. And they played into the night, stopping repeatedly to cry. Jesse recalled staying the night at Nilsson's house. The next day they went to the Bel-Air Hotel and drank cognac all day, "Crying, and doing that horseshit, and finally, Harry decided I'd had enough and called whatever chick I was with at that time to come get me. I was out of control, and I said call this number and ask her to come get me." Jesse's cousin Russell remembered Jesse calling that night: "He was disconsolate. I had never seen him so broken." Jesse remembered breaking down again when the world held a moment of silence at Yoko's request.[28]

For the rest of his life, Jesse believed John's murder was a conspiracy. "He was taken out, definitely," Jesse insisted, understandably struggling to accept what happened. "I loved the bastard," he stressed. "Him playing music and guitar was secondary. I think he was just a great guy, and he was one of my dearest friends of my whole life, and I really miss him. . . . I wonder to this day how I can carry on his work."[29]

Jesse later contributed to a controversial and widely discredited best-selling book about John Lennon by Albert Goldman. Over the years, Lennon friends, fans, and experts alike have pointed out numerous errors, half-truths, falsehoods, exaggerations, manipulations, and more. Others stand by the book, refusing to acknowledge its flaws or loving the book in spite of them. Some of the exaggerations and embellishments came from Jesse himself, who often seemed to care more about stories being entertaining than truthful, and who maybe felt pressure to tell Goldman something sensational given that Goldman paid Jesse for his involvement. Jesse died in 1988, the same year the book was published, and probably never saw the final product. But it's clear he was already feeling some regret when he wrote Goldman three years earlier in 1985 to clarify some of what he shared and ensure that he was properly framing his relationship with John:

> Whatever lunatic asides John and I participated in or sometimes encouraged, always remember that the vital connection between us was rock & roll. Sailing full tilt on a breakdown boogie beat was our passion fulfilled. All the rest was waiting. If the moments between could be livened up with a laugh or a tear, so much the better. That I loved the guy goes without saying.

Jesse's second wife and widow, Kelly Davis, disavowed Goldman's book. She told *Rolling Stone* that Jesse confessed that some stories in the book were not true, including one about Lennon kissing him on the mouth in a studio parking lot as well as a story Dr. John told about Lennon punching out one of Jesse's teeth. The latter certainly was false, Kelly noted, for the obvious reason that Jesse had all of his teeth.[30]

We often measure and discuss history according to decades. TV shows, books, documentaries, music compilations, and more all do it. *The Sixties. The Seventies.* I'm not the first to suggest the 1960s really ended on December 8, 1980. At the center of the misty memories surrounding that terrible night rest two fundamental truths: no one wanted John to die and everyone wanted to be there with him when he did.

IN A PARTICULARLY VIVID contribution to Albert Goldman's book, Jesse twice, in separate interviews, recounted a story about encountering John Lennon one day in Hawaii. It should have been obvious to Goldman that Jesse was contradicting a previous interview in which he said the last time he ever saw John was in 1976, at the Morris Levy trial. Goldman either wasn't paying attention, or, like Jesse, cared more about the show business than the truth.

One day in September 1979, Jesse and Tom Sullivan from the *Cocaine Cowboys* film had been drinking in a bar in Waikiki. They walked out into daylight and Jesse literally bumped into John Lennon, who was on his way home from a trip to Japan. "Hey, where can we cop?" John didn't hesitate. The trio hopped into a cab and headed to Ewa Beach, to a cane cutter's house where Jesse had a connection named Timmy. They scored $300 worth of heroin and even ran into Tony Cointreau, heir to the French liquor company, before getting a room at the Sheraton where they could fix in private. They then watched *Star Trek* for a while before heading out to Pearl City, where they crashed a club called John Barleycorn's and played an impromptu three-song set including "Roll Over Beethoven" and "Peggy Sue" to a packed house.[31]

But this couldn't have happened. Patti makes no mention of it in her journal from September 1979. The painstakingly thorough *Lennonology*, a daily account of John Lennon's life, does not mention it. On other occasions, Jesse himself mentioned that the last time he ever saw John was in 1976. So many questioned the story upon release of Goldman's book that the *Honolulu Advertiser* ran an article about it, interviewing several people who stressed not just skepticism but incredulity. No witnesses were ever found. No one had heard anything about John Lennon, a Beatle, one of the most famous people in the world, taking the stage at a packed Pearl City club. In fact, no club by that name ever existed in Honolulu. It also made no sense that John would fly into Hawaii unannounced and literally, not figuratively, bump into Jesse Davis on the street, before leaving the very next day. Who can say why Goldman chose to include this story in his book, or why Jesse invented the story in the first place.

It might be that Jesse missed John so much he later imagined stories he wished had happened when those that did happen were not enough to fill the absence. Maybe Jesse's story about reconnecting with his old friend and shooting heroin wasn't malicious, and not even strategic. Maybe he had no motive at all. Maybe a sunny day on the beach and a warm night onstage together in Hawaii, happy and high with an old friend who symbolized Jesse's former position at the top of the music business, was merely a reverie. Maybe it was just a dream.

Ten

THE GREAT ABANDONMENT

THREE MAJOR FIGURES moved in and out of Jesse's life during the early 1980s. They provided love and companionship, sometimes joining him in the ditch and sometimes pulling him out of it, often with mixed results. One was his new bride; one was an old hell-raising "blood brother"; and one was a new flame in the form of an old friend. All three reflected something unique about Jesse, and each of them suffered with him in their own ways.

Jesse's life in the early 1980s is difficult to track. The story becomes elusive, marked by illness and incoherence. Jesse became very sick during this time, in a way making him less knowable. Tantalayo was one of the key sources for this chapter, which features their slingshot marriage and failed musical partnership. But just when she agreed to work with me for this book and began sharing her story, she suddenly passed away at her home in Honokaa, Hawaii. One message came through. Though Tantalayo experienced a great deal of pain with Jesse, she still loved him. At the end of her life, she still dreamed about him.[1]

SMALL AND REMOTE Hawaii could not contain Jesse and Tantalayo's big music ambitions. In April 1980, prior to their marriage, they headed to Los Angeles to begin work on their first album. Signaling a break from her life in the Source Family, Tantalayo considered changing her name. She was unsure whether she even possessed legal control over her professional moniker in the first place. Her idea for a new stage name and backing band revealed something about how she envisioned herself and her relationship with Jesse. The new concept, Tondelayo and White Cargo, referred to a 1941 film starring Hedy Lamarr, who portrayed a pesky "tropical temptress" of some vague native background. She's "romantic and ruthless." She loves jewelry and she's dangerous. Tanta-layo's current name almost certainly derived from Tondelayo. Equally unsure of her ability to legally use the latter name, she finally decided to keep the former. They would be a blend of the two: Tantalayo and White Cargo.[2]

With a wish list of players and guests, including the Band's Garth Hudson and Richard Manuel, Jesse and Tantalayo hoped to record an album titled *Keep Steppin'* in a major studio. Lacking adequate funds, they instead wound up at Ricky Eckstein's modest garage studio with a smaller cast, including a drum machine. There they recorded demos they hoped were strong enough to send to Jesse's old music mogul contacts, including Clive Davis at Arista, Lenny Waronker at Warner Brothers, and Jerry Moss at A&M. None of them bit.

Alongside their version of Lennon's gift to Jesse, "Mucho Mungo," Tantalayo and Jesse had developed a series of new songs for *Keep Step-pin'*. Jesse mostly handled the music and Tantalayo wrote lyrics. They repurposed at least one tune from Jesse's catchy song "Sorry Girl," likely cowritten with Johnny Angel years earlier. Tantalayo changed the words to "Sorry Boy," reflecting a change to a female perspective, with the refrain "Things just didn't work out the way we planned." Other songs included "Goodbye Babee," "Give to Him," and "Monkey." The latter, interestingly enough, was not an ode to their pet Capuchin, Clever. The song employed the old metaphor of drugs as a monkey on one's back: "You've been looking for a lover, but stay away from my backdoor." Other new material appeared to signal their combative love for each other. "Love always seems to hurt," one unrecorded song proclaimed.[3]

Their partnership is best captured in a song called "Through the

Golden Gates," written during a "deep dark time" on a grand piano in the living room of the place they shared near Lanikai Beach. Jackie DeShannon, the hitmaker behind "What the World Needs Now Is Love" and "Put a Little Love in Your Heart" fame, and whose 1975 album *New Arrangement* featured Jesse's guitar, recorded "Through the Golden Gates" as a bonus track for a reissue of her album *Jackie* in 2004. "All your giving was for naught / But you ain't giving now half of what you got," the song goes.

Years later, still using the surname Davis, Tantalayo heard only sadness in Jesse's guitar when she listened to their collaboration. "I wish I knew then what I know now about the progression of the disease of addiction," she wrote with remorse. "Jesse and I continued to record our music through it all," she elaborated, before realizing, "We really did record our struggle."[4]

At some point, they dropped the name White Cargo, and Tantalayo made her debut with Jesse and the Glide Band at McCabe's Guitar Shop in Santa Monica, a hallowed institution among guitar players. With Jesse's old Skyhill pal Bobby Keys on saxophone, Johnny Lee Schell on second guitar, session bassist Paul Stallworth, and a drummer named Jack Spence who would soon be murdered, Tantalayo appeared in the position of "thrush." Led by Jesse and his signature sunburst Telecaster, they played a handful of covers; some of Jesse's standards, including "Bacon Fat," "Every Night Is Saturday Night," "Reno Street Incident," "Natural Anthem," and "Farther on Down the Road"; and a few new tunes with Tantalayo out front. Playing to a "packed house" of about 150 people, the band made a total of $200, which Jesse split evenly seven ways, amounting to about $28.50 per musician. It was a start. Exactly one week later, Jesse appeared at McCabe's again, this time backing his old pal from the Byrds, Gene Clark.[5]

Jesse and Tantalayo's personal life proved just as challenging as their attempt at launching a music venture. Virtually broke, they crashed at various apartments in and around Venice, including Gary Ray's duplex, Johnny Lee Schell's apartment, and a rented house off La Cienega with a domed roof. At each stop, Jesse and Tantalayo's monkey Clever wreaked havoc. "The monkey was very unhappy," Schell recalls. Trombonist

Jock Ellis also remembers Clever: "You had to be real careful with him, because he'd fuck you up if he was in a bad mood." Clever once swung down from the dome and punched Jock in the face. "If he escaped, it was all over." Telling me this over the phone, Jock imitates Clever's sinister screeching. It clearly made a lasting impression on him.[6]

An attempt at married life may have been doomed before Tantalayo and Jesse ever left Hawaii. To some, Jesse's marriage to Tantalayo in August 1980 seemed a last attempt at calling Patti's bluff. Maybe she'd suddenly appear at the sweltering wedding in Oklahoma City and protest. When she didn't, Jesse could only try to move forward. In a letter promising that a "union that is everlasting begins in the light of Yahowha," appealing to Tantalayo's Source Family lingo, Jesse professed,

I HAVE FOUND MY INNER PEACE. I REALIZED SUDDENLY THAT IT WAS ALWAYS THERE. NOW I WILL BE COMPLETE IF OUR UNION WILL BEGIN AT LAST. I'LL ALWAYS LOVE YOU. YAHOWHA, JED.

Given the on-again, off-again nature of their relationship, many of Jesse's friends and family members never met Tantalayo. Gary Ray likened her witchy power over Jesse to that of Yoko Ono and John Lennon. "He was doing that trip that talented musicians do with their girlfriend," Ray recalls. Ricky Eckstein cautiously agrees: "She was a lot for me to swallow at the time, probably an opportunist, but then Jesse could be that too." Tantalayo was "real needy," Jock Ellis suggests. "She fancied herself a singer, and she was okay."[7]

Jesse's bandmates' impressions of Tantalayo were hurt by the fact that Jesse was again spiraling into brutal heroin and alcohol binges. Sometimes she went down with him; other times she tried to rescue him. Either way, he was never the same after John Lennon's murder. "The circus left town when his dear friend John Lennon was murdered," she stressed years later.[8]

By the end of summer 1981, the couple was back in Hawaii, scrambling to pay rent on their new place in Kailua overlooking the ocean. Jesse showed the landlord all of his albums, promising he'd be good for the money once the next royalty check arrived. With their first anniversary approaching, Jesse and Tantalayo, still struggling to get on their feet, turned to family for money. They jointly wrote Jesse's Seminole aunt Allece Garrard, granddaughter of Alice Brown Davis. "We have been blessed with a wonderful two-story house overlooking the most beautiful beach in all the world," they began. "The warm Pacific waters are aqua-blue fading to lapis and the palm-lined sand is powdery white. Truly breath-taking," they described their view, while emphasizing that Jesse was set to score a film being made in Hawaii. Soon, there would be a "nice jingle in my pockets" that would foster a return on any loan. "The morning sun rises in our faces and the fruit is falling off the trees," they shared. These lovely impressions masked the reality of their situation. With no record deal in place and drugs taking a toll, the couple began breaking apart. After a conflict about possibly having a child together, there seemed little for either partner to continue fighting for or against, and though they remained legally married for some time, their relationship soon ended for good.[9]

As Jesse's health declined, he broke down in tears many times. In an unreleased song from the period called "Tell Me Any Story," he surveyed his condition in explicit terms:

> *My eyes were wide and open*
> *But now they've closed*
> *Seen so many movies it's a bore*
> *Feel like some old junkie, lost my do*
> *I'm singing my song before it's even thru*
>
> *My cigarette's half smoken, it's a drag*
> *I just wanna throw the sack away*
> *So many lines and verses like an endless tune*
> *They all seem to take me right back to you*

Friends tried to help. His old Continentals bandmates John Ware and John Selk staged an intervention. It became heated. "You're gonna kill yourself!" they pleaded. Other friends repeatedly loaned Jesse money— thousands of dollars from Bob Dylan, thousands more from drum-

mer Jeff Porcaro. Rarely did Jesse repay anyone. Working through his
list of phone numbers late one night, he called an old studio session
friend asking for $100,000. When they realized Jesse wasn't kidding,
they responded, "Jesse! I'm not John Lennon! I don't have that kind of
money!"[10]

When Robbie Robertson saw Jesse at a mutual friend's house, he
thought of Jesse's background as an Indigenous person in a way that
only a fellow Indigenous person might understand. "Jesse and I, we come
from a generation where they not only had the alcohol but they threw
in some drugs to boot," Robertson explained. "If you've got the fever,
that's what they called it in Mohawk Country, it's going to make you
very sick." Robbie was worried, having experienced many friends and
family struggling with the disease. He warned Jesse, "Man, you got to
watch the fever." "I'm trying," Jesse promised. "And he knew what I was
talking about," Robbie remembers. "He didn't get the help he needed.
He didn't know how to, and it grabbed hold of him, it strangled him, it
grabbed hold of him so hard, and he couldn't find a way out, and that
was heartbreaking to me."[11]

WITH HIS MARRIAGE in shambles and addiction overpowering him,
Jesse turned to a friend who was in almost exactly the same position.
Jesse had known ex–Byrds singer Gene Clark for years. They were self-
professed blood brothers, having actually cut their hands and exchanged
blood, as Jesse once did with Billy. Jesse and Gene made some of the best
music of their careers together. Yet they often emboldened the worst in
each other.

In 1971, facing pressure from his record company to make a new
album, Clark drove down to Los Angeles from his majestic retreat in
Little River, Mendocino County, and enlisted his friend Jesse to produce.
Gene was searching for a different sound, wanting to center his poetry
in his musical presentation. He asked Jesse to clear away instrumental
clutter and let his music breathe. He wanted the album to reflect the
peace he found since moving away from the stress of Los Angeles. Gene
wrote the songs for *White Light* in his head while walking in darkness

around his Pacific village at night. Soon they were rehearsing at Jesse's Hurricane House. Patti and Gene's wife Carlie often fell asleep listening to them play into the night.[12]

Beginning work on the album, Jesse and Gene would hit the studio around 8 p.m. and sometimes work until 4 a.m. or later. Jesse was in great shape, at the top of his game. "He loved being in the studio," the album's engineer Baker Bigsby says. "Everybody loved him—the musicians, everybody in the studio, the person carrying out the trash. He was amiable. He made everybody feel comfortable, like you were his best friend no matter who you were. Jesse could have been a politician." Jesse brought in trusted friends, including John Selk, who remembers the sessions being very creative and spontaneous, characterized by instrumental freedom. Jesse's Hurricane housemate Gary Mallaber joined on drums and recalled a similar atmosphere: "The gate came flying open, and out came the bull. . . . It was yes, yes, yes, yes, yes to everything."[13]

Jesse's first priority as producer was to ensure the feeling was right. His greatest talent as a producer was in creating a certain mood and aura. "By his very presence, he shapes the session," *White Light* keyboardist Ben Sidran puts it. Beyond that, Jesse was just one of the guys. He'd pick up a guitar and add his own parts, but he didn't like to interfere with anyone's creativity. Jesse, Gene, and company succeeded in achieving Gene's goal. They played with beautiful restraint and allowed Gene's voice to shine. Although *White Light* sold poorly, it became a retrospective classic and a favorite among both Jesse Ed Davis and Gene Clark fans.[14]

The most memorable moment of making the album stemmed not from anyone's performance inside the studio but from a disaster outside after a session that ran into the next morning. At around 6 a.m. on February 9, 1971, the Village Recorder's studio monitors began shaking above the mixing console. Baker Bigsby and Jesse's assistant Pete Waddington panicked and ran outdoors, where the massive San Fernando Earthquake created a street that looked like a rolling ocean wave, with telephone poles rocking back and forth. Waddington remembers the earthquake like it was yesterday. Jesse came running out too, at which point the team realized they had accidentally locked themselves out. So, they held on for dear life. Finally making it back inside, Bigsby realized they left the tape machine running and recorded the earthquake. "It was wonderful—the best recording I ever made!"[15]

Jesse helped bring out the best in Gene again for Gene's extravagant, over-budget album *No Other* (1974), which also initially sank before becoming a rediscovered classic. With Thomas Jefferson Kaye—sort of "Phil Spector light," as drummer Russ Kunkel describes him—in the producer's chair, Jesse joined the album strictly as a guitar player. He picks the bedrock rhythm part in "Life's Greatest Fool," a swinging country rocker that gallops out of the gate. Clark sings about winners, losers, and costs. "Do you believe . . . you held the key to your destiny gone?" he cries beneath a heavenly choir. Jerry McGee delivers an impeccable first guitar solo between verses. Then Gene continues: "Born out of pleasure / chiseled by pain," before Jesse swoops in with a brilliant slide guitar solo during the song's outro climax. Jesse's guitar voice calls back to Clark in some spectral language before spiraling upward, forming a staircase to cosmic destiny.[16]

Jesse achieves masterful interplay with fellow session guitar player Danny Kortchmar on the haunting "Silver Raven," and breathes new life into a loping version of "Train Leaves Here This Morning." In "From a Silver Phial," his guitar is a beacon through the "darkened rain" in Clark's lament to a lost lover, a "refuge from a silver phial," who escaped "fire on the borderline." Losing himself in that same milky tone that sweetened John Lennon's *Walls and Bridges* that same year, Jesse was at the top of the mountain.

Seven years later, in a new decade increasingly dominated by New Wave rock and pop, British heavy metal, Sunset Strip hair metal, and the emerging sounds of hip hop, Jesse and Gene were at the bottom of the hill. Not unlike his concurrent relationship with Tantalayo, Jesse's partnership with Gene could be turbulent—sometimes dangerous. Gene once offered a metaphor for his relationship with Tommy Kaye that just as much applied to his friendship with Jesse: "You put two bulls in a pen, and they horn each other for a half an hour, and then they say, 'Okay, man, you're a stud too.'"[17]

Gene was both a mirror to Jesse and a key to understanding him.

They were the same age. One came from Missouri and the other from Oklahoma. Both had fallen on hard times professionally, and by 1980, both had lost their partners—Patti and Carlie—who brought out their better selves. Though immensely talented, both Jesse and Gene were unreliable narrators of their own histories. Prone to self-destruction, they exhibited protean personalities, making life hard for those around them. Both suffered from a toxic relationship with alcohol—one they attributed to their ancestry. They both suffered from addiction, and as people, they were addictive.[18]

If Jesse and John Lennon's escapades have been overstated, sometimes to the point of fiction, then Jesse and Gene's exploits are the opposite. They seemed to be on a mission to test their mortality. "Those guys worked hard at dying," one mutual friend said. "You've got to remember that." The daredevil duo, or trio when *Kung Fu* legend David Carradine joined them, regularly crashed the celebrity haven Dan Tana's Italian restaurant in West Hollywood, getting in fistfights on the dining floor, practicing their knife-throwing technique on the restaurant wall, and generally courting danger with the mafia.[19]

Jesse and Gene bonded over Gene's claims of Indigenous ancestry. The Clarks had an Indigenous great-great-grandmother, possibly from Minnesota or possibly Osage, on their father's side. Supposedly, a white ancestor's marriage to the Native woman divided the family, at which point the newlyweds moved to Missouri. During the intervening years, Gene's family did not often discuss their Indigenous relative because of the racism they might invoke in their social environment. Gene embraced this story. In his friendship with Jesse, he sought a deeper connection with his Native ancestry. Gene's son Kai remembered how his father's deep interest in a spiritual view of land, water, and the cosmos informed his songwriting. Gene's then-wife Carlie noted how Jesse and Gene "brought out the Indian in each other."[20]

Gene and Jesse found further Indigenous fellowship in Apache siblings Robby and Joanelle Romero. Partly raised in Hollywood, their mother dated Elvis and Dennis Hopper was their godfather. Gene and Jesse played the role of music mentors to Robby and Joanelle, encouraging their songwriting and teaching them about the profession. The

initially productive relationship soon dissipated, especially in the wake
of John Lennon's death, which hit Gene almost as hard as it hit Jesse,
Lennon having been Gene's music hero. They went on a furious drinking binge. Robby remembers the troupe ending up at his mother's house
one night. She looked at them and began crying, refusing to let them in.
Frightening himself with these blackout episodes, Jesse expressed regret
and fear for his condition. "I'd wake up and walk out into the house
and it would just be rubble. And I'd say, 'Who did this?!' And they'd
say, 'It was you!'" Through it all, Robby loved and admired Jesse, relat-
ing to him as a fellow Native musician. He felt safe with Jesse. During
more tranquil days they loved playing music together and going to the
rodeo. "It was no surprise to me that he knew so much about rodeos,"
Robby says. "It was a sweet time far away from the studios, rehearsal
halls, and stages."[21]

In 1981, when Joanelle Romero was twenty-two, she completed her
last drinking run with Gene and Jesse. They were suffering the shakes
and flopping around LA in a "miserable condition," Gene's brother
David recalled, when Joanelle announced she was ready to go home.
Jesse and Gene encouraged her. They wanted to go home too. When
Jesse finally dropped Joanelle off at her old apartment, he gave her his
grandmother's concho belt and wished her well. When Gene's brother
visited soon thereafter with a cake baked by their mother, Gene broke
down. "Do I still have a family?"[22]

BY SUMMER 1981, tired of flirting with death in Los Angeles, Jesse and
Gene, absent Tantalayo, set a course for Hawaii, where they planned
to get clean, not through formal rehab programs but through tandem
willpower. Jesse and Gene christened their retreat to Hawaii "the great
abandonment." If things went well, they might even accomplish some
writing and recording. Alas, while they managed to escape California,
they would soon learn that their problems were more than an extension
of that environment. There would be moments of clarity, salubrity, and
productivity, but these were often compromised by the outlaw life they

claimed to have left behind in Los Angeles. They even re-created some of the scenes they were supposed to abandon, like when a rival gang drove by and shot up the dealer's house they had just stepped out of somewhere in Hawaii.[23]

Always improvising, sometimes to the point of imposition, Jesse escorted Gene to Hawaii with nowhere to stay and no real plan at all. Jesse remembered a friend named John Granito he had crashed with in 1979, back when he and Patti were attempting a similar reset. Now, two years later, with no notice of any sort, he called Granito from the Honolulu airport. He mentioned he had Gene Clark from the Byrds with him. "Can we stay at your place?" It was more of an expectation than a request, but charitable Granito was happy to accommodate them.[24]

An aspiring musician, Granito welcomed the rock star company. He also loved Jesse's stories—especially a story he told about having sex with a famous singer when her Doberman bit him on the lip, sending him to a plastic surgeon in the middle of the night, and leaving a visible scar. Jesse was comfortable enough with Granito to discuss his Native background; it may be that he more easily trusted a friend away from the Hollywood scene. Jesse told him about dancing at powwows when he was a kid; about how he learned to play piano with his mother and preferred composing music on the instrument; about his grandfather Jasper's work as a US Marshal; and about how his Kiowa and Comanche ancestors were fierce warriors on the Southern Plains. If Jesse seemed to enjoy telling these stories, it was always at Granito's urging. "Jesse was not arrogant," Granito maintains. "He was humble. He didn't brag. He was shy and quiet."

Jesse and Granito bonded over music, too. When Granito asked to hear more of Jesse's music, Jesse took him to the nearest record store, where he swiftly located the John Lennon bin and pulled out *Walls and Bridges*. Though he had been unhappy with the album, Jesse now told Granito that his work with the late Beatle was his "proudest moment." Perhaps his affection for the album grew after losing Lennon. Jesse later overheard his host playing an old Woody Guthrie song on his Martin acoustic guitar. "Way down yonder in the Indian nation," he sang, "I rode my pony on the reservation." Jesse was astonished. "I can't believe you know that song!" Woody Guthrie's "Oklahoma Hills" carried him back home.

Good times notwithstanding, Granito worried about Jesse's self-destructive tendencies and gradually realized the extent of Jesse's disease each time Jesse asked him to leave his own house for a bit so he could "take care of something." Gene was a handful too. A vitamin therapy regimen seemed to be helping Gene resist alcohol, but it didn't help him with other drugs. And unlike Jesse, Gene was prone to angry outbursts. It was exhausting looking after them, Granito sighs.

The best times were when they all played music together. Jesse, Gene, and Granito formed the evocatively named group Smokey Road, along with drummer Pat Adams and Tantalayo's old Source Family sibling Wade Cambern. The latter grew up in Hollywood, where his father was editor on numerous major films, including the hippie cautionary tale *Easy Rider* (1969). Half the time Jesse didn't show up for gigs, but when he did, he was marvelous. They packed Anna Banana's, Bullwinkle's, and other local venues. With Jesse on his sunburst Telecaster playing through a borrowed Fender Twin amplifier, the band played Gene Clark and Byrds tunes alongside Motown hits "My Girl" and "You Really Got a Hold on Me."

Preparing for a Smokey Road photo shoot one afternoon, Gene proclaimed that he would be going bare chested, extolling his lack of body hair, planning to strike a Native warrior pose. Slapping Gene's big belly, Jesse couldn't contain himself. "You look more like the Buddha!" he cried. More often Jesse was a man of few words, more enigmatic and remote than warm and inviting. When he was healthy, Jesse could be almost alienating in his talent. With Smokey Road, he enjoyed dusting off his guitar chops, but it seemed as if he resented the gig—as though it was beneath him. Cambern was at first intimidated by Jesse, but he couldn't resist Jesse's infectious laugh that shook his whole body. Neither can he forget Jesse's inscrutable mantra: "Hunger makes the best sauce."[25]

For all Jesse's charisma, he could test his friends' patience. Borrowing a guitar from Granito for a duo gig with Gene, Jesse suspiciously asked to take it into the other room and told Granito not to come in. "Okay,"

Granito granted, before finally taking a peek. "What the hell are you doing?!" Granito screamed, barging in. Jesse was using an awl to carve little notation holes on the side of the guitar neck all the way up to the twelfth fret, damaging the guitar. To Granito's astonishment, Jesse, one of the greatest guitarists of the past decade, couldn't play without them. An angry Granito grabbed Wite-Out and painted little dots up the neck. "Whoa, that's smart!" Jesse conceded. "No shit!" Granito snapped.

On another occasion, Jesse pawned Granito's Martin acoustic guitar, after having already pawned a second Martin that Gene Clark got from Jerry Garcia. "Jesse, how could you?" Granito pleaded. They drove together to the pawnshop in Pearl City and then to the home of the old woman who bought it. She threatened to call the cops, only to return it the next day. "[Jesse] knew he fucked up," Granito says.

> I just couldn't hold it against him. Sometimes you gotta look past the things people do, and try to look into their soul. There was something about Jesse that made you want to, not so much forgive, but understand that there was a hurt inside this guy. There was something deeply disturbing inside of him that caused him to be self-destructive. I don't think he did these things to be mean. He couldn't help himself.

Shortly thereafter, Gene, believing guitars take on the spirit of those who play them, found his own Jerry Garcia Martin guitar in San Francisco and bought it back.

By the end of 1981, Jesse and Gene were back in Los Angeles, where they went separate ways for a while. In 1984, Gene considered taking Jesse on the road with his group the Fyrebirds, but Jesse was in poor health. It wasn't the only major gig he would miss that year as a result. A few years later, Jesse and Gene talked again about making a record together. Leon Russell was set to produce, but they ran out of time.[26]

STILL SEPARATED FROM his first wife and waving goodbye to his partner in crime in Gene Clark, Jesse now found himself alone. His trail becomes difficult to follow here, only knowable through others' strange sightings of Jesse roving the fringes of the changing Hollywood rock scene. Los Angeles was increasingly teeming with guitar players anxious to become the next Eddie Van Halen or Randy Rhoads, who led a new generation of sweeping and tapping rock guitarists. Playing new styles of effects-laden guitars, Van Halen and Rhoads lit up their fretboards with laser runs of speed and precision, often appreciated more for their dexterity than their depth. Meanwhile, Jesse was gigging at a strip club and staying anywhere he could crash, at one point occupying a treehouse in a Topanga Canyon backyard. At another stop, in Laurel Canyon, Jesse lost all of his letters from rock star friends when a scorned friend stacked Jesse's belongings by a swimming pool while threatening violence. Jesse left the stuff behind. On another occasion an adoring fan found him walking down Sunset Strip. "You're Jesse Ed Davis!" they exclaimed. "I used to be," Jesse replied.[27]

Some friends who were outside Jesse's tenuous Hollywood orbit gradually began to understand the nature and cause of Jesse's rapidly deteriorating condition. Jesse's childhood Choctaw friend Bill Saul, who called Jesse "Snookie" on the playground in Norman, bumped into Jesse in a shoe store buying a pair of red Adidas. Shortly thereafter a friend told Saul they saw Jesse's amplifier in a pawn shop. "Why would Jesse pawn his amp?" Saul wondered.[28]

May Pang spotted Jesse thumbing a ride in Laurel Canyon in 1982. "Stop the car! That's Jesse!" "Jesse! Come over! Hey! Do you need a lift somewhere?" Sporting a Hawaiian shirt, Jesse peered into the car window with a crazed look in his eyes. "Jump in," Pang instructed. "Thanks man!" Jesse said, promptly jumping out at his destination. "Wait," Pang implored. "Let me take a last photo of you." Somehow, she knew she would never see him again.[29]

It wasn't uncommon for Jesse to crash random parties, asking for money. At one gathering, attendees were ready to call the police until *LA Weekly* editor Bill Bentley, recognizing Jesse, intervened. "Wait, this guy is a legend!" No one believed him.[30]

After Bill graduated high school, he reconnected with Jesse. Bill had his adult life ahead of him. But "Billy the Kid" couldn't rescue his substitute dad from addiction. Instead Bill got pulled into addiction's current. Soon Jesse and Bill began roaming the streets together, sometimes sleeping in the gazebos that line Venice Beach Boardwalk. Like his friend and vagabond Beach Boy Dennis Wilson, the "Mayor of Washington Boulevard," Jesse became a folk hero among people in the Venice street community. He often sat among them playing someone's guitar. But it wasn't always a picture of romantic vagrancy. Picking Jesse up from jail one day, Jock Ellis noticed he looked a little roughed up: "Gee, what happened in there?" "A cellmate kept taunting, 'Hey, buffalo head!'" Jesse said. "I knocked him the fuck out and he left me alone."[31]

Jesse's imposing nature frustrated his friends. His *Keep Me Comin'* percussionist Bobby Torres was thrilled to reconnect with Jesse in Las Vegas in the early 1980s. He likened playing with Jesse to serving in the Merchant Marine. He felt they were brothers. Then Torres, a diabetic, left Jesse in his hotel room while he went to soundcheck with Tom Jones. When he returned, Jesse was gone, and so were all of his hypodermic needles. "That left a bad taste in my mouth about him," Torres admits.[32]

When Jesse called Jackson Browne for a loan, Jackson, still grateful for Jesse's role in his first top-ten hit, didn't hesitate. He called his accountant: "I'm going to lend a thousand dollars to Jesse Ed Davis." "Oh, I'm sorry," came the reply. "I beg your pardon?" "Well, he's borrowing a thousand dollars from everybody." Jackson supplied the loan, and later helped Jesse again by arranging for him to buy his sister's Ford Mustang. One day, not long after, his sister got a call from the impound lot. Jesse had abandoned the car downtown. He never paid for it or filed the paperwork. Sometimes the infractions felt personal, like when Jesse tried to rope Jackson into a telemarketing scheme. When Jackson realized what was going on, he was confused and hurt. Yet Jackson remained sympathetic. "I see what happens when somebody is selling themselves short," Jackson said. "When an addict sells themselves short, sells everybody out, it's himself that he's betraying."[33]

His diminishing reputation notwithstanding, Jesse did make some live and studio appearances during the early '80s. Alongside his old Continentals drummer John Ware, he played on Emmylou Harris's single "Precious Love," but he was clearly distracted. "That guy you brought in has been on the phone ever since he came into my office," Emmylou complained to Ware. "I don't know who the fuck he's talking to, but I know for a fact it's long distance." It was. Jesse rang up a $600 bill talking with Tantalayo back in Hawaii before she ultimately showed up in person at the session a couple days later.[34]

In addition to occasional studio assignments, Jesse appeared live as a special guest with some famous friends. Briefly but seriously auditioning to replace his early guitar idol Robbie Robertson in the Band, Jesse sat in for a handful of California tour dates in 1983, but he blew it when the group realized he was too deep into drugs. Given the deteriorating state of the Band, in terms of some members' own battles with addiction, this spoke volumes. By this point, Jesse had no guitar. He borrowed one when he joined Leon Russell at the Trancas club in Malibu, playing alongside fellow special guest Eric Clapton and actor Gary Busey, who stalked the stage banging percussion instruments while Clapton and Jesse traded solos on "Amazing Grace" and "Somewhere Over the Rainbow." "It's guitar night at the Trancas!" Leon cheered.[35]

In fact, Clapton saw something in Jesse he hoped to salvage. Gearing up for a world tour in 1984, the British guitarist extended an invitation to join him on the road. A substantial payday was in order, so much so that Jesse could afford to bring Bill on tour with him as a guitar tech and personal assistant, and even share some of the loot. Clapton insisted on one proviso: Jesse had to stay clean for three months leading up to the tour. He made it two months and twenty-nine days. "I fucked myself up again," he said. Clapton was "leery of me now. He's Mr. A.A. and he thinks I'm fucking around." Once again, Jesse hurt Bill as much as he hurt himself. Bill had recently graduated high school and had an incredible job lined up—a world tour with his dad. "But Jesse disappeared one week before and blew it," Bill remembers, "so I got a job making bagels." Jesse then siphoned Bill's bagel money. "What a scoundrel," Bill says.[36]

WITH PATTI AND TANTALAYO in the rearview, Jesse's next romantic interest took the form of an old friend. Kelly Wallahan, better known as Kelly Brady (her father's show-business surname), was a tall, beautiful, smoky-voiced woman with Seneca Native American ancestry—"statuesque," one friend described her. Kelly grew up in the entertainment business, first running around craps tables in Las Vegas, then trekking back and forth to Mexico, where her stepbrother was killed fighting alongside the Zapatistas, an Indigenous agrarian army that fought for land reform. Kelly's father Wally Brady lived in Mexico with his second wife, who was from there, and managed arguably the most famous mariachi band in the world, Mariachi Vargas de Tecalitlán, during the Golden Era of Mariachi.[37]

Kelly forbade drugs and alcohol, partly because of early gum disease she developed from chain-smoking. Kelly became Jesse's sobriety sergeant, as she described herself. She was backed by her father, who instilled fear of God in Jesse, sometimes threatening his life. He meant it, too. Wally still boasted mob connections from his days working with Frank Sinatra and Dean Martin. Jesse's onetime bandmate Van Dyke Parks knew Wally and a young Kelly from years prior when he arranged "The Bare Necessities," with Brady producing, for Disney's *The Jungle Book*. Then as now, the music business was a small world. Growing up inside and around it granted Kelly experience that she applied to her life with Jesse. She was tough and independent. Jesse called her "BOB," as in "Beast of Burden," an apt reference to the Rolling Stones—Kelly's favorite band. "Jesse would have been dead long before if it hadn't been for Kelly," one friend insists. "Jesse was crazy about her."[38]

Before Kelly was Jesse's friend and then girlfriend, she was Jesse's fan. She first saw him at the Ash Grove playing with Taj Mahal when she was in tenth grade. Venue staff let her hang around because of her father's reputation. She became fixated on Jesse. "Have you ever seen him play?" she once enthused. "You got to see it. He would just stand there and close his eyes and play. He wasn't jumping around. He wasn't dancing. He would just play the tones that he could get out of any guitar." She would never forget what Jesse said when he approached her that night: "Don't I know you from Seattle?" Kelly had never been to Seattle.[39]

When they officially began dating on March 27, 1982, they had known each other for years. Kelly was Ray Eckstein's girlfriend and part of the Marina gang that befriended Jesse back at the Hurricane House. When Ray died, Jesse looked out for Kelly, not with any ulterior motive but from an avuncular obligation to care for her. "Somehow, he appointed himself my guardian," Kelly recalled. She had a gig bartending, and Jesse would pull up a stool for hours, chasing away anyone who tried to hit on her. In 1975, she married a man named Luis Zavala, likely a mariachi musician, but he soon died from a drug overdose. Kelly was "not dark," Gary Ray suggests, "but she experienced a lot of darkness." All three of her serious romantic partners ultimately died tragically. On New Year's Eve 1975, Kelly needed a date for a party, so she invited Jesse, who was reeling from his separation with Patti. The date couldn't help but be awkward. "I was more like his little sister," Kelly said.[40]

When they became a real couple in 1982, Kelly fell in love with Jesse's poetic sensibility, his cooking, and his paintings of American Indians, reflecting his father's influence. They would sometimes sit around and make drawings of each other for fun. "Jesse was an artist first and foremost in everything he did," she stressed. But she didn't love everything about Jesse's life. While Jesse and Kelly temporarily stayed with a friend of ex–Rod Stewart manager Bobby Daniels, Kelly struggled with Bill's enduring relationship with Jesse. "I'm going to see my son," Jesse announced one day in front of their hosts. "Well, it's not his son—it's Patti's son," Kelly grumbled after Jesse left.[41]

Kelly took a job at the car rental corporation Avis—"Slavis," she called it—to put food on the table and pay rent. But Jesse often undermined her efforts and hit the streets. Kelly and her friend Mary would form a search party to find him and bring him home. Tired of the escapades, Kelly recruited her friend Sarah to sit with Jesse by day and keep him out of trouble, "but there was only one person who could do that," Sarah remembers. Jesse and his would-be warden liked to get Carl's Jr. burgers and play Trivial Pursuit. Jesse always won. Kelly once suggested he was "too smart for his own good." Miraculously, the phone still rang with offers for work. Jesse repeatedly turned them down. One day, out of love and concern, Sarah lost her composure and berated him: "Goddammit, Jesse! All these people still want you! Why don't you take your guitar and go play?!" "Being a junkie is a full-time job," he told her.[42]

While Kelly and Jesse's love alternatingly faltered and flourished, another significant person in Jesse's life died tragically, with little fanfare beyond his hometown paper. Johnny Angel had moved back to Detroit in 1980, but he brought some of California with him. In November 1984, he was found in his car, in his garage, seated next to a glass of whisky he swigged and a Philip K. Dick novel he read while exhaust fumes washed over him. No one saw it coming. Angel seemed happy enough playing with his group the Torpedos, and he had recently joined his friend Bo Diddley on harmonica. His obituary described him as "really spontaneous; words just flew out of his mouth," not unlike they had when Jesse collaborated with him on the lyrics for *Keep Me Comin'*.[43]

Johnny Angel joined a growing list of important people in Jesse's life who met terrible ends, including keyboardist Ray Eckstein, engineer Joe Zagarino, Okie bassist Carl Radle, cosmic cowboy Gram Parsons, Beatles assistant Mal Evans, Beatle John Lennon, and his own father, Jesse Edwin Davis II. There would be more. Murders, suicides, and drugs. Jesse loved his friends deeply, and their sudden departures crushed him. The same drugs that took the lives of several of his closest friends helped him numb his anguish over their absence. Time and again, he risked joining them.

In 1984, Kelly finally convinced Jesse to enter rehab, despite resistance from both Jesse and her father, who hated the fact that she was with Jesse. Fortunately, this wasn't just any rehab venue but the American Indian Eagle Lodge program in Long Beach. The Eagle Lodge began in 1972 as part of a larger social services network supported by federal grants. It employed an all-Indian staff and housed roughly fifteen patients at a time. Native people who worked there were often recovering addicts themselves, reflecting recent national trends across addiction treatment centers. Program manager Frank DuPoint was a Kiowa person like Jesse. "Being an Indian," DuPoint stressed, "it seems as though it's the companionship and the relationships working throughout the building here are in better harmony than they would be working with the white institutions."[44]

Jesse's experience at the Eagle Lodge had such an effect on him that he later simultaneously served as a patient and a counselor at the similar American Indian Free Clinic's Main Artery program in Compton. Formed in the back of a church in 1969, the Free Clinic became the first urban Indigenous health center in the country. "When an Indian walks in here, he knows he can get help regardless of what his problem is, and he won't be shifted from one agency to another," then-director George Baker promised. In addition to providing everything from pediatric care to eyeglasses, the clinic featured an alcoholism recovery center. In his own battle with alcoholism, Jesse was not alone; as a result of the ongoing effects of colonialism, legacies of generational trauma, and more, one in three Native people fought substance dependence during the 1970s. "These people have a living problem," Baker, himself a recovering patient, said, "and it's not enough just to put the plug in the jug. . . . We have to deal with it. It's not going away."[45]

Kelly and Jesse soon became active members of the Orange County Powwow Club and traveled up and down the coast for events that took Jesse back to his childhood days dancing in Oklahoma. They would head out to a powwow on a Thursday and stay all weekend, with Jesse cooking pozole and frybread for his growing cast of Native friends. Jesse's secret frybread recipe involved prepackaged Pillsbury biscuits. (We can assume Mamacita protested, if she ever knew.)[46]

Jesse also picked up a promising gig with a new guitar partner. Mark Shark and the Hammerheads regularly played the Lighthouse, a stalwart jazz club in Hermosa Beach, and began inviting Jesse to sit in. Warming up at their first gig, Shark called for the Little Feat classic "Willin'." "I started it off," Shark recalled, "and Jesse came in and my god the tone he got from that shitty little amp and second-rate Strat blew my mind. I learned right then and there that it wasn't the equipment that made the man." After soundcheck, a towering redheaded bartender from an adjacent club shouted at Jesse, "Hey, why don't you get a haircut?!" Shark watched Jesse jump from the stage and chase the Irishman with his guitar. "You didn't say that kind of shit to Jesse Ed," Shark quickly understood. His growing partnership with Jesse seemed promising enough to reject a gig with an up-and-coming music comedian calling himself "Weird" Al Yankovic. Shark didn't regret it.[47]

NOTWITHSTANDING A DIFFICULT divorce from Tantalayo, prospects for Jesse were improving again. Benefiting from treatment, finding his way back into Indigenous fellowship, forging new musical partnerships, and falling in love with an old friend, Jesse capped this beginning of a comeback with marriage to Kelly. Together they went to the LA County Courthouse to stand before the same judge who once put Jesse in jail when Jesse was living on the street in Venice. Jesse invited Jackson Browne to be his best man, and Jackson brought his wife, the movie star Daryl Hannah. "There he was," Jackson recalls, "clean and straight, sober, and the judge was really . . . you could see that the judge liked him, in a sort of judge, magisterial kind of gruff way, saying, 'Well, Mr. Davis, I see that you've really turned the corner here.' "[48]

Things were looking up for Jesse, and another extraordinary encounter waited to unfold. Jesse would soon meet another John who would provide new perspective, purpose, and friendship. While Jesse was checked in at the Eagle Lodge, someone brought in a cassette tape of *Tribal Voice*, featuring poetry by a Dakota person named John Trudell who had lived his own hard life. With the cassette cranked on the rec room boombox, Jesse was mesmerized. He especially loved a song called "Diablo Canyon," about a protest at a nuclear power plant, which contained the powerful lyric, "It took the pain, the grief, and the dying to remember what gets forgotten in the living."[49]

When the Eagle Lodge organized a bus trip for patients to go see this John Trudell character perform at Cal State Long Beach one evening in 1985, Jesse was first to sign up. After the set, he introduced himself to Trudell. "I'm Jesse Ed Davis," he said. "I can make music for your words." When their impromptu introduction ended, Jesse mentioned that he wanted to "rediscover his roots." John could help with that.[50]

John Trudell would go on to recite the details of their first encounter many times, careful to get it right, like a story in an oral tradition. Each time, he emphasized that it was May Day, as though that connection was particularly appropriate and important. May Day is, after all, an international workers' day, a celebration of spring, and a code word for distress—three themes that would correspond with Jesse and John's collaborative turn.

Eleven

I WILL RETREAT NO FURTHER

"GOOD EVENING. This is John Trudell from Radio Free Alcatraz, welcoming you to Indian land Alcatraz on behalf of the Indians of All Tribes." The Santee Dakota Vietnam veteran's voice transmitted from a cell block in the former prison that once incarcerated Indigenous parents who refused to send their children to government boarding schools in the late nineteenth century. Beaming through the San Francisco Bay fog, Trudell earned a reputation as a compelling thinker and speaker, a skill set that lent itself to a life of music, poetry, acting, and activism. From his leadership during the watershed Alcatraz reclamation in 1969 to his performances across international music stages, Trudell delivered news from Indian Country as orator and troubadour.[1]

On important Indigenous matters, Trudell deftly shifted between past, present, and future. He talked about poverty, patriarchy, and history, as well as sovereignty, community, family, and future. He could comfortably transition from nineteenth-century Indigenous leaders' speeches to twentieth-century Bureau of Indian Affairs policies. This made him an ideal national spokesperson for the American Indian Movement, which he helped lead after the 1973 Wounded Knee defense

that resulted in a clash with US federal forces, three deaths, FBI infil-
tration, civil war on the Pine Ridge Reservation, and the incarceration
of numerous Native leaders. It also made Trudell a target. FBI agents
followed him for years, gathering a thick file.

In 1979, Trudell experienced the unthinkable loss of his family in
a fire that he considered "murder" and an "act of war." "It was like I
was in this exile of feeling that there was really no safe place, and a lot
of disillusionment set in," he described the aftermath. Seeking refuge
in his writing, he began wondering if his words could become songs.
His Warm Springs Tyghpum friend Quiltman Sahme helped him
try, providing traditional drumming and singing. After a successful
debut show supporting Bonnie Raitt, they made their first album,
Tribal Voice (1983). Jackson Browne, who first met Trudell at a No
Nukes concert in 1979, loaned out his studio, hosted Trudell at his
house, and paid to press some cassettes. All involved were impressed,
but there was a consensus that they could take the project even further. Trudell had innovative ideas for music and poetry. He was a fan
of rock and roll, from Elvis to John Lennon. He only needed another
music partner who could connect him to those sounds. Then he met
Jesse. For three electric years, they elevated each other's artistry and
sense of purpose.[2]

AFTER THEIR INITIAL ENCOUNTER in May 1985 at Trudell's poetry
performance, Jesse and Trudell promised to meet again. Later that
month, Trudell was driving to LA along Pacific Coast Highway when
he saw a sign for a powwow in Watsonville. Stopping for coffee and a
driving break, he bumped into Jesse and Kelly. Now Jesse and Trudell's
interest in working together seemed ordained, a "cosmic event," as their
future bandmate Mark Shark recalls. Having just completed a treatment
program, Jesse sought support and healing within the Los Angeles and
surrounding urban Indigenous community. They made plans to begin
working on some music.[3]

For Jesse, Trudell became a friend, comrade, music partner, and

Indian brother. Jesse wasn't just trying to find his way back to the Native community, he wanted to contribute something when he got there. Trudell encouraged it. In order for Jesse to bring something, he needed to first repair his professional reputation:

> I've got a real reputation as a lunatic, a madman. There was always that suspicion lurking in people's minds: "Will he show up? Will he show up drunk or will he not bother to come at all?" When John [Trudell] allowed me to create the music for his poetry, I had nowhere else to turn. My back was to the wall, but I had all this music inside me that just came gushing out.

Trudell was searching for something too. When officials decided against investigating the fire that took his family, he worried that it wasn't safe for his friends and loved ones to be around him. He needed a new partner and place. "Jesse dressed me up and he put me out there on stage," Trudell said. At a Grafitti Band show during the height of their partnership, before tearing into Jesse's standards "Natural Anthem" and "Bacon Fat," Trudell told the crowd the band's story. "It seems to me like I've been through a lot of worlds before this one, and things were starting to fall into place a bit," he said, "but I still didn't know how to get to where I was headed and I needed some help, and a man just showed up and helped me, my brother, Jesse Ed Davis." The crowd cheered.[4]

Jesse's professional peers also recognized the promise of their partnership. Jackson Browne saw how Jesse and John complemented one another as a formidable duo of Native American artists. Jesse could literally amplify Trudell's messages. He radiated charisma and confidence, conquering people with a fantastic smile wherever he went. Trudell introduced a different kind of magnetism, a magnetism born out of his confrontational honesty. Trudell was not a "diplomat," stresses Jackson Browne. Recalling a dinner with Trudell and the 1960s New Left activist organization Students for a Democratic Society leader Tom Hayden, Jackson says, "John put [Hayden] on a stand. It was like an inquisition. . . . That's who Jesse Ed met—a devout, powerful activist, who was dealing with the injustices." Trudell demonstrated outward anger but never hate, a subtle yet important distinction. Jesse was similar, but his anger often turned inward. Bonnie Raitt witnessed their countervailing relationship:

> The miracle of the fact that Jesse was getting sober just around the time when John was coming into needing and being open to musical background, the two of them together, it was no accident, it was divine—synchrodestiny for them to both fill a need that each other had and for the bigger purpose of getting that message out.

John brought the message; Jesse brought the music. They sacrificed for each other. "Jesse could've done a million things and he chose not to," Bonnie Bramlett affirms. "He chose to help John." Jesse's partner Kelly certainly appreciated how Trudell helped Jesse stay sober—Jesse could never get anything past him. Kelly witnessed a stronger spirit at the heart of their relationship. "The minute they hooked up [Jesse] knew they were brothers," she recalled. "That connection will go on throughout eternity."[5]

Jesse considered Trudell one of his greatest artistic collaborators, likening him to John Lennon and Bob Dylan. When asked if anyone could fill the void of Lennon's death, Jesse said no. But in Trudell, he saw the same power. "John Trudell is one of the inspirations like John Lennon," he proclaimed, highlighting the two Johns' fierce independence and commitment to their causes, be they political, artistic, spiritual, or all three at once.[6]

As they grew closer, Jesse also became convinced Trudell was the Indian Bob Dylan. He described his new partner's artistry as a "Bob Dylan imagery consciousness and I immediately heard music behind this poetry." For Jesse, partnership with Trudell would be about Indigeneity and music. Jesse felt it was important for another Indigenous artist to put Trudell's poetry to music. And where the music was concerned, he was certain it needed to be rock and roll. So Jesse concluded, "I seemed tailor-made for the job." Working with Trudell didn't make Jesse more or less Indigenous. But Trudell did provide easier proximity to Indian people and culture, something Jesse had been missing in the mainstream music industry and related social circles.[7]

IN SUMMER 1985, Jesse and John began working together in earnest, eventually adopting the name Grafitti Man. Jesse articulated three goals for their project: make sure Trudell is heard, enjoy the musical experience, and make a change in the world. John brought Quiltman into the mix and Jesse introduced his old friends Ricky Eckstein, Gary Ray, Bob Tsukamoto, and his new guitar partner Mark Shark. At various times they were augmented by keyboardists Jim Ehinger and Nicky Hopkins. Special guests such as singer Bonnie Bramlett, the Mvskoke poet Joy Harjo, and actress Daryl Hannah appeared on the group's recordings. Jesse hoped to bring some of his favorite musicians into the project, including Eric Clapton, Don Henley, and Joe Cocker, who could "bring a tear to a glass eye," Jesse liked to say.[8]

Jesse and Trudell ultimately made three albums together: *aka Grafitti Man* (1986), *Heart Jump Bouquet* (1987), and *But This Isn't El Salvador* (1987), the third an adjacent Tribal Voice project featuring traditional poetry, drumming, and songs by Trudell and Quiltman. Jesse coproduced it and contributed guitar to a track that marks the group's greatest musical creation. Predictably, Jesse liked each new album more than the last. It's an admirable trait, and significant in what it tells us about him. He was always confident in where he was going sonically, if not in life. He always imagined his next work would be his best.[9]

Grafitti Man worked on a tight budget. The group demonstrated cunning resourcefulness, sometimes to the point of comedy. When Ricky Eckstein stepped away from playing bass with the group to focus on coproducing the band, Jesse asked his friend Howard Tsukamoto's younger brother Bob to take over. Jesse gave Bob a tape of songs to learn. Strangely, it was Jesse's phone answering machine tape, still featuring old messages from John Lennon and Bob Dylan. Jesse once worked with both artists in the best studios in the world. Now he couldn't procure a blank cassette tape.[10]

Working quickly in Eckstein's garage, John would show Jesse a new set of lyrics each day while Jesse composed music on the spot, similar to Jesse's experience in the studio with Bob Dylan. Within twelve hours or so they'd have a complete song recorded. Importantly for Trudell, the experience was a family affair with his daughters in tow. "I was living with Jackson. I would take the girls with me and we would work on it all day. Then at night, they would go to sleep on the floor and we would record a rough mix."[11]

The music Grafitti Man made wasn't easily accessible. They weren't a pop group. This was serious music. The audience needed to meet it half-way. "This wasn't a comedy act," Mark Shark describes the group's seriousness of purpose. "Trudell had a message. It was no bullshit." Trudell often reminded the band that they were together to make art. As a serious group, they had obligatory serious conversations about how best to present themselves—not only their music but also their style and look. They were trying to launch this project from Hollywood, after all, or at least a garage nearby. It's hard enough for any band to develop an audience, let alone the way the Grafitti Band did, working the local club circuit at a time when hair bands with lipstick, spandex, smoke machines, and pyrotechnics dominated the rock scene. The Grafitti Band wasn't just different, it was innovative. The group had attitude, but its music wasn't about sex and drugs. It had something important to say about politics, earth and the environment, humanity and war, and more. How and where would they fit? Should stationary Trudell wear tighter pants and move around a little more onstage? Daryl Hannah wondered after seeing an early gig. "Maybe she's right!" Jesse laughed. Upon further reflection, he concluded, "I like him the way he is."[12]

The band committed to who they were and what they could do. They would be a lyrically driven project with strong instrumental backing. In style and substance, they merged early-twentieth-century talking blues and foundational 1950s rock and roll, as well as Old and New Left folk movements, traditional Indigenous music, and 1980s New Wave. Their originality was an incomparable synthesis of these genres, but then steeped in social thought anchored in Indigenous artists' political and thematic sensibilities. "There's a difference between imitation and influence," Bob Dylan suggests. "And then there's something else entirely. Like John Trudell."[13]

Jesse was a seasoned pro in the studio. Trudell, on the other hand, paced the floor for hours. He worried about comparisons to Beat poets from an earlier California scene. Unlike Kerouac, Ferlinghetti, and others, Trudell didn't want to read poetry on top of a soundtrack. He and Jesse were striving to deliver poetry *within* their music, through cohesive composition and aesthetic. They called it "talking rock." Before meeting Jesse, Trudell recalled, "I was around a lot of musicians but they didn't relate to what I was saying." He explained how his spoken word was an extension of Indigenous oratory traditions and his recent role as spokesperson for the American Indian Movement. Trudell's lyrics were carefully crafted speeches, intended to deliver power to the people. At the same time, he was influenced by his favorite popular musicians, including Jackson Browne, Bob Dylan, John Lennon, Willie Nelson, and Leonard Cohen. Jesse had played with all of them. Through Jesse, Trudell could draw from both streams. Together they could fashion something truly unique.[14]

Some Jesse Davis fans recoil at the use of synthesizers and drum machines on his tracks with Trudell. While these productions now sound dated, there was a greater purpose behind their use. This was not *just* an inevitable nod to the prevailing music-making tools of the 1980s. By engaging with the most modern and trendy sound of the day, the group proved that Indigenous music could not only exist within modern music but enrich it. "I wanted to do it with the oldest musical form and with the newest musical form," Trudell said. Indigenous musicians held rightful claims to belonging within the current trends, including '80s pop and rock music. Besides, some of Jesse's old rock star friends were doing the same.[15]

Trudell wanted to call the first album *Lavenders Blues*, but Jesse preferred another title. Each time Trudell mentioned their work on *Lavenders Blues*, Jesse interjected "also known as *Grafitti Man*." Trudell finally yielded, agreeing that the latter title better represented the aim of their project. Jesse was thrilled for people to hear *aka Grafitti Man*. He sent copies to friends and began looking for a record deal, even approaching the executive who once signed him to ATCO back in 1970. "I have a meeting with Jerry Wexler, I'm gonna lay this Sioux Indian poet tape that I got on him," Jesse announced. When that proved fruitless, Jesse asked his Apache musician friend Robby Romero to help arrange a meeting with Island Records. Everyone seemed excited when Jesse delivered his pitch to the label heads. "But then something happened," Romero recalls. "I could tell Jesse was disappointed and Island never moved forward with the deal."[16]

The group decided to embrace their friend Betty Billups's standing offer to start an independent label, Peace Company, to release the album. She loved the group and wanted Jesse and John's music to be heard. Trudell helped her organize the materials for the first album, including the cover images designed to look like mug shots. It was only after they pressed cassettes and placed ads that they realized they had misspelled "Graffiti." They were stuck with it.[17]

The label also operated on a tight budget, but the cassette became a hit in Indian Country, especially on the powwow circuit, where Native music fans scouted for albums not stocked in major record stores. Fan letters poured in from Navajo protesters at Big Mountain; the Leonard Peltier Defense Committee; and even Marlon Brando, who was himself a longtime advocate for Native rights. Billups remembers laughing with Jesse as they drove to formally nominate *aka Grafitti Man* for Grammy Awards in the rock duo and spoken word categories. It didn't advance to the final round, but it was more about getting the album heard than any serious expectation of an award, deserving as it was.[18]

Then came a boost from an unexpected source. "Hey, wanna hear the best album of the year?" Bob Dylan said about *aka Grafitti Man* during an interview with *Rolling Stone*. "Only people like Lou Reed and John Doe can dream about doing work like this," he pledged. Knowing how rarely Dylan personally endorsed other artists, the group was deeply grateful. "When Dylan did that we were in our 40s," Trudell recalled. "Here is this Indian rock and roller, ex junkie, this militant. There was no market for us." Crowds at Grafitti live audiences and bookings grew significantly after Dylan's recommendation, while Billups instantly received over five hundred new orders for the album.[19]

Meanwhile, the group's music was becoming more sophisticated as they steered closer to their envisioned sound. On the stunning "Beauty in a Fade," Trudell, Jesse, and Quiltman finally achieved it. They blended poetic oratory, round dance drumming, and weeping bottleneck slide guitar in a song unlike anything before or since. "It was the first time you could hear how to blend the electric guitar with traditional Indian music and not sound like the Hamm's beer commercial," Shark says. Jesse's circular slide guitar cries in response to Quiltman's pleading, "Wait for me, wait for me, my darling," underneath Trudell's poem about a man trying to conquer the world and a woman who became his last stand. "That song changed the musical world," Quiltman says. "He did it. Jesse."[20]

Jesse's slide guitar skill, referred to as "Night Spirits Guitar" in the credits for "Beauty in a Fade," first emerged exactly twenty years prior with Taj Mahal. But the roots of Jesse's technique can be traced much further back, to Hawaii in the late nineteenth century. Kānaka people developed the kīkā kila steel guitar prior to colonization. It traveled on ships to California, where Jesse made a career, and eventually became a feature of country and western music in Oklahoma, where Jesse was born.

Long before Jesse was born, other Indigenous people learned and advanced the style, including Mvskoke mezzo-soprano opera singer Tsianina Redfeather Blackstone, who played the lap slide guitar for American military personnel in Europe during World War I. After surviving a German U-boat attack, Blackstone appeared with the instrument in the earliest known video of someone performing it. She was a Mvskoke person from Indian Territory Oklahoma, like Jesse, playing a slide guitar invented by Indigenous Hawaiian people as part of a show called "The Indian of Yesterday and Today," for people in England and in France. Jesse's practice of the technique connected him to an important past that saw Indigenous musicians travel far and wide to deliver the healing powers of their music through a technique that passed through many Indigenous musicians' hands.[21]

Later, in 1992, Rykodisc rereleased augmented and remixed versions
of some original tracks from *aka Grafitti Man, Heart Jump Bouquet*,
and *But This Isn't El Salvador* as part of the subtly retitled *AKA Grafitti
Man* album. This marked another great opportunity to further spread
Jesse and Trudell's music. One Native American newspaper called the
album "one of the most successful attempts ever at mixing spoken word
and rock music." Some songs featured in the Robert Redford–produced
documentary film *Incident at Oglala*, about the 1975 raid on the Pine
Ridge reservation that resulted in two FBI agents' deaths and what many
have protested as the unjust incarceration of activist Leonard Peltier.
Trudell had also recently starred in the major studio film *Thunderheart*,
garnering additional attention for the group. A massive shift in popular
rock music occurred with the Alternative Revolution that ushered in a
diverse wave of both new bands and old bands earning renewed popularity. There was market room for an album like *AKA Grafitti Man*
that defied conventions. But Ryko failed to anticipate the roughly thirty
thousand orders they received, having only pressed five thousand copies.
They couldn't fill orders. By the time they tried to catch up, *AKA Grafitti
Man*'s shelf life was dead. Like *Keep Me Comin'*, it was another album
featuring Jesse's music that suffered a marketing debacle.[22]

IN A LIVE MUSIC SETTING, Jesse and Trudell endured an inauspicious
start. Before putting the complete band together, they went to Minneapolis to appear as a duo at one of Trudell's spoken word events. At
showtime, Jesse was too inebriated to perform. Trudell, furious, took
Jesse's guitar and refused to return it for months. "I know he felt bad
about it," Trudell later said.[23]

Given Jesse's unpredictability, the Grafitti Band had to remain flex-
ible. After Dylan hyped them in *Rolling Stone* in 1986, a packed house
immediately awaited at Club Lingerie. Jesse was again incapacitated.
Rolling Stones keyboardist Nicky Hopkins took the stage in his absence
to help fill the musical void. Kelly Davis left in disgust. After the gig,
Hopkins drove Jesse to a Scientology detox center. "He woke up in a
fucking Scientologist room," Trudell mused. "YOU GAVE ME TO

THE SCIENTOLOGISTS?!" Jesse cried when he got back. "He didn't do that again," Trudell said.[24]

When Jesse was healthier, the band played an impressive number of gigs, working all over Los Angeles County, and occasionally beyond, including a concert in New York City, where Jesse's mother once performed. They appeared everywhere from old establishments dating back to Jesse's earlier heyday to clubs like the Coconut Teazer, which became notorious as the headquarters for Heidi Fleiss's high-end call girl business that catered to celebrities.[25]

Jesse and company shared these diverse stages with a diverse range of artists, including other Indigenous performers. If Jesse once took his music to Hollywood, his music was now taking him to Indian Country—an urban version located in Los Angeles, which then housed one of the largest concentrations of Indigenous people in North America. The Grafitti Band played alongside popular Oneida comedian Charlie Hill, Dakota country-rocker Floyd Red Crow Westerman, and Mvskoke poet Joy Harjo. An early gig at UCLA saw the Grafitti Band take the stage after a performance by traditional Native dancers at the "Continuing Gifts of the American Indian: Painting and Poetry" event organized by the American Indian Women's Support Group.[26]

On other occasions Katey Sagal, Peg Bundy of *Married with Children* television fame, opened Grafitti Band shows with her band while sitcom star Max Gail emceed. At one gig, the Grafitti Band backed the revolutionary activist Abbie Hoffman, known for his role in the Chicago Seven trial stemming from the 1968 Democratic National Convention protest and for the radical, sometimes farcical, ideologies reflected in his work: *Fuck the System, Revolution for the Hell of It, Steal This Book*. He was now trying to launch a standup comedy career, with Grafitti Band in support.[27]

A lot of Indian people showed up for the gigs, Quiltman notes, but, "sometimes *he* wouldn't show up," he says, referring to Jesse. And though Native people often turned out, they frequently upset club owners because so few Native patrons drank alcohol at gigs. But they loved seeing one of their own onstage and many celebrated Jesse's legacy. He was humble and gracious when fans approached. Though he didn't like

to show it, it made him feel good. He knew his talent. Sometimes, however, a certain sad dejection competed with Jesse's revel in fan love. By
that point, he wondered if anyone wanted to hear him play anymore.[28]

Because they were so different and appeared on such diverse bills,
the Grafitti Band often faced tough crowds. "The band is great, but
can you lose the poet guy?" was a common refrain at early gigs. People
who came to hear the poetry complained that the band was too loud.
Conversely, those who came to hear Jesse's guitar complained that the
poetry was too loud.[29]

The Grafitti Band also endured ignorant depictions of Native artists.
One reviewer praised *AKA Grafitti Man* through almost exclusively back-
handed caricatures, referring to Trudell as "the stage-stalking, angry
spokesperson of the Indian condition" and Jesse as the purveyor of "night
club licks" and "angry slide guitar." The reviewer suggested that the
socially conscious project was better than the self-congratulatory "We
Are the World" and the cynicism of John Mellencamp's *Scarecrow* and
Farm Aid. But then, he continued, "John Trudell and Jesse Ed Davis
are latter day shamans who are connecting the ancient ways of sharing
and unity to the here and now with deeply felt sound and sense." The
piece was obviously meant to be flattering, and there was truth to the
mention of peace as a central theme in the music. But it may also exem-
plify why Jesse was often apprehensive about marketing himself as a
distinctly Indigenous artist.[30]

In 1986, Jesse appeared solo at the Drums Across America benefit concert for Navajo and Hopi people protesting removal from Big
Mountain. He was one among numerous prominent Native musicians,
including Robby Romero, Redbone, Jim Pepper, Floyd Westerman, and
more. *Exorcist* actress Linda Blair must have meant well when she lent
her celebrity to the event, telling a news reporter, "These people are like
wild animals. You can't just uproot them and expect them to live somewhere else. They die when you take them away."[31]

Native people, needless to say, are not wild animals. This is a colonial
stereotype dating back to early-sixteenth-century reports from European
explorers who cast Indigenous people as children of an untamed land
that should be taken at will. Virtually every Native nation existing today,

including Jesse's ancestors, experienced at least one episode of violent removal in their histories. While many Native people *did* die during various removals, it wasn't because they were lacking in constitution. Rather, it was because of the conditions of their removals. It's another example of a harmful stereotype Jesse had to confront from people who meant well. Now with Quiltman and Trudell, at least he had greater numbers.

Around like-minded people, the Grafitti Band fit right in. In October 1987, they joined Lucinda Williams in Los Angeles to lend support to the activist Katya Komisaruk, who had been imprisoned for breaking into Vandenberg Air Force Base and smashing a computer she believed operated a nuclear missile system. A preview for the gig likened Jesse and Trudell to Indigenous "comic book superheroes" who will "tap their Indian spirit for a blow against the nuclear empire." Despite being literally cartoonish, it's a more appropriate summation of the group's mission. If Jesse saw it, he probably liked that one.[32]

While the group achieved a sense of belonging among more enlightened musicians and audiences, their politically charged messages about nuclear empires sometimes courted police surveillance. One day in 1987, on Oregon's Warm Springs reservation, Quiltman asked his daughter to sing a traditional song. Out came "Old MacDonald Had a Farm." Determined to avoid the same with his son, Quilt planned to create an Indian survival school modeled on those in Minnesota, where Native students gained a Native education from Native instructors as an act of self-determination. To kickstart his effort, Quilt arranged a benefit concert by the Grafitti Band.[33]

Before the show, Quilt took Jesse to the radio station for a promotional interview. Jesse went straight to the shelves of vinyl and began pulling down albums. "Hey, I'm on this . . . I'm on this one too . . . And this one . . . ," he said. "Goddamn!" Quilt laughs. "Three quarters of the music they had he was on it. He was magic." That afternoon, the atmosphere before the concert was relaxed, with horseback riding, golf, and a beer garden. Then the FBI showed up. They had been trailing Trudell for years. Though the concert was sold out, few attended after word quickly spread about the FBI presence. Undeterred, the Grafitti Band played for a few dozen people while helicopters buzzed above the stage and federal agents snaked around bushes snapping pictures. This didn't ruin Jesse's experience. "I really needed that," he told Quiltman after the gig.[34]

The FBI's stunt did nothing to soothe a severe paranoia stemming from the murder of his friend John Lennon and aggravated by years of drug dependence. Jesse was convinced he was being surveilled. His phone was never shut off, he noticed, even when he couldn't pay the bill, and someone broke into his apartment and stole his letters from Lennon. Dining with his cousin Gary Davis before a Grafitti Band gig in Seattle, Jesse mentioned that he feared for his life, before pointing to two men at a nearby table. "They always follow me," he whispered.[35]

The FBI appeared at a second Grafitti gig with Joni Mitchell, Kris Kristofferson, and Willie Nelson in Costa Mesa at the Cowboys for Indians benefit for Leonard Peltier. The Grafitti Band brought out surprise guest Jackson Browne, who joined the group on a cover of Greg Copeland's "Revenge Will Come" and Jackson's own "Doctor My Eyes." This was the first time Jackson and Jesse had played the latter song together since it became a top-ten hit in 1972. "It's hard to imagine a more socially committed pop attraction than the Grafitti Band," one reporter wrote. Outside the venue, police and FBI formed a picket line. The real injustice wasn't Peltier's incarceration, they argued, but the deaths of two FBI agents back in 1975. "DON'T THROW [PELTIER] A BENEFIT, THROW HIM A ROPE!" one sign read. These benefit concerts were a far cry from the Concert for Bangladesh.[36]

WHILE STAYING BUSY with the Grafitti Band, Jesse found time to develop other projects and collaborations. He didn't just commit to a comeback; he began announcing it. Amusingly, in pencil, on wide-ruled notebook paper, he wrote a letter to his old friend Mike Piranha in Hawaii. "I want to dip my pecker in the water again with the Piranha Brothers," he wrote. Mike welcomed it, but then he never heard from Jesse again.[37]

After the Cowboys for Indians gig, Jesse, inspired by their live rendition of "Doctor My Eyes," asked Jackson Browne about working together again. "How about I play in your band?" Jackson thought about it for a while. But he wasn't touring. Putting something together with Jesse would have steered him in a new direction, one that didn't make sense at the time. "I didn't really respond," Jackson regrets. "I didn't take him up on that." Jackson would only see Jesse one more time.[38]

Alongside an assortment of artists including R.E.M., Los Lobos, Lou Reed, and Pee-Wee Herman, Jesse's song "Santa Claus Is Getting Down" was included on the *Winter Warnerland* holiday compilation in 1988. Jesse's contribution was an original tune that borrowed from his favorite blues number, "It Hurts Me Too." After a copy of Jesse's song landed on project coordinator Bill Bentley's desk, he called Kelly to invite a high-quality transfer for inclusion on the album. Kelly sent a tape with her father Wally Brady, who showed up at Bentley's office dressed like "Yukon Jack" in cowboy clothes and handlebar mustache, "like a star nobody knew, like he was auditioning for a Western or something, total character, great guy. . . . He was used to running with Dean Martin and Sinatra and that crowd, and kind of thought he still did," Bentley recalled. Wally Brady probably liked Christmas, if for no better reason than, each year around that time, he received a large royalty check for his share of Elvis Presley's gospel albums, which he later left to Kelly. Jesse loved Christmas. He was like a kid about it. It's comforting to realize his last work as a solo artist was a Christmas song, one rooted in the blues music he loved throughout his life.[39]

While working on "Santa Claus Is Getting Down," Jesse brought in Bonnie Bramlett to Eckstein's studio for another holiday tune: "Auld Lang Syne," which went unreleased. Bramlett was attempting a comeback too, and Jesse was trying to help. Their collaboration is glorious, a credit to Bramlett's soaring performance, which she significantly attributes to Jesse's production. "You allow the artist their expression first, and Jesse always knew that," Bramlett explains. "I had the freedom. I could fly like a freaking eagle. And if I went too high, he'd pull me down. If I didn't go high enough, he'd give me an updraft, push me further, higher, higher, you know. And that's how he produced me."[40]

In 1987, Jesse also made his final session appearance supporting another artist. On Scott Colby's *Slide of Hand* album, Jesse plays exem-

WASHITA LOVE CHILD

plary guitar on "At Last." First Colby took Jesse to a pawn shop to retrieve the yellow Telecaster that Bill bought him when Jesse was flat broke. Then Jesse delivered his part in one take through a small Fender amp, not unlike he did on "Doctor My Eyes" years earlier. Colby got to know Jesse well, joining him and Gene Clark for Thanksgiving and going to watch Jesse sit in with Leon Russell and Edgar Winter a few times. When Colby visited Jesse's apartment, he always had to leave before the spy drama television show *The Equalizer* began.[41]

While keeping up duties with the Grafitti Band and pursuing some projects on his own, Jesse also reconnected with his old guitar partner Walter Trout, who had a regular gig in Huntington Beach with other musicians who were determined to stay sober and form a mutual support group, including Little Feat's Richie Hayward, the Band's Garth Hudson, and guitarist Mick Taylor, whom Jesse once almost replaced in the Rolling Stones. The sobriety network seemed to help Jesse. "His playing was beautiful," Trout remembers.[42]

Finally, in early 1988, in what should have been a rewarding project for Jesse in a new direction, he and Trudell were set to compose music for the now enduringly popular, award-winning Native American film *Powwow Highway*, which featured acclaimed Native actors Wes Studi, Gary Farmer, and Graham Greene, alongside Jesse's friend Joanelle Romero. In fact, Jesse was serendipitously responsible for the film coming to life on the big screen. Screenwriters Jean Stawarz and Janet Heaney had seen the Grafitti Band at a club in Los Angeles and immediately approached Jesse to compose music for their film project. They dispatched director Jonathan Wacks to see the band at the Palomino Club the night when Bob Dylan and George Harrison showed up. Coincidentally, Stawarz had already sent the script to George Harrison's HandMade Films production company, but received no reply. Wacks leapt at the opportunity to pitch the film directly to George, mentioning that Jesse and Trudell were on board to provide music. Wacks express-mailed the script to George the next day, and HandMade immediately greenlit the project.

Frustratingly, as the project moved forward, Jesse and Trudell lost their position as music contributors. The latter accepted a consolation prize in the form of a part in the film. Stawarz and Wacks attribute this to some combination of Jesse's health and a sense that the film needed a more prominent name in the music department, though Stawarz disagreed with the latter point. George Harrison suggested Eric Clapton. However, when the film's editor began setting scenes to music from the first solo album by Robbie Robertson, Wacks fell in love with the pairing. Robertson's music was appropriate for the Indigenous-centered film, but it's difficult to resist imagining what a further boost it would have been for Jesse, on a comeback trail that ran through Indian Country.[43]

AS IT TURNED OUT, Bob Dylan's interest in the Grafitti Band extended beyond the boost he provided in the media. He became an enthusiastic fan, playing *aka Grafitti Man* as warm-up music before taking the stage. He enjoyed riding his Harley to their rehearsals at Ricky Eckstein's garage studio, where Dylan typically parked in the "No Parking" spot, trustingly hung his helmet on the back of his bike, and occupied a couch inside. Eckstein remembers the first time Dylan came over and knocked on the front door. "Go around to the gate through the backyard," his twelve-year-old son instructed, oblivious to Dylan's fame, forcing the renowned folksinger to walk through the mud. He would also go see the band live. Then Dylan fans started turning up at Grafitti gigs, hoping to see Dylan. When Bob Tsukamoto introduced himself at Club Lingerie, Dylan immediately hugged him and proclaimed, "I love the Grafitti Band." His genuine fandom was a boon to Jesse, who worked with Bob during an earlier career peak, and to Trudell, who counted Dylan among his greatest influences.[44]

On March 5, 1987, not long after the Taj Mahal and Grafitti Band gig at the Palomino, Dylan invited the Grafitti Band into Sunset Sound studio with him. Dylan was struggling with writer's block and suggested that they record some cover songs. Grafitti Band members suspected this was also likely Dylan's way of seeing if he might work with the group in a greater capacity and possibly take them on the road. Everyone was thrilled. Jesse was simultaneously working with the Indian Bob Dylan and the real Bob Dylan.[45]

Looking like he just woke up, Dylan rolled in a few hours late. Nevertheless, he made a sincere attempt at capturing something and seeing what the band could do backing him. He sang and played electric guitar in an isolation booth, with the band set up live on the main floor. With Shark, Jesse, and Dylan all on electric guitar, Bob Tsukamoto on bass, Gary Ray on drums, and Jim Ehinger on keys, they cut five songs across thirteen total takes.[46]

Among the songs they played was a Dylan original I refer to as "Involved with You." It's perhaps the strongest song of the bunch, with a tight groove and guitar hook reminiscent of the Rolling Stones' "Tumbling Dice." Dylan tries different lyrics across three takes, but always keeps the chorus: "To fall in love / to fall in love with you," he croons. "Let's get one!" Jesse exclaims as they launch into their first attempt. I look at the session notes, assuming "Sugaree" is the Jerry Garcia tune. To my surprise, it's not. It also isn't the 1950s rock and roll song performed by various artists including the Sonics and Hank Ballard. It's an up-tempo 4/4 rocker, like that older number, but the lyrics, aside from the chorus, are entirely different. Dylan might have worked up his own version based on the original, in the folk tradition. The song features strong interplay between Shark and Jesse, and Jesse delivers his best solo of the day.

"My Prayer" is a cover of the classic song popularized by the Platters. The mix is rough, obscuring what's otherwise a beautiful solo by Jesse that recaptures his milky sweet tone on Lennon's *Walls and Bridges*. Dylan's all over the place vocally, in a way that at first sounds insincere, but might actually be a product of him trying too hard. "You sang your ass off! That was great!" the engineer exclaims. "I'm not shitting you!" Dylan responds with laughter. Each of the five takes of Solomon Burke's "Sidewalks, Fences, and Walls," some eclipsing seven minutes, is impressive, though many suffer from a bungled ending. "What's that? A bad chord?" Dylan stops the group. "Yeah," says Jesse, the guilty party.

The reggae tune "Street People" is more obviously a cover. Apparently, Dylan had to call the writer and ask them to dictate the lyrics over the phone while they recorded it. Dylan sings about homelessness with great conviction, but I can't help but feel it's an odd choice. The lyrics are out of character for him. He probably could have bested them in less time than it took to call the songwriter. Nevertheless, the song features excellent guitar interplay between Jesse, Shark, and Dylan. In fact, Dylan played great electric guitar all day, something Shark and Jesse perhaps brought out in him. Tsukamoto and Ray's bass and drums groove is strong, and Ehinger enhances the tune with the Hammond organ. "That was a good one!" Jesse enthuses after an especially long take with some lively jamming.

All this music remains unreleased. Even the Grafitti guys haven't heard the material since they recorded it. With some editing and a proper mix, it could fit nicely on one of Dylan's archival releases. Dylan seems more relaxed with the Grafitti Band. They played a swinging groove and their guitar trio could have opened some interesting possibilities in Dylan's live presentation and his setlist.

Unfortunately, nothing more came from the session. That summer, Dylan toured with the Grateful Dead. He had been genuine in his interest, and his performance was impassioned, but he seemed more determined to achieve fun than focus in his sessions with Grafitti Band. Or, it could be that Jesse failed to make a better impression on Dylan, not unlike his rehearsal back in the winter of 1977–78. Jesse's physical skills hadn't left him, but his usual creativity and musicality seemed muted. It's hard to know if it was a failing or a determination on Jesse's part to play more reservedly with Dylan. Jesse was also struggling with his illness. Coming off and on methadone at the time, he understandably seemed tired and a little less sharp by the hour. Finally, as Jesse began nodding off, Dylan said, "I guess that will be enough for the day." Shark could tell Dylan was dismayed by Jesse's condition. While Jesse was his brilliant self in spots, it would sadly be the last time he worked with Dylan, whom he adored.[47]

While enjoying Bob Dylan's renewed endorsement, Jesse also regained valuable support from another friend he hadn't seen in some time. After catching up a bit by phone, Jesse told Taj Mahal, "I'm working with John Trudell, and we've got this thing called Grafitti Man." Jesse was hoping Taj might grant them an opening slot at an upcoming gig. Taj was happy to do it, leading to a series of concerts where the

Grafitti Band would open a gig and then return as Taj's backing band. With Taj, Jesse wasn't only gaining strength from the company of Native people, he was also reconnecting with his musical brother from his first artistic peak in the late 1960s.

The exuberant Taj Mahal and Grafitti Band show at the Palomino, where Dylan, George Harrison, and John Fogerty joined the bands onstage for a lengthy jam, was a great testament to Jesse's power and the love his friends still had for him. Since then, that Thursday night at the Palomino has become a classic rock folk tale. Though physically sitting on a chair to the side, Jesse was center stage that night. He was the hub that connected those great musicians. They gathered around him, lifted him up, and played through him. And they did it the way Jesse liked it, with an emphasis on having fun.[48]

JESSE'S HEALTH WAS up and down during his last years. At times he was completely sober. He might go months, and then suddenly it would come crashing down in one day. "As with anyone who has been involved with the tragic cycle of addiction, everyone suffers, everyone loses, everyone is brought to their knees and everyone grieves," Mark Shark says. Jesse showed up at one Grafitti gig in a bad state that wasn't, however, a result of inebriation. In fact, Jesse had been healthy for months before he was pulled over in the Mustang he got from Jackson Browne. He may have been sober, but he lacked license or registration. Finally arriving at the club, Jesse beelined for the bar and ordered a double bourbon. A confused Shark tried to intervene. "Jesse, don't do it man. What happened?!" "FUCKING COPS FUCKING WITH ME BECAUSE I'M A FUCKING INDIAN MAN!" Jesse roared. He drank six double shots, made it halfway through the first set and then started to stumble. Shark called for a break. After the gig, he took Jesse to crash in a friend's basement. The episode clearly indicated that the racism Jesse experienced as a Native American person was one source of the pain he tried to extinguish through harmful means. Only recently has there been growing acknowledgment of how Native people are arrested and killed by police, and receive and serve longer sentences, than any other demographic group in the nation. These trends have deep historical roots.[49]

In desperate moments, Jesse continued to take advantage of his friends. Drummer John Ware, who played with Jesse in Oklahoma when they were teens, regularly received calls from Jesse asking for money. "He was excited about the music he was making with Trudell," Ware said. "In a way, I didn't mind getting the phone calls, even if the end of the call was him asking for money."[50] After asking to borrow a dobro guitar from Betty Billups, who financed Grafitti cassette releases, Jesse pawned it. "Why didn't you tell me? I could have gotten it out!" Betty pleaded. "I'm so sorry," Jesse said. "I was embarrassed."[51]

It was around this time in 1987 that Cars guitarist Elliot Easton met Jesse and witnessed the depths of his condition. Easton and the Cars had been on a long run of chart-topping singles and albums, but it was Easton who was initially starstruck by Jesse. Jesse was one of his greatest guitar heroes, dating back to the Taj Mahal albums. Jesse heard Easton mention this one night during a radio interview and got in touch. Thrilled by his hero's invitation to hang out, Easton brought a guitar, hoping Jesse would show him the right way to play the Taj Mahal tune "The Cuckoo." The only problem was that Jesse didn't have a guitar, so they passed Easton's back and forth.

Jesse played his answering machine microcassettes that contained old messages from John Lennon before sending Easton away with a couple cassettes Jesse dubbed for him. They were branded "Jesse Ed Davis's Greatest Hits," featuring Jesse's personal favorite cuts from his solo albums. Typically modest about his career, Jesse remained proud of his work and the celebrity he once enjoyed. He wanted this newer popular guitarist and fellow Telecaster player to know his greatness. But Easton didn't need any convincing.

Returning home from Jesse's apartment, Easton kept thinking about how his guitar hero didn't have a guitar. "I knew something was up, and I knew drugs were part of it," Easton recalled. He phoned Dan Smith, the president of Fender, which had once sponsored Jesse, and asked for help getting Jesse a nice guitar. Smith warned Easton what would happen. "I didn't care," Easton says. "It was Jesse Ed Davis and I wanted him to have a guitar." He drove Jesse to the Fender factory, where they selected a beautiful sunburst Stratocaster. Sadly, but predictably, Jesse pawned it, "which was heartbreaking," Easton never forgot.

A few weeks later, Easton was at home in Boston when Jesse called at around three or four in the morning, speaking frantically, wanting to borrow $15,000 to record a Bonnie Bramlett Christmas single. "Jesse, I can't send you $15,000. If I could send $15,000 it would be to my parents," Easton said. "It's an eye opener," Easton says now, decades later. "[Addiction] takes away any sense of shame or pride, and you just do what you gotta do. And that was my last encounter with Jesse. And I wasn't mad at him. I was just sad. . . . I hoped and prayed that he would find a way out of it."[52]

It wasn't for lack of sympathy that people weren't able to do more to help. Jesse's friend Mike Johnson, who worked for the Warner Brothers archive that managed Jesse's catalog, was happy to loan Jesse twenty bucks here and there, buy him cigarettes, and give him rides around town, though Johnson regretted a particular drive to a Venice alley where he saw Jesse trade a Telecaster for junk. Johnson and Jesse would grab tacos at Tito's in Culver City and relax at Jesse's spartan apartment, which he shared with Kelly and their white cat named White Kitty. It was like a bachelor pad: a TV sat on a rickety dinner tray, with a shoebox containing memorabilia and cassette tapes (one featuring John Lennon's bone-chilling primal scream therapy sessions) underneath. Sometimes Jesse went with Johnson to folk jams in Redondo Beach, where he'd pick up a guitar and share joints with the group. On one occasion, Jesse showed Johnson a bootleg black-and-white copy of the 1968 *Rock and Roll Circus*. When Johnson asked Jesse about the fate of his career, Jesse replied, "One day the circus left town."[53]

THERE WERE DAYS WHEN Jesse's health seemed to be further suffering, but in a greater sense he remained determined to achieve a comeback and he just as often seemed capable of one. Like his relationship with his music, he always believed he was one move away from the promised land. In Jesse's thinking, now reflecting a little more wisdom and experience, that didn't have to be in the spotlight.

Quiltman first heard the name Jesse Ed Davis years before he met him. Quilt was at a Sun Dance hosted by Deganawidah-Quetzalcoatl tribal university in Davis, California, when he recognized a man sitting on the hood of a car. To Quilt's confusion and surprise, it was Taj Mahal. "How'd you find us here?" Quilt asked, after introducing himself. "My guitar player told me to come here," Taj replied. "Do you know him? His name is Jesse Ed Davis." Taj had his dobro guitar and asked to play some songs for the people. An impromptu crowd formed to hear "Farther on Down the Road." When he returned to his car a little over an hour later, Taj was glowing. This was a credit to Jesse. While he was finding his way back to Indian people, community, and spirituality, it was apparent in sending Taj to the event that Jesse already knew the power of the Sun Dance. Jesse didn't need to learn to become Indian or be Indian again. He instead needed community where his Indigeneity could belong.[54]

Quilt first met Jesse in person with Trudell in Malibu to discuss a possible partnership. Trudell warned Quilt in advance that the first thing Jesse would do is ask to borrow $75. "Don't give it to him!" "When Jesse got there," Quilt remembers, "we visited for a while sitting outside, and Jesse said, 'Can I borrow $75?'" Quiltman laughs hysterically. "Crazy Jesse! I loved the guy. He was a great character." Acknowledging Quilt's own Indigenous background, Jesse often talked with him about his people in Oklahoma, and how he wanted to learn the Kiowa language. Occasionally, Jesse called his cousin Lowell Russell, who is a fluent Kiowa speaker, asking for help. "Jesse was searching for something," Russell could sense.[55]

Everyone, including Jesse, understood he had more to give. Quilt and Trudell tried to speak with Jesse about his illness. They wanted to get him into the sweat lodge. Jesse liked the idea; he was looking for ways to get back to his culture. "The feeling I got with Jesse is that he wasn't around his people much," Quilt observed, "but I think it was always there, his family, his people. . . . He knew what he wanted to do." When the Grafitti Band played the Warm Springs reservation in Oregon for Quilt's school benefit, Jesse didn't want to go home. "He seemed so happy," Quilt remembers. "He had really good intentions of getting away from the other side." Jesse told Quilt he needed to get out of Los Angeles, and even asked Quilt to see if his people would hire him to play guitar full-time in the lounge at the Kah-Nee-Ta Resort. Impatiently, Jesse himself called the resort manager asking for an opportunity. But for some reason it didn't happen, though it says something that he tried. He was trying to get back home. "He was so proud to be a Kiowa man. He wanted to come back to the sweat lodge. But it was hard to pin him down, I guess too many demons chasing him, you know," Quilt says. "He was a good guy. Jesse was a good guy." I tell Quiltman I don't want Jesse's demons to become the story. "Right," he agrees. "He was bigger than that."[56]

IN THREE YEARS, Jesse and Trudell, with support from the Grafitti Band, wrote twenty-three songs and performed together live more than fifty times. They drew strength from their past and purpose from their present, with a view of the future as Indigenous artists. "It takes a giant inspiration like that to draw out the music in me," Jesse said about Trudell, noting that only John Lennon had previously affected him that way. "His poetry just reaches something in me that makes me do more than I thought myself capable of."[57]

Trudell's commitment to social and political causes changed Jesse's relationship with his own. "It's so rare to meet another Indian artist who has the concepts and values that I do," Jesse said, adding, "It's so rare to meet somebody who has a global concern like that." An interesting assertion, maybe, given the wave of Red Power activism and global Indigenous rights movements that had recently emerged, but also a reflection of how Jesse's career was removed from those trends, even as he, an Indigenous person, made an indelible impression on the world of rock and roll. In 1986, when asked what he envisioned for the future, Jesse said he wanted to see the nation's entire defense budget "dismantled," and the money reallocated to make the country a "paradise." He alone couldn't possibly achieve that, he acknowledged, but he wondered if he could do his part to "plant some seeds."[58]

Trudell's influence had been mutually regenerative. He helped give Jesse a cause, and in turn, Jesse helped give John confidence as an artist. "[He] literally gave me music, gave me a band, put me onstage, and experienced me," Trudell said.[59]

Grafitti Man's social mission was just as powerful and significant as its music. Their work in the 1980s advanced a legacy of Indigenous activism that was rooted in the Red Power era, in which Trudell had been a major figure. With Jesse's talent and experience to help amplify its message, the Indian movement was able to reach a new and wider audience. Jesse's chanting at the beginning of *aka Grafitti Man* signals what the album later emphatically declares in the title track—Grafitti Man's got something to say. Indigenous people have something to say.

What Grafitti Man achieved was something greater than activism, but also less divisive and complicated. "John believes that, not just Indians, but *everyone* is his people," Jesse stressed. Grafitti Man's agenda was humanity and respect for the earth. "I think that it's everybody's responsibility to head in that direction," Trudell said. "Those who will take the identity of poet or activist or any of that are no more responsible to do that than everyone else."[60] To the degree that Grafitti Man's music was an extension of activism, Jesse had a stake in that, too. Though Jesse was always careful about how he appealed to his Indigeneity, he thought of his career as a form of activism. Trudell understood better than anyone that Jesse's experience, even his existence, was not only artistic but also political. "I imagine it had to be really hard to be an Indian trying to make it through that world," Trudell suggested. "There were those who romanticized the Indians so that it's hard to be real there and there are those who want to exploit it so it's hard to be real there." Jesse showed Trudell that music could be an effective means toward recognizing each other's humanity and right to a dignified existence, which was needed to underwrite sovereignty expressions and claims. Music, more than any other language, more than any other human power, can cross borders and boundaries. Music is from the soul. In Jesse's family, art and music had long been a medium for advancing sovereignty rights and Indigenous belonging. Jesse and his family demonstrated how art and activism are born from each other.[61]

It wasn't that Jesse stood apart from or disagreed with the more visible proponents of Red Power. He simply understood he had to be careful with art and politics. In Jesse's world, being overtly political was professionally and commercially inadvisable, especially for new artists. Those who engaged in politics were typically further along in their careers and could withstand potentially alienating some of their audience. Moreover, Jesse had by coincidence become musical partners with two artists named John who had been outspoken in politics, and both paid a price for it. Still, reflecting on Trudell's effect on Jesse, Kelly Davis affirmed, "[Jesse] became more outspoken."[62]

In John and Jesse's work with the Grafitti Band, twin currents of art and activism merged powerfully, vocally, and musically. In combining art with activism, the Grafitti Band presaged future artists like Rage Against the Machine who married incisive human and political oratory with powerful music. It was people's music.

Like musicians before them and since, Jesse, Trudell, and Quiltman came together as Indigenous artists commenting on the issues of their time. "My mind drifts a lot about my time with Jesse . . . ," John later reflected. "Jesse and I believed in each other. . . . In our own way, we both went to the last doorway and we opened that sucker, we saw what was back there and we handled it in our own ways, but it affected both of us. . . . It gave us a bond." Across three years, that bond created a comeback and mutual, if imperfect and incomplete, recovery. Jesse only needed more time.[63]

Twelve

YOU SACRIFICE YOURSELF
FOR YOUR PEOPLE

Life was clear
Close your eyes
——HARRY NILSSON,
"REMEMBER (CHRISTMAS)"

BEGINNING WHEN he was a kid, Jesse had recurring nightmares in which he would walk into a room containing a crowd of people. Then some sort of cloud or gas would emit from the ceiling and he knew he was going to die. I believe in the premonitory power of dreams; Jesse's Indigenous ancestors did too.

What did Jesse's nightmare mean? I first thought of World War II Nazi genocidal gas chambers. The details of the Holocaust spread widely when Jesse was a boy, and Jesse, born during the war, was the son of a veteran. Maybe something he heard stuck with him. He had certainly heard stories about Native American kids who were shipped to boarding schools where they were forced into rooms and showered with DDT, in some cases forced to wear the pesticide on their bodies for a week. Maybe somewhere in his subconscious, the Jewish Holocaust became analogous to Indigenous genocide.[1]

Then I think about how Jesse died. Heroin kills through asphyxiation. A lethal amount suffocates the blood as the brain tells the lungs to stop breathing. I thought about Jesse's nightmare as I became tasked with writing his death. Did he know it was happening, like he did in his nightmare? Then again, while I've gotten to know Jesse a little, I can't say I know the meaning behind his dream. Maybe it's just something he saw in a movie or a book.

I do know Jesse was haunted by death, and not just a nightmare depicting his own. He lost so many people close to him, to drugs and other terrible circumstances: John Lennon, Carl Radle, Joe Zagarino, John Angelos, Ray Eckstein, Mal Evans, his own father. During an interview concerning John Lennon's legacy, Jesse reflected on the dangers of substance abuse. "Recreational drugs . . . we all thought they were such harmless things," he began. "Some people thought this was a way to see God. . . . Recreational drugs did have quite a bit of attrition. There was a lot of us that went down. . . . Unfortunately, we lost a lot of our best friends . . . Gram Parsons, Tommy Bolin, I remember a lot of those people real well."[2]

In 1986, shortly before his own passing, one more tragic loss hurt Jesse deeply. Richard Manuel, the singer and pianist from the Band, took his own life in a moment of despair after years surviving addiction. Jesse and Richard went back to the days when the Band was still called the Hawks. Teenage Jesse used to watch them play in Oklahoma City. Later he shared stages with Manuel. "I was just devastated by that," Jesse said. "That was a shame, a real loss for me." Having just completed a course in suicide prevention, Jesse also had nightmares about failing to save Manuel.[3]

Jesse penned a heartbreaking obituary for his friend in *Rolling Stone* magazine. "When Richard Manuel and I were both seventeen, we were already seasoned road dogs," Jesse wrote, noting that Manuel "always had a ready song or a timely laugh," before shifting to a more urgent reflection. "Much later, as a counselor for the American Indian Free Clinic, I tried to get across the idea that suicide is a permanent solution to a temporary problem. I'm gonna miss you, 'Beak.' You made the music really mean something to me." Jesse's memory of his friend's greatest qualities—laughter, songs, making the music mean something—can mutually apply to his own importance to those who knew him.[4]

IN EARLY JUNE 1988, Jesse took a job as a doorman at the vaudevillian Ventura Theater and underwent an intense new treatment program nearby. He called old friends and loved ones to let them know he was doing well. This wasn't out of character; he loved talking on the phone. But people remembered these particular calls and how Jesse radiated renewed spirit. His marriage with Kelly had become strained, and she was hopeful he was improving.[5]

On June 19, he called Patti and Bill at Patti's parents' home in Apple Valley, on the southern edge of the Mojave Desert. It was both Patti's birthday and Father's Day. Patti still considered Jesse her best friend and greatest love. Bill, meanwhile, remained upset about the last time he saw Jesse, when they were arrested together after Jesse wrote bad checks through Bill's account. The three of them now talked about collaborating on some projects, like the old days when they were a team behind Jesse's exciting solo career. They planned to get together soon in Los Angeles.[6]

On June 21, Jesse called Grafitti bassist Bob Tsukamoto and left a message: "Hey, I heard the Grafitti Band are big in Japan! Let's go over there! Call me back when you get this. I'll be back home tomorrow." Bob got home late that night and decided to call Jesse back the next day. Trying several times and getting no answer, Bob left for Solana Beach, where Grafitti had a gig with Taj Mahal. They had already decided to play this gig without Jesse, partly because it would have been difficult for him to travel to and from Ventura, and partly out of hesitation, hoping that Jesse really was getting better. They would check on him when they got back, and hopefully he would rejoin them the following night, June 23, at the Palomino with Taj.[7]

The morning of June 22, Jesse did his laundry in Ventura before catching a ride to Los Angeles. He visited a handful of pawn shops, and later ended up at an apartment complex on Rose Avenue. He had fixed there many times. His friend lived at the complex and never forgave himself for not being home that day. Sometime between 4:30 and 5 p.m., an apartment resident found Jesse in the building's laundry room and called the police.[8]

When Detective David Straky arrived at the scene, he noted a fresh needle mark on one of Jesse's arms and burned matches and tinfoil on the ground. The police report mistook forty-three-year-old Jesse for

being in his sixties. "It appears to be a drug overdose," Straky told the
LA Times. The toxicology report found heroin, alcohol, and Librium,
a benzodiazepine, in Jesse's system. Combined with alcohol, Librium,
prescribed to treat alcohol withdrawal symptoms, can create a synergis-
tic effect capable of producing unconsciousness or a conscious blackout.
Jesse had used Librium as early as 1968 on the plane ride to London for
the *Rock and Roll Circus*. Aside from the needle mark, "there was no
trauma on his body," Straky noted.[9]

The detective did, however, observe features at the scene that seemed
suspicious. Apart from the matches and tinfoil, there was no drug para-
phernalia. Moreover, someone had taken Jesse's shoes and watch. "That's
how cold those motherfuckers were," Mark Shark says. "There's a dead
Indian in the laundry room, and they steal his motherfucking shoes."
Detective Straky informed a reporter that the case was open, suggesting
it could turn out to be homicide. Writing in her journal that day, Patti
noted that Jesse was pronounced dead on the way to a hospital.[10]

KELLY WAS THE FIRST to call Patti and tell her the news. Then Kelly
called the Belly Up Tavern in Solana Beach and asked to speak with John
Trudell. He hung up and returned to the green room where the Grafitti
Band and Taj were waiting to go on. "Jesse's dead," he announced, his
voice shaking. Gene Clark also made several phone calls, telling people,
"Brother Jesse died." The loss of his dear friend inspired Gene to get
clean and get back to work, but he was never the same. "It is still, after all
these years, excruciatingly painful," Mark Shark says about losing Jesse.
Shark drove back to LA with Trudell late that night. Pouring a tumbler
of whisky when he got home, hoping to numb himself to sleep, he played
a phone message from earlier that day. It was Jesse: "Sharkington! We're
going to Japan! Gimme a buzz! We'll talk soon!"[11]

That same week, an announcement for a Taj Mahal and Grafitti
Band show at the Palomino on June 23 ran in the *LA Weekly*. Urging attendance, the paper alluded to Bob Dylan and George Harrison's
appearance last time Taj and Grafitti played the Palomino. "Will it hap-

pen again? Don't count on it, but you can be sure this place is going to be *packed* with people wondering the same thing." Alas, the fact that that night couldn't be re-created had nothing to do with Dylan or Harrison.[12]

Jesse's friends and family struggled with the circumstances of his passing. Kelly told Patti how the pawn shops Jesse visited on June 22, which knew Jesse well, claimed he was with a few strangers. Ming Lowe heard the same. So did Bill's old babysitter and Jesse and Patti's friend Vince. Kelly told friends she wasn't satisfied with the police report. Some members of Jesse's family in Oklahoma became convinced there was foul play, noting a bump on Jesse's head that conflicted with the police report. They struggled with the fact that his shoes were missing. John Trudell specifically struggled with the conclusion that Jesse died from an overdose. He heard someone was seen running away from the laundry room. Both Trudell and Quiltman were confused, confident Jesse was beating his illness. Bill remains confused by the fact that Jesse mixed alcohol and heroin that day. Jesse only turned to alcohol when he couldn't afford or couldn't find heroin. But Jesse obviously had money for heroin. "I don't really know if I really believe . . . just how he died—an overdose," Bill admits.[13]

Friends and family understandably cycled through competing emotions as they processed their grief. Betty Billups began mourning Jesse's passing before she knew it had happened. He visited her in a dream that night as he went on his journey. She was walking down a street in New York City, passing sidewalk cafes. From a crowd Jesse stood up: "HEY, SWEET BETSY FROM PIKE!" he called out. Jesse loved that old cowboy ballad, and often used it as a pet name for Betty. "JESSE!" Betty exclaimed, running over to him. They hugged, and then, walking away, she looked back and Jesse was still there, "smiling his beautiful smile." In the morning, Betty received a phone call informing her of Jesse's death the previous day.[14]

Many were shocked. Jesse was experienced with heroin. Many times, he underwent treatment and emerged healthy. People had become conditioned to the cycle. Why would this time be different? With the Grafitti Band and rekindled connection with Taj, Jesse seemed to be going somewhere again. "He was ready to hang those demons up," Quiltman recalls. "His intentions were good. His words, his eyes, they told me his heart was in it, but it didn't happen."[15]

Others weren't shocked. Bob Tsukamoto reported Jesse's death to his brother Howard, who had been Jesse's bandmate in the Hurricane House days. Howard wasn't surprised or overly responsive. He personally understood something about Jesse's illness. He died from a heroin overdose six months after Jesse passed.

Pete Waddington had long since moved to Alaska, where he was working on tugboats when he heard Jesse had passed. "It really bothered me," Pete says, choking up. "But you know, I anticipated it. Just because he would take everything to the nth degree." Similarly, Robby Romero remembers last seeing Jesse in Hollywood, where they were trying to develop a music project. "He looked good," Romero remembers, "but I had a sad feeling, like I might not see him again." Jesse's Kiowa cousin Russell Saunkeah understood Jesse's struggle as something he inherited. "[Jesse's] confidence in his ability to perform with anyone, anytime, anywhere at such a high level of quality obscured a deep-seated pain in his soul," Saunkeah said. "Sadly, a family trait which contributed in some way."[16]

For some, a sense of anticipation nevertheless yielded to frustration and anger when it finally happened. "We felt so fucking helpless," Shark confesses. "Looking back, as a totally different person myself, I wish I could have helped him," Jim Keltner says. Taj Mahal too realized how much Jesse was suffering. Was there something more someone could have done? "No," Taj answers. "I'd look at him, I'd look right in his eyes. He knew I knew what was going on. . . . All you gotta do is make one slip, man, with that stuff, and you're dealing in the underworld." Yet as Jesse was laid to rest, Taj struggled with anger at his friend. "I was so goddamn mad at him. You know, a major beautiful player, but I didn't walk in the man's moccasins." Incapable of making peace with Jesse's death, Van Dyke Parks vents, "Nobody did enough. Damnit. Nobody did enough, and that's a fact. It's a goddamn shame. And I take no pride in it. . . . He died alone there. On the end of a needle. And I'm very sorry for it all because of his spectacular ability."[17]

Still others thought Jesse's death was a suicide. "He knew about drugs, honey," says Bonnie Bramlett. "He didn't OD." From 1988 onward, Bramlett called Jesse's mother every Mother's Day until Mamacita passed. Joe Cocker, who collaborated with Jesse and who covered Jesse's "Where Am I Now (When I Need Me)," was also under the impression that Jesse chose to take his own life. "Jesse Ed Davis committed suicide," he said, reflecting on Jesse's passing in 1992. "After the tour [in summer 1988] I was in the Sunset Marquis in Los Angeles having lost a lot of weight, thinking, 'Is this what it's all about?' "[18]

Beneath the shock, confusion, anticipation, and anger ran a profound pain. Patti wrote notes and letters to cope with the absence of her love. "I miss that crazy Indian," she wrote to George Harrison on the first anniversary of Jesse's death. "I shall always desire that magic feeling I felt when he played the guitar. He was powerful, and he's left a void in my heart." Patti also wrote Jesse's mother, describing her broken heart and soul. "Mamacita, this past year has been a hard one on me, both physically and mentally," she wrote in one letter. "Jesse, Bill & I had a family together; that none of us have been able to let go of!!!" Patti often wrote to Jesse too: "Wherever your soul is . . . 4:54 Sunday . . . I am watching American Indian dances . . . Oh, how my heart crys-out for you to be near to me . . . I am missing you Kiowa chief, my Warrior of the Rainbow—Dance On—Hear my Prayers!" One final message from Patti brings me to tears:

> *i'm reaching out to you, JED,*
> *In the only way*
> *I know how . . .*
> *Flow*
> *Thru vibrations of tone . . . music*
> *You were*
> *A master*
> *Of subtle tone*
> *Turning my soul*
> *Until my heart soared*
> *With yours . . . We were home . . . if 2 could become 1,*
> *it's you and I . . . JED.*

On the day Jesse died, Patti wrote to herself and to all of us who have been moved by Jesse's music. "Today a great man died, Jesse Ed Davis III," she began. "Play pretty on the night shift! You took a part of me with you." We can be forgiven for thinking Jesse heard her. Shortly before Jesse left our world, he said, "[I] and most Indians believe that there's another reality beyond the last breath we take in this life."[19]

THE GRAFITTI BAND date with Taj Mahal at the Palomino on June 23 became a gathering of friends to mourn Jesse's passing and lift each other's spirits through music. Jackson Browne encouraged Shark to keep the Grafitti Band going, to honor Jesse's legacy and continue spreading his music. A few weeks later, Leon Russell hosted a Rock for Sobriety fundraiser at the Ventura Theater for the 12 Friends Alcohol Recovery House in Jesse's memory. Jesse had organized the event shortly before he died.[20]

Kelly and Mamacita decided that Jesse's body would be returned to Oklahoma for a Kiowa ceremony. Jesse would be buried in Oklahoma City's Memorial Park Cemetery, next to his father and his Kiowa grandparents Jasper and Anna. Jackson Browne paid for the Grafitti Band to fly to Jesse's funeral. Taj Mahal adjusted his schedule to fly down to Oklahoma from Toronto, where he was appearing at the annual Mariposa Music Festival, which he first played with Jesse in 1969. Before Jesse's ceremony began, some of Jesse's Kiowa kinfolk conducted a smudging to bless the venue while Kelly dressed Jesse for his final viewing. She tied a medicine pouch around his neck. Trudell stuffed some tobacco and a dollar into Jesse's shirt pocket. "Hey, what's that for?" Gary Ray asked. "Well," Trudell replied, "every time I saw Jesse, he asked me for a buck."[21]

The traditional Kiowa service was deeply moving. Many of Jesse's friends had never experienced anything like it. Kiowa women sang heart-wrenching songs. As Jesse's casket was lowered into the ground, lightning flashed. A sudden thunderstorm began pouring rain. "It matched my tears," Betty Billups says. "It felt like the whole world was crying." From Kelly's vantage point, it looked like the lightning was coming up from Jesse's grave. That night, Jesse's friend from Hawaii, Tim Garon, composed a song about his impressions of the ceremony called "Jesse's Rain." "Mamacita's memories cry / his tears they fall down from the sky," the song begins. "There is no way to hide your pain / so soothe your heart in Jesse's rain." Jesse's Kiowa-Comanche relation Thomas Mauchahty-Ware laid an Indian flute across Jesse's chest before the casket closed. Thomas had danced at powwows with Jesse when they were kids. More recently, he had been teaching Jesse to play the flute. When the service finally ended, Taj Mahal walked over to talk to his old friend one more time. "Goodbye Chief," he said.[22]

That evening, everyone gathered at Mamacita's house. She showed Jesse's friends and bandmates the painting Jess senior made for Jesse's first solo album. Then she proudly took them over to the piano she had taught Jesse to play on when he was a boy. "Even as her heart was broken, she made each one of us in the band feel welcomed and loved," Mark Shark says. "She was like her boy," Quiltman adds. "She was like Jesse."[23]

Jesse always stayed in touch with his first love and fiancée, Mary Carol Kaspereit. She still cared about him and loved speaking with him. Sometimes he called in the middle of the night, as late or early as 2 a.m. Occasionally, Mary Carol had to beg off the call. "I don't think he ever considered time differences," she says. One of the last times they spoke, Jesse talked about an old mansion on Oklahoma City's Pennsylvania Avenue that was once a beautiful estate with a large plot of farmland. (It's now a bank headquarters, crowded by fast-food restaurants.) The house was owned by two land developers and art collectors who were caught in a kidnapping plot involving their daughter, which resulted in the father's murder. Jesse remembered the place from when he was a kid. Then, it was marked by thick trees, gravel roads, fish ponds, hen houses, cattle, and barns. He dreamed of moving back to Oklahoma City, buying the old place, and leaving Los Angeles behind. "I was thinking that I should come back and live there," he told Mary Carol. Oklahoma was always on his mind. It never stopped calling him home.[24]

JESSE ED DAVIS'S REPUTATION and legacy persisted just long enough to be rediscovered and elevated as an important figure in Native American and music history. Now, in the wake of growing attention to his legacy, Jesse has become retrospectively hip. He's perhaps more popular in the twenty-first century than he was during his lifetime. The growing circles of Jesse fandom didn't immediately extend from the moment of his death, like they did for Hendrix, Janis Joplin, Jim Morrison, and Kurt Cobain. Jesse's legacy has been nurtured on a smaller—yet profoundly loyal—level.

In 2002, Jesse was inducted into the Oklahoma Jazz Hall of Fame, followed by the Oklahoma Music Hall of Fame in 2011 and the Native American Music Institute Hall of Fame in 2018. In 2015, acclaimed Seminole-Mvskoke director Sterlin Harjo used Jesse's "Keep Me Comin'" during a stirring scene in the film *Mekko*. In 2023, in another nod to Jesse, Harjo featured "Washita Love Child" in an episode of his sensational TV series *Reservation Dogs*. In 2017, the award-winning documentary *Rumble: The Indians Who Rocked the World* included a segment focused on Jesse alongside surveys of other prominent Indigenous artists. Also in 2017, Atlantic/Real Gone Music began reissuing Jesse's music on compact discs, and then vinyl; special editions sold out immediately. In 2021, Pamunkey musician Kevin Blackwater recorded his tribute song "The Ballad of Jesse Ed Davis" for his album *Wiindigo Is Real*. Likewise, in 2023, Former R.E.M. guitarists Scott McCaughey and Peter Buck's group the No Ones included their song "J.E.D." on an expanded version of the album *My Best Evil Friend*. Most recently, NTVS clothing, created by Indigenous designers, printed a run of Jesse Ed Davis t-shirts that were out of stock within minutes.

Throughout Indian Country, Jesse is a rare example of an Indigenous rock star. His Kiowa cousin Russell Saunkeah idolized him. After a series of recurring dreams in which Jesse motioned him to a live stage, Saunkeah learned guitar and hit the road. "I think he should be known as the greatest Native American guitarist of all time," Jesse's Comanche cousin Gary Davis suggests. Jesse's Apache friend Robby Romero idolized him too. "Of all the musicians I have had the pleasure of playing with," he said, "Jesse is the one I looked up to the most." For Jesse's Mohawk musician friend Robbie Robertson, Jesse was "a long-lost brother. He's somebody that will live in my heart forever."[25]

First as John Trudell and Grafitti Man, then as Bad Dog, John Trudell continued working with Quiltman, Shark, Eckstein, Gary Ray, and Bob Tsukamoto. They made several more albums and traveled North America and Europe, appearing at Farm Aid and other major festivals, while logging tours with Peter Gabriel and Australian stars Midnight Oil. Trudell reunited with Jesse in the next world in 2015. Reflecting on his Indigenous musical brotherhood with Jesse and Trudell, Quiltman thinks about what's been missing since those days. "We need more Jesse Eds," he stresses. "There might be horn players and guitar players here on the rez now, but they don't have any access. I know we got some Jesse Eds in this world. Goddamn he was so good. He made music grow with his guitar." Jesse made access possible.[26]

Indeed, Jesse remains an inspiration to Native kids picking up a guitar for the first time. "We're still living in a time when it's so hopeless to young people," says Jesse's Kiowa relation LB Chalepah. "He showed how it's possible to be successful and maintain your culture." Especially in and around Oklahoma, young Native musicians are inevitably compared to Jesse Ed Davis, says his Seminole relation and guitarist Chebon Tiger. Thinking about the histories Native people have survived, he concludes, "We're lucky to have even had a Jesse Ed Davis."[27]

As I approach the end of Jesse's story, I'm overwhelmed with sympathy for the central women in his life. They all tried to help him in their own ways. Mary Carol Kaspereit has long been a leader in the Oklahoma City community in far too many roles to summarize here. Ming Lowe continues working as a multimedia artist and recently published a book of photographic essays on her trip along Highway 61. Tantalayo Saenz embraced adoption by an Indigenous Hawaiian grandmother named Mona Kahele, who carried the old stories and helped Tantalayo heal. Tantalayo helped others working as an addiction counselor in New Mexico. She passed away suddenly in 2020. Despite the great anguish she experienced before and after Jesse's death, she loved him until the end. "I hold him in my heart and highest light always," she told me.[28]

Patti Daley loved Jesse until the end too. "Now, when I remember those days, years, we had it all," she wrote about life with Jesse, "us, the music, the excitement of it all." She hoped to honor her promise to

Jesse to one day write a book about him, but she struggled with health issues. A perennial beach girl, Patti lived in Hawaii for several more years, before returning to California, where she lived with Bill until she passed away in 2016. In 2022, Bill fulfilled her wish for her ashes to be spread in the ocean off Lanikai Beach in Hawaii.[29]

Kelly Davis continued managing Mariachi Vargas, traveling throughout North America with the popular group. Though she struggled to leave home after injuring her back in a horse-riding accident, she made exceptions for traveling to see her favorite band, the Rolling Stones. She loved her cats and sometimes rescued wounded animals. She never remarried. Jesse told her that it was Kiowa tradition for him to pick an acceptable replacement husband, a variation on the traditional Kiowa custom in which one brother is obligated to marry another brother's widow. Jesse chose the best man from their wedding, Jackson Browne, who never became available. Kelly passed away in California in 2017, just before the premiere of the film *Rumble*, in which she appeared during the segment on Jesse. Until Kelly died, she always left Jesse's boots out in her apartment, hoping he would find her.[30]

Growing up with Jesse, Bill Noriega experienced equal amounts of happiness and hardship. "I was Billy Davis in his world. It's an honor or a curse, however you look at it," he says. Bill has lived a lot since those days. He cared for his mother in Victorville as she battled lung disease. When she passed, Bill moved into his biological father's home in Ojai and cared for his father, who suffered the same disease as his mother. His father passed during the making of this book. "I missed out on a whole family," Bill regrets. "I don't really know anything else to do except to just keep on keeping on. I know I like to grow my own vegetables. Just trying to be as healthy as I can."[31]

Long after Jesse's passing, Mamacita kept the Davis tradition alive, singing and spinning records at friendly gatherings with other Native people. For the rest of her life, she visited local record stores and made sure they stocked Jesse's albums. In 2006, she rejoined both of her Jesses in the spirit world.[32]

Others among Jesse's Kiowa, Comanche, Cheyenne, Seminole, and Mvskoke families still call Oklahoma home today. Jesse's memory and meaning is grounded in their persistence as Indigenous peoples from these lands. His artistic influence advances through the work of his numerous professional partners and protégés who still make music. From Taj Mahal and Grafitti to solo albums and session spots, Jesse's music forms an expansive and accessible archive. His music is good medicine. He was a red dirt boogie brother, all the time.

CODA

Satanta's Bugle

I SPENT THE MONTH OF August 2022 in Venice, working on this book, exploring Jesse's old stomping grounds. Though much had changed, there were numerous remnants of his life and career. I found the late Leon Russell's old Skyhill house at the foot of the Hollywood Hills; it still has the same basic structure, even if the grassy green exterior has been repainted gray. (I would guess the funky aqua and fuchsia carpets no longer cover the interior.) The winding hills leading to the house are so relentless that my wife and I had to quickly pull over, no more than half a block from Skyhill, which had just come into view, so our four-year-old son could get sick on the side of the road. I also found the old Plantation house in Sherman Oaks, where Jesse crashed with other Okies and rehearsed with Taj Mahal until he moved with Patti to Venice. The two-story house with a garage apartment extension remains virtually identical. The family residing there now knew just a little about its history and appreciated me telling them more. Shortly after they moved in, before they knew the home's history, their young son suddenly and inexplicably became fascinated with guitars. There is power in that place.

I found the apartment complex on Sawtelle Boulevard where Jesse and Kelly rented a unit. It was in the early stages of conversion to the Windward School Innovation and Arts Center—a perfect future for a plot of earth that holds Jesse's memory. I visited the stalwart McCabe's Guitar Shop and saw the stage where Jesse and Gene Clark played some concerts during their windswept years jetting between Hawaii and Los Angeles. The McCabe's trucker cap I bought was too small; I gave it to my son and he wears it every day. I grabbed food at some of Jesse's favorite grub spots, including Pink's Hot Dogs and Johnnie's Pastrami. Jesse liked good junk food. Me too. I went to the famed Whisky a Go Go, where the Rolling Stones once caught Taj Mahal's set and then invited Taj and the Great Plains Boogie Band to their circus in London. I met many of Jesse's close friends and music partners. I walked the streets he roamed when he couldn't go home to Kelly. Of course, the Pacific Ocean, Pacific Coast Highway, sandy beaches, buzzing communities, and California summer sun are still there. I had been to California many times, both as a historian and as a musician. But driving there from Oklahoma, on some of the same roads Jesse took, further revealed its appeal.

Toward the end of my trip, Jesse's son Bill came to visit me in Venice. He drove down from Ojai, from the home he shared with his biological father, who had recently died. We spent the day driving around, locating old landmarks from his sometimes charmed, sometimes painful life there. We broke for some unpretentious tacos at Tito's, another of Jesse's favorite fast-food joints, then headed over to Marina. We parked my truck at 20 Hurricane Street, where we met the current owner Tammy, who was anxious to show us around. I watched Bill breathe an ocean tide of memories. Out back, we found the exact garage door to the hidden house across the alley that provided a backdrop for promo pictures Jesse took with Patti and Billy for his first solo album. Everything is exactly as it was. Bill re-created his boyish pose, sitting on the ground with legs outstretched, leaning back on his hands. Above him I saw Patti and Jesse, smiling.

Before Bill departed my Surf Chateau, he brought from his car an old trunk overflowing with what remains of his mother's archive preserving pieces of life with Jesse. The trunk is weary and weathered, but full of materials that told me so much, sometimes too much, about the world that created it.

Bill also shared something special and personal that I hope signaled his trust in me. I began crying, and he did too. We hugged and then he told me something else, something that I can share here. Patti, long ago, had promised Jesse she would write a book about him if, in her words, "something would ever happen to him and he would leave this planet." I saw evidence of this in Patti's archive. She planned to call the book "Warrior of the Rainbow," reflecting her rebuffed suggestion that Jesse call his solo band the Rainbow Warriors. At some point, she arrived at a different name for the book: "Heart Chanting." She contacted several of Jesse's old friends and colleagues, even gaining a promise of support from industry giant Jerry Wexler, who signed Jesse to a major label deal in 1970. Writing Yoko Ono on Bill's birthday in 1989, Patti explained how she promised Jesse a book back during their life at 20 Hurricane Street. "Nobody knows me like my baby," Jesse always said. Alongside a book, Bill would make a film, drawing on his recent work at a film editing studio. Finally, they'd compile a tribute album. Patti's dream was to get Jim Keltner, Taj Mahal, Bill Rich, Keith Richards, Dr. John, Eric Clapton, George Harrison, Joe Cocker, Bonnie Bramlett, and others to contribute, with Wexler at the helm. She hoped Jesse's Kiowa relative Al Momaday would paint something for the cover.[1]

Alas, she didn't complete the project and was forced to sell some of her memorabilia in order to pay down her massive medical bills before she passed in 2016. Since then, Bill always imagined some greater force would eventually send someone to write this book. That's you, he said. That both frightened and emboldened me. This had already been such a physically, intellectually, and emotionally exhausting project—hearing, thinking, reading, discussing, breathing, and sleeping Jesse Ed Davis every day for three years. Now I'm fulfilling some greater promise? Why me? What can I possibly say?

As Bill drove away, I rushed back to my rented shack and placed the heavy trunk on the dining table. Bulging at the hinges, its latch was already unclasped. I switched on the plastic chandelier, put on one of Jesse's favorite albums, Grady Martin's *City Lights*, and began exploring. Completely enthralled, I arrived at the first piece that made me stop surveying materials for a moment. It was one of those old roadside vendor Wild West postcards of the famous Kiowa war chief Satanta (Settainte, meaning White Bear). Jesse knew Satanta's story and counted him as an ancestor. I knew Satanta from my work in Native American history. He's a subject in my class.[2] Among the few old stories Jesse shared with others about his Indigenous ancestors was one about Satanta's bugle. It's a story well known among Kiowa people.

Satanta fought against some of the most famous United States army leaders of his day, including William Sherman, George Custer, and Philip Sheridan. During the 1864 Battle of Adobe Walls, Satanta hid and watched a US Cavalry bugler under Kit Carson's command sound his horn and signal his fellow soldiers to either attack or retreat. Satanta captured the bugler and took his horn. During the next cavalry charge, Satanta blew the horn to confuse his enemies. He was eventually captured and died mysteriously in a Texas penitentiary.[3]

At Fourth of July ceremonies, Kiowa people still hang Satanta's bugle from their center pole and invite a white reenactor to wear old US Cavalry clothing and come up and blow it, "As if the Kiowas opened up a portal into the late 1800s by way of Carnegie," says Wichita writer S. E. Ruckman. During the ceremony, the Kiowa Gourd Dance Clan, of which Jesse was a member, reenacts Satanta's acts of bravery.[4]

Jesse knew Satanta's death song. He also knew the death song of a second Kiowa war hero, Ghee-ale (Gi-edel, meaning Big Meat), who died in battle against US soldiers in the winter of 1874–75. The two songs go like this:

SATANTA'S SONG
No matter where I fall in battle,
Do not mourn for me.
For I will not know it.
Somewhere in some far-off land
My body will be devoured by wolves.
But I will not know.

GHEE-ALE'S DEATH SONG
Now I am ready to go,
I hear my comrades calling me

Over on the other side,
I am going to join them.[5]

With relatives in the Black Leggings Society, Jesse upheld the Kiowa warrior traditions. He admired how they used to form a first line of defense by tying ropes around each other's shoulders, sacrificing themselves as other warriors helped women and children retreat. "They would actually take their long trailers, their long ropes," Jesse described, "and spear themselves with the magic arrow to the ground and say, 'I will retreat no further.'" Jesse sometimes recited a mashup of Satanta and Ghee-ale's death songs. Jesse's version went like this:

I can hear my comrades calling.
I can hear them calling me from
the other side.
To the place where all great warriors go.

Do not mourn for me.
For that is the end all great
warriors face.
Do not mourn for me.
For I will never know.[6]

Satanta's music protected Kiowa and Comanche people when their lives were endangered. He helped them resist attack by white settlers, and he did it with a horn, an instrument that featured prominently in Jesse's music. Like Satanta, Jesse wielded a magical instrument. As a Native kid in Oklahoma, he watched people play guitars and make music that settled conflict and conquered pain. He watched guitars bring people together, across tribal lines, across racial and political lines, across space and time. He watched guitars save and protect people. He played a guitar to protect himself. His music can protect others. "You sacrifice yourself for your people," Jesse vowed.

Just as the bugle didn't take Satanta's life, music didn't take Jesse's life. It was instead the conditions of making it. Who he was, where he came from, and what he carried shaped his experience and struggle. The music business can be tough on young artists. Not only was Jesse not immune, he was a little more vulnerable. But when he played his guitar, he could make people change direction. Jesse Ed Davis won that battle.

ACKNOWLEDGMENTS

Jesse Ed Davis remains connected and important to so many people still living. This can present numerous challenges. Some might feel inclined to protect the subject. Emotional attachments or grudges might result in potential contributors either avoiding my invitation or trying too hard to shape my understanding of Jesse and his story. Others might struggle too much with lingering pain over Jesse's ultimate fate. Because Jesse's historical record is so minimal, I understood I needed help from those who knew him, and I was willing to face potential obstacles. I therefore was not merely delighted, but inspired, when I was met with overwhelming energy and enthusiasm for this book. "It's about time," I heard repeatedly from those who lent support in varying forms.

Many of Jesse's surviving friends, family members, music partners, and professional peers trusted me with their insights and stories. The sincerity of their support for Jesse's legacy made me realize very quickly that he was someone special, in spite of his flaws. I was party to some deeply emotional exchanges, and I learned a great deal from them. At times, interview subjects insisted they were learning as much from me. Some of his closest friends were astonished by some things they didn't know about him. I sensed that, for many, talking about Jesse was not just enjoyable but therapeutic. Sadly, several contributors, including Jim Karstein, Alan White, Mike Nesmith, Robbie Robertson, and Tantalayo Saenz, passed away while I was working on this book. Others have become friends.

I cannot contain the depth of my gratitude within these acknowledgments. While hoping my appreciation is also evident in the foregoing book, a handful of individuals deserve special mention for the critical roles they played in helping this project succeed. Jesse's Comanche cousin Richenda Davis Bates was the first person I contacted with the idea for this book. She granted me her blessing and provided ongoing support. She also equipped me with a starter kit of material she had gathered and a family tree containing important ancestral information. She hopes to one day see Jesse receive an honorary degree from OU, be recognized by the Rock and Roll Hall of Fame, or even just get a nicer gravestone.

From there, I reached more individuals who not only shared their important reflections, but also functioned as nexuses in my developing interview pool. When Jackson Browne's manager Cree Miller replied to me expressing Jackson's interest in contributing, I started feeling confident I could do this. Richenda put me in touch with more family and friends, and Cree connected me with more musicians. From there, Bob Glaub, Jim Keltner, Mark Shark, John Ware, Mike Brewer, and Jim Karstein were especially instrumental in recommending me to others. Taj Mahal's support was essential, as many people I contacted first asked me: "Did you speak with Taj?" It wasn't long before the project exhibited real stature by virtue of the people behind it. Finally, Laura Garon played an essential role in connecting me with many of Jesse's friends, and, most importantly, Jesse's first wife Tantalayo and Jesse's son Bill Noriega. Not only did Laura and Bill share numerous contacts, photos, and memories, they also became close friends who lent perspective during times when I struggled with a project so inherently difficult.

Numerous other people provided extensive help in many forms. Gary Gilmore granted me several interviews and provided some of the best surviving photos of Jesse. Ann Shultz, Pete and Cheryl Waddington, Bob Tsukamoto, Mike Smith, Ming Lowe, Ben Sidran, Carol Furr, Mike Boyle, John Ware, Ricky Eckstein, John Granito, Andy Schwartz, David Brendel, Betty Billups, Sarah James, Larry Hollis, Mike Johnson, Rick White, and several others shared photos, music, and other valuable materials. The Western History Collections at the University of Oklahoma, the Oklahoma Historical Society, the National Cowboy and Western Heritage Museum, the Philbrook Museum of Art, the Bob Dylan Center, the OKPOP Museum, and Columbia University also provided valuable research materials. In addition to always keeping his dedicated Jesse Ed Davis vinyl bin stocked at Monkey Feet Music in Oklahoma City, Ed Commander helped with some important contacts and shared some good stories. I also benefited from Wovoka Trudell's support, friendship, and the insights he shared about his father.

I appreciate numerous Indigenous people who provided insights into the Native American cultural and historical dimensions of Jesse's story, including his family members Mary Helen Deer, Richenda Davis Bates, Gary Davis, Alvin Deer, Lowell Russell, LB Chalepah, and Ray Doyah, as well as Wovoka Trudell, Marc Wilson, Caleb Garcia, Mark Bolin, Kent Sanmann, Chebon Tiger, Robby Romero, Robbie Robertson, Phil Deloria, and Quiltman Sahme.

I owe special thank-you to Eric Hisaw, Bertrand Bouard, Larry O'Dell, Stephen Foehr, Lisa Roth, and Catherine Bainbridge, who provided me with interviews they conducted for previous projects concerning Jesse. I appreciated not only the interviews they shared, but also the emotional benefit of connecting with others who worked at documenting and advancing Jesse Ed Davis's legacy.

Within my Oklahoma State University community, I enjoyed enthusiastic support from my department head Brian Hosmer, who helped make some important connections and joined me in some good discussions about Jesse Davis. I am also grateful for the helpful feedback I received from colleagues in our writing group who read an early conference paper on Jesse. Likewise, I benefited from my research assistants Ramsey Thornton, Savannah Waters, and Katanna Davis, who helped transcribe interviews. As well, I continue to benefit from my connection to the Clements Center for Southwest Studies and I appreciate Andy Graybill's guidance and support in this project.

The good folks at Liveright/Norton have been as excited about this book as Jesse's friends, family, and professional collaborators. As they learned about Jesse through this project, I never felt I needed to convince them that his story is important and worthy of attention. I credit the vision they shared alongside me. In particular, Haley Bracken and Robert Weil have been everything I hoped to experience in great editors, as they challenged me to elevate my work while recognizing and harnessing my strengths. I am also grateful to Liveright's art department for the wonderful cover image and all the impressive talent in Liveright's marketing and promotion department. At a relatively late stage, I invited Mvskoke poet Joy Harjo to contribute a foreword. I am so grateful for the time she made to produce something so beautiful. Her reflections on Jesse elevate this book. Finally, I am so indebted to my agent Faith Childs, who nurtured my entry into new dimensions of the publishing world and who champions my work at every turn.

It was a blessing to speak with people who knew Jesse personally and made music with him. It was something else entirely to speak extensively with the person Jesse called his "son." In addition to the reflections Bill Noriega shared, the trunk containing materials his mother Patti collected over the years helped animate Jesse to a degree I couldn't have anticipated. Bill became a good friend to me. I love checking in with him and hearing what music he's listening to. I'm looking forward to him teaching me how to play backgammon.

Speaking of family, I couldn't have done this without my own. Everything begins with and depends on their love, and I received a lot of it. Thank you to my mother Donna, who always encouraged my interest in music, and my brother Nick, who, for years, long unbeknownst to me, borrowed music from my collection and learned something about his big brother. Thank you to my larger family, including Chris, Mary, Kathy, Stan, Margaret, AJ, Seth, and Duncan for all the love and encouragement they provided through many forms. Thank you also to Matt Mahurin and Lisa Desimini, who provided valuable professional insights when I was in the contract stage of advancing this project.

Finally, how can I explain the significance of my partner Exa and our son Kit's relationship to this book? Exa heard every sentence as it came to life and then read them all again on paper. Music has always been central in our marriage and friendship. Her reflections elevated this book. Meanwhile, our son Kit entered our lives shortly before I started on this book. He quickly became my music buddy, especially during the pandemic, when we turned to our guitars, keyboards, drums, shakers, horns, harmonicas, bells, whistles, and more to pass long days and fashion our bond, between spinning seemingly countless records featuring Jesse Ed Davis that increasingly filled our home. Now Kit is a music fan to a degree that far exceeds my fandom at his age. That's saying a lot.

On that note, I must conclude by thanking Jesse Ed Davis for all the fabulous music he made. I discovered so much music through this project, and that alone made it all worth it. I take some comfort in how so many of Jesse's friends tell me he would be secretly proud of this book. I'm grateful for all the friendships I've made through this project and our mutual concern for Jesse's memory and legacy. Jesse and his music brought so many people together, and I hope that will be the lasting legacy of this book.

Side A

JESSE ED DAVIS, "ANYWAY YOU WANNA DO, OR: ETERNAL JIMI HENDRIX"

With mixed feelings I remember watching many of my friends excitedly preparing to leave for Monterey. That summer in 1967, I had hoped to attend the great pop festival myself. But two days before it was to begin, I knew it would be impossible. I had just elected to go in the studio with a man I had only just met: Taj Mahal. A week later we had Taj's first album in the can and my friends were returning from Monterey. There was only one topic of conversation: The Jimi Hendrix Experience.[1]

Not only had Hendrix set his guitar on fire, he had fucked it, bit it, beaten it, and above all played the greatest shit you ever heard. My repeated questions let me know only that he was black, wore flash gear, and his music defied description. These were trusted musician friends I was talking to, so you can imagine my anticipation as I rushed home a few weeks later with a fresh copy of "Purple Haze." Ten seconds after I had set the needle on the disc, I lifted it off and began the record again. "What is it? What is it?" I wondered to myself. I honestly did not know what to think. Several joints and many listenings later, I decided that behind all the obvious sound effects and theatrics that amazingly came across on record, there lurked a master blues guitarist. Having never been one to pigeonhole music, or even art in general, I nevertheless felt the solid blues roots could not be mistaken. Over two years would pass before I would realize how short my categorization had fallen.

Days, weeks, months, all become a blur when you're on the road with the band. Those years with Taj let me rack up over one hundred thousand miles with TWA, lose at least three Hertz rent-a-cars, smash up countless Holiday Inns—booze, girls, dope, and at least three invitations to meet and play with Jimi Hendrix, each of which I decided to pass. How could I? I suppose something akin to jealous rivalry caused my reluctance to meet Jim Hendrix. Listening to reports from our drummer, who recorded with him, and our bass player, who jammed with him, led me to believe he was a very nice fellow who just happened to play his ass off. How many times have we all seen musicians adopt an ambitious gunslinger attitude? Such a description fit me perfectly. What a turkey.

As it turned out, I have cursed a thousand times the fact that I never met Jimi Hendrix face to face. I have also given thanks that the one time I heard him play, he really played. He completely fried me. About the middle of the summer 1969, I was invited to the Whisky a Go Go to see the Buddy Miles Express. My good friend Bill Rich, who was playing bass with Buddy's band, had said that Jimi Hendrix may sit in. My sweetness and I took a seat in the balcony and enjoyed an excellent set by Buddy's band. The club was hot and thumping. Truly something special was happening or expected to happen. As the horn section left the stage, as well as Jimmy McCarty the guitarist, and the organist too, I had thought the set was over. But Buddy had stayed behind the drums. Bill Rich hadn't moved either.

The whole audience of the nightclub was suddenly on its feet crowding toward the stage. A girl was screaming. The noise level was suddenly deafening. A tall black man with long skinny legs and huge Afro stepped easily from the dance floor to the stage. He carried a shiny black Stratocaster with a maple neck and a single wah-wah pedal. After he had plugged into McCarty's Sun amp, he turned around and I could see that it truly was Jimi Hendrix. He smiled at his two fellow musicians and seemed eager to play. At once he began playing the opening figure to Purple Haze and people crowded around the stage went totally nuts. The tune was clearly unrehearsed and after singing the first chorus, Hendrix began a long solo that seemed to last more than two hours.

Actually, it was the only tune he played all night. I sat enthralled. Hendrix never made the same sound twice. I had never heard one electric guitar and a single pedal used to such an extent. It could easily have been two or three guitars on stage, for he gave his solos fantastic accompaniment all on his own. As he played stinging lead lines, he pushed the wah-wah pedal all the way to the treble position and then punctuated all this with chugging comp chords, pushing the pedal all the way to the bass position. The total effect was devastating. This was no mere blues player. This was no mere guitarist. I had truly misjudged him. I was bearing witness to spontaneous creativity with the ultimate artistic vision of Jimi Hendrix. I was stunned. What a show.

Side B

EXCERPTS FROM
AKA GRAFITTI MAN FAN LETTERS

"My husband and I heard the tape at the Bob Dylan/Tom Petty/Dead concert in Buffalo, NY recently and absolutely flipped for it! It's wonderful to hear such political, social, and universal concerns and truth coming out from 2 speakers. What a great combination: poetry and music!! Please Rush."

"After hearing rave reviews about Grafitti Man, I decided that I couldn't resist."

"I was listening to Jesse Ed play some tasty guitar with Albert King the other day, and as I look through my record collection I find him playing on quite a few albums. My question is this: Is there anybody this man hasn't played with? I really like the music on Grafitti Man and I have enjoyed Jess's guitar work with Taj Mahal for some time now."

"What a tape! Absolutely powerful, righteous Native American Blues Rap Fusion. . . . The band itself has a really powerful, driving sound. Very fluent, very assured. Shaman Chant should be required listening for everyone! Hurry Hurry Hurry! Because there are a lot of folks who need to hear this stuff!"

"I heard their album being played on the PA system before the Bob Dylan show in Buffalo Ny and it sounded great!"

"Jesse Ed Davis—Where have you been hiding all these years? I have all of your solo albums and a lot of your session work. Still hear your solo once a week off 'Doctor My Eyes.' Keep on Keepin on—Glad to see you have resurfaced!"

"It was good to hear something about Jesse Ed Davis again in *Rolling Stone*. I haven't read anything about him for seven or eight years. I have his first two LP's which I still like and some of his LPs with Taj Mahal. I know he had a third LP, 'Keep me Comin' which I couldn't get hold of as yet. I really felt good to hear of him again. Is it possible to contact Jesse Ed Davis through your address?"

"Great to see a new album by Jesse Ed Davis, this time with John Trudell. I think he's a terrific guitar player and I've been an admirer of his playing since his days with Taj Mahal's band. Later on his own albums and with Roger Tillison, Gene Clark and Jim Pulte. After albums with Nilsson and David Blue I lost track of Jesse Ed. So I'm very pleased to see him working again!"

"I encountered a group of young people in Portland traveling together for world peace. I gave the tape to them. As they say in Ireland, 'God Bless the Work.'"

"Davis is one of my favorite guitarists from way back, Taj Mahal days. But he doesn't put out enough of his tasty work. So I look forward to his alot!"

"Dylan played this before his show in Vancouver and it sounds great."

"This person heard it first in between sets at the Dylan/Dead Party. This person was very impressed. Thanks for making art and for making art that says something."

"There are two Indian brothers who felt the same as I, World Peace. They are very gifted in music. Signed An Indian Sister"

"It is in my opinion, the most inspiring, challenging and insightful piece of work I have heard in a long time."

"During the Dylan/Dead show in Buffalo, I had the delicious treat of hearing what I suspect was AKA Grafitti Man."

"I love it."—Relocation of Indian Residents from the former Navajo-Hopi Joint Use Area

"I am wild about the tape. The music is hot. The poetry is hot. This mix is outstanding. The entire tape flows smooth and expressively. You have a masterpiece here. I've listened to it over and over without tiring because the music never fails to get under my skin, that message goes straight to my heart. This is great. What you have done should be heard and when it is, it will certainly leave a lasting impression on the fortunate listener. I play the tape for everyone who comes to visit me."

"A first rate, magnificent effort captured on cassette."

"Attend[ed] two Dylan concerts in Buffalo and was fortunate to hear AKA Grafitti Man being played. May I say that I found it very mesmerizing lyrically and it swayed me to want to hear more. Tell John Trudell and Jesse Ed Davis that they've made one hell of an album and they should collaborate more."

"Yesterday I picked up AKA Grafitti Man and played it. I have almost continually played it through the night and also now in the morning. Even brought it to work. I don't just like it, I love it!! It's great and I am thankful to Dylan for talking about it in *Rolling Stone*."

"A friend from Columbia River gorge tells folks that Trudell and Davis are some stomp down dudes as well as heavy musicians."

COURTESY OF BETTY BILLUPS/PEACE COMPANY

Side C

JESSE'S MIXTAPE FOR PATTI

ULULU SIDE

Jesse Ed Davis, "Ululu"
Aretha Franklin, "You and Me"
Aretha Franklin, "I Say a Little Prayer"
Bonnie Bramlett, "Superstar (Groupie)"
Marvin Gaye, "Pretty Little Baby"
Junior Walker, "Come See about Me"
Cat Stevens, "Wild World"
Jesse Ed Davis, "Keep Me Comin'"
Jesse Ed Davis, "Farther on Down the Road"

REMEMBER CHRISTMAS SIDE

Jesse Ed Davis, "She's a Pain"
George Harrison, "Don't Let Me Wait Too Long"
John Lennon, "Bless You"
Harry Nilsson, "Many Rivers to Cross"
Harry Nilsson, "Mucho Mungo"
Harry Nilsson, "Remember (Christmas)"
Marvin Gaye and Tammi Terrell, "Ain't No Mountain High Enough"
Derek and the Dominos, "Bell Bottom Blues"
John Lennon, "Happy Xmas (War Is Over)"

Side D

DISCOGRAPHY

WITH TAJ MAHAL

Taj Mahal (Columbia, 1968)
The Natch'l Blues (Columbia, 1968)
Giant Step (Columbia, 1969)
Happy Just to Be Like I Am (Columbia, 1971)
Taj (Gramavision, 1987)
The Rolling Stones Rock and Roll Circus (ABKCO, recorded in 1968, released in 1996)

SOLO ALBUMS

¡Jesse Davis! (ATCO, 1971)
Ululu (ATCO, 1972)
Keep Me Comin' (Epic, 1973)

WITH THE NEW BREED

"Just Another Bird Dog" b/w "You'll Be There" (Boyd, 1964)

WITH JOHN TRUDELL

aka Grafitti Man (Peace Company, 1986)
Heart Jump Bouquet (Peace Company, 1987)
But This Isn't El Salvador (Peace Company, 1987)
AKA Grafitti Man (Rykodisc, 1992)

WITH OTHER ARTISTS

Junior Markham and The Tulsa Review, "Let 'Em Roll Johnny" b/w "Operator Operator" (Uptown Records, 1967) and "Black Cherry" b/w "Gonna Send You Back to Georgia" (Uptown Records, 1967)

Delaney & Bonnie, *Genesis* (GNP Crescendo, recorded 1968, released 1971)

Daughters of Albion, *Daughters of Albion* (Fontana, 1968)

The Asylum Choir, *Look Inside the Asylum Choir* (Mercury, 1968)

Various Artists, *Live at Bill Graham's Fillmore West* (CBS, 1969)

Bob Dylan, "Watching the River Flow" and "When I Paint My Masterpiece," *Bob Dylan's Greatest Hits Vol. II* (Columbia, 1971)

Roger Tillison, *Roger Tillison's Album* (ATCO, 1971)

Marc Benno, *Minnows* (A&M, 1971)

Ben Sidran, *Feel Your Groove* (Capitol, 1971)

Albert Collins, *There's Gotta Be a Change* (Tumbleweed, 1971)

Booker T. Jones and Priscilla Coolidge, *Booker T. & Priscilla* (A&M, 1971)

Charles Lloyd, *Warm Waters* (Kapp, 1971)

Buffy Sainte-Marie, *She Used to Wanna Be a Ballerina* (Vanguard, 1971)

Leon Russell, *Leon Russell and the Shelter People* (Shelter, 1971)

The Asylum Choir, *Asylum Choir II* (Shelter, 1971)

John Lee Hooker, *Endless Boogie* (ABC, 1971)

Albert King, *Lovejoy* (Stax, 1971)

Gene Clark, *White Light* (A&M, 1971)

George Harrison and Friends, *The Concert for Bangladesh* (Apple, 1971)

Joe Cocker, "High Time We Went" b/w "Black-Eyed Blues" (A&M, 1971)

Marc Benno, *Ambush* (A&M, 1972)

Jim Pulte, *Out the Window* (United, 1972)

Alex Richman, *Salty* (Capitol, 1972)

B.B. King, *L.A. Midnight* (ABC, 1972)

Lightnin' Hopkins, *It's a Sin to Be Rich* (Verve, recorded in 1972, released in 1992)

Jackson Browne, *Jackson Browne* (Asylum, 1972)

Steve Miller Band, *Recall the Beginning . . . A Journey from Eden* (Capitol, 1972)

Rod Taylor, *Rod Taylor* (Asylum, 1973)

Arlo Guthrie, *Last of the Brooklyn Cowboys* (Reprise, 1973)

Mick Jagger, "Too Many Cooks," *The Very Best of Mick Jagger* (Warner Music, recorded in 1973, released in 2007)

John Wonderling, *Day Breaks* (Paramount, 1973)

Wayne Berry, *Home at Last* (RCA, 1974)

Arlo Guthrie, *Arlo Guthrie* (Reprise, 1974)

Bert Jansch, *L.A. Turnaround* (Charisma, 1974)

Gene Clark, *No Other* (Asylum, 1974)

John Lennon, *Walls and Bridges* (Apple, 1974)

Ringo Starr, *Goodnight Vienna* (Apple, 1974)

Harry Nilsson, *Pussy Cats* (RCA, 1974)

Pointer Sisters, *That's a Plenty* (Blue Thumb, 1974)

Brewer & Shipley, *ST11261* (Capitol, 1974)

Guthrie Thomas, *Sittin' Crooked* (Singing Folks, 1974)

Mac Davis, *Burnin' Thing* (Columbia, 1975)

Jimmy Cliff, *Follow My Mind* (Reprise, 1975)

Tom Jans, *The Eyes of an Only Child* (Columbia, 1975)

Valdy, *See How the Years Have Gone By* (A&M, 1975)

Cher, *Stars* (Warner Bros., 1975)

Keith Moon, *Two Sides of the Moon* (MCA, 1975)

George Harrison, *Extra Texture (Read All About It)* (Apple, 1975)

John Lennon, *Rock 'n' Roll* (Apple, 1975)

Harry Nilsson, *Duit on Mon Dei* (RCA, 1975)

Eric Mercury, *Eric Mercury* (Mercury, 1975)

Susan Webb, *Bye-Bye Pretty Baby* (Anchor, 1975)

Dion, *Born to Be with You* (PSI, 1975)

Jackie DeShannon, *New Arrangement* (Columbia, 1975)

The 5th Dimension, *Earthbound* (ABC, 1975)

David Bromberg Band, *Midnight on the Water* (Columbia, 1975)

Rod Stewart, *Atlantic Crossing* (Warner Bros., 1975)

Rod Stewart, *A Night on the Town* (Warner Bros., 1976)

Harry Nilsson, *Sandman* (RCA, 1976)

Harry Nilsson, *That's the Way It Is* (RCA, 1976)

Dunn and Rubini, *Diggin' It* (Prodigal, 1976)

David Blue, *Cupid's Arrow* (Asylum, 1976)

Long John Baldry, *Welcome to Club Casablanca* (Casablanca, 1976)

Tracy Nelson, *Time Is on My Side* (MCA, 1976)

Geoff Muldaur, *Motion* (Reprise, 1976)

Attitudes, *Attitudes* (Dark Horse, 1976)

David Cassidy, *The Higher They Climb, the Harder They Fall* (RCA, 1976)

David Cassidy, *Home Is Where the Heart Is* (RCA, 1976)

Neil Diamond, *Beautiful Noise* (Columbia, 1976)

Donovan, *Slow Down World* (Epic, 1976)

Eric Clapton, *No Reason to Cry* (RSO, 1976)

Ringo Starr, *Ringo's Rotogravure* (Atlantic, 1976)

Van Dyke Parks, *Clang of the Yankee Reaper* (Warner Bros., 1976)

Eric Andersen, *The Best Songs* (Arista, 1977)

Leonard Cohen, *Death of a Ladies' Man* (Warner Bros., 1977)

Various Artists, *Blue Collar* (soundtrack) (MCA, 1978)

Brian Cadd, *Yesterdaydreams* (Capitol, 1978)

Ben Sidran, *A Little Kiss in the Night* (Arista, 1978)

Piranha Brothers, "Alibi," "Down in Cairo" (unreleased, 1979)

Emmylou Harris, "Precious Love" b/w "The Boxer" (Warner Bros., 1980)

Johnny Cash, Paul Kennerley, Emmylou Harris, Levon Helm, et al., *The Legend of Jesse James* (A&M, 1980)

Frank Stallone, "A Case of You" b/w "Sea Song" (Scotti Bros., 1980)

Various Artists, *Kent State* (soundtrack) (RCA, 1981)

Michael Hardie, *Michael Hardie* (Punch, 1982)

Tim Garon, "Goodbye Dear Friend," "Incurable Romantic," "Baby It's You" (early 1980s, unreleased)

Guthrie Thomas, *Hobo Eagle Thief* (Eagle, 1983)

Scott Colby, *Slide of Hand* (SST, 1987)

INTERVIEWS AND COLLECTIONS

INTERVIEWS WITH THE AUTHOR

Kika Acevez, November 2021

Diana Allen, October 2022

Richenda Davis Bates, June 2022

Marc Benno, June 2021

Bill Bentley, May 2022

Baker Bigsby, December 2022

Betty Billups, May 2021

Valerie Blue, August 2021

Victor Bockris, June 2022

Mark Bolin, February 2023

Pattie Boyd, February 2021

Mike Boyle, May 2021

Bonnie Bramlett, September 2020

Mike Brewer, October 2020

Bob Britt, September 2020

Jackson Browne, February 2021

James Burke, February 2023

Wade Cambern, February 2021

Jim Catalano, May 2021

LB Chalepah, July 2023

Scott Colby, October 2020

Ed Commander, April 2024

Dave Copenhaver, January 2022

Erik Dalton, May 2022

Gary Davis, January 2021

Alvin Deer, June 2022

Mary Helen Deer, June 2022

Mark Dempsey, June 2022

Ray Doyah, October 2023

Tammy Dunkley-Nikolov,
    August 2022

Ian Dunlop, January 2023

Elliot Easton, March 2023

Ricky Eckstein, August 2020

Jim Ehinger, March 2023

Mike Eldred, October 2021

Jock Ellis, August 2022

Chris Frederickson, May 2021

Caroline Furr, November 2020

Albhy Galuten, August 2022

Laura Garon, August 2020

Gary Gilmore, October 2020

Bob Glaub, September 2020

John Granito, October 2021

Mary Hauschild, April 2021

Boyd Hickox, September 2021

Larry Hollis, July 2021

Neil Hubbard, April 2022

Sarah James, April 2022

Mike Johnson, April 2022

Daniel Jones, April 2022

Kenney Jones, January 2021

Jim Karstein, September 2020

Mary Carol Kaspereit,
    January 2021

Jim Keltner, August 2020

Paul Kennerley, May 2022

Sandy Konikoff, November 2020

Danny Kortchmar, March 2021

Robby Krieger, August 2023

Russ Kunkel, March 2021

Jim Layton, September 2020

Gary Lewis, May 2022

Ming Lowe, February 2023

Charles Lloyd, January 2023

Taj Mahal, October 2020

Mona Maiman, March 2022

Gary Mallaber, October 2020

Bill Maxwell, February 2021

Scott McCaughey, September 2023

Tracy Nelson, August 2021

Mike Nesmith, March 2021

William Davis Noriega,
    March 2021

Chris O'Dell, December 2021

May Pang, October 2022

Van Dyke Parks, November 2020

Gene Parsons, December 2022

Bill Payne, April 2021

Mike Piranha, August 2021

Don Preston, October 2023

Bonnie Raitt, January 2022

Gary Ray, November 2020

Randy Resnick, April 2023

Bill Rich, December 2022

Robbie Robertson, February 2021

Robby Romero, July 2021

Karen Rudolph, April 2021

Lowell Russell, May 2023

Tantalayo Davis Saenz, June 2020

Quiltman Sahme, January 2022

Scott Sanger, April 2022

Kent Sanmann, December 2021

Bill Saul, March 2022

Bobby Saunkeah, September 2020

Johnny Lee Schell, June 2023

Ann Shultz, January 2023

John Selk, January 2021

Mark Shark, October 2020

Ben Sidran, January 2021

Judy Sidran, January 2021

Leland Sklar, September 2021

John Simon, September 2022

Michael Smith, January 2021

Jean Stawarz, July 2023

Rod Stewart, April 2023

Rob Stoner, September 2022

Carl (Rogel) Summers,
    February 2021

David Teegarden, July 2023

Chebon Tiger, August 2023

Bobby Torres, August 2022

Walter Trout, September 2020

Bob Tsukamoto, April 2022

Gary Vogensen, February 2022

Klaus Voormann, April 2023

Jonathan Wacks, July 2022

Cheryl Waddington, August 2022

Pete Waddington, January 2021

John Ware, January 2021

Cleve Warren, October 2021

Alan White, February 2021

Rick White, November 2021

Bobby Whitlock, October 2022

Sweet Mama (Marie) Janisse Wilkins,
  December 2023

OTHER INTERVIEWS

Jesse Ed Davis Audio Interviews

With Albert Goldman, Albert Goldman Papers,
  Columbia University Rare Book and Manuscript Library:
February 28, 1983, Parts I and II
December 20, 1983
May 28, 1984
December 17, 1984
April 2, 1985
February 28, 1986, Parts I and II
March 6, 1986, Parts I and II

With Maurice Goldman, 1972, promotional for *Ululu* LP, ATCO
  Records, copy in author's possession

With B. Mitchell Reed, 1973, bonus 45 rpm in *Keep Me Comin'* LP,
  Epic Records

With Westwood One Radio Network for "The Lost Lennon Tapes" episode, aired July 1988

Interviews by Eric Hisaw
Rick Eckstein
Moon Martin
Gary Ray
Mark Shark
Bob Tsukamoto

Interviews by Bertrand Bouard
Jackson Browne
Gary Gilmore
Jim Karstein
Jim Keltner
Taj Mahal
Junior Markham
Bill Maxwell
John Selk
Butch Trucks
John Ware

Interviews by Oklahoma Historical Society
Chuck Blackwell
William Graham Davis
Jim Karstein
James "Junior" Markham
Moon Martin
Thomas Mauchahty-Ware
Joe Bob Nelson
Leon Russell

Interview by Stephen Foehr
Kelly Davis

Interview by Catherine Bainbridge in 2014 for the documentary film *Rumble: The Indians Who Rocked the World,* **directed by Bainbridge and Alfonso Maiorana (Rezolution Pictures, 2017)**
Kelly Davis

Interview by Karen Rudolph
John Trudell

Interview by Scott Lunsford for Arkansas Memories Project, Center for Arkansas Oral and Visual History, University of Arkansas
John Ware

COLLECTIONS AND PAPERS

Garrard Ardeneum Collection, Sequoyah National Research Center, University of Arkansas Little Rock

Patti Daley Collection, unpublished collection of photos, letters, journals, and other materials in author's possession, courtesy of Bill Noriega

Jesse Ed Davis Collection, including photos, letters, vinyl records, and various ephemera, Hard Rock Casino, Catoosa, OK

Bob Dylan Center Archive, unreleased studio recordings from 1971 and 1987, Tulsa, OK

Indians for Indians radio broadcast recordings collection, Western History Collections, University of Oklahoma Libraries, Norman

Philbrook Collection, Oklahoma Historical Society, Oklahoma City

Rock and Roll Hall of Fame Library and Archives, Cleveland, OH
Nesuhi Ertegun Papers
Jerry Wexler Papers

NOTES

Prelude: Farther on Down the Road

1. Voormann.
2. Keltner; *Concert for Bangladesh*, directed by Saul Swimmer (1972: Apple Film/Rhino Entertainment, 2005), DVD.
3. J. E. Davis with M. Goldman.
4. Chris O'Dell, *Miss O'Dell: My Hard Days and Long Nights with The Beatles, The Stones, Bob Dylan, and Eric Clapton and the Women They Loved* (New York: Touchstone, 2009); *Concert for Bangladesh*.
5. Tom Whittle, "In the Footsteps of the Greatest," *Freedom Magazine*, September 1986, 33–37.
6. *Concert for Bangladesh*.
7. Whittle, "In the Footsteps of the Greatest."
8. *Fort Lauderdale News*, April 10, 1987.
9. *Trudell*, directed by Heather Rae, written by Russell Friedenberg (Appaloosa Pictures, 2005), DVD.

Overture: My Ship Has Come In

1. Tom Whittle, "In the Footsteps of the Greatest," *Freedom Magazine*, September 1986, 33–37.
2. Easton; Cliff Jones, "I'm Peter Green," *Mojo*, September 1996; Johnny Rogan, *Byrds: Requiem for the Timeless, Volume 2* (London: Rogan House, 2017), 701.
3. Nesmith.
4. K. Davis with Bainbridge; Garon; B. Sidran; Billups; Gilmore; Shark; Ray.
5. Whittle, "In the Footsteps of the Greatest," 33–37; Ray; Gilmore; Romero; Nesmith.
6. Noriega; Garon.
7. Payne.
8. Parks.
9. Robertson; Trudell with Rudolph.

10. Steve Rosen, "An Interview with Jesse Ed Davis," *Guitar Player*, March 1974, 10, 26; Ray with Hisaw.

11. Keltner; Raitt; Britt.

12. J. E. Davis with A. Goldman, March 6, 1986, Part I.

Chapter 1: Natural Anthem

1. M. H. Deer, A. Deer, and Bates.

2. Jesse Davis, live radio broadcast from the Red Creek Inn, April 1973, WCMF Rochester, New York, recording in author's possession, courtesy Rick Eckstein.

3. Donald J. Berthrong, *The Southern Cheyennes* (Norman: University of Oklahoma Press, 1963), 305, 326–330.

4. This quote is from a conversation I had with one of Quanah's relations while working on this book in Medicine Park, OK, in 2023.

5. Dustin Tahmahkera, "Hakaru Maruumatu Kwitaka? Seeking Representational Jurisdiction in Comanchería Cinema," *Native American and Indigenous Studies* 5, no. 1 (Spring 2018): 100–35.

6. Jacki Thompson Rand, "Medicine Lodge Treaty (1867)," *Encyclopedia of Oklahoma History and Culture*, Oklahoma Historical Society (OHS).

7. W. P. Bliss, "Tah-pui or Tahpony, Comanche," Kansas Historical Society: Kansas Memory; William T. Hagan, "Kiowas, Comanches, and Cattlemen, 1867–1906: A Case Study of the Failure of U.S. Reservation Policy," *Pacific Historical Review* 40, no. 3 (August 1971): 333–55; *Lawton Constitution-Morning Press* (Lawton, OK), January 12, 1964.

8. *Lawton Constitution-Morning Press*, January 12, 1964.

9. *Lawton Constitution-Morning Press*, January 12, 1964.

10. J. E. Davis with A. Goldman, February 28, 1986, Part II.

11. Vance H. Trimble, *Alice & JFB: The Hundred-Year Saga of Two Seminole Chiefs* (Wilmington, DE: Market Tech Books, 2006), Chapter 9.

12. J. G. Sanders, compiler, *Who's Who Among Oklahoma Indians* (Oklahoma City: Trave Company, 1928), 49; Trimble, *Alice & JFB*, Chapter 9; W. G. Davis with OHS; Jon D. May, "Jennings, Alphonso J. (1863–1961)," *Encyclopedia of Oklahoma History and Culture*, OHS.

13. Sanders, *Who's Who Among Oklahoma Indians*, 49; Trimble, *Alice & JFB*, Chapter 9.

14. Trimble, *Alice & JFB*, Chapter 9.

15. Trimble, *Alice & JFB*, Chapter 9.

16. Trimble, *Alice & JFB*, 209, 235–38, 252–54.

17. Jesse E. Davis Obituary, *The Okemah Ledger* (Okemah, OK), April 28, 1921.

18. Alice Marriott and Carol K. Rachlin, *Dance around the Sun: The Life of Mary Little Bear Inkanish* (New York: Crowell, 1977).

19. Benjamin R. Kracht, "Kiowa," *Encyclopedia of Oklahoma History and Culture*, OHS.

20. N. Scott Momaday, *The Way to Rainy Mountain* (Albuquerque: University of New Mexico Press, 1969), 8.

21. Kracht, "Kiowa."

22. Momaday, *Way to Rainy Mountain*, 4, 59; Shark.

23. William C. Meadows, *Kiowa Ethnogeography* (Austin: University of Texas Press, 2008), 153–54.

24. Laura E. Smith, "Modernity, Multiples, and Masculinity: Horace Poolaw's Postcards of Elder Kiowa Men," *Great Plains Quarterly* 31, no. 2 (Spring 2011): 125–45; Thomas Poolaw, "Horace Poolaw: Photographer, Mentor, Grandfather," *Great Plains Quarterly* 31, no. 2 (Spring 2011): 147–48; Maurice Boyd, *Kiowa Voices: Ceremonial Dance, Ritual and Song*, Volume 1 (Forth Worth: Texas Christian University Press, 1981), 86.

25. *Mountain View Times* (Mountain View, OK), December 16, 1943.

26. Hadley Jerman, "Acting for the Camera: Horace Poolaw's Film Stills of Family, 1925–1950," *Great Plains Quarterly* 31, no. 2 (Spring 2011): 105–23; Daryl Meador, "Amateur Settler Cinema in Early Texas: Old Texas" (Charles Goodnight, 1916), Orphan Film Symposium, New York University, May 28, 2020.

27. Smith, "Modernity, Multiples, and Masculinity"; Amy Connors, "Horace Poolaw's Kiowa Nation," *New Yorker*, November 28, 2014; Poolaw, "Horace Poolaw: Photographer, Mentor, Grandfather," 147–48.

28. Sanmann.

29. N. Scott Momaday, "The Photography of Horace Poolaw," *Aperture*, no. 139 (Summer 1995): 12–19.

30. W. G. Davis with OHS; *The Topeka Daily Capital*, October 19, 1919; Embarkation Passenger List, Hoboken, NJ, May 26, 1918.

31. W. G. Davis with OHS.

32. *Lawrence Daily Journal-World*, December 30, 1920; Steve Gerkin, "They Might Be Giants," *This Land* 3, no. 17 (September 1, 2012).

33. W. G. Davis with OHS.

34. W. G. Davis with OHS; William Graham Davis Obituary, *Muscogee Nation News*, January 1992.

35. Sanmann.

36. "38 Useful Years of Service to End," *Daily Oklahoman* (Oklahoma City), June 28, 1953.

37. *American-Democrat* (Anadarko, OK), June 11, 1924; May 16, 1923; November 19, 1931.

38. *American-Democrat*, December 11, 1930; *Oklahoma Game and Fish News* 1, no. 12 (December 1945); *Daily Oklahoman*, August 16, 1947.

39. *Daily American-Democrat* (Anadarko, OK), January 6, 1936; *American-Democrat*, October 24, 1928; *Harlow's Weekly* (Oklahoma City), June 16, 1934.

40. *Tushkahomman, the Red Warrior* (Stroud, OK), April 2, 1935.

41. *Harlow's Weekly*, June 16, 1934.

42. *Harlow's Weekly*, June 16, 1934; *Daily American-Democrat*, April 19, 1935.

43. *Daily Oklahoman*, June 28, 1953.

44. *The Mangum Daily Star* (Mangum, OK), September 14, 1938.

45. Muriel Wright, "The American Indian Exposition in Oklahoma," *Chronicles of Oklahoma* 24 (1946): 162; E. R. Gaede Jr., *An Ethnohistory of the American Indian Exposition at Anadarko, Oklahoma: 1932–2003* (PhD dissertation, University of Oklahoma, 2009); *The Leader-Post* (Regina, Saskatchewan, Canada), October 18, 1947.

46. J. E. Davis with A. Goldman, February 28, 1986, Part II; *Mexia Daily News* (Mexia, TX), January 23, 1951.

47. *Ventura County Star-Free Press* (Camarillo, CA), June 4, 1952.

48. Jessica Farren (Fowler), "Toby Blackstar Discusses Funeral Customs in the Native American Communities," *Funeral Pro Chat #12* (podcast), ASD, November 12, 2015;

Tom Whittle, "In the Footsteps of the Greatest," *Freedom Magazine*, September 1986, 33–37.

Chapter 2: A Kiowa-Comanche Tipi

1. Gilmore.
2. Bates; M. H. Deer; A. Deer.
3. "Pops Wilted by Tots in Annual Contest," *Oklahoma Daily* (Norman, OK), May 18, 1948.
4. 1930 and 1940 censuses; Oklahoma Baptism Records.
5. "Brightest Tackle Prospect, Wewoka, Oklahoma," *Wewoka Capital-Democrat* (Wewoka, OK), September 24, 1937; Jesse Edwin Davis Draft Card Registration, February 12, 1942; "How NYA Girls Learn Radio," *Radio and Television: The Popular Radio Magazine* 11, no. 12 (April 1941): 714; Tally D. Fugate, "National Youth Administration," *Encyclopedia of Oklahoma History and Culture*, Oklahoma Historical Society (OHS).
6. US Department of Veterans Affairs, Jesse Edwin Davis Death File; "City Painter Wins Indian Art Award," *Daily Oklahoman* (Oklahoma City), May 8, 1957; "Former Grid Father Watches Son in Zoomer Scrimmages," *Daily Oklahoman*, October 3, 1943.
7. "Peace Pipe to Be Smoked," *Norman Transcript*, November 13, 1946; "To Feature Indian Art at Festival," *Black Dispatch* (Oklahoma City), November 8, 1957; "It Can't Be for Art's Sake for OU Student," *Daily Oklahoman*, March 29, 1949.
8. *Time Magazine*, May 31, 1943.
9. This distinction between Oklahoma and Texan blues comes from my interview conversation with Marc Benno.
10. *Indians for Indians* radio show, June 24, 1947, tape 12, Western History Collections (WHC), University of Oklahoma Libraries.
11. Oklahoma County Marriage Records; *Anadarko Daily News* (Anadarko, OK), February 9, 1944; Ivy Coffey, *The Urban Indian* (a reprint from *Sunday Oklahoman* and *Oklahoma City Times*), WHC; "Indians Brave Harsh New Life in City," *Daily Oklahoman*, July 16, 1967.
12. "Indians Brave Harsh New Life in City."
13. J. E. Davis with A. Goldman, February 28, 1986, Part II; Fifteenth Annual Contemporary American Indian Painting Exhibition, Philbrook Art Center brochure, 1960, Oklahoma Historical Society (OHS) Philbrook Collection.
14. "O-k-i-e Is Becoming an Honorable Name," *Daily Oklahoman*, January 15, 1956.
15. Oscar Jacobson, *American Indian Painters* (Nice, France: C. Szwedzicki, 1950), 45.
16. Jacobson, *American Indian Painters*.
17. "City Painter Wins Indian Art Award," *Daily Oklahoman*, May 8, 1957; Twelfth Annual Contemporary American Indian Painting Exhibition, Philbrook Art Center brochure, 1957, OHS Philbrook Collection; Thirteenth Annual Contemporary American Indian Painting Exhibition, Philbrook Art Center brochure, 1958, OHS Philbrook Collection; "Prize Indian Art Returns to City Home," *Daily Oklahoman*, September 23, 1959.
18. Jeanne Snodgrass, *American Indian Painters: A Biographical Directory* (New York: Museum of the American Indian, 1968), 44–45.

19. Mahal.

20. Gilmore; Noriega; Mahal; Elaine Larecy, "Calling the Roll of Sooner Classes," *Sooner Magazine* 15, no. 5 (January 1943): 15–20; "Dealers' Security Program Is Taking Hold," *Harvester World* 34, no. 4 (April 1943): 7.

21. Bureau of Land Management Patent, March 26, 1952.

22. "Popejoy Music Club Broadcasts Over WKY," *Cement Courier* (Cement, OK), October 27, 1932; *Anadarko Tribune*, June 22, 1932; Nancy Ruth, "Leon Russell: The Early Childhood Years," *The Church Studio* (blog), January 6, 2023.

23. "Kiowa Indians Go to Treaty Festivity," *Caddo County Tribune* (Anadarko, OK), October 12, 1932; "Old Folk Lore of Many Lands Given Realistic Staging," *St. Louis Star and Times* (St. Louis, MO), April 30, 1934.

24. *Carnegie Herald* (Carnegie, OK), May 8, 1940.

25. "State Indian Girls Leave Soon for NY," *Stillwater Gazette* (Stillwater, OK), August 11, 1939; *Clinton Daily News* (Clinton, OK), August 8, 1939.

26. Classen High School 1938 Yearbook; Saunkeah; *Oklahoma City Star*, June 5, 1942; *Oklahoma Daily* (Norman, OK), November 7, 1940; "Cherokee Heads State Indians," *Stillwater News-Press* (Stillwater, OK), November 16, 1941.

27. *Daily Oklahoman*, June 17, 1942; "Princess Wins," *Daily Oklahoman*, June 2, 1943; *Daily Oklahoman*, May 18, 1945.

28. "Minutes of a Regular Meeting, The University of Oklahoma Board of Regents," Share, OK, September 11, 1946; Davis Obituary, *Daily Oklahoman*, August 25, 2006.

29. "Taj Mahal's Band," *Hit Parader* (January 1970).

30. J. E. Davis with M. Goldman; Steve Ellerhoff, "Red Dirt Boogie: Autobiography in the Songs of Jesse 'Ed' Davis," *American Indian Quarterly* 40, no. 2 (Spring 2016): 118.

31. J. E. Davis with M. Goldman; "Older Than America: Resisting the Predator—An Interview with John Trudell," *Border/Lines* 23 (Winter 1991/1992); Chuck Blackwell with OHS.

32. "It Can't Be for Art's Sake for OU Student," *Daily Oklahoman*, March 29, 1949.

Chapter 3: Six-Gun City, or, You Can Take the Boy out of Oklahoma . . .

1. J. E. Davis with A. Goldman, March 6, 1986.

2. J. E. Davis with Reed.

3. J. E. Davis with Reed.

4. Tom Whittle, "In the Footsteps of the Greatest," *Freedom Magazine*, September 1986, 33–37.

5. Larry O'Dell, "All-Black Towns," *Encyclopedia of Oklahoma History and Culture*, Oklahoma Historical Society (OHS); David Chang, *The Color of Land* (Chapel Hill: University of North Carolina Press, 2010).

6. Chet Baker and Charlie Christian as representative figures in Oklahoma's musical landscape comes from my interview conversation with singer Diana Allen; Selk.

7. Saul; *Norman Transcript* (Norman, OK), May 1, 1949.

8. Maiman; Mauchahty-Ware with OHS; Gilmore.

9. *Daily Oklahoman*, March 1, 1953; Bolin.

10. High school reunion photo, 1972, Daley Collection; Ray; K. Davis with Bainbridge.

11. Furr.
12. "Taj Mahal's Band," *Hit Parader*, January 1970; *Daily Oklahoman*, November 20, 1955; Furr; Boyle.
13. Furr; Maxwell.
14. Kaspereit; Tsukamoto; Shark.
15. Ware; Bramlett; K. Davis with Foehr.
16. Layton; Ware.
17. "Into the Roots—Taj Mahal," *Guitar Player* 4, no. 5 (August 1970); "Taj Mahal's Band"; Bramlett; Browne.
18. Brianna Bailey, "Musical Finale: Closing at Year's End, Midwest City's Jenkins Music Can Trace Its Roots to Long-Gone Kansas City Chain," *Daily Oklahoman*, December 4, 2014.
19. Ware; Joe Edwards, "I'll Fly Away Hymn Classic," Associated Press/*Kentucky New Era*, March 13, 1987.
20. Allen; *Daily Oklahoman*, October 20, 1963; "Radio Man Can't Talk Back," *Daily Oklahoman*, September 4, 1966.
21. "Into the Roots—Taj Mahal."
22. Smith.
23. Colby; Ray.
24. "Youngsters Wild about 'Cat' King," *Daily Oklahoman*, April 20, 1956; J. E. Davis with Reed; Steve Rosen, "An Interview with Jesse Ed Davis," *Guitar Player*, March 1974, 10, 26.
25. Allen; Ware; Rosen, "Interview with Jesse Ed Davis," 10, 26; Whittle, "In the Footsteps of the Greatest."
26. Hollis.
27. Doyah; Martin with Hisaw; Ray; "Taj Mahal's Band."
28. Whittle, "In the Footsteps of the Greatest"; "Taj Mahal's Band"; "Into the Roots—Taj Mahal."
29. Doyah; WCMF Rochester Concert; Rosen, "Interview with Jesse Ed Davis"; J. E. Davis with Reed.
30. "J. Julian Adkins," *Daily Oklahoman*, April 7, 1996.
31. Rosen, "Interview with Jesse Ed Davis"; "Taj Mahal's Band"; *Daily Oklahoman*, November 20, 1955; Furr; Boyle; Layton.
32. Layton.
33. Layton.
34. J. E. Davis with M. Goldman.
35. "Taj Mahal's Band"; Brewer; Burke.
36. "Taj Mahal's Band"; Brewer; Burke.
37. *Northwest News* (Bethany, OK), August 6, 1959; Allen.
38. Smith.
39. Smith; Furr.
40. Frederickson.
41. Boyle; Smith; Furr.
42. Frederickson.
43. Smith; Kaspereit; Burke; Doyah.
44. *Keep Me Comin'* LP (Epic Records, 1973); Ray.
45. The next several paragraphs are from my interview with Mary Carol Kaspereit.

46. Leonard Cayton, "School Racial Plan Granted Tentative OK," *Daily Oklahoman*, August 9, 1963; Leonard B. Cayton, "A History of Black Public Education in Oklahoma" (PhD dissertation, University of Oklahoma, 1977), 121; James Traub, "Oklahoma City: Separate and Equal," *The Atlantic*, September 1991.

47. Cayton, "School Racial Plan Granted"; Cayton, "History of Black Public Education," 121; James Traub, "Separate and Equal"; Brewer; Kaspereit.

48. Lynne Ames, "About Westchester; 'Hottest,'" *New York Times*, February 21, 1988; Roy Johnson, "What It Was Like to Be an African-American Freshman in 1962," *Stanford Magazine*, August 31, 2017. For examples of Indigenous peoples' relationship to twentieth-century race-making between white, Black, and Native people, see David A. Chang, *Color of the Land: Race, Nation, and the Politics of Landownership in Oklahoma, 1832–1929* (Chapel Hill: University of North Carolina Press, 2010) and Malinda Maynor Lowery, *Lumbee Indians in the Jim Crow South: Race, Identity, and the Making of a Nation* (Chapel Hill: University of North Carolina Press, 2010).

49. J. E. Davis with Reed; Rosen, "Interview with Jesse Ed Davis."

50. *Daily Oklahoman*, August 25, 1963. This was probably during Twitty's Springlake engagement August 30–September 2, 1963. I find no appearance by Twitty at Springlake between this date and August 1962, when Jesse had not yet replaced guitarist Al Bruno.

Chapter 4: . . . But You Can't Take Oklahoma out of the Boy

1. Robert E. Lee, "Andy Still Whips Up His Salad," *Daily Oklahoman*, July 16, 1990; R. L. Smith, "'Old-Time Chef' Still Cooking," *Daily Oklahoman*, September 28, 1987.

2. Hickox.

3. Summers; *Keep Me Comin'* liner notes (Epic Records, 1973).

4. Unless otherwise noted, material in the next several paragraphs comes from interviews with Selk, Ware, and Summers.

5. Ware; John Ware with Scott Lunsford for University of Arkansas Oral and Visual History: Arkansas Memories Project, February 18, 2011.

6. Ware; Martin with Hisaw.

7. John Ware with Scott Lunsford; Maxwell.

8. Levon Helm, *This Wheel's on Fire: Levon Helm and the Story of the Band* (Chicago: Chicago Review Press, 1993), Kindle edition; Tom Whittle, "In the Footsteps of the Greatest," *Freedom Magazine*, September 1986, 33–37; Robertson.

9. Ware.

10. Summers; Keltner with Bouard.

11. Summers; Selk; Ware.

12. Summers.

13. Selk; Ware.

14. Ware.

15. Frederickson.

16. Selk.

17. Selk.

18. Dalton.

19. Selk; Ware; Maxwell.

20. Selk; Martin with Hisaw.

21. "Taj Mahal's Band," *Hit Parader*, January 1970; Ware.

22. Sam Blakelock, "What Was Joe Pass' Approach to Solo Jazz Guitar?," *Medium*, October 21, 2015.

23. Joe Pass interview, *Guitar Player*, June 1974; Joe Pass interview, *Rolling Stone*, December 13, 1979.

24. Steve Rosen, "An Interview with Jesse Ed Davis," *Guitar Player*, March 1974, 10, 26; Summers; Frederickson; Mary Jo Ruggles, "Songs of the Peoples of the North American Plains," in *Remaining Ourselves: Music and Tribal Memory*, ed. Dayna Bowker Lee (Oklahoma City: The State Arts Council of Oklahoma, 1995), 27.

25. "Taj Mahal's Band."

26. Warren.

27. Ware; Kaspereit.

28. "Connecting the Dots," *Daily Oklahoman*, July 14, 2019; *Country Social* videos on YouTube; Bud Mathis, "Blackberry Boogie," Country Social Girls, "I'll Lose My Mind Before I'm Over You," and Conway Twitty, "Lonely Blue Boy" and "Walk Me to the Door," YouTube channel GatorRock789. Thank you to Scott Sanger for sharing his discovery of these rare video clips.

29. Whittle, "In the Footsteps of the Greatest"; "Taj Mahal's Band."

30. Wilbur Cross and Michael Kosser, *The Conway Twitty Story: An Authorized Biography*, 2nd ed. (New York: Paperjacks, 1987), 90–92, 103–105.

31. Cross and Kosser, *The Conway Twitty Story*, 90–92, 103–105.

32. "Taj Mahal's Band"; Karstein; *The Dispatch* (Moline, Illinois), August 22, 1961. It's incredibly challenging to pinpoint the exact dates of Davis's tenure with Twitty. As of August 1962, Conway Twitty's band still included Joe Lewis on bass, Al Bruno on guitar, Porkchop on drums, and Dumpy Rice on keys. *Daily Oklahoman*, August 5, 1962. "Into the Roots—Taj Mahal," *Guitar Player* 4, no. 5 (August 1970): Here Davis said he began playing with Conway Twitty when he was eighteen, which squares with John Selk's recollection.

33. J. E. Davis with A. Goldman, March 6, 1986; Robertson; Helm, *This Wheel's on Fire*, Chapter 4.

34. J. E. Davis with M. Goldman; On the Steel Guitar Forum, Gene "Deacon" Jones said he played pedal steel with Conway Twitty in 1965 and Jesse Ed Davis was in the band that year. Photo evidence suggests this is correct.

35. J. E. Davis with M. Goldman; William Kelly, "Act II Episode 14—Tony Marts Bids Farewell to the Hawks and Conway Twitty," *Summer of '65* (blog), August 21, 2015; *New York Times*, August 24, 1965; *Atlantic City Press*, June 30, 1965.

36. Cross and Kosser, *The Conway Twitty Story*, 90–92, 103–105.

37. William Kelly, "Episode 12 Conway Returns to Tony Marts and the Second Coming of Tito Mambo," *Summer of '65* (blog), July 30, 2015.

38. Warren; Ware.

39. Selk.

40. The New Breed, "Just Another Bird Dog" b/w "You'll Be There," 45 rpm single (Boyd Records, 1965), copy in author's possession. During the session, the group cut a third Davis-penned song, an up-tempo number called "Pulling Up Stakes," which Mike Boyle sang. Gene Sullivan made a small number of 78 rpms that the band gave to fans during live engagements. I don't know if any survive. See Rhett Lake and

Teb Blackwell, *Oklahoma Guide to 45 rpm Records and Bands, 1955–1975, Volume 1e.* Excerpts courtesy of Larry Hollis.

41. Kaspereit.

42. Boyle.

43. Boyle.

44. Jesse Edwin Davis III, University of Oklahoma transcript, in possession of author.

45. Donald J. Berthrong interviewed by Ronald McCoy, vol. 23, no. 1 (2012), Heritage of the Great Plains Collection, Emporia State University.

46. J. E. Davis with A. Goldman, February 28, 1986, Part II; J. E. Davis OU transcript.

47. Donald J. Berthrong, *The Southern Cheyennes*, rev. ed. (1963; Norman: University of Oklahoma Press, 1986), 405.

48. Donald J. Berthrong interviewed by Ronald McCoy.

49. J. E. Davis in the National Guard: email correspondence with Robin Brewer, head of state records branch for the Oklahoma National Guard, May 19, 2022; Jesse Ed Davis, "Washita Love Child," *¡JESSE!* (ATCO Records, 1971).

50. J. E. Davis OU transcript; Brewer; J. E. Davis, "Washita Love Child."

51. Brewer; R. White; Frederickson.

52. Allen; Layton; Maxwell.

53. Jeffrey M. Moore with Larry O'Dell, contrib., *Another Hot Oklahoma Night: A Rock and Roll Story* (Oklahoma City: Oklahoma Historical Society [OHS], 2009), 127–31; Payne.

54. Ellerhoff, "Red Dirt Boogie: Autobiography in the Songs of Jesse 'Ed' Davis," *American Indian Quarterly* 40, no. 2 (Spring 2016).

55. "Taj Mahal's Band"; "Into the Roots—Taj Mahal."

56. R. White; photos from R. White; Maxwell; Warren; Ware with Bouard.

57. In 1965, Jesse was still taking classes at OU, playing with Conway Twitty and the Continentals/Joe Banana/New Breed, and serving in the Oklahoma Guard. He appeared on television in Oklahoma City, in photos with the New Breed, and cut the New Breed single that year. Cleve Warren recalls Davis not being at OU when he enrolled in fall 1966, and recalls Davis going back and forth once or twice before a permanent move. Erik Dalton moved with his group the Disciples, who became Southwind, to LA in 1967 and feels confident Ed Davis moved there right around the same time.

58. "Taj Mahal's Band."

59. "Taj Mahal's Band"; Warren; Ellis.

60. Nelson with OHS.

Chapter 5: Turned On in Tinseltown

1. "Taj Mahal's Band," *Hit Parader*, January 1970.

2. "Taj Mahal's Band."

3. Konikoff.

4. Tarquin Campbell, "Bobby Keys: Sax Sideman Extraordinaire," *Rock's Backpages*, May 2010; "Bobby Keys, The Rolling Stones," *Classic Rock Online*, December 2014.

5. Benno; B. Sidran; Whitlock.

6. Whitlock; Karstein; Markham with Oklahoma Historical Society (OHS); Benno.

7. Bramlett; K. Davis with Bainbridge; *Ann Arbor Sun*, January 9, 1975; "Edward M. Davis," *LA Weekly*, February 28, 2013.

8. John Wooley, "Ending a String of Bad Luck," *Oklahoma Magazine*, June 21, 2018; Markham with Bouard; Dunlop; Bobby Keys, *Every Night's a Saturday Night: The Rock 'n' Roll Life of Legendary Sax Man Bobby Keys* (Berkeley: Counterpoint, 2012); "Taj Mahal's Band"; Markham with OHS.

9. Wooley, "Ending a String of Bad Luck"; Markham with Bouard; Markham with OHS; Lewis.

10. Dunlop; Steve Rosen, "An Interview with Jesse Ed Davis," *Guitar Player*, March 1974, 10, 26.

11. Keltner; Lewis.

12. Gilmore; Karstein; Whitlock, Bramlett.

13. Karstein; Gilmore; Whitlock; Leon Russell, "Shoot Out on the Plantation," *Leon Russell* (Shelter, 1970).

14. Benno.

15. Karstein; Benno; Keltner; Mahal with Bouard.

16. Russell with OHS.

17. O'Dell; Karstein; Browne.

18. Karstein; Keltner.

19. Whitlock.

20. Mahal; "Taj Mahal's Band."

21. Mahal; Gilmore.

22. Mahal; Gilmore; Konikoff; Karstein.

23. Gilmore; Blackwell with OHS.

24. Mahal; Mahal with Bouard.

25. Easton.

26. Mahal.

27. Gilmore.

28. *Los Angeles Times*, September 30, 1969; *Topanga New Times*, April 7, 2023; Mona Maiman interview with Dan Danner, *Conversayor*, August 1, 2021.

29. Dunlop; Gilmore; Wilkins.

30. *Long Beach Independent*, November 19, 1967.

31. Jim Shelly, "Bullfrog 3 Festival 1969," *The Woodstock Whisperer* website, August 21, 2017; "Bullfrog Drug Use Debated by Officers," *Statesman Journal* (Salem, OR), August 25, 1969.

32. J. E. Davis to Patti Daley, March 28, 1969, Jesse Ed Davis Collection, Hard Rock Casino, Catoosa, OK (Hard Rock Collection). Jesse wrote from Philadelphia, where the Taj Mahal band played the Electric Factory; Krieger.

33. Gilmore; Mahal; *Dayton Daily News*, May 12, 1969.

34. Gilmore; Mahal; Rich.

35. *Daily Utah Chronicle* (Salt Lake City), February 16, 1968; Jerry Gilbert, "Taj: Thinking the Blues," *Sounds*, December 22, 1973; Mahal; "Taj Mahal: Still One of the Hardest Rockers," *Melody Maker*, April 25, 1970.

36. Blackwell with OHS; Gilmore; Mahal.

37. Robertson; Mahal.

38. Mahal.

39. On the counterculture's appropriation of Native culture and its complicated conse-quences, see Sherry Smith, *Hippies, Indians, and the Fight for Red Power* (Oxford, UK: Oxford University Press, 2012).

40. Nelson. Ed and Tracy Nelson's bond deepened when Ed later contributed guitar to several songs on Nelson's 1974 album *Time Is on My Side*, including the reggae-styled "Anything You Want," for which Nelson "can't think of any other guitar player who could have nailed that groove that well." We might interpret Jesse's recognition of a Cherokee tradition as an example of Native people in Oklahoma sharing cultural practices during the nineteenth and twentieth centuries, when even former rival tribal nations worked in common cause to survive colonization.

41. Garon; Maiman; J. Sidran.

42. Noriega; Maiman; Gilmore; Bramlett; Patti Daley to Jim Keltner, December 19, 1988, and Patti Daley to Taj Mahal, January 30, 1993, Daley Collection; Twin Talk with Jose and Angel, "Rock and Roll Treasure, Part 1, 2 & 3," YouTube, March 30, 2011. In this Los Angeles NBC News segment, Patti mentions that she met Jesse in 1966, but her recollection must be off by one year. Jesse and Taj began working together in 1967.

43. Patti Daley to Jesse Ed Davis, April 18, 1969; Patti to Jesse, April 15, 1969; Jesse to Patti, March 28, 1969; all letters are in the Daley Collection.

44. Mahal; Gilmore.

45. Blackwell with OHS; Jesse Ed Davis to Patti Daley from Londonderry House, December 1968, Hard Rock Collection; Gilmore.

46. Jesse to Patti from Londonderry House, December 1968, Hard Rock Collection.

47. Jesse to Patti from Londonderry House, December 1968, Hard Rock Collection; J. E. Davis with Westwood One; Tom Whittle, "In the Footsteps of the Greatest," *Freedom Magazine*, September 1986, 33–37; J. E. Davis with A. Goldman, February 28, 1986, Part I; J. E. Davis with A. Goldman, February 28, 1983.

48. Jesse to Patti from Londonderry House, December 1968, Hard Rock Collection; J. E. Davis with A. Goldman, March 6, 1986, Part II; J. E. Davis with A. Goldman, February 28, 1986, Part I; J. E. Davis with A. Goldman, February 28, 1983.

49. "Rock And Roll's First Indian Superstar: Jesse 'Ed' Davis," *Los Angeles Free Press*, June 1973; Jesse to Patti from Londonderry House, December 1968, Hard Rock Collection.

50. J. E. Davis with A. Goldman, February 28, 1986, Part I.

51. Mahal; Gilmore.

52. Mahal; Gilmore.

53. Mahal; Gilmore.

54. P. Waddington; Gilmore; Rich; Jesse Ed Davis to Patti Daley from New York, April 17, 1969, and Jesse to Patti from New Haven, April 14, 1969, Hard Rock Collection.

55. Rich.

56. Karstein; Rich; Simon. Drummer James Otey played on the session for "Chevrolet" and "Oh Susanna."

57. Taj Mahal 1970 tour itinerary, Daley Collection; Ruben Chagoya, "Pop Rock & Blues Festival Essen 1970," YouTube, January 16, 2017; Rich.

58. Taj Mahal with Stephen Foehr, *Taj Mahal: Autobiography of a Bluesman* (Sanctuary Publishing Ltd., 2001), 158–63; Taj Mahal, "West Indian Revelation," *Happy to Be Just Like I Am* (1971).

59. Rich; Mahal; "Into the Roots—Taj Mahal," *Guitar Player* 4, no. 5 (August 1970).

60. Mahal; "Rock Star on the Rise," *Long Beach Independent*, May 4, 1973.

61. "Taj Mahal's Band," *Hit Parader*, January 1970; "Taj Mahal: *Giant Step* Production Notes," *Hi-Fi News & Record Review*, n.d.
62. Mallaber; Benno.
63. Benno; Whitlock.
64. Gregg Allman, *My Cross to Bear* (New York: William Morrow Paperbacks, 2013), 123–24; "Southern Men: The Long Tall Saga of the Allman Brothers Band," *Mojo* 109 (December 2002).
65. Easton; Kortchmar; Whitlock; McCaughey; Gilmore; Payne.
66. Raitt.
67. Whitlock.

Chapter 6: ¡Jesse Davis!

1. Patti Daley, letter to David Wood (attorney), April 18, 1989; Patti Daley, email to Richard (surname unknown), Daley Collection; J. E. Davis with M. Goldman.
2. Boyd; O'Dell; Keltner.
3. Glyn Johns, *Sound Man* (New York: Plume, 2015); B. Sidran; A. White.
4. B. Sidran.
5. J. E. Davis to Jerry Wexler, Rock and Roll Hall of Fame, Wexler Papers.
6. J. E. Davis with M. Goldman.
7. J. E. Davis with M. Goldman.
8. J. E. Davis with M. Goldman; ¡*Jesse Davis!* (ATCO, 1970).
9. Mahal; Warner Brothers Tape Archive, Burbank, CA; Jesse Davis to Mark Meyerson, August 20, 1970, Nesuhi Ertegun Papers, Rock and Roll Hall of Fame, Cleveland, document courtesy of Andy Schwartz.
10. *Jesse Davis!*, *Rolling Stone*, January 21, 1971.
11. *INK*, no. 9 (United Kingdom), June 26, 1971; *Gazette* (Montreal), May 27, 1972; Steve Rosen, "An Interview with Jesse Ed Davis," *Guitar Player*, March 1974, 10, 26.
12. Jesse Davis to Mark Meyerson (ATCO A&R Representative), First Album Cover Instructions, undated, Nesuhi Ertegun Papers.
13. J. E. Davis with M. Goldman.
14. J. E. Davis to Jerry Wexler, Rock and Roll Hall of Fame, Wexler Papers; Taj; Daley Collection.
15. P. Waddington.
16. Russell Saunkeah message to Laura Garon, April 17, 2019; P. Waddington; B. Sidran; Benno.
17. O'Dell; Karstein; Mallaber; B. Sidran; Catalano; Noriega; Selk; Konikoff; Russell.
18. Selk.
19. Noriega; P. Waddington; Summers; Dalton; O'Dell; J. E. Davis with M. Goldman.
20. Daley Collection; P. Waddington.
21. C. Waddington; Glaub; P. Waddington; Noriega.
22. Konikoff; Glaub; Noriega; Karstein; B. Sidran; Ray.
23. Konikoff; C. Waddington; Selk; Noriega; Ron Kovic, *Hurricane Street* (Brooklyn: Akashic Books, 2016), 54.
24. Noriega; P. Waddington; Bramlett.

25. J. Sidran; Noriega.

26. Voormann; Noriega. Noriega is the principal source for the next several paragraphs.

27. Ann Arens, "The Canal Festivals 1969–75: Fighting City Hall Venice Style," *Free Venice Beachhead*, no. 277 (September 2004); "Venice Canal Festival May Attract 10,000," *Los Angeles Times*, September 23, 1973; Noriega; C. Waddington.

28. Arens, "The Canal Festivals 1969–75";"Venice Canal Festival May Attract 10,000"; Noriega; C. Waddington.

29. Arens, "The Canal Festivals 1969–75"; "Venice Canal Festival May Attract 10,000"; Noriega; C. Waddington.

30. J. E. Davis with M. Goldman.

31. "XIT: Indian Musical Sensation Makes It Big," *Navajo Times*, December 20, 1973.

32. Mallaber.

33. Speaker of "smoke signals" quote prefers to be anonymous here; P. Waddington.

34. Mallaber; P. Waddington; Torres.

35. J. E. Davis with M. Goldman; Russell with Oklahoma Historical Society (OHS).

36. J. E. Davis with M. Goldman.

37. *Concert for Bangladesh*, directed by Saul Swimmer (1972: Apple Film/Rhino Entertainment, 2005), DVD.

38. Johnny Rogan, *Byrds: Requiem for the Timeless, Volume 2* (London: Rogan House, 2017), 749; Martin with OHS.

39. Galuten.

40. Galuten.

41. J. E. Davis with M. Goldman.

42. C. Waddington.

43. J. E. Davis with A. Goldman, February 28, 1986, Part II.

44. J. E. Davis with M. Goldman; Keltner with Bouard.

45. *The Times* (San Mateo, California), April 29, 1972.

46. *The Montreal Star*, April 1, 1972.

47. "*Ululu*," *Rolling Stone*, April 27, 1972.

48. *Punk Magazine* 1, no. 1 (May 7, 1973): 11; "Indians 'Ululu Proud,'" *Springfield Leader and Press* (Missouri), August 6, 1972.

49. *Zoo World*, March 2, 1972.

50. "Rock and Roll's First Indian Superstar: Jesse 'Ed' Davis," *Los Angeles Free Press*, June 1973.

51. Ellis; P. Waddington.

52. Mallaber.

53. Browne; P. Waddington.

54. Ellis; *Los Angeles Times*, March 3, 1972.

55. "Jesse Ed Davis Live" review, unidentified newsprint source in author's possession, 1973.

56. Karstein; *Orlando Sentinel*, December 1, 1971; *New York Daily News*, December 23, 1971.

57. Karstein; B. Sidran.

58. J. E. Davis with A. Goldman, March 6, 1986; P. Waddington.

59. Glaub; *Buffalo Evening News*, March 6, 1971.

60. Copenhaver; June 1972 photo in Daley Collection; B. and J. Sidran; Maiman.

Chapter 7: The Circus Comes to Town

1. Album liner notes, *The Section*, Warner Brothers, 1972; Nesmith.
2. Browne.
3. Kortchmar; Kunkel.
4. Ware; Brewer; Kunkel.
5. Ray; Sklar; P. Waddington.
6. "Rock Star on the Rise," *Long Beach Independent*, May 4, 1973; "Even Under the Guise of Hank Wilson, Leon Russell Is a Legend in His Time," *Goldmine*, September 11, 1998; Russell with Oklahoma Historical Society (OHS).
7. "Leon Russell Is a Legend in His Time"; Russell with OHS; Keltner.
8. There has long been misinformation that indicates that Don Preston played on this recording. This isn't true. Jesse plays electric guitar and it's actually Leon Russell who played the dobro part. This is according to my interview with Don Preston, who insists he was not on this session.
9. Keltner; Raitt.
10. Browne; Kunkel.
11. Browne; Kunkel; Sklar; Steve Rosen, "An Interview with Jesse Ed Davis," *Guitar Player*, March 1974, 10, 26.
12. Browne; Kunkel; Sklar.
13. Browne; Sklar.
14. Browne.
15. Browne; Sklar; Kunkel; Noriega.
16. Hubbard; Nesmith.
17. Benno; Lloyd.
18. Bigsby; "Albert Collins: The Ice Man," *The Wire* (1987).
19. Konikoff.
20. Keltner.
21. Ray; P. Waddington.
22. B. Sidran; Krieger.
23. *San Francisco Examiner*, November 26, 1973.
24. Dalton.
25. J. E. Davis with M. Goldman; P. Waddington; Ray with Hisaw.
26. Shark with Hisaw.
27. "Rock and Roll's First Indian Superstar: Jesse 'Ed' Davis," *Los Angeles Free Press*, June 1973; Tom Whittle, "In the Footsteps of the Greatest," *Freedom Magazine*, September 1986, 33–37; Steven Rosen, *Zoo World*, December 6, 1973.
28. Maiman.
29. Eckstein; Tsukamoto; Ray; Glaub.
30. Eckstein; Tsukamoto; Ray; Glaub.
31. Glaub.
32. Torres; Glaub.
33. "Rock and Roll's First Indian Superstar."
34. Maiman.
35. "Rock and Roll's First Indian Superstar"; Patti Daley to David Wood, June 22, 1989, Daley Collection; *Buffalo Evening News*, January 6, 1973; Torres.

36. Steven Jae Johnson, *Walk, Don't Run* (Wilkes-Barre, PA: Kallisti Publishing, 2015), 260–69; P. Waddington; Bigsby; Whitlock.
37. Maiman.
38. "Rock and Roll's First Indian Superstar"; J. E. Davis with A. Goldman, February 28, 1986, Part II; Maiman; P. Waddington; Torres; Jann S. Wenner, "John, Yoko, and Me," *Rolling Stone*, September 2, 2022.
39. "Rock and Roll's First Indian Superstar"; J. E. Davis with A. Goldman, February 28, 1986, Part II; Maiman; P. Waddington; Torres.
40. *Binghamton Press and Sun Bulletin*, May 26, 1973; *Pensacola News*, May 17, 1973; *Zoo Magazine*, May 10, 1973; *Buffalo News*, June 30, 1973.
41. *Buffalo Evening News*, April 20, 1973; Glaub; Shultz.
42. *Long Beach Independent*, May 7, 1973.
43. "Nicky Hopkins: Sixth Stone Rolls Alone," *Melody Maker*, August 11, 1973.
44. Resnick.
45. "Interview with John and Yoko," *Rock Magazine* 3, no. 10 (January 3, 1972): 28–29.
46. "Interview with John and Yoko"; Pang.
47. Pang; Catalano; Noriega; J. E. Davis with A. Goldman, February 28, 1986, Part I; "Another Day in the Life," *Creem*, June 1974. The next string of paragraphs concerning the incident at Harold Seider's house all draw from these foregoing sources.
48. Pang; J. E. Davis with A. Goldman, February 28, 1986, Part I.
49. J. E. Davis with A. Goldman, February 28, 1983; Pang; Catalano; Noriega; Daley Collection.
50. Pang; O'Dell.
51. Pang: J. E. Davis with A. Goldman, February 28, 1983, Part II.
52. Trucks with Bouard.
53. J. E. Davis with A. Goldman, February 28 1986, Part I.
54. J. E. Davis with A. Goldman, February 28, 1986, Part I.
55. J. E. Davis with A. Goldman, February 28, 1986, Part I; J. E. Davis with A. Goldman, February 28, 1983, Part II.
56. J. E. Davis with A. Goldman, February 28, 1986, Part I; J. E. Davis with A. Goldman, February 28, 1983, Part II; Noriega.
57. J. E. Davis with A. Goldman, April 2, 1985; J. E. Davis with A. Goldman, February 28, 1983; Noriega.
58. *London Observer*, September 28, 1997.
59. "Random Notes," *Rolling Stone*, April 11, 1974; "Random Notes," *Rolling Stone*, April 25, 1974; Keltner.
60. "Dining and Dancing with Pop Stars," *Los Angeles Free Press*, September 13, 1974.
61. Furr.
62. P. Waddington; Noriega.
63. "Employee Slain in Burger Shop Holdup," *Los Angeles Times*, August 18, 1974.
64. Glaub; Eckstein.
65. Pang; J. E. Davis with A. Goldman, March 6, 1986, Part II.
66. J. E. Davis with A. Goldman, March 6, 1986, Part II; J. E. Davis with A. Goldman, December 20, 1983.
67. "Two Questions About John Lennon," *Rolling Stone*, August 29, 1974.
68. J. E. Davis with A. Goldman, March 6, 1986; Voormann.

69. J. E. Davis with A. Goldman, March 6, 1986; Granito.

70. Voormann; Granito; Pang.

71. Keltner; Keltner with Bouard.

Chapter 8: Where Am I Now (When I Need Me)

1. Robert Greenfield, *Ain't It Time We Said Goodbye* (Boston: Da Capo Press, 2014), 251; Mahal.

2. Maiman; Ellis; Karstein with Bouard.

3. *Albuquerque Journal*, September 19, 1975; K. Jones.

4. "Rod and the Faces," *Miami News*, October 17, 1975; K. Jones.

5. Ian McLagan, *All the Rage: My High Life with The Small Faces, The Faces, The Rolling Stones and Many More* (New York: Macmillan, 2000); *Miami News*, July 25, 1975; *Miami News*, July 30, 1975.

6. Patti Daley email to Carol Lee, April 12, 2012, Daley Collection; *Creem*, November 1975.

7. "Rod and the Faces"; *Miami News*, July 25, 1975; K. Jones.

8. *Asheville Citizen-Times*, August 19, 1975; *Los Angeles Times*, August 23, 1975.

9. "Stewart Faces the HIC," *Honolulu Star-Bulletin*, September 10, 1975; *Albuquerque Journal*, September 19, 1975; Faces live cassette recording, Asheville, NC, August 19, 1975, Daley Collection.

10. K. Jones.

11. K. Jones.

12. K. Jones.

13. McLagan, *All the Rage*; Piranha; "Rock and Roll Animals," *Buffalo News*, December 7, 1986.

14. Piranha; "Rock and Roll Animals."

15. Mahal; R. White; Hollis; Ray; Shark; Lowe; Glaub; Torres.

16. Tom Whittle, "In the Footsteps of the Greatest," *Freedom Magazine*, September 1986, 33–37.

17. McLagan, *All the Rage*.

18. Dave Marsh, "Ron Wood: Rolling Stones Are Born, Not Made," *Rolling Stone*, November 3, 1977; McLagan, *All the Rage*.

19. Barbara Charone, "Lean and Hungry Rod," *Crawdaddy!*, September 1976; Tom Nolan, "Faces Break Up—Wood a Stone?," *Rolling Stone*, January 29, 1976.

20. Noriega; *Asheville Citizen-Times*, August 23, 1975.

21. Noriega.

22. Pang.

23. Noriega.

24. Catalano; Noriega; Vogensen.

25. Parks; John Pidgeon, "Eric Clapton: Return of the Reluctant Hero," *Creem*, April 1978; Michael Schumacher, *Crossroads: The Life and Music of Eric Clapton* (Westport, CT: Hyperion, 1995), 201.

26. *Long Beach Press Telegram*, September 13, 1987.

27. "Lean and Hungry Rod."

28. Stewart.

29. *Los Angeles Times*, February 23, 1977.
30. Trout.
31. Trout.
32. Shark; Lowe. Discussion of Jesse's relationship with Ming Lowe is informed by my interview with Lowe.
33. Konikoff.
34. Kaspereit.
35. Catalano.
36. Some Internet websites list the dates for these Leonard Cohen sessions in June and July 1977, but that information is false. Leonard Cohen's friend and foremost biographer Sylvie Simmons confirmed that these sessions in fact took place in January and February 1977.
37. Catalano; Sylvie Simmons, "Leonard Cohen, Phil Spector: Death of Ladies' Men," *Please Kill Me*, April 21, 2021.
38. Kaspereit.
39. Scott James, "Family Opened Up the Door to John and Yoko," *New York Times*, October 8, 2010; J. E. Davis with A. Goldman, Part II, March 6, 1986; Pang.
40. Stoner.
41. Interviewee prefers anonymity.
42. Sklar.
43. Shark; Ellis.
44. I benefited from some very powerful conversations with many people about this subject. I am especially grateful for a discussion about the subject with Karen Rudolph. My feelings and position here are also an extension of deep experience with the subject in my own family.
45. Terri Roman-Szynkowski, "Remembering the Longest Walk 1978 in St Louis," video footage, *Censored News*, August 30, 2013.

Chapter 9: Was It Just a Dream?

1. I appreciate Hugh Aldersey-Williams's essay on the history of the tide as metaphor in literature. I'm inclined to use it here given my agreement with him, demonstrated in this book, that every outgoing tide will be met with a new one coming in. See Aldersey-Williams, *Tide: The Science and Lore of the Greatest Force on Earth* (New York: W. W. Norton, 2016). I also stress the fact that Patti and Jesse's story is set in Hawaii and Venice Beach, where the tide is not merely a geographically dislocated metaphor but a very real physical element of daily life.
2. Piranha.
3. Piranha; Garon; D. Jones; Granito.
4. Patti Daley journal from Daley Collection.
5. Granito.
6. Next several paragraphs stem from interview with Daniel Jones.
7. D. Jones.
8. Piranha; Daley journal from Daley Collection.
9. Piranha.
10. Margaret Trudeau, *Consequences* (New York: Bantam, 1982).

11. Bockris.
12. Kennerley.
13. Kennerley; Glyn Johns, *Sound Man* (New York: Plume, 2015), 307–13.
14. Daley journal from Daley Collection.
15. Daley journal from Daley Collection.
16. Garon.
17. Garon.
18. Garon.
19. Garon; Ray; Granito; J. E. Davis to Tantalayo, undated letter in author's possession.
20. "The Chants Are Safe," *Daily Oklahoman*, October 7, 1951.
21. J. E. Davis with Westwood One; J. E. Davis with A. Goldman, February 28, 1983, Part II; Eckstein; Cambern.
22. J. E. Davis with A. Goldman, December 20, 1983; Chip Madinger and Scott Raile, *Lennonology* (Chesterfield, MO: Open Your Books, 2015), 465.
23. J. E. Davis to A. Goldman, February 28, 1983, Part II; Jay Bergen, *Lennon, the Mobster and the Lawyer: The Untold Story* (Memphis: DeVault-Graves Books, 2021), 228–34, 314–46, 388–92.
24. J. E. Davis to A. Goldman, February 28, 1986, Part I; Piranha.
25. Keltner; Voormann.
26. Tantalayo S. Davis, Facebook post, September 21, 2019.
27. Ray.
28. Russell Saunkeah, email conversations with Laura Garon, 2019. When I asked Van Dyke Parks about his recollection of Lennon's murder, he replied in his typically erudite and enigmatic way: "I'll tell you, it was just as dismal as it gets down there dear, I'm sorry, we had a very hard time," he begins. "I just, it was very sorrowful, that's all there is to it. Of course, you want to leave a situation anyway when you figure these things out. You want to get some confirmational value, and I'm just telling you I'm no Pollyanna, I don't need a happy ending. I don't need the happy ending to enjoy the exposition. There is a great deal of tragedy." In so many words, I think Parks was trying to tell me it's painful and he doesn't want to think too much about it.
29. J. E. Davis with A. Goldman, April 2, 1985; "In the Footsteps of the Greatest," *Freedom Magazine*, September 1986, 33–37; J. E. Davis with Westwood One.
30. Both Kelly's comments and a transcript of Jesse's letter to Goldman from May 20, 1985, were included in the October 20, 1988, issue of *Rolling Stone*.
31. J. E. Davis with A. Goldman, April 2, 1985, and March 6, 1986; *Honolulu Advertiser*, October 24, 1988.

Chapter 10: The Great Abandonment

1. Saenz.
2. J. E. Davis early 1980s music notebook, courtesy of John Granito.
3. Jesse and Tantalayo Song and Gig Notebook, circa 1980–1982, in author's possession.
4. Tantalayo S. Davis, Facebook post, October 11, 2019.
5. Jesse and Tantalayo Song and Gig Notebook; Schell.

6. Ray; Schell; Ellis.
7. Hisaw with Ray; Ray; Ellis; Eckstein.
8. Thomas Patterson with Mike Johnson, "Jess Ed Davis: Washita Love Child," *Shindig Magazine*, comments: Tantalayo: Posted on August 7, 2019.
9. Jesse and Tantalayo to Allece Garrard, August 19, 1981, Garrard Ardeneum Collection, University of Arkansas Little Rock.
10. Jesse and Tantalayo Song and Gig Notebook; Selk; Ray.
11. Robertson.
12. John Einarson, *Mr. Tambourine Man: The Life and Legacy of the Byrds' Gene Clark* (San Francisco: Backbeat Books, 2005), Kindle edition; Patti Daley journal from Daley Collection.
13. Bigsby; Mallaber.
14. Bigsby; Selk; Mallaber; B. Sidran.
15. Bigsby; P. Waddington; Selk.
16. Kunkel.
17. Gene Clark radio interview with B. Mitchell Reed, 1974, *Two Sides to Every Story*, CD (Universal, 2014).
18. Johnny Rogan, *Byrds: Requiem for the Timeless, Volume 2* (London: Rogan House, 2017), 10–13, 208–10.
19. Rogan, *Byrds: Requiem for the Timeless*, 210–18.
20. Rogan, *Byrds: Requiem for the Timeless*, 210; Einarson, *Mr. Tambourine Man*.
21. J. E. Davis to A. Goldman, December 17, 1984, Part I; Romero; Einarson, *Mr. Tambourine Man*.
22. Einarson, *Mr. Tambourine Man*.
23. *Honolulu Star-Bulletin*, September 18, 1981; Rogan, *Byrds: Requiem for the Timeless*, 218; Cambern; Colby.
24. The next several paragraphs draw from my interview with John Granito.
25. Cambern; Colby.
26. Einarson, *Mr. Tambourine Man*; Rogan, *Byrds: Requiem for the Timeless*, 469.
27. Karstein with Bouard; J. E. Davis to A. Goldman, February 28, 1986, Part I; Eckstein.
28. Saul.
29. Pang.
30. Bentley.
31. Noriega; Ellis.
32. Torres.
33. Browne.
34. Ware; Schell.
35. Jesse sat in with the Band, July 23, 1983, at Paramount Theater Oakland, and July 24, 1983, at Nevada County Fairgrounds, Grass Valley, California; childang, "The Band with Jesse Ed Davis/ July 24, 1983," YouTube (1:35:30); Ray with Hisaw; Britt.
36. Noriega; Granito; J. E. Davis to A. Goldman, April 2, 1985.
37. Acevez.
38. Noriega; James; Blue; Acevez; Billups; K. Davis with Bainbridge; Obituary, *Billboard Magazine*, August 1, 1998; Parks; Ray; Hauschild.
39. K. Davis with Bainbridge; K. Davis with Foehr.

40. K. Davis with Bainbridge; K. Davis with Foehr; Ray.
41. K. Davis with Foehr; Hauschild.
42. Hauschild; James.
43. Ricky Phillips, "20th Century Boys," *Detroit Metro Times*, December 25, 2002; "Metro Area Rock Musician Johnny Angelos, 37," *Detroit Free Press*, November 27, 1984; "Torpedos," *Detroit Free Press*, February 18, 1980.
44. Hauschild; Nicolas G. Rosenthal, *Reimagining Indian Country* (Chapel Hill: University of North Carolina Press, 2014), 144–45.
45. *Long Beach Independent Press-Telegram*, July 4, 1974.
46. K. Davis with Bainbridge.
47. Shark.
48. J. E. Davis to A. Goldman April 2, 1985; Carlie Clark obituary, *Mendocino Beacon*; Browne.
49. Tom Whittle, "In the Footsteps of the Greatest," *Freedom Magazine*, September 1986, 33–37; "Older Than America: Resisting the Predator—An Interview with John Trudell," *Border/Lines* 23 (Winter 1991/1992); "America's Most Wanted," *The Daily Telegraph*, July 15, 2000; Trudell with Rudolph.
50. "Older Than America; "America's Most Wanted"; Trudell with Rudolph.

Chapter 11: I Will Retreat No Further

1. On boarding schools, see Brenda Child, *Boarding School Seasons: American Indian Families 1900–1940* (Lincoln: University of Nebraska Press, 1998); on Trudell at Alcatraz, see Paul Chaat Smith and Robert Allen Warrior, *Like a Hurricane: The Indian Movement from Alcatraz to Wounded Knee* (New York: New Press, 1997).
2. Trudell with Rudolph.
3. Rudolph; Shark.
4. Shark; Tsukamoto; *High Times*, "Greats: Interview with John Trudell," February 14, 2020; Don Snowden, "Indian Rights Activist Finds Outlet in Rock," *Los Angeles Times*, December 27, 1986; *Trudell*, directed by Heather Rae, written by Russell Friedenberg (Appaloosa Pictures, 2005); Trudell with Rudolph.
5. Browne; Raitt; Bramlett; Acevez; *Trudell*.
6. Tom Whittle, "In the Footsteps of the Greatest," *Freedom Magazine*, September 1986, 33–37.
7. Whittle, "In the Footsteps of the Greatest"; Snowden, "Indian Rights Activist Finds Outlet in Rock."
8. Whittle, "In the Footsteps of the Greatest"; In interviews with me, Ricky Eckstein and Bob Glaub note how often Jesse employed this expression.
9. John Trudell, *The Collection 1983–1992* (Effective Records, 2011), CDs.
10. Tsukamoto.
11. Trudell with Rudolph.
12. Shark; "Older Than America: Resisting the Predator—An Interview with John Trudell," *Border/Lines* 23 (Winter 1991/1992); Whittle, "In the Footsteps of the Greatest."
13. Bob Dylan, *Philosophy of Modern Song* (New York: Simon and Schuster, 2022).

14. "Older Than America"; Whittle, "In the Footsteps of the Greatest"; Christopher Luna, "With Words and Song: An Interview with John Trudell," *Rain Taxi*, Fall 2009; *Long Beach Press Telegram*, September 13, 1987.
15. Trudell with Rudolph.
16. "Older Than America"; J. E. Davis with A. Goldman, March 6, 1986; Romero.
17. Billups.
18. Billups; "Older Than America."
19. *Rolling Stone*, July 17, 1986; Billups; Shark; Trudell with Rudolph.
20. Sahme; Shark.
21. *But This Isn't El Salvador* album notes; John W. Troutman, *Kīkā Kila: How the Hawaiian Steel Guitar Changed the Sound of Modern Music* (Chapel Hill: University of North Carolina Press, 2016), 1–2.
22. Billups; Browne; "Tribal Voice: John Trudell's 'AKA Grafitti Man,'" *On Indian Land*, Spring 1993.
23. Trudell with Rudolph.
24. Billups; Trudell with Rudolph.
25. Hauschild.
26. Nicolas G. Rosenthal, *Reimagining Indian Country* (Chapel Hill: University of North Carolina Press, 2014); Douglas K. Miller, *Indians on the Move: Native American Mobility and Urbanization in the Twentieth Century* (Chapel Hill: University of North Carolina Press, 2019).
27. Sahme.
28. Sahme; Billups.
29. Ray; Sahme.
30. "Sounds '86," *Rapid City Journal* (Rapid City, SD), June 27, 1986.
31. *Santa Maria Times* (Santa Maria, CA), July 1, 1986.
32. *LA Weekly*, October 1, 1987.
33. Sahme; on survival schools in Minnesota, see Julie Davis, *Survival Schools: The American Indian Movement and Community Education in the Twin Cities* (Minneapolis: University of Minnesota Press, 2013).
34. Tsukamoto; Sahme.
35. G. Davis; Whittle, "In the Footsteps of the Greatest."
36. Robert Hilburn, "Benefit for Convicted Indian: Willie Nelson Heads the All-Star Lineup," *Los Angeles Times*, October 29, 1987; "Two Stations Ban Singers Recordings," *Los Angeles Times*, October 29, 1987.
37. Piranha.
38. Browne.
39. Bentley.
40. Eckstein; Ray; Easton; Bramlett.
41. Colby.
42. Trout.
43. Wacks; Stawarz; Whittle, "In the Footsteps of the Greatest"; *Daily Hampshire Gazette* (Northampton, MA), January 13, 1988.
44. Tsukamoto; Eckstein.
45. Tsukamoto; Shark; Ray.
46. Tsukamoto.

47. Tsukamoto; Shark; Ray; Ehinger; Shark and Eckstein with Hisaw; Grafitti Session, March 1987, Bob Dylan Center Archive, Tulsa, OK.
48. Mahal.
49. Shark; Douglas K. Miller, "The Spider's Web: Mass Incarceration and Settler Colonialism in Indian Country," in *Caging Borders and Carceral States: Incarcerations, Immigration Detentions, and Resistance*, edited by Robert T. Chase, 385–408 (Chapel Hill: University of North Carolina Press, 2019).
50. Maxwell; Ware.
51. Ware; Billups.
52. Easton.
53. Johnson; Mike Johnson interview with Thomas Patterson, "Jesse Ed Davis: Washita Love Child," *Shindig Magazine*; Russ Saunkeah message to Laura Garon, April 17, 2019.
54. Sahme.
55. Sahme; Russell.
56. Sahme.
57. "Older Than America"; J. E. Davis with Westwood One; Whittle, "In the Footsteps of the Greatest."
58. Whittle, "In the Footsteps of the Greatest."
59. "Older Than America"; J. E. Davis with Westwood One; Whittle, "In the Footsteps of the Greatest."
60. Whittle, "In the Footsteps of the Greatest"; Luna, "With Words and Song."
61. "Older Than America"; Snowden, "Indian Rights Activist Finds Outlet in Rock"; Billups.
62. K. Davis with Bainbridge.
63. "Older Than America."

Chapter 12: You Sacrifice Yourself for Your People

1. Brian James Schill, "Truth and Reconciliation" (blog), University of North Dakota School of Medicine and Health Sciences, September 20, 2022.
2. J. E. Davis with Westwood One.
3. Tom Whittle, "In the Footsteps of the Greatest," *Freedom Magazine*, September 1986, 33–37.
4. "Richard Manuel Obit," *Rolling Stone*, June 5, 1986.
5. Shark; Tsukamoto; Lowe.
6. Patti Daley, letter to David Wood (attorney), April 18, 1989; Patti Daley journal, June 25, 1988, both from the Daley Collection.
7. Tsukamoto; Tsukamoto with Hisaw; Shark; Shark and Eckstein with Hisaw.
8. Shark; Noriega; Ellis; Daley Collection; Colby; "Backed Up Major Artists: Jesse Ed Davis, 43; Noted Rock Guitarist," *Los Angeles Times*, June 24, 1988.
9. Ellis; Noriega; Tsukamoto with Hisaw; Shark; "Backed Up Major Artists"; Shark and Eckstein with Hisaw; "RIP JED: Jesse Ed Davis in Memory, June 22, 1988, 4:30PM," Daley Collection; Jesse Ed Davis to Patti Daley, from Londonderry House, December 1968, Hard Rock Collection; "Librium and Alcohol: Mixing Effects," American Addiction Centers, January 17, 2023.

10. Ellis; Noriega; Tsukamoto with Hisaw; Shark; "Backed Up Major Artists"; Shark and Eckstein with Hisaw; "RIP JED: Jesse Ed Davis in Memory," Daley Collection.

11. P. Daley to D. Wood, Daley Collection; John Einarson, *Mr. Tambourine Man: The Life and Legacy of the Byrds' Gene Clark* (San Francisco: Backbeat Books, 2005), Kindle edition; Johnny Rogan, *Byrds: Requiem for the Timeless, Volume 2* (London: Rogan House, 2017), 469; Shark; Tsukamoto; Granito.

12. *LA Weekly*, June 17–23, 1988.

13. Noriega; Colby; Lowe; Bates; Rudolph; Sahme; Mauchahty-Ware interview with Oklahoma Historical Society (OHS).

14. Billups.

15. Sahme.

16. Karstein; Billups; Tsukamoto; P. Waddington; Romero; Russ Saunkeah message to Laura Garon, April 17, 2019.

17. Shark and Eckstein with Hisaw; Mahal; Kortchmar; Keltner with Bouard; Parks.

18. Bramlett; Mat Snow, "All Together Now: Joe Cocker," *Q*, May 1992.

19. Daley notebook, n.d; Patti Daley to David Wood, April 18 and June 22, 1989; Daley to Vivian Davis, June 17, 1989; Daley, "RIP JED: Jesse Ed Davis in Memory"; Daley to George Harrison, April 20, 1989—all from the Daley Collection; J. E. Davis with Westwood One.

20. Daley journal, June 25, 1988, Daley Collection.

21. Shark; Browne; Tsukamoto; Mahal; Ray with Hisaw.

22. Shark; Ray; Billups; James; Garon; Mauchahty-Ware.

23. Shark; Tsukamoto; Sahme.

24. Kaspereit.

25. "OK Music Hall of Fame Inducts 3 Native Artists," *Native Times*, November 14, 2011; G. Davis; Romero; Robertson.

26. Sahme.

27. Chalepah; Tiger.

28. Lowe; Saenz.

29. P. Daley to D. Wood, June 22, 1989, Daley Collection.

30. Acevez; Blue.

31. Noriega.

32. Chalepah; Hollis; Commander.

Coda: Satanta's Bugle

1. Patti Daley to Yoko Ono, September 13, 1989, and Patti Daley to Vivian Davis, June 17, 1989, Daley Collection.

2. James.

3. S. E. Ruckman, "Kiowas Celebrate Settainte During Independence Day Dance," *Native American Times*, July 9, 2010.

4. Ruckman, "Kiowas Celebrate Settainte"; C. C. Rister, "Satanta: Orator of the Plains," *Southwest Review* 17, no. 1 (1932): 86n29.

5. Maurice Boyd, *Kiowa Voices: Myths, Legends and Folktales, Volume II* (Fort Worth: Texas Christian University Press, 1981), 75, 245.

6. Tom Whittle, "In the Footsteps of the Greatest," *Freedom Magazine*, September 1986, 33–37.

Side A: Jesse Ed Davis, "Anyway You Wanna Do, or: Eternal Jimi Hendrix"

1. Author's transcription of J. E. Davis, reading essay, audio cassette, Daley Collection.

INDEX

Page numbers after 330 refer to endnotes.